FAY WRAY AND ROBERT RISKIN

Fay Wray and Robert Riskin

A HOLLYWOOD MEMOIR

Victoria Riskin

PANTHEON BOOKS, NEW YORK

Names: Riskin, Victoria, author.
Title: Fay Wray and Robert Riskin : a Hollywood memoir / Victoria Riskin.
Description: First edition. New York : Pantheon Books, 2019. Includes bibliographical references and index.
Identifiers: LCCN 2018027978 (print). LCCN 2018030875 (ebook). ISBN 9781524747299 (ebook). ISBN 9781524747282 (hardcover).
Subjects: LCSH: Wray, Fay, 1907–2004. Riskin, Robert. Motion picture actors and actresses—United States—Biography. Screenwriters—United States—Biography.
Classification: LCC PN2285 (ebook) | LCC PN2285 .R565 2019 (print) | DDC 791.4302/80922 [B] —dc23 | LC record available at lccn.loc.gov/2018027978

www.pantheonbooks.com

Jacket photographs: (Fay Wray) AF Archive/Alamy; (Robert Riskin) Irving Lippman
Jacket design by Jenny Carrow

Printed in the United States of America
First Edition

9 8 7 6 5 4 3 2 1

FOR MY DAVID

God gave us memory so that we might have roses in December.

—J. M. BARRIE

FAY WRAY AND ROBERT RISKIN

For my mother, it had already been A Great Adventure. A sometimes wild ride.

She had been put on a railroad train from Salt Lake City to Los Angeles at age fourteen, somehow entrusted by her strict Victorian mother to the care of a charming twenty-one-year-old man who had said he could, maybe, get her into movies. There had been no money in their tiny home, no man to provide for them, six hungry mouths and some days nothing to feed them but bread soup. Later she said, "Maybe Mama put me on the train so there'd be one less mouth to feed." My mother had dreamt of a better life and perhaps Los Angeles, where she knew no one and had no family within hundreds of miles, could provide it.

The year was 1920 and Los Angeles was a rough, busy, unfinished town.

Her young man proved as good as his word. He took her to a respectable rooming house where she stayed for a dollar a night, which he paid, and then found a family who promised to look after her. Walking in Hollywood, she was seen by a producer who offered her a bit part as a clown at five dollars a day. After another small part or two, she went alone to the Hal Roach Studios, told them of her acting experience, and asked for a weekly contract. They gave it to her, six months at sixty dollars a week that soon was seventy-five dollars, a handsome salary for the time.

By 1933 she had grown into a beautiful young woman and was atop the world, literally. The immortal scene played out on the Empire State Building where she dangled in the giant hand of King Kong, the largest and most terrifying gorilla the world had ever seen. As audiences gasped, airplanes swooped around, firing machine guns at the beast. Before Kong fell to his death a hundred stories below, he made sure the woman he loved was safe on a ledge.

My mother made more than a hundred films, some with the outstanding producers and directors of the era and opposite the greatest leading men: Gary Cooper, Spencer Tracy, William Powell, Victor Jory. She used her earnings to buy her family a home in Hollywood and support them in comfort.

But along the way there were challenges: an overbearing mother and marriage to an Academy Award–winning writer who soon revealed himself to be an alcoholic. Then came an infatuation with Cary Grant after they had starred together on Broadway, a brief romance with Howard Hughes, and a serious one with the playwright Clifford Odets.

Real love, a man she could love and who loved her back, had eluded her.

In 1930, on the day my father arrived in Hollywood on the 20th Century Limited from New York, he went to the Columbia studio on Poverty Row, where second-tier movie companies were situated. He was ordered to report immediately to Harry Cohn's office, where the famed, tyrannical studio boss was conducting an inquisition among Columbia's executives and contract writers about a stage play, *Bless You, Sister,* he had just bought, to be directed by Columbia's top director, Frank Capra. Cohn turned to the newcomer and demanded to know if he had anything to say.

My father had written the play and, with his brother, produced it on Broadway, where it had failed despite positive reviews. He told Cohn he thought it would fail as a film, too, and gave his reasons. Cohn and Capra went ahead anyway, and the film failed.

From that shaky and inauspicious start, my father went on to have a celebrated career as a screenwriter, working mostly with Cohn and Capra. The films he wrote are still considered classics that helped define America to itself and the world: *Lady for a Day, The Whole Town's Talking, It Happened One Night, Mr. Deeds Goes to Town, Lost Horizon, You Can't Take It with You, Meet John Doe. It Happened One Night* was the first film to sweep the five top Academy Awards—Best Picture, Director, Writer, Actor, and Actress, a record matched only twice in the three-quarters of a century since: by *One Flew Over the Cuckoo's Nest* and *The Silence of the Lambs.*

My father's films reflected love for his characters, especially the ordinary people he cared about and the smart, independent women who were equal to—at least equal to—the men they were paired with. His films were admired for their wit and charm, and the spirit that even in the middle of a grinding Depression, problems could be solved if we only worked together.

He was called on by Harry Cohn to give judgments on most pictures Columbia put into production after *It Happened One Night.* He mediated heated arguments between Cohn and Frank Capra, Columbia's top director.

Outside the studio he was a strong and active supporter of FDR and the New Deal. He helped his fellow screenwriters establish a union, and as the 1930s wore on he became increasingly concerned about America's isolationism and went to England to help Great Britain in its fight for survival against Hitler.

He also had relationships with actresses Glenda Farrell, Carole Lombard, and Loretta Young. Involved and busy as he was, by his early forties he was increasingly aware that something fundamental and important was missing in his life.

My parents met at a Christmas Eve party in 1940. My mother's first marriage had ended in divorce, and although she was spending most of her time with Clifford Odets in New York, she was briefly in Los Angeles to make a film and see friends.

My father crossed the room to talk to her. By the end of the evening he had invited her to see an acclaimed new movie, *The Grapes of Wrath.* And that night or very soon thereafter he fell, hard, whether because of her intelligence, her wit or infectious laugh, or the way she listened to him with undivided attention. The morning after their first date he sent her a dozen red roses and in the following days he saw her as often as he could. After she returned to Odets in New York, he told friends he was heartbroken.

It would be the following December, two weeks after Pearl Harbor, before they found each other again. And this time when they connected my parents both knew they had found the intimacy they had longed for. When my father was slow to propose, *she* proposed to *him,* and they married in New York in a small ceremony attended by a few close friends, including Irving Berlin, David O. Selznick, and William "Wild Bill" Donovan, and set out to make up for all the time they had missed together.

1

Life is all memory, except for the one present moment that goes by you so quickly you hardly catch it going.

—TENNESSEE WILLIAMS

My first memory is of a snowstorm in Los Angeles. The land of eternal sunshine had never in its known history been blanketed in white the way it was on January 10, 1949—*The Old Farmer's Almanac* gives the date—and never has again.

I was three years old. My brother Bobby, five, had already dressed himself and run downstairs to join our thirteen-year-old sister, Susan, outside. I fidgeted impatiently while our English nanny, Miss Haesloop, in her starched white uniform, secured the buttons of my blue corduroy trouser suit and put rubber overshoes over my Buster Browns.

My father organized a snowball fight that morning on the front lawn of our Bel-Air home. Bobby and I pelted each other until a snowball hit me in the face and I burst into tears. My father scooped me up and deftly distracted me into helping him make a snowman. He also recruited Bobby, who was a genius at building things, and let me tuck in stones for the snowman's eyes and a carrot for his nose. This, he emphasized, was the most important job of all. "There you go, rascal. You stick that carrot right in the middle of his face."

In the photographs of that day, my mother is absent. For years, I imagined she was in the kitchen having the cook prepare the hot chocolate to warm us when we came in, or rearranging the living room rugs and furniture for an evening of square dancing that was all the rage in the late 1940s, or readying a dinner party for the friends who regularly came to our house: Jack Benny, Rosalind Russell, Ronald Colman, Cary Grant, Jimmy Stewart, Irving Berlin, Harpo Marx, Darryl Zanuck, Edward G.

Robinson. I now understand that she was outdoors with us all along, taking the photos with her Leica camera, recording our lives, memorializing our family's landmark moments as was now her passion. Snow and snowman and, indelibly, my father in his tweed newsboy's cap, woolen scarf and heavy overcoat, tortoiseshell glasses, tanned olive skin, his head tilted to the side with a smile starting to form as if waiting for me to finish telling him a funny story.

Today, looking at pictures of that day, I still smell his Old Spice aftershave and the scent of his cigarettes, and see his smiling eyes.

Life with my father had warmth and adventure. He took us to Gilmore Field to see the Hollywood Stars play baseball, leading us in singing "Take Me Out to the Ballgame" on the way. He took us to his bungalow at Twentieth Century–Fox, where we could play while he wrote, or to the commissary for lunch, or for the world's best hot fudge sundaes at C. C. Brown's on Hollywood Boulevard.

Evenings were an unchanging ritual. At five o'clock Bobby and I ate dinner in the playroom upstairs as Miss Haesloop turned the Grundig radio to Edward R. Murrow or Cecil Brown, and mostly we followed her orders to be quiet. Her rapt attention, turned to the news from London, was a clear indicator of how she worried about war, even though the war had been over for three years.

After our baths, we were sprinkled with talcum, put into pajamas, and ushered into our parents' bedroom for the children's hour. My father, in his armchair with the rose floral print, waved us in. He held his beer, or sometimes neat Scotch, in his left hand, his Lucky Strike in the right. Two fingers were yellowed from chain-smoking, one calloused from writing. He wore cashmere sweaters and handmade shoes from London and the best silk ties and shirts money could buy. My mother might be wearing a clingy black crepe dress if they were going to dinner at Romanoff's or Chasen's, her dark wavy hair combed back to frame her warm, welcoming face, her red lipstick carefully drawn outside the line of her lips to give them fullness. Her rosewater eau de cologne spiced the air.

"Hey, rascal," my father said, pulling me onto his lap. "Tell me how your day was." I told stories from school or pretended I was a ballerina and climbed down and danced for him. He watched as if nothing in the world were more important than my awkward ballet twirls. He let me sip foam from his beer while Bobby was using the bed as a trampoline.

"Hey, Bobby! Think you can crack us open some walnuts?"

Bobby did what my father had taught us, punching a hole in the corner of a pillow—not too deep, not too shallow—and tucking a walnut inside

Fay Wray and Robert Riskin and their children, 1948. Wray (right) memorializing the family's landmark moments with her Leica. My father (left) with Bobby, five . . . and me (below), age three, with Bobby

Fay and Robert in black tie at a Hollywood restaurant, 1949

and throwing the pillow up a foot or two in the air, then smashing it hard on both sides as it came down. The walnut flew up, hit the ceiling, and exploded. Walnut pieces rained everywhere. My mother said that years later, when we moved, she found walnut bits behind the painting over the fireplace, under the bed, even in the closet. She said wistfully, "It made a mess but you kids were having such a good time."

My father's tricks engaged our sense of wonder. None was more exhilarating or terrifying than when he held the burning butt of his Lucky Strike between his lips and, with a grin, flipped the smoldering butt backwards into his mouth where it disappeared for an interminable time. When our screaming and excitement reached its peak, he flipped the burning butt out, no hands—that would have been cheating—and took a long easy puff while we collapsed in relief.

"You like that one, hey?"

Those were the Eden days, the first six years of my life.

We looked forward to Christmas all year.

In 1950, as every year, an enormous Christmas tree draped with popcorn and cranberry garlands we had strung ourselves—a sticky business—occupied one corner of the living room. With our father's guidance, we placed lights and beautiful ornaments and glass icicles on the pine branches and pitched fistfuls of tinsel onto the tree, with Bobby imitating a baseball pitcher.

The house turned into a noisy party, which my father preserved on his wire recorder. Listening to it today, Christmas chaos bubbles through the scratchy sounds, with my father opening Christmas cards and reading aloud—"Look at this one, Faysie! The Bernsteins from London!"—and instructing Susan and Bobby to hang them on a string spanning the living room archway, then asking me to come sit on his lap, where he handed me more envelopes. "Hey rascal, can you open this one?"

The housekeeper, Bertha, added two leaves to the mahogany dining table to accommodate the entire family, whose arrival was imminent. She polished and set it with fine linens, china, glassware and a large centerpiece of anthuriums. My mother closed the velvet curtains and lit candles in the silver candelabras on the credenza.

"Company!" called my father.

First came Essie, my father's eldest sister, born in Russia and speaking Yiddish-English. To my six-year-old eyes, Essie, though still in her fifties, looked shriveled. "How is you, darlink? So beeg you got since I saw you!" Uncle Everett came with tempestuous Aunt Katya, who swept in wearing an ankle-length turquoise Native American skirt, a black velvet shirt, and heavy silver jewelry. Bobby and I found her exotic and exciting. My father's sister Rose followed, and close behind was the youngest Riskin, Murray, a lawyer, with his wife also named Rose. Bobby and I were on tiptoes looking at the presents they brought, hoping to find our names on the largest.

My mother's brother Richard, a film editor at Universal Studios, five feet five inches tall, came with his five-feet-ten-inch part-Cherokee wife, Laura. Her youngest brother Victor, who had an office job at Douglas Aircraft, brought his wife, Ginny. Victor sang "Ave Maria" in his magnificent tenor voice each year, making everyone teary. My mother's older sister, Willow, now divorced, came alone. She, too, sang like an angel—mostly opera—and had a large bosom like a down pillow I loved to snuggle into.

Wrays and Riskins. Two families, one from a poor dusty Mormon mining town in Utah, the other first-generation Jews from the Lower East Side, gathered as one around our dining table. My father loved having family around. He told stories and my mother led the laughter with abandon. Everyone shared a passion for liberal politics and the arts—ballet, music, movies, theater—and whiskey and cigarettes, probably too much of both. At thirteen, Susan was sophisticated enough to join their conversation about the recent smash New York opening of *Guys and Dolls* that my father's best friend, Jo Swerling, had written based on the stories of Damon Runyon, or their concerns about friends caught up in the Hollywood anti-communist witch hunts.

Unobserved, Bobby and I slid under the table and crawled the length of the rug, liberating everyone's napkin from their laps, almost wetting our pants trying not to giggle. When we emerged napkins in hand— "ta-dah!"—aunts and uncles looked in their laps, shocked, shocked, to find their napkins missing. On my journey the length of the table, I had pressed the buzzer my father used to summon the kitchen staff. The cook flew in and my father apologized, saying, "The rascals are up to no good."

I heard my father sound uncharacteristically impatient when he told us we now should settle down and rejoin the table. I was old enough to detect the strain on his face and sense something was wrong.

Monday morning, December 26, 1950, my father left at nine o'clock for a full day at the studio.

At ten-thirty his Buick pulled back into the driveway.

My mother rushed to open the door. Without a word, he walked past her and slowly and with difficulty climbed the stairs.

My father was at this moment suffering a stroke that would leave him partially paralyzed, with his mind impaired.

I didn't understand at first, and when I did, I felt like Humpty Dumpty, unable to put myself back together.

My mother was left to do everything. She had to keep us afloat financially, not easy with all the hospitals, doctors and nurses, and with no health insurance, no Medicare, no Writers Guild health or pension plans, all of which lay far in the future. She had given up her movie career when she married my father and now there was no money coming into the house, which was large and expensive to maintain. Only later did I grow to appreciate her strength and determination to buoy her children with her optimism and cheer.

Despite all she did to lift my spirits, everything seemed gray, as if someone had turned off all the lights in our home.

The house was arranged for my father's comfort and rehabilitation, but after a year he was no better. He was taken to a convalescent home where he remained, not improving, for the three years left to him.

Once he left home my fantasies took hold. Just as children of soldiers off at war imagine their fathers as superheroes, slayers of dragons and bad men, in my imagination my father had been banished by my mother. Surely she was powerful enough to make him well and restore our life together. One day I would find him on a beach in the south of France and be reunited with him. This was the story I told myself so often I came to believe it, even though I knew he was a few miles away, in a full-care convalescent home.

My mother found a modest house for us in the Brentwood Hills of the Santa Monica Mountains, and in 1953 reluctantly packed us up, moved us there, and went back to acting.

My father never recovered from his stroke and died in 1955.

His Oscar for *It Happened One Night* sat on the television in our living room as a reminder of him, but life had to go on. Occasionally when my mother told us a story about Daddy, her eyes filled remembering him. But for Bobby, Susan, and me, the pain of remembering him was almost unbearable. Over time Bobby withdrew, spending hours by himself in his workshop, tinkering with gadgets or his radio transmitter, or developing photos or reading science and science fiction books and magazines, or playing his guitar. Susan, who had read to us and entertained us with games when we were little, became tense and uncommunicative and she, too, withdrew to her room where she listened to opera for hours on end. Through her closed door, I could hear the doleful arias of *Madama Butterfly* and *La Bohème* repeated endlessly.

I found salvation in school and with friends, and especially at summer camp in Arizona, riding horses, swimming, listening to ghost stories, sitting around a campfire, being far from home and the reminders of my loss.

Dreams of childhood are hard to surrender. As I grew, I understood my story of finding my father on the beach in France was an illusion, but the need to reach across time and bring him back never left and the longing to know him became more pronounced.

In my search for him I combed through countless old boxes of his notes, outlines, scripts, essays, studio contracts, press clippings, photos, and correspondence. I spoke to friends and relatives and read the work of biographers, historians, and film critics to understand his life and career. Going through the hundreds of newspaper stories and interviews, it was clear that while he would talk openly about the work he was engaged in and the world as he saw it, he shied away from personal revelation. He was a private man who expressed his deeply held values and philosophy largely through his writing.

To begin to know my father, I started with his movies and his scripts. His screenplays still make marvelous reading today and are a treasure trove for any screenwriter. But nowhere does he come alive more vividly than in the letters he wrote to my mother when they were courting and after they married, when he was overseas during World War II. My mother kept a leather pouch with every letter, including telegrams and V-mail ("V" for Victory), written on a single piece of paper and censored to disguise the writer's whereabouts and protect military secrets, and as a wartime economy measure photographed and shrunk before mailing. His letters spill over with affection and urgency, breezy anecdotes and observations about Hollywood, human nature, the war, writing, relationships with family and friends—and most of all his devotion to his wife and children. "My dear darling Faysie: I loved your letter. I love them when they are long and 'talky' and intimate . . . This one was a kiss and a long embrace. It was sunshine and a cool summer evening and a warm spring shower."

For years, I kept the letters hidden away, unable to bear to read them. Today they make me laugh and cry. My father's mind, his passion for life and the people he cared about, his love of country, all shine through.

· · ·

My mother lived ninety-six full years and I knew her in all her brilliance and complexity. On many occasions, I asked about her life and she was always forthcoming. Her autobiography—titled *On the Other Hand,* a reference to the classic image of her in Kong's hand—is filled with memories. Still, there were parts of her life that remained in the shadows, with many questions I wanted to answer.

My mother had a pioneer resilience, a vulnerability, a need for admiration. She could sweep into a room and enchant anyone she encountered. She laughed with infectious, unbridled enthusiasm. Her china blue eyes took hold of anyone she met. Cab driver, doorman, saleslady, prince—all were captivated by her genuine interest in them. Her aquiline nose was almost imperceptibly misaligned, broken while filming an early Western. She never rose from the dining table until she had carefully reapplied her bright red lipstick.

She judged people quickly and embraced or dismissed them. She became a successful handicapper at horse races at Santa Anita and Hollywood Park, where movie stars and executives regularly came up to her for betting tips. She was my brother's Cub Scout den mother. She sewed labels in my clothes and packed my trunk for summer camp. She squeezed fresh orange juice for my breakfast, made peanut butter and jelly sandwiches for my lunch box, and took her turn at carpooling the neighborhood kids.

Without my father around, none of this could have been as easy as she tried to make it appear. I felt her mood swings as if they were my own. I worried about her when she was sad or anxious.

Sometimes she was my mother. Other times she was the actress Fay Wray. When I was young it felt special to be born into Hollywood royalty, into "the business," a private club the world admired, but when I became a teenager, friends' questions made me shy. I sometimes felt we lived in a fishbowl with people watching and judging. It wasn't just teenage self-consciousness, it was the realization that my mother's celebrity meant we could be the subject of gossip at school or in newspapers, although the press in general was far more restrained than it is now.

When people stopped my mother for an autograph in the supermarket, their fawning made me uneasy. Her movie star personality switched on and sometimes confused me. I worried about how she dressed in public, although she always dressed fashionably, but try telling that to a teenager. I longed for an ordinary, *Father Knows Best* family.

Mark Twain famously said, "When I was a boy of fourteen, my father was so ignorant I could hardly stand to have the old man around. But when I got to be twenty-one, I was astonished at how much he had learned in seven years." By my twenties, my mother had become a woman of exceptional wisdom, and my confidante. We were close the rest of our lives. She called me "Vicola." I called her "Faysie," my father's favorite name for her.

2

Parents lend children their experience and a vicarious memory;
children endow their parents with a vicarious immortality.

—GEORGE SANTAYANA

My father was far more interesting than the errant, far-off knight of my
childhood invention. He was the smart, scrappy, talented son of warmhearted Jewish immigrants, born on March 30, 1897, third child of Jakob
and Bessie Riskin who had come to the United States in 1891 from what
is now Belarus. The details of my grandparents' origins survive in a 1943
Western Union telegram from Jakob, which my father needed for his government security clearance in World War II. Three-quarters of a century
later I unearthed the telegram in a box of family keepsakes, a brittle piece
of yellowing paper.

> Born Orsha White Russia September 25, 1868. Arrived this country
> last part of August 1891. Do not remember date. Naturalized June 19,
> 1901, in New York Southern District Court. Mother was born May 15,
> 1866, in Korsovka Vitebsk Province Russia. Her maiden name Bessie
> Shetzer. Expect your letter. Love, Dad

Like countless Jews of their era, Bessie and Jakob had found life under
Tsarist rule harsh and cruel. The assassination of Alexander II in 1881,
blamed falsely on Jews, had unleashed a wave of pogroms, massacres, and
persecutions, and led to restrictions that confined Jews to poverty-stricken
districts like Vitebsk and Orsha. Jakob's formal education was limited,
but he was drawn to progressive ideas, doubtless inspired by the Jewish enlightenment then sweeping Russia that rejected traditional religious
teachings in favor of modern ideas of freedom, equality, and justice. He

was also drawn by the idea of starting a new life in a new country, America, which promised justice and jobs and streets paved with gold.

Bessie and Jakob's first baby, Essie, was three years old when they landed in New York. Here Everett was born and, in short order, my father, Rose, and Murray. Their first Lower East Side apartment over a whiskey store was typical: small cramped rooms, sweltering summers, freezing winters, minimal sanitation, constant noise both from the street and baby Rose inside crying. Still, in America there was the hope of a better life for the children.

Jakob worked as a tailor in the garment industry for sixteen dollars a week. A gentle-natured man with a large nose, handsome moustache, and smiling eyes, he took pride in his appearance and fashioned for himself several high-style three-piece suits that made him look like a Park Avenue gentleman. Although my father never remembered him having a permanent job, Jakob always cobbled together enough piecework to feed his family.

At the turn of the twentieth century, garment factories were sweatshops with hellish working conditions. Jakob became a devoted reader of *The Forward,* the Yiddish Socialist newspaper that campaigned for trade unionism and humane workplaces. The newspaper's message, and his own progressive ideas and experiences, made for stimulating conversation at the dinner table, where Jakob engaged his children with stories of the lives of the disadvantaged and exploited. My father was the most curious of all the children. He asked questions incessantly and Jakob never tired of talking to him.

Jakob was a romantic, with unconventional ideas about marriage, as seen in a letter to his future daughter-in-law, Rose, on the eve of her marriage to Murray.

My dear Rosy,

You must forgive me for writing in Yiddish because in English it will be difficult for me to express the right thoughts. I probably make mistakes in spelling, so I don't want you to laugh at me. Mother will read the letter for you and you will understand it very good.

Your letter has brought me great pleasure but one thing does not please me, when you sign "your daughter-in-law." With me you are not a daughter-in-law but a child equal with all my children. Murray and you are one for me, his life bound up with your happiness and his happiness also mine. I hope you will live out your lives in peace.

I have a preference for wise and diplomatic people and you will understand how to travel the road of life. It is not said that people, especially young ones, should not make mistakes, but even for a mistake you have to have diplomacy.

I have always in my lifetime been opposed to marriage. I have considered love and marriage two different things. Love is holy, love is sweet, and marriage poisons love—that is how I always felt, but I came to the conclusion that we have no other way to put order in society. We have no better system. That's why we have to conduct ourselves according to the old system and people with sense can adapt themselves to all circumstances and enjoy the best you (they) can.

Your loving father,

Yankiff [Jakob]

Seeking a better life, Jakob moved his family from New York to Baltimore, where black neighbors invited them in for fishcakes, which Everett remembered fondly sixty years later. They next moved to Philadelphia before settling in Brooklyn, where Jakob worked as a cutter, a position more prestigious than a mere tailor and a source of pride to his family.

Brooklyn was abuzz at the start of the twentieth century. Ferries still went to Manhattan but were losing business to the horse-drawn carriages and pedestrians now clogging the Brooklyn Bridge. The family lived in Brownsville and then Canarsie, where the Irish fought the Jews and the Italian gangsters had money, snappy clothes, and style. Someone described my father at the time as being "short and streetwise, developing a satirical tongue in self-defense against the Irish boys who tormented him and against the equally combative Italians who lived in the adjoining neighborhood." Over time he became friendly with some of the Irish and Italian boys and interceded when they picked on boys who couldn't defend themselves.

It was in Brooklyn that my father, always a keen and sympathetic observer of people, started to acquire the humanity that would be his hallmark in his life and his writing. He also acquired a sense of style, buying suits and ties as soon as he could afford them, and shoes he waxed to a high sheen. He later said if he hadn't been a writer he might have been a gangster because of their stylish spats and pin-striped suits, not to mention the sleek cars they drove. For his first big hit movie, *Lady for a Day* in 1933, he relied on the gangsters of Brooklyn with their well-hidden kindness as models for Dave the Dude and his posse.

As he moved on from Canarsie, my father also moved on from the world of street fights and gangsters. In Robert Riskin's scripts, a punch was almost never thrown, a gun almost never fired. No one was killed, no one hurt—with one exception in his own life years later, and it made headlines when it happened.

It was 1936 and he was a top screenwriter in Hollywood. The endlessly curious child had matured into an adult concerned about the major affairs of his time—national politics, the rise of Hitler, union activism. He was considered good company, especially by women, and seen regularly with Hollywood's most glamorous stars in the toniest nightclubs. The leading movie columnist of the period, Louella Parsons, awarded him the title "Most Eligible Bachelor in Hollywood."

One night at the black-tie Trocadero Club, he was dining with Barbara Stanwyck, Carole Lombard, and Zeppo Marx (the fourth Marx brother) when a writer named Harry Ruskin, known for the Dr. Kildare film series, approached. He bragged to the table that his technique for seduction was to take advantage of the similarity of their names, Ruskin and Riskin, with success in the bedroom inevitably following. My father who, according to all who knew him, never said an unkind thing about anyone, was as offended by Ruskin's coarse and cocky manner as by what he said. He stood and punched Ruskin on the jaw, knocking him cold. The next day, headlines read FILM WRITER KAYOES COLLEAGUE IN THIRD. It was his only fight post-Brooklyn, but ladies were present and to a street kid from Canarsie, the one-punch fight was justified. You can take the boy out of Brooklyn but you can't take a swift punch to the jaw, when appropriate, out of the boy.

My father's mother, Bessie, was loving, buoyant, volatile, energetic, and devoted to her children. She was round and rosy-cheeked, looking in old photographs like a Russian nesting doll. Everett remembered her as exciting with a warm sense of humor. She spoke English with barely an accent, a matter of pride to her American-born children. A skilled seamstress, she took her daughters to the best stores in New York, and when they saw something they liked she fixed it in her mind and sewed it at home.

Bessie was serious about religion, and tried to corral her boys on Friday nights to go to *shul* to help make a *minyan*, the ten adult men necessary to conduct a worship ceremony. But the boys, eager to assimilate and shed old-world trappings, were not easily lassoed. My father preferred to sneak into vaudeville theaters in Brooklyn like the Bushwick, where he was entranced by the comic routines. He taught himself the Pitman shorthand system to write down the jokes as fast as possible. In a 1941 interview he said he was still using those gags, "with a touch of polish on them."

Riskin (above, left), age eight, jousting with his brother Everett, age ten, in 1905, and their parents, Bessie and Jakob (right), in a Brooklyn park, 1920s. Jakob, a tailor, made his own suits and Bessie sewed her own dresses.

Along with Everett, my father sold *The Saturday Evening Post* on street-cars for pocket money. By the time he quit school at age thirteen, he had saved enough to rent a typewriter for three months, teaching himself the touch system and transcribing all the jokes he had collected. At fifteen, he became secretary/office boy for the owner of a textile company, Joe Golden. Golden saw that during my father's lunch break he wrote stories and poetry and, marginally literate himself, offered my father a promotion to "executive" if he would write love letters for him. Golden was mad for a famous operetta star he wanted to marry but seemed barely to know. Her name was Trixie Friganza and my father did his best, writing Cyranoesque mash notes to Trixie. Alas, Trixie wasn't moved, or maybe she just pre-ferred being Trixie Friganza to Trixie Golden—who could blame her?—and she never responded to his pleas. In his disappointment, Golden fired my father.

He next found a job with two well-known New York shirtmakers, Heidenheim and Levy, who recognized him as a smart kid who liked to

Riskin as a rakish teenage office boy in New York's garment industry, 1915. When his employers sent him to Florida to supervise comedy films they were financing, he affected a Panama hat and moustache for age and credibility.

tell stories. After giving him a brief, unsuccessful tryout as a traveling salesman in New England, they, too, made him their office boy/secretary. The partners had a side investment in silent movie comedies being shot in Florida, to be sold to Famous Players–Lasky for distribution. One day they were showing some of the two-reel comedies in the office and my father's bosses called him in. In a forerunner of his first experience with Harry Cohn at Columbia, my father was not shy in offering his opinion: "Famous Players–Lasky will throw you out on your asses when you show them these. Even I could be funnier." Heidenheim and Levy ignored him until Famous Players–Lasky rejected the films whereupon, having nothing to lose, they dispatched my seventeen-year-old father to Florida to take charge and salvage their investment.

At seventeen my father became a movie producer. To look older he grew a serious mustache and used mascara to paint over a patch where his hair wouldn't grow. He hired well-known Broadway comedian Victor Moore and his wife, Emma Littlefield, to star in his new movies.

The short films my father produced in Florida for Heidenheim and Levy between 1916 and 1918 are mostly lost, but film historians think he produced more than a hundred Klever Komedies. One *Variety* reviewer called the films "screamingly funny," saying audiences "laughed uproari-

Riskin, in checkered cap (center), and his crew turned out more than a hundred Klever Komedies. At eighteen, he was in charge of writing, directing, producing, and selling the pictures to the hinterlands.

ously at the screening." In a 1941 interview, my father said he did everything on the pictures; making up stories, writing the scripts, producing, sometimes serving as an extra, taking care of all the business details, and "worrying how the darn thing would do in Waukegan." Searching through old newspapers, I found announcements for Klever Komedies up and down the eastern seaboard. Recently I saw one of the few surviving prints, *Rough and Ready*, starring Victor Moore, and there was my seventeen-year-old father sporting a three-piece suit and mustache as an extra cheering at a boxing match.

By the time he was twenty, in 1917, my father had earned $6,000, the equivalent of $130,000 today, and sent most of it to his family. Soon after America entered World War I, he enlisted in the Navy—his naval Registration card lists his occupation as actor-manager of Klever Pictures, Inc.—and rose from seaman second class to yeoman third class, where he filled a desk job. He was stationed at New York Naval Headquarters for his nine months of service while his movie career was sidelined.

Discharged in early 1919, unemployed and almost broke, he and his brother Everett rented a room at the Green Room Club at Forty-Seventh

Riskin (top right) with his lead actor, Broadway comedian Victor Moore (top row, second from the left). Their financial backers are in the front row.

Street and Broadway, a boardinghouse for young impoverished actors and writers, several of whom—S. J. Perelman, Lee Tracy, Edward G. Robinson—went on to major film careers. The residents had barely enough money for cheap meals and provided their own entertainment, putting on plays and comedy sketches in the sitting room. My father and Everett shared their room with Robinson, and my father and Robinson remained friends long after they came to Hollywood, in 1935 making *The Whole Town's Talking* and staying close through the nightmare years of Robinson's blacklisting.

With Everett, my father set up a small film production office off Times Square, at 220 West Forty-second Street. They made a series of silent bathing beauty shorts, "Facts and Follies," one of which touted muscle building as the best way to meet girls. Another used puppets called Riskinettes hooked to tubes inflated by a clacking typewriter. The venture foundered but, undaunted, they decided to try producing plays for Broadway.

It was the Roaring Twenties, with Prohibition the new law of the land. Speakeasies sprang up around the city and theaters opened on every corner. The Riskin brothers cobbled together enough financing to get into the game. Their younger sister Rose, proud of her older brothers, kept detailed records of everything they did. In her scrapbook of clippings, begun almost a hundred years ago, I found press stories from the five years my father and Everett produced plays on and around Broadway.

Their first play, *The Mud Turtle,* opened in 1925 at the New Bijou The-ater. It starred Helen MacKellar—from her photograph a lovely ingénue—and the billing said the play was presented by A. E. and R. R. Riskin. "A good piece of theater," wrote the *Daily News.* My father didn't have a mid-dle name, nor did Everett, but in what was clearly a bow to the past, the initials were a reminder that my father Robert had been born Rouven and Everett born Avraham—thus R. R. and A. E. The brothers were assimilat-ing, probably not abandoning their Jewish roots so much as making their way in the new world, and the added initials may have sounded American to them. The initials also lent a touch of class or sophistication, and when did a little invention hurt a career in show business, anyway?

The Mud Turtle ran more than fifty weeks—not a bad beginning.

Their second play, a revival of *The Bells* in 1926, opened to respectful reviews. They hired Florence Moore to star in a new farce, *She Couldn't Say No,* at the Booth Theater.

My father and Everett were both short, stylish, energetic, with an imp-ish quality that suggested they were thinking of something funny, on the verge of laughing. Rose's scrapbook includes a profile of the brothers in the popular *New York Journal-American*: The brothers "are young. The sunny side of thirty. A. E. is perhaps the more serious of the two . . . R. R. has the talent . . . They laugh at failure. They scoff at success. They know how to enjoy life."

My father was especially drawn to spirited, attractive, independent women. Edith Fitzgerald was the first in his life.

Years later Everett remembered her as "a pretty, tough, Irish gal." She had doe eyes and wore her hair in a bob which, together with her dramatic early life, irreverent tomboy spirit, and Kentucky accent—half twang, half Southern drawl, to my father's delighted ear—combined to make her unlike anyone my father had known.

Edith was the sixth of ten children of John Morgan Fitzgerald, a cabi-netmaker in the backwater logging town of Burnside, Kentucky, in the heart of Appalachia, where he had built the family a large, rambling home. Edith was a gifted child, her father's favorite, and he told her he would help her go to college to become a teacher.

But when Edith was sixteen her father, an innocent bystander, was killed in a gunfight between the town marshal and a moonshiner. Devas-

Riskin, successful Broadway
writer and producer, 1927, at age
twenty-nine

RISKINS WILL OPEN "THE BELLS" AT BAYES' TUESDAY EVENING

Rollo Lloyd Will Act Henry Irving's Role of Mathias

A. E. and R. R. Riskin will present a revival of Sir Henry Irving's famous stellar vehicle, "The Bells," by Leopold Lewis, at the Bayes Theatre on Tuesday evening next. This is a dramatization of the story, "The Polish Jew," by M. M. Erckmann and Chatrain. Rollo Lloyd staged the production and Nicholas Yellenti designed the stage settings.

tated, feeling she had no future in Burnside, she married a local boy and ran off with him to Chicago. The marriage was over as quickly as it began and she made her way alone, still in her teens and one year out of Appalachia, to New York.

Her life in New York is a story both unique and familiar. She landed a small part in a play produced by Sam Harris, *Wake Up, Jonathan!* After a brief Broadway run, she barnstormed with the play through the Midwest. Admiring her judgment and moxie, Harris kept her on as a play reader and assistant when she returned to New York, while he kept his eye out for a good part for her. He found it as Go-to-Hell Kitty in the original production of *Chicago*.

In 1926 my father went to theater once or twice, or more, every week. Whether he sparked to Kitty Baxter, the betrayed wife who machine-guns her husband and two mistresses, or to Edith, he arranged to meet her.

They discovered a shared passion for theater and writing. They were both in their twenties and unattached, and soon were a steady item. Edith was free-spirited, unconventional even for the Jazz Age, and not long after meeting they took an apartment together in Forest Hills.

Edith Fitzgerald, actress, writer, and Riskin's first girlfriend, followed him to Hollywood under contract to M-G-M in 1930.

My father was producing on Broadway but wanted to write. Edith also wanted to write and they began a play together. My father hoped to explore universal themes such as the restraints of social conventions. Edith brought to the collaboration her keen observations about people. My father's style called for elliptical and offbeat, witty dialogue; Edith's characters said just what they meant. They agreed to try a romantic comedy, and somehow they made it work.

They shared one typewriter on the kitchen table, where my father chewed gum and smoked endlessly, two lifetime habits. He got up every few minutes to pace, jiggling the coins in his pocket.

Edith was an important influence on my father. She not only introduced him to the pleasures of domestic life, she brought to his life her innate caring and concern without compromising his independent spirit.

Edith showed *With the Help of Emily* to Sam Harris, who bought it on the spot. He took it to Chicago, where the press release noted, "It represents the combined writing talents of Robert R. Riskin and Edith Fitzgerald. Miss Fitzgerald, when not a playwright, is an actress. Mr. Riskin, when not a playwright, is a producer. And Miss Fitzgerald, when not Miss Fitzgerald, is Mrs. Robert Riskin."

Not exactly, but couples who lived together in Forest Hills or a hotel room in Chicago in the 1920s were expected to be married, and it would not have occurred to either of them to protest the journalistic license. Living together without benefit of marriage was a modern arrangement which suited them both. Like Jakob, each believed that the institution of marriage could stifle independence and kill romance, and they were content as they were.

With the Help of Emily closed out of town. While my father and Edith looked for their next play together, he resumed producing with Everett and Edith wrote the first of a number of short stories she would sell to *The Saturday Evening Post*. By 1929 her stories appeared virtually monthly alongside those of F. Scott Fitzgerald and Booth Tarkington. Her well-crafted tales were usually set in the theater, a world she knew well. She worked hard and nonstop and sent a generous portion of her earnings back to her family in Kentucky, where a *Saturday Evening Post* cover highlighting one of her stories hung in the family parlor long after Edith died.

One night my father went to a heavyweight fight in Yankee Stadium to see Jack Dempsey knock out Jack Sharkey. On his way home, a billboard promoting a revival meeting featuring Uldine Utley, a famous evangelist and contemporary of Aimee Semple McPherson, caught his eye. He had recently read Sinclair Lewis' *Elmer Gantry* about religion and its abuses, and thought a woman evangelist could be the basis for an interesting play. Edith was working on her short stories so he enlisted John Meehan, an experienced playwright, to collaborate with him.

Bless You, Sister concerns a minister's daughter who is disillusioned when her father's congregation dismisses him after years of devoted service. Persuaded by a con man to become an evangelist, Mary soars to wealth and fame, but her success is without spiritual meaning to her; it feels hollow and distances her from the man she loves. At heart a decent woman who knows she is being corrupted by money, she sets out to regain her integrity and true self.

Belief in the inherent decency of people, the price of corruption, the human capacity for redemption, all are themes that would occur regularly in my father's screenplays. A central character whose moral compass has spun out of control wants to find the

WOMAN EVANGELIST IN 'BLESS YOU, SISTER'

Alice Brady Wins Ovation in Play That Treats Religion Like Any Other Commodity.

BLESS YOU, SISTER, a play in three acts, by John Meehan and Robert Riskin. staged by Mr. Meehan and George Abbott; settings by Yellenti; produced by A. E. and R. R. Riskin. At the Forrest Theatre.
Rev. Robert MacDonald........George Alison
Sandy MacDonald.........Mildred MacLeod
Mary MacDonald.................Alice Brady
Freddy Gribble.................Robert Ames
Senator Gribble.............George Lessey
Timothy Bradley...........Charles Bickford
Esther Lewis.............Dorothy Estabrook
Tony Nazarro................Eugene Donovan
Daisy.......................Eloise Keeler
Miss Hyde.....................Marie Ilka
Miss Quigley.................Marjorie Dalton
George Hunter.................Denis Gurney
Choir Leader.................Olivia Martin

way back. "I still contend, despite all their larceny, people are good," he wrote my mother years later. "Most larcenous behavior is acquired—and the extent to which the individual practices it is dictated by necessity. Create a society of abundance—for all—and the need for larceny is reduced to a minimum. Of course, it will never be perfect—unless that green snow falls and changes the nature of men—but our jungle existence can be eradicated to some extent—and eventually to a great extent."

Bless You, Sister attracted director George Abbott, who left another production to sign on. "I could not help myself," Abbott told a journalist. "The idea of *Bless You, Sister* fascinated me."

It was a critical success for the Riskin brothers and their star. A headline in *The New York Times* read: WOMAN EVANGELIST IN "BLESS YOU, SISTER." ALICE BRADY WINS OVATION IN PLAY THAT TREATS RELIGION LIKE ANY OTHER COMMODITY. But that theme seemed to be the play's undoing as well; the idea that religion was sometimes marketed for profit kept audiences away, and the payroll for its enormous cast of seventy-five nearly bankrupted the Riskin brothers.

Still, the experience of *Bless You, Sister* inspired my father to keep writing. Working again with Edith, he wrote *Many a Slip*, starring Sylvia Sidney. The play opened at the Cort Theater in February 1930, with my father directing. The comedy centered on a writer whose girlfriend has tricked him into marriage by pretending to be pregnant. One reviewer said that the play gave "the Cort Theater the best acting it has seen in many a moon." It ran fifty-six performances and was voted by critics one of the best plays of the season.

Through the 1920s my father and Edith lived the high life in New York. He loved the horse races at Aqueduct and Saratoga Springs, the music of Tin Pan Alley, poker with pals, going to speakeasies and nightclubbing at Jack and Charlie's 21, the Cotton Club, and Café Deluxe. He was a natural dancer.

Fridays were reserved for trips to Brooklyn with Everett for Shabbos dinner when the family gathered in Bessie's cramped kitchen. The family loved Jakob's stories, all familiar, including his oft-told version of how the family left Russia, when he had stolen a Cossack's horse—so Jakob said—and then sold it back to him. When the Cossack figured it out, he and his friends came and pounded on their front door as Jakob and Bessie went out the back, and kept going all the way to America. Is that really true? the boys asked. Bessie, who had mastered the ancient Jewish art of answering a question with a question, said, "What—you think your father would ever tell you anything that wasn't true?" Then—she couldn't help herself—she laughed with the boys, and with abandon.

Everett also enjoyed the good life New York had to offer, and he and my father and Edith became an inseparable trio. For most of their lives my father and Everett shared one bank account, each putting in what he had and taking out what he needed. Money came quickly and easily and they spent it generously, helping Jakob and Bessie, and family and friends, with gifts and loans, paying their youngest brother Murray's tuition for law school. Moshe, as he was called, graduated from high school and enrolled directly in Fordham Law School, which did not require a college degree. Bessie said, "A lawyer?! What do you want—to make yourself crazy?!"

The threesome of Everett, my father, and Edith, expanded to include Katya Minassian, a stunning twenty-two-year-old actress/singer/dancer of Armenian-German descent. Before long, she and Everett were sharing an apartment on the Upper West Side. Unlike Edith, Katya expressed unhappiness with her unmarried status, and so did her strict German mother. Everett finally succumbed. Later, when serious domestic troubles arose in their marriage, he would look back wistfully at his carefree bachelor days of the late 1920s.

Like virtually everyone in the Roaring Twenties, my father and Everett invested on Wall Street. When the stock market crashed in 1929, their joint bank account was soon as empty as everyone else's. It had been a great decade-long ride but almost overnight my father was, like millions of others, virtually penniless and with few prospects. Broadway theaters, now an unaffordable luxury for many, started to shut down. Newspapers and magazines were hard hit, too, and Edith's income from *The Saturday Evening Post,* modest as it was, evaporated. Neither they nor Everett had money or any prospects.

When my father talked five years later about how grim times were, he said, "For days I paced Broadway aimlessly. No job, no money, no work, no breakfast. Next week's room rent and, as a matter of fact, tomorrow's breakfast were things only vaguely to be hoped for. I spent my last $1.20 to wire an important executive in Hollywood in a frantic plea for a job, and was rewarded with the most thunderous silence."

He took to wandering the boarded-up and nearly lifeless streets of Broadway. One day he ran into a friend who had been hired as an agent for Warner Bros. His friend had been trying to reach him on the telephone, he said; my father did not explain that he had been unable to pay the phone bill and his service had been disconnected. The friend knew of *Illicit,* the play my father had written with Edith, and thought maybe, perhaps, possibly Warners might be interested.

My father raced home and brought the play to him that day. Then he prayed.

It was weeks before he heard. His friend sent a note inviting him to the office, where he asked what my father wanted for the rights, saying that if he pushed Warners very hard he thought he might get $5,000.

"Something in his voice sounded like hidden anxiety," my father later remembered. "I said I would sell it for $50,000, no less, digging my nails into the palms of my hands in an effort to be casual . . . I have never been ushered out of an office as quickly as I was that day. I found myself on the sidewalk, swaying uncertainly, my mind blank."

He was still wandering aimlessly in the neighborhood, wondering how he could have been such an idiot, when his friend came out for lunch and, seeing my father, said, "You're a madman, but maybe I can get you $7,500."

Illicit, based on an Edith Fitzgerald–Robert Riskin play, was turned into a film starring Barbara Stanwyck in 1931.

My father again thought he detected a faint note of anxiety and decided to follow his hunch. "Look," said my father, whose worldly assets consisted of his train ticket back to Forest Hills, "Let's stop wasting each other's time. The price is—no, wait—if you'll close immediately, I'll sacrifice the play for $40,000."

"You have really blown your topper. I couldn't get you more than $10,000 for this if you were my own brother!" But they went back to his friend's office where they continued to argue. My father said he still had a "constant recurring hunch that they wanted the play badly."

"Well, I guess there's no sense discussing it further," my father finally said. "Mail the play back to me, will you? I'd take it with me, but I have an important tennis date."

He left the office and began the long slow walk to the elevator. He wanted to look over his shoulder to see if his friend was following, but that might show weakness. He pushed the button and when the doors opened, the operator said, "Down, sir?"

"No, up," he lied, stalling, still hoping to hear his friend following him. Twice more he let the elevator go down, now sure he had finally gone too far. The third time, just as the elevator door opened, the friend's secretary came running out, asking him to return. He walked back slowly, nonchalantly, but with legs like Jell-O. Now the real bargaining began.

"$20,000," said the friend.

"$30,000," my father came back.

"$30,000," conceded the friend and they sealed the deal. Had he known the movie of *Illicit* was already in production and the studio was panicked about securing the rights, he might have stuck to $50,000.

Illicit was the story of a couple "living in sin," as it was then called by those not doing it. The woman, convinced marriage poisons love, resists her boyfriend's proposal. When she relents, their marriage suffers from petty jealousies, mundane routines, and social obligations, and they agree to live separately to reignite their romance. When the film, starring Barbara Stanwyck, was released in 1931, its raciness so alarmed New York censors they demanded numerous cuts.

Now the studio executive on whom my father had spent his last $1.20 in a pleading telegram called to offer an overall deal. While he was thinking about it, Columbia purchased *Bless You, Sister* and asked him to come out under contract. He phoned around to find what other writers at Columbia were earning and asked twice as much. When the studio agreed, he scooped up Edith, who had been offered her own writing deal at M-G-M, and together they took the 20th Century Limited to California.

3

Tell me, what is it you plan to do with your one wild and precious life?

—MARY OLIVER

My mother came from pioneer stock and would need every ounce of their frontier strength and resilience to navigate the challenges of her early years.

Her mother, Elvina (Vina) Marguerite Jones, a complex woman composed of equal parts mountain granite, imagination, and emotional fragility, cast a long shadow over the lives of her children. She was the proud daughter of Daniel Webster Jones, a famed Westerner and Mormon missionary immortalized by Wallace Stegner in *The Gathering of Zion* as "The Man Who Ate the Pack Saddle." Stegner recounts the terrible winter when my great-grandfather was part of a posse that rescued more than a thousand starving travelers trapped in a blizzard on their way to the Mormon settlement at Salt Lake. Stegner called him a true hero.

Fay's maternal grandfather, Daniel Webster Jones (center), famed Western frontiersman and missionary in the early Mormon Church

Elvina (Vina) Marguerite Jones, Fay's mother, and Joseph Heber Wray, her father, 1890s

Jones' daughter, my grandmother, grew up in Utah and blossomed into a striking woman with a Victorian sensibility and an intense nature. While in her teens, her mother and baby brother were killed when a storm blew down a tent pole that crushed them. Vina raised her younger brothers and sisters while helping her father write his autobiography, *Forty Years Among the Indians*. Before she was twenty, she graduated from the University of Utah with a degree in education, a considerable achievement at a time when few women went to college.

Everyone agreed Vina was beautiful. My mother described her as having "an impudent kind of beauty—a retroussé nose, gray-green eyes, very fair skin, and an abundance of curly Titian-red hair."

By twenty-two, Vina had married, but her husband was physically unable to consummate the marriage, so the family story goes. At age thirty, she fell in love with Joseph Heber Wray, thirty-nine, an Englishman who had come to Utah from Yorkshire. His wife had died in childbirth and the child had died six months later. He had "clear blue expressive eyes," my mother remembered, "and a wonderfully kind nature." He too was Mormon. Joe and Vina fell in love and, clearly in the grip of passion, she left her husband and ran off to Canada with Joe. The episode, reported in the local newspapers, shocked Mormon society, but my mother told me she cherished this part of her parents' past, picturing them as desperately in love and willing to give up everything to be together.

Vina and Joe settled in a remote area of the Rocky Mountains, in Mountain View, Alberta, a tiny, isolated, scenically magnificent Mormon enclave fourteen miles southwest of Cardston, across the Montana bor-

Fay Wray, age three.
Born at home on
September 15, 1907,
near Cardston,
Alberta, Canada

der. Joe built a handsome two-story log-and-stone house on their 156-acre parcel. The house no longer exists, but a photograph shows that even by today's standards it was grand. Joe was a talented woodworker and crafted a houseful of furniture and later a playground for the children. At the front gate sat a large stone into which he proudly carved WRAYLAND. Seventy years later, when my mother returned to the hamlet of Cardston as their most famous citizen, the stone was presented to her, and the Kaini First Nation elders anointed her with an official Indian name, Little Beaver Woman.

Joseph Wray's handcrafted home in Alberta, where Vina gave birth to their first four children

At first, all went well for Joseph and Vina.

Joe started a sawmill that became successful. Babies came—a boy, Joseph Vivien, followed by three girls, Vaida Viola, Willow Winona, and, on September 15, 1907, my mother, Vina Fay. Fierce Canadian winters came, too, and somewhere in all this came a melancholia that seized Vina and unhinged her from her moorings.

Melancholia in that era could mean anything from depression to mania to undefined madness. What it was about Vina's behavior that alarmed her and Joe is not clear, but her life had become hard and joyless. As Vina's emotional world became jagged and turbulent, it was clear she needed help. Joe arranged a long stay for her in an asylum in Brandon, Manitoba, 650 miles away.

Without her, Joe could not manage both to make a living and raise a family. My mother, not yet three, was sent to live with a Doctor Stack-poole and his wife, and her brother and sisters were also sent to other families.

It may have been the relentless hardships that pushed Vina to the edge; the piercing winter cold with temperatures as low as 55 below zero, four babies born at home, a miscarriage, the whipsaw of hormones, a romance torn apart by the endless drudgery of laundry and cleaning, chopping wood, backbreaking work in the garden, schooling the children. The lone-liness of an isolated young woman longing for her heroic father, Daniel Webster Jones, the weight of her unmarried status and a complete absence of culture for an educated woman now living in a remote hamlet, all must have combined to make her life brutally hard. The asylum may even have been a relief.

After months of hospitalization, she was allowed to come home. The first thing she did was reclaim her children. My mother remembered the day clearly. "She knelt down outside the white picket fence and she told me she had come to take me with her. She seemed magical."

They were a family again, but life was never to be easy. In 1910, ten hard years after arriving in Mountain View, Vina and Joe sold their ranch and sawmill and left Canada for the warmth of Mesa, Arizona, where Vina's father and two of her brothers now lived. Before leaving, Joe and Vina were married, in St. Mary's Ukrainian Catholic Church in Brandon, Manitoba. My mother never knew whether Vina had divorced her previ-ous husband. Vina's claim, years later in a government document, that she was married to Joe as early as 1900 may have been more prideful than precise.

Vina's father and her brothers welcomed them to Mesa, the town Daniel Webster Jones had founded as a Mormon mission. He was still living there, now eighty-four, a godlike figure with a flowing white beard. From her earliest childhood, Vina had regaled my mother with stories about her grandfather, including the time when, in his teens, he accidentally shot himself in the groin and was left to die by his companions, only to be rescued by Indians.

At first everything was harmonious in Arizona. Vina and Joe stayed with her brother and it was here that my mother remembered first experiencing small pleasures—"a meal of fresh bread, milk still warm from the cow, and the tartness of just-picked gooseberries." Another baby boy, Richard, was born.

But Arizona had blistering heat, 120 degrees in summer, and Joe could not make a go of the new farm. The chickens died, the alfalfa withered, and two years after they had come to Arizona, Joe left in defeat to find work in Salt Lake City. Vina and the children followed shortly. It was in Salt Lake City where she delivered her last child, Victor, in 1914. She sold her wedding ring to pay the doctor for the delivery.

Again, life was hard. In a box of my mother's personal effects, I found letters Vina wrote to relatives asking for help. The grammar, penmanship, and style show Victorian perfection, but underneath her desperation is apparent. She tells how Joe had to go to other communities for work, sometimes for long periods. Once he was away all summer working at odd jobs for three dollars a day—painter, day laborer, a repair gang. In his absence, to make a little money, Vina wanted to sew dresses at home for other women but Joe wouldn't hear of his wife working. On Sundays Vivien, the oldest boy, got up at five in the morning, bought fifty newspapers for five cents each and sold them for a quarter. Joe's sister sent them some chickens and clothing, and Vina was once able to borrow $100 from an aunt and uncle, but in the three years they were in Salt Lake City there was never enough food and, my mother wrote, "Our stomachs were often growly with hunger."

It was at this time that my mother first sensed, without really knowing, that her parents' marriage was troubled. Joe had always been good-humored, a dreamer whose inventions were supposed to make them millions—one of which was a can opener for condensed milk that also resealed the can to keep out the flies—but now his optimism faded and he complained frequently about not feeling well. Vina said it was hard for Joe, who had built and managed his own sawmill, to work for someone else and see his family barely scraping by. He wanted to keep the children out of school, feeling they were not getting enough food at home to keep up their strength, but Vina insisted they go, fearing the humiliation they were sure to face when the school asked why they'd dropped out.

After three years subsisting—"living" is too grand a word—in Salt Lake City, Joe was offered a job as night watchman in a copper mine in the small town of Lark, Utah. Vina and the six children joined him in what was from the first day a life of grim and unrelenting poverty.

In 1977, I learned for myself what their life had been like in Lark.

My mother, then seventy years old and living in a high-rise condominium in Century City, California, received a letter from a childhood friend, a retired Utah Supreme Court Justice she had not heard from in sixty years. He enclosed a newspaper story about Lark, the Kennecott Copper company town, soon to be leveled and returned to the slagheap of time. The only thing standing in the way of the bulldozers was an eighty-one-year-old woman, the town's last surviving resident. Hilda Grabner, a former schoolteacher, a widow and obviously not a woman to be pushed around, refused to leave under any circumstance except death. According to the clipping, she remembered saying to her husband on their first day in Lark in 1928, "This is the last place God made and He forgot to finish it."

My mother shared the letter and clipping with me and I proposed we fly to Utah for a last visit to Lark, where she had lived from seven to twelve. She agreed at once. She wanted to reconnect with her childhood and I wanted to learn firsthand about her growing up.

We spent the night in Salt Lake City at the Hotel Utah—built in 1912, the year my mother came to Utah and, like her, still elegant and enduring—and set out in the morning for Lark. Before we left, my mother said, "We have to pack provisions, darling. It'll take all day to get there." I'd never heard her, or possibly anyone, use the word "provisions," which that morning sounded quaint and long-ago. We bought tuna fish sandwiches and bottles of Coca-Cola before setting off in our air-conditioned rented Mercury sedan on the daylong trip to Lark.

Fifteen minutes later, we saw a sign for the Lark turnoff.

"That can't be," my mother said firmly. "It takes all day to get there!"

I suggested we take the turnoff anyway. At first she resisted, then dubiously agreed but only to accommodate me. Within a mile, we were in a deserted, decaying town of boarded-up houses and empty ramshackle buildings.

"Oh my goodness," she said. "This is it."

What seventy years earlier had been a full day's trip in a horse-drawn wagon on a rough dirt path with no stores, so if you hadn't brought provisions you didn't eat, was today fifteen minutes on a four-lane highway with convenience stores all along the way.

She got out of the car and looked around the town. Her eyes were shining. For a long time she was silent. Amid the dilapidated shacks was one freshly painted house with a garden of orange and yellow ranunculus. It was obviously the schoolteacher's. My mother didn't want to bother her. Hilda Grabner had come to Lark long after my mother had left for Hollywood, and today was about her own memories.

She led me to an empty lot flanked by boarded-up houses.

"Our house was here, honey, but it's gone now. I guess it looked like that one." She laughed, pointing to a crumbling building. "Pretty awful, don't you think?"

I thought I should feel sad that she had been so poor, but I didn't. She never gave way to self-pity—that was beneath her—so why should I? "Children are never really aware of deprivation," she once told me. "If it snows, there's a ride on a sled or snow patterns forming on the window, and in the summer there's maybe a cactus flower to look at. If you haven't got very much it is twice as exciting when something good comes along."

She talked to me that day about her older sisters.

"Vaida and Willow and I sat on the porch for hours, singing in harmony to 'Alice Blue Gown.' They had clear, beautiful contralto voices. I could barely sing at all. And we were always making up stories, playing." She was silent a long time before continuing.

"Dick and Victor were always inside with Mama. They were imps, hellions really. Mama seemed so overburdened sometimes, taking care of the six of us . . . We couldn't play with the other children in town . . . she said they were 'ruffians,' . . . although sometimes we snuck off and played anyway. She was frightened they'd be a bad influence on us." More silence.

"I longed for my mother to be happy," she said. "She never was, really."

My mother led me up a hill, pointing to where the livery stable once stood, the little post office, the four-room schoolhouse. We stopped across the dirt street from a two-story boardinghouse that housed the unmarried miners.

"I loved watching the miners come home in the evening in their horse-drawn wagons, carrying their kerosene lanterns. They looked tired, but so proud. But Mama said, *You stay away from there now! Those men are single!*"

There was one other place she wanted to show me and she saved it for last. She led me to a small building which had been a pool hall on one side, a movie house and church on the other. We went into the crumbling wooden shell and she showed me where she sat hypnotized on a bench as the earliest black-and-white movies flickered on a bed sheet nailed to the wall. She pointed to where an organist played, dramatizing the scenes.

"I saw Mabel Normand, Charlie Chaplin, and Harold Lloyd here, little Mary Pickford and Douglas Fairbanks and Lillian Gish—she was my favorite. I loved her so—I never dreamed I'd meet her one day and we'd become friends . . . Oh my . . . it was all so long ago . . ."

After two hours we got back in the car. In 1990, Hilda Grabner died and the town was bulldozed flat. On her tombstone were engraved the words JOAN OF LARK.

The mill in Lark burned when my mother was twelve and Joe left to find work in another town. But this time was different. Vina didn't miss him. "Street angel, home devil," she said to someone in Lark one day, and when it was reported back to the children, they knew their father wasn't coming back. "There wasn't anything said about them separating. One day Papa was just gone and Mama seemed happy. There was a vague awfulness about that," my mother said. A few months later, she packed up the household and children and moved back to Salt Lake City.

They struggled as before, this time with no financial contribution from Joe. Vina did sew dresses at home, for a pittance. Vivien got a meager-paying job as an out-of-town laborer. My mother folded circulars during the Christmas holidays and earned enough to buy shoes and stockings and a sash ribbon for herself. Vic and Dick were old enough to be a double handful of mischief. The older girls, Vaida and Willow, found small jobs in town.

Vaida was my mother's guardian angel. Seventy years later she would still say she had never seen anyone as beautiful. They shared everything, including a bed, and in the winter, with no money to heat the house, they wore sweaters to bed and Vaida pulled my mother in close. "She was a warming person," my mother said.

Then came the flu epidemic of 1918. All the children were seriously ill, especially Vaida. My mother later wrote, the flu was "a dark force that must have moved through the whole Salt Lake Valley looking for Vaida, saying to her, 'I'm going to take you with me. You're mine.' But that dark, mysterious force had no shape and no face, so you couldn't go and find it and say, 'No. She's mine!'" Vaida died and my mother, age twelve, was devastated.

Lark, Utah, was a company town, built by Kennecott Copper to house its miners.

To her lifelong regret, my mother never saw her father again, with two very brief exceptions. Twice in Salt Lake City she saw him watching their house from across the street. My mother thought he was hoping to get a glimpse of his children but was afraid to come to the door. "I never told Mama," she confessed, lifting a hand to wave away the sadness. "I didn't want to be disloyal to her. I took my mother's side and believed what she told me."

She never knew what had caused the rift between her parents, only that she yearned for her father. As she grew older, she came to understand that Vina, so complicated and turbulent, had driven him off. She recalled how in Lark, before they separated, her mother had pushed Joe away physically and had grown to resent him, how she criticized him repeatedly in front of the children, often about money and his failure to provide it.

Without Joe, Vina had no outlets but her children. She was determined that they succeed where Joe had failed. She brushed the girls' hair for hours every night to make it shine, and creamed their hands and put gloves on them to keep their hands soft before they went to bed. She lectured them regularly on behavior and had ironclad rules about conduct, manners, education. She filled their heads with stories about seeing the great Swedish soprano Jenny Lind perform, and Maud Adams in the role of Peter Pan. She repeatedly told the children that Chief Justice John Marshall might have been an ancestor of theirs, although my mother doubted this was true. "Sometimes I actually enjoyed the special aura Mama created around our family," my mother said.

My mother and Willow took care of the tempestuous Vina more than Vina took care of them and were responsible for bringing joy and pleasure into their own lives.

A photograph of the family outdoors in Lark around the time of her parents' separation shows Vina strained and tired, bracing against the cold, her children huddled around her, with not a sign of the beautiful young woman Vina once had been. And there is little Fay, my mother, looking demure, poised, and confident, as if to say, *No matter where I am now, no matter what we are enduring, I know I will have a good life. I have a special destiny.*

In 1920, the *Salt Lake Telegram* offered a prize of a screen test to the person who sold the most subscriptions. My mother, now thirteen, eagerly entered the contest and Vina, determined as she was in all things, set out to make sure she won. She made my mother a plaid suit, curled her hair, and sent her door-to-door through the neighborhood hawking subscriptions. My mother won handily. When Vina heard that the screen test might include posing on a horse, she rented a pony so my mother could practice riding. Years later my mother described the screen test. "I sat on a bench holding a bunch of red roses. The director told me to lift the roses to my face and then look up to heaven as though the fragrance was just wonderful."

The test was shown in a local movie house. It went by so fast it was hard to tell much, but my mother was thrilled to see herself on the screen. And Vina, who seldom found anything my mother did praiseworthy, decided

Fay's beloved older sister, Vaida (right), died at eighteen in the 1918 flu epidemic.

Fay's other older sister, Willow (left), sixteen. They remained close all their lives.

little Fay might have some talent after all. My mother later said, "Everyone else in the family could sing beautifully. Finally, it seemed I could do
something, too, that got Mama excited."

Willow was a boy-crazy, dreamy fifteen-year-old working in a Salt
Lake City photography studio, touching up photographs with hints of
color, when one day she brought home a handsome coworker, William
Mortensen, and introduced him as her boyfriend. Mortensen was twenty-
one and an art teacher who had studied at the legendary Art Students
League in New York. His intense and passionate nature intoxicated the
family. His sophisticated talk of his travels in Greece and references to his
favorite novels, poetry, and theater was like a drink of cool water to my
mother's family, and especially to culture-parched Vina.

After Mortensen had made several visits to the house, Vina announced
that Willow and William were "sort of engaged" and he was going to
Hollywood and would take with him not Willow but my mother, to

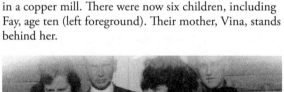

Lark, Utah, 1917, where Joe worked as night watchman
in a copper mill. There were now six children, including
Fay, age ten (left foreground). Their mother, Vina, stands
behind her.

Fay, thirteen, practicing riding for a screen test in Salt Lake City.
The test led nowhere, but got her excited about movies.

seek opportunities for her in the movie business. She would stay with
Mortensen's friends in Los Angeles and he would look after her.

Why would Vina, a Victorian, a perfectionist with unbending social
mores, who had warned her daughters against even speaking to men her
entire life, send my fourteen-year-old mother on a train to Hollywood? "I
never really knew why," my mother said.

But that night, barely more than a child, she had stars in her eyes and
asked no questions. "California! California! I went upstairs and sat in the
window, looking at the night sky. There was a large crescent moon with a
star near the lower tip of the crescent. I saw them as glowing symbols of
everything in the future."

She packed her few clothes and the next day said good-bye to her family and boarded the train to Los Angeles with Mortensen.

With the exception of the months her mother had been hospitalized for
melancholia, my mother had never spent a night apart from her family.
At fourteen, she was completely innocent. When the train was passing
through the Rocky Mountains, Mortensen told her how beautiful she
was. He praised her many virtues and told her he was in love with her,
not Willow. "My sister. It's Willow you like!" she insisted. "No, it's you,"

William Mortensen, photographer and artist, who took Fay, fourteen, to Hollywood, promising to help her get into movies

he said. She was alarmed and stricken with guilt over the betrayal of her sister, but there was no turning back. Years later my mother wrote, "I felt old, as old as a fourteen-year-old could feel." But being free from her mother's domineering hand was a relief and she never allowed herself to be saddened by her separation from the family.

Los Angeles rejuvenated her. It was still not much more than a frontier town, experiencing an explosive expansion with a monthly influx of thousands of people, booming oil and film businesses, and all the predictable tensions and conflicts based on race, religion, country of origin, and economic and cultural status. To my mother it was all beautiful and exciting. She described her first impression of the City of the Angels as "Poinsettias, red poinsettias, fields of poinsettias, poinsettias everywhere!" as if Los Angeles were glowing and electric with color.

The night of their arrival, Mortensen took her to a rooming house where she fell asleep, exhausted. In the middle of the night she awoke to a noise when Mortensen tiptoed into the room. Her heart pounding, she held her breath, not daring to move, but he curled up on the floor on the other side of the room fully clothed and went to sleep. This did not reassure my mother, who had overheard a conversation about a cousin who had slept with a man and become pregnant. She feared that sleeping in the same room with a man would result in a baby.

The next day, true to his word, Mortensen arranged for her to stay with a family. The people who took her in were, like Mortensen, Christian Scientists, and they praised the refined manners Vina had taught her.

Mortensen moved into a Hollywood apartment where he set up his photographic studio. He worked there during the week and on weekends took my mother in the sidecar of his Harley-Davidson motorcycle to parties and on day trips to the Santa Monica Mountains. Sometimes they went with his friends for dinner at the Musso and Frank Grill, then and now one of Hollywood's famous restaurants.

Life was full of adventure and freedom. Mortensen enrolled her in the Thirtieth Street Junior High School where he presented himself as her guardian. He also served as an extraordinary tutor, filling her mind with stories from Greek classics and introducing her to the work of the great Italian painters Titian and Tintoretto. He designed highly stylized photographs for which she sometimes posed, and he made elaborate masks for her to wear. He took her on outings to the famous Mack Sennett Studios to see the earliest slapstick comedies being shot. One weekend, he arranged for her to be the houseguest of a famous producer and his wife, hoping this would help her get work in the movies. When the producer tried to force his way into her bedroom, she leapt out of bed, locked the door and jammed a heavy dresser against it to thwart him. She could be feisty when she had to be.

Only once, shortly after their arrival in Los Angeles, did Mortensen cross the line. My mother, who was circumspect in discussing her private life, wrote that he sat next to her on the sofa and ran his hand over her dress to feel the shape of her breasts. "I sat absolutely still, not moving at all, even to look at him," she wrote with an honesty that startled me. Then Mortensen "got up and left the house, leaving me worried and wondering why, when I stood up, there was moisture on my skirt." He never troubled her again, and in the months following he resumed his role as her mentor protector.

Mortensen's efforts to help my mother get into movies led to her being hired for a bit part in a silent at Century Com-

Mortensen got Fay, fifteen, a part as a clown in a silent comedy. She loved the experience.

One of the Mortensen photographs of Fay that survive. Fay's mother ordered the destruction of hundreds more.

edy Studio. "I was to perform a clown dance in a theater scene," she said. "Bill got me a dark-green, white-trimmed clown suit and when they were ready for me to go up on stage and dance, I improvised what I thought was a screamingly funny little dance— part clownish, part Charleston— and I felt just marvelous showing off that way." In the days that followed she felt a glow, and bold enough to entertain her school friends with made-up stories, making herself popular.

A year after arriving in Los Angeles, she looked through the window to see Vina marching up the walkway with her little brothers Victor and Dick "and what looked like an invisible army on either side of her." Vina ordered her to gather up her things and, in stony silence, led her out of the house without even a word of thanks to the people who had cared for her child. Vina stayed silent all the way to a boardinghouse where she had rented rooms. At dinner and through the next day, she was steely and silent. Then she took my mother to nearby MacArthur Park, away from the boys. She told my mother she had visited a spiritualist who had spoken to her in the voice of Vaida, who warned Vina to get to California as quickly as possible to save my mother from Mortensen. *He is dangerous,* Vaida's voice said. My mother, believing the mystical communication, was hurt that her beloved sister Vaida would say such a cruel thing.

Vina began to interrogate my mother; "Now, what's the worst thing that happened? Did he have his way with you?" My mother, not really knowing what that meant, described how Mortensen took her to the beach one day where she posed in a chiffon dress like the famous movie star vamp, Theda Bara. She was so proud of her grown-up Theda Bara look that she had sent Mortensen's photos home to Vina. She had changed clothes behind a large rock and then run on the sand with the chiffon floating in the wind as Mortensen snapped his pictures. A policeman came over to say a passerby had reported someone on the beach was taking nude photographs, but that was not the case.

Vina turned to ice and steel. She marched my mother to Mortensen's studio and ordered him to produce every Graflex negative of my mother. "I stood near the door," my mother wrote. "He was across the room. I saw his expression of astonishment and nonresistance as my mother smashed each negative. Each plate of glass splintered down on the one just smashed until she had destroyed them all. *It wasn't good,* her fury was saying. *It was evil, evil, evil . . . !* It wasn't Mortensen alone her fury was directed at. "In her eyes, all the time I had been in California, I had been a very wicked person," my mother wrote. Vina forbade her ever to see or speak of Mortensen again. Years later, long after Vina's death, my mother talked about the education and opportunities he had given her. She remembered the sadness she felt knowing she might never again see the "great, lit-up look of Mortensen's blue eyes" when she came into the room.

Vina stayed in Los Angeles and continued to treat my mother as sinful. She took her out of school and did not let her leave the house unaccompanied. "All I had was an instinctive knowledge that I could survive any wrongful accusation," my mother later wrote. "I had that understanding about myself. What I did not have was an understanding about her. And the love I felt for her blurred any possibility of seeing her clearly. If I could have, perhaps I would have loved her more."

A lady from the Board of Education came to the boardinghouse and insisted my mother return to school, rescuing her from Vina's absolute

In 1923, Fay landed her first leading role, in *Gasoline Love* (1923), a Century Pictures comedy.

Publicity still, circa 1925

control. My mother always believed Mortensen had alerted the school authorities. She registered at Hollywood High School and from the beginning did well academically. The drama teacher saw in her a talent for acting and cast her in several school plays.

One day my mother was walking with Vina near their house when two men from Century Studios approached. They said they remembered her from her small role as a clown and offered her the lead in a movie. One of the men was a friend of Mortensen's but my mother said nothing. Within days she was acting in a new comedy.

Had Mortensen arranged the role for her? She was sure he had. The part led to another, more important role as a young leading lady in another Century film, and soon she felt confident enough, at age fifteen, to go alone and unprompted to the important Hal Roach Studios to ask for work. On the spot, they gave her a six-month contract.

Vina borrowed $600 to buy a Model-T Ford, and my mother's brother Vivien, who had joined them in Hollywood, taught my mother to drive. She dropped out of school and early each weekday morning, long before the sun was up, drove to Culver City with her new friend Janet Gaynor, another young actress at Hal Roach. Their daily assignments were in the short comedies the studio churned out, one each week, starring and directed by Charley Chase or Stan Laurel. I have my mother's yellowed time sheet from 1924 when she was earning $75 a week, about $1,000 today, enough for Vina to rent a house for the whole family.

When my mother's contract with Hal Roach ended,

At sixteen, she went unaccompanied to the Hal Roach Studios to ask for work and was given a six-month contract. She is featured in *Madame Sans Jane* (1925).

she and Janet Gaynor were offered more lucrative contracts at Universal Studios, run by the warmhearted Carl Laemmle; "Uncle Carl," everyone called him, both because he was avuncular and had brought his entire family, including future director William Wyler, from Europe and given them all jobs.

Uncle Carl took a protective interest in my mother. He cast her in a series of two- and four-reel Westerns where she mastered the art of applying her own heavy greasepaint and dark lipstick. "Actors were given the general outline of the story," she said, "and began shooting at sunrise. The crew used reflectors to capture the sun and light up the actors' faces, nearly blinding them. It was almost painful when I had to look up adoringly into the eyes of the leading man." I have seen some of the films. They show her to be spirited, beguiling.

In 1925, Fay, eighteen, starred in the independent silent feature *The Coast Patrol,* playing the innocent ward of a lighthouse keeper who falls prey to a gangster.

She filmed six days a week, from sunup to sundown, in scorching heat and swirling dust, making a new movie every week—*The Saddle Tramp, The Show Cowpuncher,* or *Lazy Lightning* directed by William Wyler. She trusted the cowboys to protect her when they started a mad horse

At Universal Studios, Fay appeared in dozens of two-reel silents, costarring in Westerns like *Wild Horse Stampede* (1926) with Jack Hoxie.

Fay Wray (center, above the second A) as a WAMPAS star, 1926. The
WAMPAS Baby Stars, a promotional campaign of the Western Association
of Motion Picture Advertisers, featured actresses on the threshold of
stardom. WAMPAS stars that year included Mary Astor (third from left),
Janet Gaynor (to Fay's right), Dolores Del Rio (third from right), and Joan
Crawford (last, right).

or cattle rush in her direction, although in *The Wild Horse Stampede* a
wagon crashed, which may have caused my mother's broken and ever-
after slightly misaligned nose. When she went on location, as far as Lone
Pine in the mountains northeast of Los Angeles, Uncle Carl made sure the
studio tutor went along so all the school-aged children could keep up with
their studies between scenes.

At eighteen, my mother was the sole financial support of her family.
She was nominated by the Western Association of Motion Picture Advertisers (WAMPAS) as a WAMPAS Baby Star, on a par with being a Hollywood debutante or Rose Bowl Princess. The list of honorees at their
black-tie gala, the WAMPAS Frolic of 1926, included, in addition to my
mother, Joan Crawford, Mary Astor, and Janet Gaynor.

Erich von Stroheim was clearly a man who understood the importance
of image and dramatic narrative, especially his own. He was born Erich
Oswald Stroheim, son of a Jewish hatter in Austria, and changed his name
to Erich Oswald Hans Carl Maria von Stroheim while en route by boat
from Bremen to America, where he encouraged all to believe he was a military officer from a royal Austrian family. In the world of film, a good story

has on occasion been known to trump the truth; or as a character in the film *The Man Who Shot Liberty Valance* says, "When the legend becomes fact, print the legend."

With his new legend and commanding bearing and personality, von Stroheim was accomplished at persuading Hollywood to finance his movies, which revealed him to be both a genius at filmmaking and wildly profligate with other people's money.

In 1926 von Stroheim, already famous after his epic movie *Greed,* was preparing his new big-budget film, *The Wedding March,* but was stymied by his inability to find a young actress with the necessary blend of innocence and sensuality. An agent took my mother to the great man's office. Years later she remembered her heart racing with excitement as von Stroheim, dressed in a pristine sleeveless white linen suit and wearing a monocle, paced back and forth recounting in exquisite and dramatic detail the story of his epic film set in Viennese society.

A dissolute Hapsburg prince, von Stroheim, is at the head of a grand parade when his horse spooks, causing a beautiful young girl, Mitzie, daughter of a beer garden owner, to fall and break her leg. The prince visits her in the hospital where, charmed by her innocence and sweet playful nature, he falls in love. But there are problems. The royal family, facing bankruptcy, is pressing the prince to marry Zasu Pitts, the lame and homely daughter of a wealthy businessman, and Mitzie's family is pushing her to marry a rich but smarmy local butcher. In the end, true love does not triumph. The prince gives in to his family and marries Zasu Pitts, breaking Mitzie's heart.

As von Stroheim was telling the story, he was gauging my mother's reactions, peering at her sideways through his monocle. She was paying the closest possible attention. "I wanted to show him I understood *everything!*" When he finished, he walked her to the door and said, "Good-bye, Mitzie." It may have been a slip of the tongue, or that he didn't know or had forgotten my mother's name, but to my mother the fact that he had called her by the character's name meant he was telling her she had the part. She burst into tears and hugged him, saying, "Thank you, thank you, thank you!" And the great director, whether he was nonplussed or perhaps now had seen a level of emotion in my mother which he felt would serve the part, said, "Ah, well um . . . yes, I guess I can work with you."

A press headline the next week read:

THE FAIRY WAND OF HOLLYWOOD LIGHTS ONCE MORE: FAY WRAY, CHOSEN OUT OF HUNDREDS BY VON STROHEIM FOR *THE WEDDING MARCH,* WAS SCHOOL GIRL A YEAR AGO

Fay on the set of her first starring role in a major feature, *The Wedding March,* costarring and written and directed by Erich von Stroheim, 1927. To her immediate right is Pat Powers, the producer who was nearly bankrupted by the production. Slumped in his chair is Matthew Betz, who played her evil fiancé, the butcher.

Von Stroheim was magnetic both as actor and director. He kept a musical trio on set—piano, cello, and violin—playing Viennese waltzes and marches to put the actors into the right mood. In one of Mitzie's romantic scenes, set in an apple orchard, he ordered 50,000 handmade apple blossoms (some accounts say 500,000) to be fixed to the trees. Extras were

dressed in authentic Austrian military uniforms, including underwear, all shipped in from Vienna.

Von Stroheim drove his cast and crew relentlessly, working them thirteen-hour days, but they were devoted to him. At age nineteen, my mother was—and was known around the studio to be—still a complete innocent. For almost a month in the middle of production she was not allowed in the studio, much less on the set, because von Stroheim was shooting scenes in a brothel. She felt lonely, and when she finally was allowed back, she was desperate to tell von Stroheim how much she had missed him and the work. Feeling a rush of emotion as they were walking to the set, she said, "I love you!" In an instant, von Stroheim had her pinned against the wall and was pressing his body against hers. She was too shocked to say anything or to push him away. All she could say, years later, was that she could hear her own heart beating, saying, "What has happened? What have I done?" Then, just as quickly as he had seized her, von Stroheim let her go.

What until now had been joyous became anxious and tense. Every day von Stroheim told her he had thought of her the night before. He arranged for her to come to his office and again pressed himself against her, bending her backward over the desk, but she gasped, "I hear someone coming!" and he released her. She felt she had started something she did not want to face. "It all seemed so urgent, so physical, so unrelated to the lyrical joy I wanted it to be," she wrote later. Von Stroheim scheduled an assignation, telling her where and when to show up. She handled it the only way she knew how, by not going.

For weeks after, von Stroheim was grim and curt with her on the set. "This was where I belonged, in a feature film with a great director," she thought, but now she was miserable.

Christmas came, and he showed up at her dressing room in uniform, bringing a beautiful box of chocolates, an alabaster powder box with a pink dancing lady on top, and an invitation to the Christmas Eve party he and his wife were giving at their home. She went and everything was wonderful again.

On and on went the filming, grand, extravagant, never-ending. One day they shot the climactic scene in which von Stroheim's character says his final good-bye to Mitzie. It is a scene emphasizing fate and destiny, and forever after was a matter of sad irony to my mother that although the picture was still not complete, it was the last day she worked with von Stroheim. The producer and financier of the film, Pat Powers, unable to rein in von Stroheim or control the escalating costs, stopped production and the next day told my mother he had given control of the picture and its 200,000 feet of film, the almost thirty hours already shot, to Paramount Pictures. He had also assigned my mother's contract to Paramount.

The news was hard for the cast and crew to accept, but my mother knew how much more painful it was for von Stroheim. She did not see him again for fourteen years, when he invited her to visit backstage on Broadway where he was starring as Jonathan Brewster in *Arsenic and Old Lace*. They had a nice reunion, but did not talk of the past. Except for the unfinished *Queen Kelly* and a few minor assignments, von Stroheim's directing career faded away. "The music would not begin again," my mother wrote.

The denouement at Paramount was predictably sad. Von Stroheim, eager to stay with the film, told the studio he would cut it to 44,000

Fay as an innkeeper's innocent daughter who falls in love with a prince, Erich von Stroheim. Their romance was destined to end unhappily. Here with von Stroheim, who prepares her for a scene

feet and they could release it as two three-hour movies. Paramount was not interested; one movie only, they insisted. The resulting impasse led Paramount to fire von Stroheim and assign the film to Josef von Stern-berg, who then cut the film to 10,000 feet for American release and added a second film, as von Stroheim had wanted, for European release only. The only known print of the second film, called *The Honeymoon,* was destroyed in a fire at the *Cinématheque Française* many years later.

Despite the fact that only the one film, representing a fraction of von Stroheim's vision, survives, film historians place *The Wedding March* in the pantheon of great silent movies.

Von Stroheim is magnetic and romantic as the prince. The qualities von Stroheim had long sought for Mitzie, combined innocence and youthful sensuality, come to life in my mother's performance. The movie was my mother's favorite, and of more than the one hundred she made, it's my favorite too, with her beauty and innocence encircled by filmmaking elegance from a time gone by.

Yet the film makes me sad. Perhaps it's the Romeo and Juliet theme, two people in love struggling to cross family barriers, and the sorrowful ending. Her inner light radiating goodness makes me pray she doesn't have to go back to the loveless fate we know awaits her.

4

Many years later, after they had become partners and close friends, my father described his first impression of Frank Capra. "The guy looked like a mug," he said. "He was telling a story, badly. He still tells stories abominably, but the thing is, he directs them brilliantly." Capra, who enjoyed bantering with my father, smiled amiably and said he agreed on all counts.

They met in 1930 in Harry Cohn's office at Columbia. Capra, short and dark and at this moment very intense, was relating the story of his next film to a roomful of captive executives and screenwriters when my father, a brand-new arrival from New York, entered late and took a seat in the back. He listened with a growing shock of recognition as Capra told, badly, the story of his play *Bless You, Sister,* which Cohn had bought and assigned to him to direct. When Capra finished, Cohn ordered my father to give his opinion.

"I wrote that play," my father said. "My brother and I produced it on Broadway. It cost us almost every cent we had. And if you make a picture of it, Mr. Cohn, I'm afraid it only proves that you"—he paused as everyone leaned forward—"are no smarter than we were."

The executives and writers, unused to hearing anyone speak so bluntly to the volcanic Cohn, were startled. Capra, seeing his next film imperiled, was outraged and demanded my father explain himself. My father said his experience with the play had convinced him audiences did not respond well to the story of religion being peddled as a commodity by an unprincipled evangelist. Despite positive reviews, Broadway audiences had stayed away and he thought movie audiences would as well. He also told Capra and Cohn that, no thank you, he had no interest in writing the screenplay.

Cohn and Capra nevertheless went ahead with the film, retitled *The Miracle Woman* and starring Barbara Stanwyck, from a screenplay by Jo Swerling. It failed, not so much critically as financially—the first failure Cohn and Capra had suffered together. Stanwyck earned rave reviews, but the depiction of religion being exploited for profit didn't appeal to movie audiences any more than it had to theatergoers.

Cohn never held it against my father that he had challenged him publicly, and over the next decade they did more than twenty pictures together, some with Capra directing, many of them good, some truly great. Cohn had two qualities my father came to admire. Rough and ruthless though he could be, he recognized and appreciated talent, especially in writers—Cohn knew he couldn't write and respected those who could—and he liked people who spoke their minds. My father may not have spoken Cohn's language—no one ever heard my father curse or heard Harry when he wasn't turning the air blue—but he and Cohn respected and even liked each other. My father found Cohn honest in his business dealings, loyal, and charming when he chose to be, and he admired Cohn's passion for moviemaking and his intuitive sense of what audiences wanted.

He also appreciated the hardscrabble path Cohn had taken to build his studio. Cohn was, like my father, the son of a tailor who grew up on the streets of New York and left school after the eighth grade to go to work. He was a short, tough kid on the make who had hustled his way through the pool halls and vaudeville palaces of the city, plugging songs and appearing in a comedy act, before getting a low-level job in a movie lab. Soon he was unstoppable, within two years making his way to Hollywood and then creating a film company on Poverty Row, where fly-by-nighters set up shop. Even in this world of hangers-on and bottom-feeders he became legendary, for his parsimony if nothing else. Once when he had gone to the unprecedented expense of hiring a makeup artist for an actress, he ordered that only one side of her face be made up and that she be photographed only from a side angle.

The 1920s would be a decade of relentless struggle for Cohn, making small movies on small budgets, before he outgrew his humble beginnings and found his place among the moguls who ran the major studios. Nothing he did in these ten years was as important as hiring a young director, Frank Capra.

As hard as my father's and Cohn's paths may have been, Frank Capra had to fight every day of his childhood just to survive. He was six years old when his family emigrated from Sicily, one of six surviving children of a peasant family where seven other children had died in childbirth. His father couldn't adjust to the new country and turned down any job offered him. Capra felt his mother never loved him. "She didn't like me at all . . . Between her and my brother Tony I took many a punch and slap in the face. Home was not for me a house of joy, it was nothing but a house of pain."

Everything was a struggle. In the first grade he had to work long hours selling newspapers on the street. Small, dark, with an Italian accent, he was taunted mercilessly at school. "I was dressed so poorly all the time, and if anybody said a word about my clothes, I'd kick him right in the ass or in the balls."

What saved him was hard work and education. He went to high school where he kept up his studies while working as a janitor and playing guitar in a brothel. Encouraged by his teachers, he went on to attend what became the California Institute of Technology with the goal of becoming an engineer, but from the start it was theater and Shakespeare that excited him. It was here that his point of view changed, he said, from "alley rat to the viewpoint of a cultured person."

Unable to find a decent job after college, he hung around the house. His mother disapproved of what she saw him becoming and handed him a bag of bread and sausages and ten dollars and threw him out. He tried to be a writer but the short stories he wrote led nowhere—"a pretty amateurish lot," he later described them—and he found himself wandering around California, tutoring, selling door to door, promoting phony mining stock to farmers.

At times, it seemed a dark cloud followed him. His father was killed in a gruesome farm machinery accident. A brief early marriage collapsed under his wife's accusations of abuse and of his alcoholism and infidelity.

He told of a day he came home expecting her to be ready to accompany him to an important screening and "she was standing next to the piano, blotto. *Blotto!* There was nothing in my mind but 'What a bitch you are!' I didn't say a word. I went over to her and hit her. She was lucky I didn't kill her."

One day chance led him past a new motion picture studio in San Francisco. They needed a director for a one-reeler, *Fulta Fisher's Boarding House,* and Capra talked himself into the job—and at the same time into a life and career that finally would make him world-famous and successful beyond his dreams.

But even now the path forward was not easy. He returned to Los Angeles and worked as a director for Mack Sennett, but was demoted to gag man when Sennett found his directing insufficient. He directed three silent films for Harry Langdon, but when Langdon publicly minimized Capra's contributions, telling *Variety* he could have done it better and would direct himself from now on, Capra lashed back and a nasty brawl

Harry Cohn, cofounder and president of Columbia Pictures Corporation (left) and Frank Capra, Columbia's top director and Riskin's long-term partner (right)

ensued in the Hollywood press, damaging both men. Capra was "flat on my ass again" when Harry Cohn offered him the chance to direct a feature film if he also provided writing and producing services as needed, all for the miserly sum of $1,000.

Cohn came within an inch of firing Capra the first week. What Capra did, so imaginative it's surprising no one had done it before, was shoot only close-ups one day, only long shots the next, saving precious hours in lighting and camera moves. It made watching rushes an unsettling experience, but Cohn was persuaded when he saw the finished picture, well directed and shot on a pinchpenny budget in a lightning-quick twelve days, and he assigned more pictures to Capra. When all did well, Cohn surprised Capra and probably himself by tripling and then quadrupling his salary; he also awarded him the prestigious screen credit, "A Frank Capra Production." The following year when Columbia followed Warner Bros. and *The Jazz Singer* into the sound era, Capra demonstrated he could handle the new creative and technical challenges, cementing his importance to Cohn and the studio.

At his first meeting with Capra in Cohn's office, my father also met the man who would become his closest friend and, fifteen years later when I was born, my godfather.

Harry Cohn understood from the beginning that to succeed in talkies he needed talented writers. Two years before he hired my father, he started bringing newspapermen and playwrights out from New York. In Jo Swerling he brought out one of the best.

Swerling had emigrated to New York from Ukraine as a small child. By his early twenties he had become a successful journalist, cartoonist, and playwright. Standing five-foot-six, he was a wide-ranging intellectual with passionate liberal politics. He also was gentle-natured, intense, emotional, and his thick glasses made his eyes look very large. He always looked rumpled. His son, Jo Junior, told me, "Your father was always stylishly dressed. If it weren't for my mom, I doubt my dad would ever have changed his pants."

My father and Swerling formed an instant, lifelong bond. Apart from their Lower East Side roots, both looked at the world with wry good humor. They swapped stories and together explored film, theater, literature, and classical and popular music. Each had a sympathy for the underdog that was reflected in both their lives and their writing. Their closeness quickly grew to include Swerling's wife, Flo, and eventually my mother.

Flo's dinner parties were storied in Hollywood, with regular attendees including my father, Edward G. Robinson, Bertolt Brecht, Harpo Marx, and Hollywood's intellectual and liberal elite. It mattered not at all to Flo that Jo looked as if he'd been dressed at the Goodwill; she had strawberry-blond hair cut short, wore brightly colored dresses from Paris, fashionable high-heeled shoes, charm bracelets that jangled, and a liberal sprinkling of Chanel #5, all in perfect tune with her effervescent spirit. After dinner, guests gathered around the piano while she played and led them in singing popular songs of the era—"It Don't Mean a Thing" or "Brother, Can You Spare a Dime?"—and then a long evening of conversation would follow, on FDR's efforts to lead the country out of the Depression or the growing menace of Hitler and Mussolini.

Frank Capra, whose politics and social attitudes were marked by devout conservatism, often stood apart in these liberal-leaning discussions. He disliked the New Deal, never voted for anyone not a Republican, admired Mussolini's firm hand, feared communism, and hated taxes. Capra had worked hard and fought his way out of poverty, and had no use for the little people or their New Deal advocates who wanted to take his money and give it to those who had not pulled themselves up as he had. My father, understanding that Capra's outlook had been shaped by the circumstances of his childhood, never allowed their differences to affect their friendship or working relationship.

Jo Swerling, a top Columbia writer, in 1933, and at the Malibu home with his wife, Flo, 1953. They were Riskin's closest friends and were soon to become Fay's as well, and in 1945 became my godparents.

It confounded some that, despite his views, Capra became known as Hollywood's "champion of the little man," a progressive mantle that fit him uncomfortably. That the movies he directed may have been at odds with his own views never troubled him. If the public wanted stories about the lives and dreams of so-called ordinary people, he would make them. The scripts my father wrote, reflecting sympathetic understanding of all the ordinary people around him, when coupled with Capra's great prowess with actors, camera, visuals, and pacing, came to define a "Capra film."

Robert Riskin, and other writers like Jo Swerling and Sidney Buchman, provided the answer to the problem Capra identified as his own limitation when he said, "This director doesn't know what the hell to say."

Working together, they made great movies. In their heyday, no one did it better.

•   •   •

My father was thirty-three years old when he arrived in Hollywood, never having written, nor likely read, a feature screenplay. He quickly learned the screenwriter's craft is different from the playwright's. Scenes tend to be longer on stage, with dialogue used to advance the drama. The screenwriter has tools—cuts and wipes, dissolves and fades—that allow easy changes from time to time and place to place. Film gives writers freedom to tell stories visually, often without dialogue, and to focus an audience's attention with camera directions, all in the service of keeping things moving and interesting.

It was not only playwrights who had trouble making the transition to film. Novelists, among them William Faulkner and F. Scott Fitzgerald, came to Hollywood and struggled to master the form; some never succeeded. A frequent criticism of both novelists and playwrights was that they overwrote for film, taking precious time to go into subtleties and interesting but unnecessary side excursions when film requires getting on with it.

My father's first effort at Columbia was a disaster. No one told him that Cohn had decreed no screenplay could be longer than ninety pages. When his first weighed in at 200 pages, Cohn fired not my father but the producer who was supposed to be supervising him. He immediately gave my father another assignment.

The pressure on writers to meet studio production deadlines was relentless. What enabled my father to maintain the pace was his understanding of dramatic structure from theater, his experience with character and fast, breezy dialogue, and a great deal of very hard work. In his first two years at Columbia, he wrote entire screenplays or the dialogue for nine films; all nine went into production.

The projects he was given, chosen by Cohn and overseen by the head of Columbia's story department, Dorothy Howell, were often adaptations of short stories. With two exceptions, all featured characters from different social milieus weaving their way through romantic tangles while trying to straighten out or improve their own lives. Bright, high-spirited, motivated women were often featured. The films included *Arizona* with Laura La Plante and promising newcomer John Wayne, *Men in Her Life* starring Charles Bickford and Lois Moran, *Three Wise Girls* starring Jean Harlow, *The Big Timer* with Ben Lyon and Constance Cummings, and *Shopworn* with Barbara Stanwyck. Screwball comedy with its fast-paced repartee and struggles between economic and social classes, generally thought to have come of age in my father's script of *It Happened One Night* in 1934, is already becoming evident in these early films.

Within a year, the hallmarks of a Riskin screenplay had begun to appear: Care about your characters . . . Women are smart so listen to what they're saying . . . Most people are good and rich people are not inherently bad . . . Having a lot of money creates as many problems as not having any . . . Humor is important, but probably best avoided if at somebody's expense.

Of his early films, nowhere does his personality come through more vividly than in *Platinum Blonde* (1931), where he wrote all the dialogue. Everybody who knew him recognized in Stew Smith my father's own breezy manner, his quips and observations about human foibles, his romantic style.

Stew is the easygoing and quick-witted newspaperman who falls for rich society girl Jean Harlow and sets about romancing her. When he tells her he wants to write a play, she finds that eccentric. "Me?" he says. "No— most ordinary guy in the world . . . Only one thing wrong with me. I'm color-blind . . . I've been sitting here half an hour looking at you and I don't know yet whether your eyes are blue or violet." When he moves in much, much closer to see her eyes better, she reassesses her earlier opinion. "I'm beginning to believe something can be done with you," she tells him. He agrees. "Putty—just putty—that's me."

When they marry and move into her opulent home, Harlow sets out to remake Stew into the high-toned gentleman she wants him to be, even hiring a personal valet to look after and train him. He soon becomes a bird in her gilded cage, bored to distraction by the manners and money of the idle rich. He wonders what Smythe, his valet, does all day. "I mean when you're alone and you want to amuse yourself."

"Well, sir, I putter."

"Do you have to have a putter to putter? . . . How about me? Do you think if I concentrate and put my whole soul into it, that someday I might be a putterer . . . ?"

"Not a good putterer, sir. To be a putterer, one's mind must be at ease. For instance, a fish can putter in water but not on land because he'd be out of place . . . Now sir, if you'll pardon me, with all respect, as Smythe to a Smith, you are an eagle in a cage."

All it takes for Stew to unlock his cage is Smythe's common sense. He leaves Harlow and goes back to his newspaper pal Gallagher (Loretta Young), who has loved him all along. She encourages him to write a play about what he knows and cares about, and of course they will live happily ever after.

Like Stew, my father found himself in a world of glamour and money in Hollywood and at risk of finding himself in his own gilded cage. It concerned him. Each day when he left the upscale apartment he shared with Edith, he drove to the studio down streets where the homeless slept under newspapers on sidewalks and apple sellers hoped for a customer with a nickel. When the poorest of the poor appeared as characters in his scripts, it was clear he liked and respected them and wanted the audience to as well. He would endow seventy-five-year-old Apple Annie, who peddles apples at night on Broadway in *Lady for a Day*, and homeless former baseball player Long John Willoughby in *Meet John Doe,* with humanity and dignity.

He never viewed screenwriting as a step down from Broadway or journalism as did some newly arriving writers. Legendary wit and writer Herman J. Mankiewicz (*Dinner at Eight, Citizen Kane*) lured Ben Hecht, coauthor of the stage play *The Front Page,* to Hollywood with the telegram, "You've got to get out here. Millions are to be grabbed and the only competition is idiots." Some directors, too, weren't immune to feeling they were in a field beneath their talents; Frank Capra referred to his career in film as "marrying the harlot."

Once he was in a position to have a say, my father tried never to work on a screenplay that didn't reflect values he believed in, that wasn't *about* something. His characters often had to struggle to maintain their integrity against forces of cynicism or greed, a theme he first explored in his play *Bless You, Sister.*

He worked without respite for the first two years but understood and lamented that there was a price to be paid for writing at the breakneck speed the studios demanded. Few writers dared complain publicly, but in his second year at Columbia, when he was working nonstop from picture to picture, he told the *Los Angeles Herald,* "The producer and director who expect the writer to turn it on like a water faucet are bound to be disappointed in originality, if not quantitative output. To turn around in two weeks an idea derived from a title is an obstetrical feat nothing short of a miracle."

Those who knew him at the time described him as having a subtle wit and an easy, unpretentious style. His closest friends saw other sides—determination, and a restless, searching mind. He was also a private man who generally kept his deeper feelings to himself. Producer Irene Selznick said he had "a quiet nobility."

• • •

Platinum Blonde came out in 1931. Jean Harlow's kittenish, sometimes elegant performance confirmed her stardom. Loretta Young earned strong reviews for being believably down-to-earth, tender and loyal. And my father showed he was getting the hang of things. One critic wrote, "Bob Riskin (former New York producer) turned out the most perfect dialogue job ever heard on a soundtrack." Another said the picture was a "perfect blending of the director's astute visual composition with the writer's lean, articulate dialogue."

The director was Frank Capra. He brought to the picture a vitality, a fluid, moving camera, warm and rich lighting, and superior casting down to the smallest parts. Actors responded to his direction. "Capra was not a talker," one actress said, "but he was forceful. He knew what he wanted and he knew how to create the right feeling with the actors. When he smiled, it went all over his face. And it was natural, the warmth that he had."

Capra's gifts and passion were not lost on my father, nor my father's on Capra, who would later write, "Bob was a fine writer, a simpatico man. Natty, witty as they come, he loved life, sports and women and vice-versa. We had many things in common, but two stood out: 1) our skulls vibrated to the same lady's hair massager and 2) our funny bones vibrated to the same tuning fork in humor . . . and never was there a better ear for the spoken word than Riskin's."

Although it would be a while before they worked together again, the stage was now fully set for their remarkable collaboration.

My father and Edith had settled into Colonial House, a stylish West Hollywood apartment building with high ceilings and working fireplaces which was at various times home to Carole Lombard, Cary Grant, Clark Gable, and Bette Davis.

They no longer wrote together, or even saw each other during the day. The theater they both loved was hard to find; movies were the staple in Los Angeles. Each morning they set out in opposite directions, my father to the humble Columbia lot in Hollywood, Edith to the grand and expansive M-G-M studio in Culver City.

Columbia had at any time perhaps a dozen writers under contract. M-G-M was, like its famous symbol, the roaring lion of Hollywood. The studio made forty to fifty pictures a year, many of them important, and was home to the greatest assemblage of movie stars in Hollywood. Edith joined the studio's army of 150 writers, which included some of the most renowned in town: Donald Ogden Stewart, Anita Loos, F. Scott Fitzger-

In his first two years at Columbia, Riskin wrote or cowrote on ten films, mostly romantic comedies. For *Platinum Blonde* (1931), his dialogue added charm and spice to Jo Swerling's screenplay. Directed by Frank Capra, the film starred Jean Harlow, Loretta Young (below), and Robert Williams.

ald. They each answered to the studio's all-powerful executives—Louis B. Mayer, Irving Thalberg, and Hunt Stromberg—and were cogs in a well-oiled machine that operated, not always but frequently, with one writer assigned to lay out the story, another to do a first draft of scenes, another to flesh them out, and another who specialized in dialogue, working in sequence, assembly-line fashion. The studio system—all studios functioned more or less alike—was not designed to bring out the greatest creativity a writer had to offer, nor to allow much opportunity to personalize a story, but under the stewardship of fellow Kentuckian Hunt Stromberg, Edith carved out a more than respectable ten-year career that included some notable highlights, beginning with *Susan Lenox: Her Fall and Rise* for Greta Garbo in 1931. She was awarded sole screenplay credit for *Today We Live* based on a Faulkner story, with Howard Hawks directing and Joan Crawford and Gary Cooper starring. She went to Columbia for *Brief Moment* with Carole Lombard (1933), and later went on to do *Small Town Girl* with Janet Gaynor and *The Wedding Night* with Gary Cooper and Anna Sten. Her greatest success was as one of three top screenwriters on Somerset Maugham's *The Painted Veil* starring Garbo, which earned rave reviews.

Eighteen months after settling into their new lives in Los Angeles, my father and Edith decided to end their relationship. Edith wanted to marry but he did not, and that decided things. Years later, when he gave a full account to my mother, my father said that while they had been collaborators and best friends, faithful to each other and mutually supportive, he had come to feel something was missing. He finally had to face the fact that he was not in love with Edith.

Their separation was amicable, yet not easy after so many years. He continued to take an interest in her and did what he could to be helpful. It was he who had arranged for her to come to Columbia to write *Brief Moment,* and they celebrated when they sold their play *Ex-Lady,* which had never been produced, to Warner Bros.

On her own for the first time in almost a decade, Edith soon married a champion tennis player; she became a serious player herself but the marriage ended after three years. She worked in Hollywood until 1939, when she wrote one last film, *Within the Law,* and a last story for *The Saturday Evening Post* titled "Suggestions for a Happy Ending." By 1942, Hedda Hopper wondered in her column what had become of Edith Fitzgerald, who was "a fine writer." What is known is only that she moved back east to live with her mother in North Carolina and died there in 1968 at seventy-five.

Now a top screenwriter, fellow writer Sidney Buchman described Riskin as "a very cultivated, nonchalant playboy." Below, by his shiny new 1932 Ford roadster

My father, on his own for the first time in years, began a relationship with Glenda Farrell, the actress who played Missouri Martin, the wise-cracking and sexy moll in his movie *Lady for a Day.* She had also been a villainous wife in *I Am a Fugitive from a Chain Gang* (1932), a blonde bombshell in *Gold Diggers of 1935,* and a hard-boiled newspaper woman opposite my mother in *Mystery of the Wax Museum,* but at the time she was probably best known as Torchy Blaine, a spirited, self-reliant, fast-talking—400 words in 40 seconds—sleuth in a series of seven popular films of the 1930s.

Farrell was the opposite of the brassy characters she often played. She was warm and charming, a great confidante, generous, a devoted mother and daughter. When a journalist asked about love in her life, she said, "I love several men, three cats, and one city." The city was New York, two of the cats were the Siamese my father had given her, and the men were her young son, Tommy, from an early marriage, her father, and her fiancé, Robert Riskin.

Fiancé? Not exactly, but it would have been ungentlemanly to deny it and they were having too much fun to care. They often dined at Ciro's or the Brown Derby in Beverly Hills, or Sardi's when they went to New York where they immersed themselves in theater. He delighted in finding special gifts for her, and on one of the trips spent three days searching for twin Siamese cats. "I always wanted a pair of them, and he remembered!" she said.

New York trips allowed him to spend time with Jakob and Bessie, now in their mid-sixties, living comfortably on what income he and his brother Everett provided. My father hoped his parents would move to California where he and Everett could fix them up with a place of their own; maybe Essie and Rose and Murray and their growing families would move out, too. Jakob and Bessie promised they would "someday, when we're old . . . there's still plenty of time." They had made a good life for themselves in New York with close friends, pinochle and cribbage games for Jakob, weekend trips to the Jersey shore with cousins, grandchildren starting to arrive. My father didn't argue but planned to renew his appeal on his next trip.

His relationship with Glenda was carefree. "We never quarrel," she told the press. Their only problem was hard work and too little time together. After twelve-hour workdays, Farrell preferred simple dinners at home

Riskin met actress Glenda Farrell on *Lady for a Day* shortly after his relationship with Edith Fitzgerald ended. Farrell became the woman in his life for two years. Farrell on a weekend outing with her son, Tommy, and my father

Farrell with one of the twin Siamese cats my father
gave her

with her son, which my father sometimes joined, and he liked to take
them on weekend picnics.

But the studio PR machine had to be served, too; they expected Farrell, indeed ordered her, to go to parties and nightclubs where she could
be photographed and written—and gossiped—about. My father was her
steady date on these evenings and the press quickly began buzzing about
wedding bells.

Reporters were also quick to invent and report imagined troubles. One
columnist wrote in the *Los Angeles Times* about what Farrell thought, and
my father agreed that it was all gossipy foolishness.

> Glenda Farrell says it is the gossip columnists who are breaking up
> romances. After going with Bob Riskin, the writer, for something
> over a year and being seen with him nearly every evening somewhere,
> there came a night when Glenda, tired of the games in a certain
> famous club, wandered downstairs and fell into conversation with an
> actor. The following day all the gossip sheets had her romance with
> Riskin broken up. The fact is, she says, Riskin was upstairs all the
> time—had brought Glenda there and was taking her home!

Another installment in the ongoing saga, this one by Louella O. Parsons from "Dateline Hollywood," August 21, 1934:

> Robert Riskin is mighty glad to be back in Hollywood. He was in
> Lake Como when Mussolini summoned his troops to get ready to

meet any invasion from the Nazis after the assassination of Dollfuss. Bob got lots of material for his stories and he reports at Columbia immediately. Glenda Farrell assures me that there is no change in her affection for Bob, that he is still headman in her life.

After four intense years in Hollywood, with no time off except for trips to New York, my father was eager for a break and the chance to finally see Europe. He traveled alone to London—he fell in love with London—and went on to Paris and Italy before taking a freighter through the fjords and into Lapland. Along the way he heard dark, fear-filled talk about the rise of Hitler and concerns about a possible Spanish Civil War, which in fact broke out two years later.

He came back to America to be greeted with more gossipy headlines.

DATELINE HOLLYWOOD: OCTOBER 21, 1934, LOUELLA O. PARSONS:

The Glenda Farrell–Robert Riskin heart attack is over. It was one of Hollywood's hottest romances while it lasted. Miss Farrell and the boyfriend have definitely split romantically speaking, although according to the lady's own word, they are still good friends.

After two years together Farrell, who had long feared that the intrusive pressures of Hollywood might ruin their relationship, told the press it was over. She wanted to earn enough money from acting to secure a good future for her son and her father, she said, a responsibility she did not feel my father, or any man, should share—unless they were married.

My father told Everett he was crazy about Glenda but wasn't sure he was suited for marriage. His life was filled with writing, friends, political and union causes, reading, and playing golf and tennis and the horses and poker. And he may have worried, too, that he had not yet found whatever he was seeking in a lifetime partnership.

After the split, he and Glenda remained good friends and a few years later traveled to Europe together.

In 1932 Harry Cohn gave my father an assignment unlike either of them had ever contemplated. Cohn wanted him to write a serious original drama about a bank in imminent danger of failing, with the head of the bank to be the hero.

No story could have seemed less promising. The country was still mired in the Great Depression, and banks and bankers were in low repute. On the heels of the crash in 1929, of 25,000 banks in the country more than 11,000 had failed, wiping out countless depositors and $2.5 billion of their savings. Ticket sales to movies had dwindled dramatically and the studios were in trouble. While Columbia was in better shape than most thanks to Cohn's legendary frugality, in 1932 the studio was facing a crisis. For ten years, Cohn had depended for financing on the San Francisco–based Bank of Italy, later the Bank of America. But now the bank was losing $3 million a day and in peril of going under. Cohn feared Columbia would go down with them.

Cohn could have assigned the screenplay, which was so important to him personally, to anyone, but in a clear sign of confidence and trust, gave it to my father. Cohn had no story to suggest but told him about the Bank of Italy and its founder, A. P. Giannini, who with his brother A. H. (Doc) promoted it as "the bank of just plain folks," and earned the reputation of lending money not on assets but on character. Doc in particular had taken an early chance on the movies and lent Cohn money beginning in 1919, and supported him through the worst of the Depression.

My father had wanted to write an original screenplay and leapt at the chance. People in trouble, the economy, the crisis in banking, all interested him as subjects for drama. He subscribed to the agenda of Franklin D. Roosevelt, whom he hoped would soon be president. FDR was urging people to put their money back to work again: "Keep your dollars moving," he said. Banks can help, taking deposits and making loans. "Back to the Good Times" was his theme, as "Happy Days Are Here Again" would be his anthem.

My father asked Doc Giannini about his banking philosophy, and with that in mind constructed his story.

A banker named Dickson has lent money all his life on his belief that character, not credit, is what matters. Dickson's lending practices have concerned and now angered his board of directors who, certain the loans will not be repaid during the Depression, want to save their investment by selling out to a big New York bank. They confront Dickson who wants to stay independent and serve his town and his people.

"Jones is no risk," he tells them. "Nor are the thousands of other Joneses through the country who have built up his nation to be the richest in the world, and it's up to the bank to give them a break . . . Where is all the money today? In bank vaults—socks—old tin cans buried in the ground. We've got to get the money in circulation before you'll get this country back to prosperity." Pure FDR optimism, pure Riskin.

A robbery ignites rumors about the bank's solvency and leads to a run on the bank, which threatens to bring it down. Getting no sympathy and no help from his directors, Dickson puts up his own money to keep the bank afloat. But his personal resources are limited and he can't do it all by himself. The bank is on the brink of failure when the businessmen he has helped for years show up with deposits to save the bank, and Dickson, and their city and the day.

A sympathetic banker who puts his customers ahead of his directors? Who'll put his own money at risk to help others? Who believes in people, not their credit? Here was a novel idea.

With those bare bones, Riskin the screenwriter went to work, adding characters, subplots, dramatic tension. Dickson, to be played by Walter Huston, is married to the stylish Constance Cummings, a smart and independent woman who feels abandoned when her husband's devotion to the bank occupies him day and night. One of the conspirators in the robbery works for the bank and, clearly up to no good, arranges to be alone with her at the Dickson house on the evening of the robbery and . . . complications ensue.

Harry Cohn was delighted with the script, now titled *American Madness,* and ordered production to begin immediately, with Allan Dwan directing.

After seeing three days of rushes, Cohn knew something wasn't right. Cinematographer Joe Walker said, "The whole thing was turning out to be a dreary mess. [Dwan] even made Walter Huston look bad." Cohn fired Dwan and brought in another Columbia director, Roy William Neill, who lasted one day. "It shook the company up and put everyone on their toes," Walker said.

Frank Capra had taken a vacation in Europe after finishing *Platinum Blonde.* He had just returned to the studio and was preparing a new picture, *The Woman I Stole,* to star Fay Wray, when Cohn pulled him off it and told him to take over.

American Madness shut down for three days while Capra read the script. He brought in a new designer to reimagine the set along lines he wanted, placing Dickson's office at the rear of the sound stage with bank activity in the foreground to energize the atmosphere. He did not change an actor in the cast nor a word in the script, following the screenplay shot for shot, including notably the montage leading to the climactic bank run, the bank's telephone operators phoning friends, piling rumor on rumor, spreading fear and hysteria, until soon there is a mob of hundreds of peo-

American Madness (1932), an original Riskin screenplay based largely on the banking philosophy of the Gianninis, founders of the Bank of America. Walter Huston (above) played the banker who lends money based not on a man's financial assets but on his character. Frank Capra came aboard to direct after Harry Cohn fired Allan Dwan and Roy William Neill.

ple storming the bank—and then the arrival of the cavalry in the form of borrowers Dickson has helped over the years, putting their dollars back in the bank.

Capra brought life and energy to every frame of film. Edward Bernds, soundman on the film who later became a director, said, "I fully realized for the first time what directing really was. Scenes that had been dull became lively, performances that had been dead came alive."

American Madness touched a familiar chord with Depression-era audiences—the rumors and realities of depositor panic and bank runs—while assuring audiences that there were decent bankers like Dickson on their side. Critics praised it for its "timeliness and for bringing to the screen the dramatic situation touching everyone in the world these past two years."

Over the years Capra grew to remember

the origins of the film differently. "I got the idea for the story from the life of Giannini . . ." he said in 1973. The following year he told interviewer Richard Schickel, "Prior to that I had been making films that were sort of escapist films, entertainment, comedies. But this time I thought, why don't we make a picture about the contemporary hang-ups—you know, bank runs and things?" And in his autobiography, Capra writes, "Riskin and I concocted a wild story about a bank president who is filled with youthful optimism and a cheerful trust in men."

Capra's propensity to claim credit for all aspects of the films he directed would grow more pronounced over the years. He would become a leading advocate of the "one man, one film" concept, later refined as the "auteur" theory—the idea that each film has only one "author," and that is the director. As with *American Madness,* he was not above reimagining history to support the theory.

With two back-to-back hits together, Riskin and Capra were eager to team up again, but first each had another project to finish.

In 1933 my father was writing *Ann Carver's Profession,* to star my mother as an important lawyer whose husband becomes jealous when she becomes the breadwinner in the family. Harry Cohn invited my mother to his office to impress upon her that she was playing the title role in his important new film, and that Columbia was becoming a first-class international film company. He even invited her to join him and his wife on a trip to Italy to meet Mussolini, but never followed through.

Surprisingly, my parents never met during the filming, but my mother appreciated the screenplay, which "had more insight and humanity than most"; she thought the story about a high-powered woman lawyer ahead of its time. "Fay Wray's and Gene Raymond's performances give emphasis and emotional impact to the changing domestic fortunes of two young persons who are very much in love . . ." said *The New York Times.* But

favorable reviews did not guarantee a financial hit, and *Ann Carver's Profession* had the singular misfortune of opening immediately after *King Kong,* which was still playing in theaters. Although my mother's name and picture were now on billboards everywhere, her involvement with a mere human being was pale competi-

Riskin wrote the screenplay for *Ann Carver's Profession* (1933), starring Fay Wray and Gene Raymond. Riskin and Wray didn't meet during the filming. In a modern take on women's roles, Carver is a high-powered lawyer whose success poses problems in her marriage. Directed by Eddie Buzzell

tion for the tumultuous response to the character of Ann Darrow and the mighty gorilla, and Ann Carver faded quietly away.

While *Ann Carver's Profession* was being made, Capra, who had fallen in love with Barbara Stanwyck while making *Ladies of Leisure*, got another chance to work with her in the interracial love story *The Bitter Tea of General Yen*. It received largely favorable reviews but was a box-office failure, Capra's first since *Miracle Woman*—and his last for a long time.

Finally my father and Capra were free from their other assignments and would work together, but again they were not partners from the beginning.

Lady for a Day owed its existence to Damon Runyon, newspaperman and popular writer of short stories about New York City full of colorful characters—gangsters, gamblers, hard-boiled newsmen, pols, cops, dolls in love with guys—who were forever getting into and out of trouble in the streets and speakeasies of the city. They spoke a New York slang that sounded pitch-perfect.

Columbia acquired rights to Runyon's magazine story "Madame La Gimp" and showed it to Capra, who said he thought it couldn't be made into a picture. They gave it to my father, who said he thought it could. While Capra was on loan to another studio for four months, my father wrote the script, which he retitled *Lady for a Day.*

An aging, destitute, heavy-drinking, and much-loved flower seller on the streets of New York gets a letter from her daughter in Spain, telling of her engagement to the son of an aristocratic family and that she is bringing them all to New York. The woman, changed in my father's adaptation to an apple seller, Apple Annie, is terrified by the letter. For years she has been writing her daughter, pretending she is living in New York among the highest of society with not a care in the world. Now she is about to be exposed in front of the one person who means most to her, probably ruining her daughter's life, and is almost suicidal.

Annie's friends from the streets of New York are loyal to her and rally to her rescue. Gamblers and cops, chorus girls and politicos, all the guys and dolls put their own problems on hold and pool their talents to transform Annie into the most high-toned grande dame society lady Gotham has ever seen. Dave the Dude and his posse move her into the best apartment in the best hotel in the city and set about preparing her to navigate through high society, using the swells' own language, style, and manners—not easy when some of the gangsters and gamblers have more than a little to learn about society comportment themselves. They finish the job of transforming Annie just as the boat from Spain pulls in.

It's the same theme as *American Madness,* people with heart working together to help a friend in trouble, with a lot of Runyon and a lot of Riskin in the mix. My father had a wonderful time writing the screenplay. The pols and cops and good-hearted but disreputable underworld characters were familiar to him from his days on the streets of Canarsie and the Lower East Side and here he was tipping his hat to them.

While he was writing the script, Capra was on loan to M-G-M for a picture that ultimately didn't get made. When Capra came back to Columbia and was given the script, he agreed to direct it.

He tried to assemble an all-star cast as insurance. He proposed Marie Dressler for Annie and James Cagney, William Powell, Robert Montgomery, and W. C. Fields for other key parts. Harry Cohn was willing, but Columbia was still viewed as a cut-rate Poverty Row studio and no actors would sign up, nor would other studios rent their valuable actors to a studio whose history of lower-quality movies might devalue them. Capra had no choice but to put together a cast of character actors and unknowns, no major stars.

Riskin and Capra with May Robson on the set of *Lady for a Day* (1933).
The film was based on a Damon Runyon story and was nominated for four
Academy Awards: Best Picture, Actress, Writer, and Director. Its great success
was the first step off Poverty Row for Columbia.

He was plagued by doubts. A few days before shooting started he went
to Cohn's office.

"Harry," Capra said, "I want you to face the fact that you're spending
three hundred thousand dollars on a picture in which the heroine is seventy years old."

Cohn rose from his desk and looked out his window onto Gower
Street. He turned back to Capra, "All I know is the thing's got a wallop.
Go ahead."

Capra was a master at casting, and his choices of character actors—May
Robson, Walter Connolly, Guy Kibbee, Glenda Farrell—could not have
been better. Starting shooting only eleven days after reading the script for
the first time, he finished in a highly economical twenty-four days. He
directed his cast brilliantly.

Lady for a Day was a major triumph, artistically and financially. Someone said the money came into Columbia so fast that "a very short time
later pencils and paper clips became available all over Columbia, as many
as you wanted. Before that you had to requisition them." Audiences loved
the picture and so did the Motion Picture Academy, which nominated it

for four major Academy Awards: including my father's script, Capra's direction, and for seventy-five-year-old May Robson, wonderful as Apple Annie. The nominations were the first ever for a Columbia picture.

Harry Cohn could not have been prouder. What Poverty Row? Asked what the studio's secret was, Cohn told the *New York Telegraph,* "We believe here that writers are more important than either star or director . . . Look at *Lady for a Day* . . . More credit is due to Riskin for that picture than to Damon Runyon."

Another who felt that way, remarkably, was Runyon himself. Feelings can easily be bruised when one writer adapts the work of another, but Runyon read the script and sent my father a telegram thanking him for improving "my feeble story . . . Your understanding of the characters amazed and delighted me . . . You made the yarn a hundred times better than the original."

Left to right: Hobart Bosworth, May Robson, Barry Norton, and Walter Connolly

My father had been on the set for much of the shooting and he and Capra found they had the same sense of when a scene worked, when it didn't. They were learning to trust and respect each other. Seeing the results, Cohn also saw the light. From now on it would be Capra and Riskin, Riskin and Capra, his best writer and best director working together. They would be given all the plum assignments and wide latitude in picking their own projects, and Cohn would essentially leave them alone.

5

A woman is like a teabag—you can't tell how strong she is until you put her in hot water.

—ELEANOR ROOSEVELT

When I was four and Bobby six, my mother told us never to go into the attic. She said something about black widows, which sounded exotic. We wondered if there might even be ghosts or monsters, or if we were lucky a dead body. We waited a few days until our parents were out and Miss Haesloop, the nanny, was busy downstairs before we snuck up the back stairs and tried the door. It was unlocked! We tiptoed into the dark space, not turning on a light for fear we might be caught. A sliver of light through the window gave shape to dozens of boxes and enormous steamer trunks covered with labels from around the world that Bobby could read, sort of: Switzerland, Sweden, England.

All the trunks were locked but one, and it had a sticker which read in large, bold print, FAY WRAY SAUNDERS. Saunders? We both thought it odd and troubling that another name was appended to our mother's. We strained to be sure no one was coming and then Bobby, schooled in *Dick Tracy* comics, whispered, "The coast is clear." We lifted the lid of the trunk and found inside swimming trophies, a purple and gold letterman's sweater, and scrapbooks filled with photographs of a tall man we had never seen with his arms around our mother, who was looking up at him adoringly.

We had discovered something entirely secret and confusing, something we both wanted and didn't want to know. We closed the lid, ran back to our playroom, and promised each other to keep our discovery secret forever.

· · ·

The first time my mother saw John Monk Saunders— college football hero, Rhodes Scholar, swimming champion, fighter pilot and screenwriter of *Wings,* the movie that would win the first Academy Award for Best Picture—he took her breath away. She remembered the moment with perfect clarity. As she was walking out the main gate at Paramount, he was entering. He called her name. She turned to see "a very handsome man. It was a warm summer afternoon. He was dressed in white flannels, a dark-blue blazer, and wore a white Panama hat. I thought he was astonishingly   good-looking . . . and wonderfully well-groomed."

The year was 1927 and, like everyone else in Hollywood, she had heard about Saunders. People at the studio called him "Golden Boy." He was already

John Monk Saunders, thirty, screenwriter of *The Legion of the Condemned* (1928), known as the Golden Boy at Paramount

writing a script for her at Paramount, at the time the premier studio in Hollywood.

The success of Paramount Pictures was due to the ambition and drive of an immigrant from Hungary, Adolph Zukor, who ran the business with power, precision, and rectitude. According to one historian, "almost everyone found him unbending, puritanical and chilling" as he made his relentless way to the top, forming Famous Players and in 1916 persuading rival producer Jesse Lasky to join him in Famous Players–Lasky. Zukor then bought Paramount, a nationwide distribution company, and merged the companies under the Paramount banner. He built a countrywide chain of two thousand theaters, giving Paramount and the entire movie business the status of a major American industry.

Of the early movie moguls, Zukor was first among equals. The foundation of his empire lay in bringing together, under contract and under his

In 1929, Fay was under contract to Paramount, where Adolph Zukor (left), a
Hungarian immigrant, assembled an impressive roster of stars including Rudolph
Valentino, Mary Pickford, and Douglas Fairbanks, and ran his studio with iron control.
Zukor merged his company with Jesse Lasky's Feature Play Company to create Famous
Players–Lasky and ultimately Paramount Pictures Corporation. Lasky (in straw boater)
with John Monk Saunders

control, a roster of important stars that included Mary Pickford, in her era
arguably the most famous person in the world, Douglas Fairbanks, and
Rudolph Valentino. His hand was not always benign. In time, Pickford
and Fairbanks bridled under his domination and left to create United Artists with Charlie Chaplin and D. W. Griffith. By then the pictures they
had made together had made Zukor, Fairbanks, and Pickford rich beyond
the dreams of avarice.

Zukor's partner Jesse Lasky also became wealthy. An ebullient one-
time vaudeville entrepreneur, showman, and film distributor, Lasky was
now an executive vice president, producer, and shareholder at Paramount,
answerable only to Zukor. When my mother signed a three-year contract
with Paramount, these were the men who held her destiny in their hands.
It was Lasky who told the press, "Unquestionably this girl is the find of
the year. She is headed straight for stardom . . . She has been carefully
educated and has culture and poise."

She was nineteen when she arrived at Paramount and earning $500 a week, the equivalent of $350,000 a year today, although a greedy agent took 25 percent; it would be another decade before the Screen Actors Guild was born and limited agents to 10 percent commission. Her salary enabled Vina to buy a small Spanish-style adobe house in Hollywood, where they lived with my mother's three brothers; her older sister Willow was out of the house, married with a child. Dick and Vic were young teenagers and roamed Hollywood in search of adventure, while Vivien, her oldest brother, stayed home writing poetry. Using my mother's salary, Vina provided the family with a baby grand piano, a full-time cook and, unusual for the time, a telephone.

My mother had never had a boyfriend, had never even gone on a date, when she met John Monk Saunders. Stories described her as shy and protected and remarked on her beauty, innocence, and sparkling intelligence. She lived at home under Vina's control, which had never relaxed after the Mortensen episode four years earlier. But now she was feeling confident and ready to spread her wings.

Pat Powers, producer of the still-unfinished *Wedding March*, had a paternal interest in her. He was a hearty, convivial, kindly Irishman, and when he invited my mother and Vina to visit his estate, Flintridge, my mother dreamed he might fill the void in her mother's life. Vina, now fifty-eight, had never shown interest in a man after Joe left, and my mother thought not only would Vina benefit from a relationship, she would be glad if her mother had someone else to focus on. The hoped-for match was wishful thinking. Neither Vina nor Powers sparked to the idea. But indirectly, Powers did help my mother to a freer life.

He invited her and John to be his guests at a gala evening at the Biltmore, and suggested John be her escort. Powers didn't know that shortly before the gala John had come to watch my mother filming his screenplay, *The Legion of the Condemned*, at a small airfield in the San Fernando Valley. It had been a hot day and John's white shirtsleeves were rolled up to the elbows. He pulled up a chair next to her. As my mother would later recall, "There was dust everywhere; only he seemed immaculately clean. During our conversation, as he touched my arm, a current of sensory feeling went through me. I knew, instinctively, it meant there would probably be no turning away from him if his thoughts should turn toward me."

On the night of the gala she dressed in high style, a white velvet gown trimmed with seed pearls. John sent a corsage of gardenias, the first time any man had sent her anything, and picked her up in a limousine. It was an elegant evening, beyond her imagination. On the way home John embraced her hard and told her he loved her. Nothing like this had ever

Fay is paired with Gary Cooper in *The Legion of the Condemned* (1928), the first of their three films together, produced by Jesse Lasky and directed by Wild Bill Wellman.

happened to her, and as soon as she came through the front door, she told her mother.

To my mother's relief, Vina was pleased. John was a perfect catch. She encouraged my mother to enjoy herself, which the young couple was happy to do.

They embarked on a dizzying round of dinners, parties, and theater with John's friends, who were part of the ultra-smart set. John provided an introduction to the worlds of alcohol, long drives through the Hollywood hills in his high-powered roadster, and lengthy kisses. After spending a long evening with him and lunch the following day, my mother remembered feeling "My body was no longer my own, that the sensory changes were so great I would never go back to being just me but was now a part of him."

She started spending evenings and nights at John's house. "The oneness was there, and very physical." Vina said nothing when my mother told her, in code they both seemed to understand, that "we are now one." In fact, Vina wrote Willow with excitement that "maybe Fay will have some very interesting things to tell you. I must be mum though . . . Oh my, John is so lovely with her."

The more Vina learned of John's background, the more eager she was for him to marry my mother. His classmates at Oxford included Lord Ivor Churchill, the Marquess of Blandford, Anthony Asquith, Henry Luce, and John Masefield, later poet laureate of the United Kingdom. Despite being American, he had been captain of the Oxford swimming team and had twice won his event against Cambridge. His manners were impeccable. Only on rare occasions when he came to pick up my mother was he "lit," his expression for being drunk, and that was no different from many of his contemporaries.

The new film he had written, *The Legion of the Condemned*, directed by the great William Wellman, was a World War I flying-and-fighting film. Paramount was clearly hoping to capitalize on the success of *Wings,* also directed by Wellman from a John Monk Saunders story, and the aviation craze that gripped the world after Charles Lindbergh's solo flight to Paris earlier that year.

To costar with my mother in *Legion*, Paramount picked a newcomer who had a bit part in *Wings* and, the studio felt, showed promise. His name was Gary Cooper.

The studio was exhilarated when they saw my mother and Cooper together on film and launched an advertising campaign promoting "Paramount's glorious young lovers," knowing audiences fall in love with movie couples—as they later

did with Tracy and Hepburn, Bogart and Bacall, Rogers and Astaire, even Newman and Redford—and set out to find more pictures for them.

My mother was less certain how well she and Cooper worked as a movie couple. Sadly, copies of their silent films together, *The First Kiss* and *The Legion of the Condemned,* no longer exist, but my mother felt she and Cooper both had a tendency to underplay and be reactive rather than assertive. Years later, she laughed at herself. "Shame on me that I didn't know then Gary was going to be one of the greatest movie stars of all time, that he would be attractive to women, that he would become a symbol of the heroic American." They never quite caught fire as a romantic team, and each would have to wait to hit it really big with other costars—Cooper with Jean Arthur in *Mr. Deeds Goes to Town,* which my father wrote, and my mother with her own most famous leading man, in *King Kong*.

After *The Legion of the Condemned*, she worked nonstop with some of the great leading men of her time: Richard Arlen, Clark Gable, Ronald Colman, Spencer Tracy, Victor Jory, William Powell—she made four films with Powell and admired his "grace, style, wit, and technique." She worked with directors who were great or destined to become so— Merion C. Cooper, Raoul Walsh, Howard Hawks. Several were Europeans who had emigrated, and sometimes their direction demanded translation, or at least close attention. In *The Street of Sin* with Emil Jannings (1928), Scandinavian director Mauritz Stiller, who had discovered Greta Garbo, talked to actors all through the scenes, telling my mother, "Don't go before you don't start, Faywray," merging her two names into one and confusing her as to what he wanted. Jannings conflated her names, too, saying, "Have zee ans in zee pans, Faywray."

For a brief time after *The Jazz Singer,* the studios made both silents and talkies. More than 80 percent of all silent films, and many of my mother's, do not survive today; some were thrown into the trash for no reason other than to make storage space. But virtually all my mother's sound movies have survived and, together with the remaining silents, provide a vivid impression of her at the dawn of the sound era. She was at ease, often sparkling and impish, or graceful and guileless, beautiful

Wray made one of her last silent films, *The Street of Sin*, in 1928. The film costarred Emil Jannings (below, with Fay) and was directed by Mauritz Stiller, who discovered Greta Garbo.

In 1929, Fay made the transition to talkies in *Thunderbolt*, directed by Josef von Sternberg, costarring Richard Arlen and George Bancroft (above). In the film, she wants to leave the gangster and go back to her childhood sweetheart.

and confident. Beginning with the Charley Chase one-reel comedies and through the scores of sound films she made, her innocence and optimism shine through. Even in her first talking role, in *Thunderbolt* (1929), playing a gangster's glib, sultry, hardened girlfriend, she has poise and grace. One reviewer wrote, "Fay Wray has a class that makes you wonder if she could ever have been a gangster's girlfriend."

John was ten years older than my mother and vastly more experienced. He had a great deal to teach her and she soaked it all up. He introduced her to his favorite authors—Shakespeare, Chaucer, Dante, Donne—and the one who became her lifelong companion, Ralph Waldo Emerson, whose transcendentalist philosophy and ideas of self-reliance and freedom she found intellectually stimulating and spiritually comforting.

John's rocket ride had begun in Hinckley, Minnesota. One of eight children, he walked barefoot to the village school carrying his lunch, and from his earliest days was precocious in all he did in school and athletics. He mocked himself as "THE

BRIGHT LITTLE BOY THE TEACHER CALLED ON TO RECITE WHEN VISITORS COME." He went on to the University of Washington, and at the start of the Great War left college to enlist in the most glamorous of the services, the Army Flying Corps. To his everlasting disappointment, he was made an instructor in aerial acrobatics Stateside and saw no combat. When the war ended, he leaned against his airplane and wept.

He finally made it overseas after the war as a Rhodes Scholar at Oxford, studying English literature while also apparently excelling in drinking and women, for which he seemed to have a natural aptitude. He came back to America with the dream of becoming a writer and was an immediate success. He first took a job on the editorial staff of the prestigious *New York Tribune*, leaving after a year to become associate editor of *The American Magazine*. He sold the first short story he wrote to *Cosmopolitan;* it was bought by Famous Players–Lasky for the handsome sum of $4,000. He wrote for *Vanity Fair* and *Liberty,* selling the rights to another story to Lasky for $5,000. His passion for flying, excitement, and heroism was present in everything he wrote.

In 1926, he hit the big time. He approached Lasky with an idea for a novel about two young Americans who volunteer for the Flying Corps and go to fight behind enemy lines in France. Lasky was hooked from the opening sentence: "A lad you know is born to be a flier from the moment you see him as a young boy, lying on his back watching an eagle in flight . . ."

Lasky, thinking ahead, and already imagining the wrath of Zukor who watched budgets like a hawk, agreed to buy the unwritten novel—if John could get the War Department to underwrite the enormous expense of making it into a movie. Still in his twenties and not lacking in confidence, John went to Washington, where he and a Paramount executive talked the War Department into providing airplanes, an airfield, and 3,500 servicemen for the big scenes. Zukor gave his blessing and committed to the picture.

Lasky had a gambler's instinct. He and John now agreed that John should forgo the novel and go right to the screenplay, for which Paramount paid him the unprecedented sum of $39,000 plus a share of the profits.

The movie was *Wings,* and John dedicated it to "those young warriors of the sky whose wings are folded about them forever." William "Wild Bill" Wellman, a first-rate fighter pilot in World War I, directed the film with its famously spine-chilling dogfights. It became a smash hit and Lasky signed John to a multi-picture commitment.

My mother reveled in John's attention. He was an exceptional athlete and taught her golf, tennis, and skeet shooting. He was welcomed in the highest echelons of Hollywood society and took my mother everywhere with him. He repeatedly expressed "sweet regret that there was no escape from the overwhelming power of his love" for her.

She was losing herself in their relationship. "The awareness of possibly being totally enveloped and absorbed by him placed a shadowy figure between me and what I hoped would be the fullness of working and growing as an actress." But she dreamt that he would propose and he did, over dinner at their favorite Russian restaurant.

He then told her something she would have been much happier not knowing. He was having an affair with Bessie Lasky, the artistic, flame-haired wife of Jesse Lasky, who was both John's and my mother's employer. He said further that, while Bessie was special, she did not have an exclusive hold on his affections.

Despite this revelation, my mother accepted John's proposal. That women were drawn to him was no surprise to her. He was one of the handsomest men in Hollywood, with graceful manners, a superior education, a golden future. It helped that he said he was counting on her, and marriage, to protect him from the attention of women. She did notice in the days following their engagement that he seemed more secure and at ease.

Then, little by little, John volunteered more details of his life that she also didn't want to know. She said, "He liked telling. He told a lot about a lot of ladies." He also told her she was different from the others. She became his confessor and confidante.

John told my mother about his unhappy marriage and divorce from a woman named Avis Hughes, who was an alcoholic and had been unfaithful to him. For a brief unhappy time, they had lived with Avis' stepfather, novelist Rupert Hughes, a verbal abuser of everyone under his roof. Hughes' wife regularly drank herself into insensibility. The marriage to Avis had scarred him, he said, and he hoped my mother could help him heal from the experience. "I love you more than all the houses and all the people. I will love you until you are a little lavender old lady," he said.

My mother wanted to do whatever she could for John, to heal his past wounds and be his wife, friend, and muse. John went to Vina and formally asked for Fay's hand in marriage; Vina agreed at once.

Now formally engaged, my mother proudly took John to a preview of the now-completed *The Wedding March*. Soon after, there was a showing of *Wings*, and John said with apologies that Bessie Lasky expected him to

escort her to the dinner and the screening. Would my mother mind? "Yes," she said, she really would mind.

So John took my mother to the opening night of *Wings* in Hollywood, and to the party where Bessie was present. She found herself sitting across the table from a woman with bright red hair and a delicate face, who, at forty, was twenty years older

John Monk Saunders wrote *Wings* (1927), directed by William Wellman and winner of the first Best Picture Academy Award. Saunders escorting Fay to the Los Angeles opening

than my mother and ten years older than John. Curiously, my mother said she felt no jealousy. "She looked at me in what seemed a purposefully detached manner. The detachment, I soon felt, was not because of me but was part of her personality, giving her an air of apparent serenity."

Bessie was a painter who preferred her own studio to the baseness of the "Hollywood factory," as she called it. "I was not influenced by Hollywood," she wrote. "My heart sang gaily of landscapes, still lifes, flowers, and water subjects."

Over time my mother came to realize the extent of Mrs. Lasky's involvement with John, how frequently she entertained him at the

Bessie Lasky, wife of Jesse Lasky of Paramount Pictures,
also mistress of John Monk Saunders of Paramount Studios

Lasky apartment in New York or their bungalow at the Ambassador Hotel
or their beach house in Santa Monica. About the beach house my mother
said, "She may well have bought it to please John, who, being a champion
swimmer, loved being at the ocean. She had a sort of Bridge of Sighs built
between his room and hers."

If the transition from silent movies to talkies was worrisome to the studios, requiring new personnel and new techniques and skills and additional costs, which were daunting even before the Depression hit, it was
terrifying to every actor.

At first my mother thought audiences would find talking an unwel-
come intrusion in movies. But the enormous success of *The Jazz Singer*
meant there was no turning back. Acting careers ended overnight when a
voice or accent didn't measure up, or a performer couldn't modulate the
gestures and mannerisms that had worked so well in silents but seemed
exaggerated in talkies. Major stars like Vilma Banky, Raymond Griffith,
and Norma Talmadge never made the transition. Sound curtailed the
careers of pantomime comedians like Harold Lloyd and Harry Langdon,
and even to all the organists and orchestras that played in movie palaces
around the country.

Pat Powers insisted his young protégée prepare for sound movies. John
helped her through the tense time by introducing her to the head of Para-

mount's sound department and having him personally supervise her test, where she recited from *Alice's Adventures in Wonderland*. She worried she sounded tinny but she could be heard distinctly and was cleared for talkies as soon as she completed *The First Kiss*. In time, like other stars of the era—including, memorably, Bette Davis, Rosalind Russell, and Katharine Hepburn—she adopted for film a "transatlantic accent," a style cultivated by theater actors and American aristocrats which required softening vowels, dropping the *r*, and sharpening the *t*.

Before leaving for location on *The First Kiss*, Pat Powers arranged a publicity photo session for her with a young photographer whose dramatic portraits of Janet Gaynor, Jean Harlow, and Anna May Wong had impressed Hollywood. The photographer was William Mortensen and to my mother's relief Vina said nothing when the photo shoot was arranged at Western Costume Company where Mortensen had a studio. My mother was overjoyed to see her friend again and they set about working with the same connectedness they had once felt. They did not discuss the past nor Vina's suspicion-fueled fury that had severed their friendship.

As my mother was preparing to leave for location with Gary Cooper, an event occurred which even today seems so harrowing as to be unendurable for a young woman.

Her brother Vivien, whom my mother adored, was twenty-eight years old and working at being a poet. Vina had given him his own room at the back of the house where he could write in peace while crafting his long spiritual poems. The room had a separate outside entrance so his friends, painters and poets and actors, could visit him privately.

Vivien was gay in an era when homosexuality was little understood or tolerated. My mother did not know he was gay and would not have understood much about it if she had. Only years later, in reading a letter Vivien had sent to Vina, did she come to understand his innermost feelings.

One day when Vina was out of the house, my mother was alone playing the piano when Vivien came in and sat on the bench next to her. He leaned close to her and breathed heavily onto her face. Then he seized her, pinning her arms, and kissed her fully on the mouth, holding her tight, not letting her go. Horrified, she struggled until she broke free and ran from the house. Dazed and uncomprehending, she found her mother and told her what had happened.

What had possessed Vivien? Did he want to prove he was not homosexual? Did he resent the attention Vina focused not on him but on my mother? Vina did not seem surprised and may have had a premonition.

The second, and last, silent feature starring Gary Cooper and Fay was *The First Kiss* (1928).

She had written Willow that Vivien had been trying to get my mother to finance a film he wanted to make that was, to Vina, very silly. "He is acting very strangely and has not spoken to Fay or me for more than a week. He seems to have cut himself off from all his friends and I certainly feel very badly about the way he is doing."

After hearing my mother's story, Vina went with John to the family doctor and together they decided Vivien should be sent on a long vacation to family friends in Canada.

My mother later said how grateful she was that Vina, who could be rigid and intolerant, was so understanding of Vivien. At the same time, she knew she could never go back to the house while Vivien was there, so she accepted Vina's and John's solution and, with Vina and the cast and crew, quickly got on a train to Maryland, where *The First Kiss* was to be filmed.

A week later Vivien boarded the train to Canada. When the train got to Lodi, California, he intentionally jumped or accidentally fell between the railroad cars and was crushed to death.

When my mother heard the news on the set in Maryland, she turned numb. "Professional people are supposed to be able to handle these moments," she said later, "but I wasn't yet such a professional." Shooting a scene with Gary Cooper, she looked up at him and saw looking back at her the face of her brother. They stopped filming for the day but the shock lasted much longer.

John called from California to tell her how miserable he was without her and how much he loved her. He came to Maryland and asked Vina for permission to go ahead with the wedding immediately. Vina agreed, and they were married in a little Methodist church in St. Michaels with Vina, the film's director and his wife, and Gary Cooper as witnesses. My mother was nineteen and John thirty.

The coda to Vivien's story came almost two years later when a nurse, who was taking care of my mother's father, Joe, sent my mother a letter that her father was hospitalized somewhere in Los Angeles and dying of cancer. There was no return address or information that indicated where he was. Unknown to my mother, Joe had moved to Hollywood to be near his family. My mother had not seen him since she left Utah, nor had Vina, but Vivien had been in regular secret contact with him.

After Joe's death, a cousin sent my mother a collection of her father's simple poems, written during the last years of his life. They express his longing for Vina and his children and his terrible loneliness. Some are wistful and romantic, others full of anger and betrayal. One was written to Vivien days after Vivien's death, and two years before Joe died.

My Dear Vivien,

The last time you called in to see me
The sun shone so bright in the room
The handclasp you gave as you entered
I shall feel till the day of my doom

It's been so long since I saw you
Since you called in to see your old dad
How happy I was then to meet you
That day when my heart was so sad

For a time we talked of the future
And then we went over the past
How could I have known when you left me
That kiss you gave was the last

That day as you left me you promised
You'd call back and see me right soon
How long must I wait for your coming
My heart filled with sorrow and gloom.

                                        Your loving father . . .

When *The First Kiss* finished production John and my mother drove to New York for their honeymoon, and Vina and the rest of the company returned to California. On their way north, they stopped in Virginia to see friends of John's first wife, Avis. The friends threw a party where John sat on the floor before an attractive woman. My mother watched as he rested his arms on her lap. "You have the most beautiful teeth I have ever seen," he told her. My mother knew he meant not her teeth but her breasts, which were very large. Because he was a little drunk, she forgave him.

In New York, they went to Cartier where he bought her an emerald-cut diamond ring. Then he left her at the Plaza Hotel and went to the Laskys' Fifth Avenue apartment to tell Bessie he was now married and was ending their affair. Her son, Jesse Lasky Jr., later wrote, "When John Saunders married Fay Wray, it almost broke Bessie's heart. She considered him her own admirer." My mother felt compassion for Bessie, now over forty years old and being displaced, but was of course happy finally to be free of her rival.

John and my mother were enjoying the life of newlyweds in Manhattan, going to elegant parties and speakeasies most nights and to Adolph Zukor's majestic five-hundred-acre country estate for fancy weekends with high society, when a personal scandal rose up and threatened to consume them. The scandal involved not John but my mother.

A motion picture magazine had published some of the photographs William Mortensen had taken of my mother at age fourteen. One showed her barefoot, her body draped in silk. Another had her sitting in the sidecar of his motorcycle, bare legs, bare shoulders, nothing else uncovered. The story told how my mother, little more than a child, had come unsupervised to California with the free-spirited Mortensen, and left the reader to draw conclusions.

Vina broke the news to them by telegram. She insisted the pictures were composites, my mother's head on someone else's body. They were not. John rushed out to buy the magazine. He returned to the hotel wild with fury directed at my mother. "I thought you were *pure!*," he said.

My mother was stunned, almost sick, waves of nausea flooding over her. She was in a whirlpool of desperation, she later wrote, as though life itself were over. "All the guilt my mother had made me feel was compounded a thousand times . . . All my feelings were for the chasm that had opened between John and me. If he thought this was so devastating, perhaps it was. He was well-educated, he was sophisticated, he was the first person I had loved."

John was certain the scandal would end my mother's career as scandals had ended the careers of Fatty Arbuckle and Mabel Normand. Paramount would cancel her contract. His fears were not irrational. Throughout the 1920s the motion picture industry had been under attack from church groups and women's organizations who saw Hollywood as a hotbed of immorality. Wanting to avoid anything that might offend audiences, the studios hired a savvy politician, Will H. Hays, to establish the Motion Picture Producers and Directors Association.

As the Association's first president, Hays instituted a Production Code to sanitize Hollywood's image. He ordered publicists to tone down references to movie stars' extravagances and required that affairs between stars be described as marriages. Morals clauses appeared in actors' contracts, my mother's included, giving studios the right to terminate contracts if actors were caught up in scandals. The Hays Office enforced draconian rules of what could be shown on screen, not even allowing a husband and wife to be seen sharing a bed.

It wasn't just John who was concerned about repercussions from the Mortensen photographs, it was the studio. A photograph of Mae West with an undraped shoulder might not have caused a stir. Not so for my mother, the fresh young ingénue. Adolph Zukor conducted his own life with fierce rectitude and tolerated no deviation from his personal code among those who worked at his studio.

Because the magazine had published these photos, John was certain there must be others. Nothing my mother said could reassure him. He insisted they immediately take the train to Hollywood to deal with the crisis. John was silent and sullen the entire trip.

At Paramount, my mother waited alone in her dressing room while John and Vina met with Barney Hutchinson, head of the studio's Publicity Department. They divided responsibilities. Hutchinson would speak to the editor of the magazine to make sure there would be no more articles. My mother would go to Mortensen and ask him to sign a paper saying that each time he had been with my mother, Vivien had been present, which was untrue but might tamp down criticism that Vina had sent her young daughter to California with Mortensen and without protection. John assigned himself the task of searching Hollywood shops that sold photographs of movie stars for the incriminating ones he was sure existed. John and Vina told my mother that they, and mighty Paramount, might be able to save her.

My mother remembered how sick and miserable she was, how responsible she felt for the mess. Years later, when she found the paper Mortensen had been made to sign, she tore it up, ashamed of what she had been responsible for putting him through. Mortensen soon left Hollywood. He set up a photography school in Laguna Beach, south of Los Angeles, where he made artistic and avant-garde and sometimes even bizarre pictures instead of the glamorous movie photos from his Hollywood days.

The crisis ended quickly, with no effect on my mother's career. John continued to suffer, obsessed with the belief that somewhere, sometime, a compromising picture of my mother might surface.

John and my mother temporarily took a suite at the Beverly Wilshire Hotel. She felt lonely even as they practiced putting golf balls together in the carpeted hallways and went to fancy parties. How much lonelier she became one night when John told her he was going to the beach to restart the affair with Bessie. My mother begged him not to go but he went anyway. She was ashamed she had begged and resolved never again to let John, or anyone, define her or make her feel she was at fault when she was not.

Before they married, John rented a beautiful English country house for them on Selma Avenue in Hollywood. It had wide-plank oak floors and beamed ceilings, and the generous grounds featured wide lawns, rose gardens, a guesthouse, and a tennis court. Even before they moved in, they learned the house was for sale. King Vidor, noted director of such silent films as *The Big Parade* and *The Crowd*, and his wife, Florence, were divorcing; she had fallen in love with the great violinist Jascha Heifetz.

John had no money of his own, having given everything to his first wife in exchange for freedom from alimony, so my mother used her film earnings for the down payment. Florence was very generous and left behind, or sold to my mother at modest prices, some of her fine china, silver, and antiques. She gave my mother books on antique furnishings and bequeathed her an additional treasure, the family's cook, Mattie.

My mother was happy in her new Selma Avenue home. It was a sanctuary where she could restore herself between films, read books from John's considerable library, and host gatherings of their growing number of

Fay Wray, at twenty, and John Monk
Saunders, ten years older, married in 1928
and began life in their new home on Selma
Avenue in Hollywood. It was not a secret
to Fay that John divided his attentions
between her and Bessie Lasky.

friends. In the movie industry, people were judged not just by their films but on their reputations as party givers, and she became a popular and gracious hostess, inviting friends for cocktails and the best caviar, which was John's obsession. Friends often stayed for the elegant dinners Mattie prepared. My mother arranged tennis matches and lawn parties during the days and parlor games and ping pong, which she was helping to popularize in Hollywood, in the evenings. She was soon able to beat most guests at ping pong, including Jascha Heifetz, who announced it was his great mission to one day vanquish her.

Most of all, she wanted John to be happy in the house.

The one discordant, only-in-Hollywood, note was struck regularly on Sundays, when my mother was expected to drive John to the Riviera Country Club for his weekly golf game with his good friend and employer, Jesse Lasky, Bessie's husband. She was expected then to drive back to the Lasky beach house at five o'clock for cocktails and a dinner party. On these evenings, she watched Bessie through the crowd and admired her rival's grace and serenity. "Bessie seemed to make no effort at all, moving through the parties as though through a grove of trees," she wrote. She learned the Laskys had an open marriage. Once, to make clear that things were not one-sided in their arrangement, John pointed out Jesse Lasky's young mistress.

Although my mother and Bessie never spoke, she seemed grateful my mother could drive John home safely when he had drunk too much.

At twenty-one, my mother struggled to understand what marriage was all about.

She thought perhaps John was only doing what everyone did in Hollywood, where rules of behavior were famously loose. If only she had had someone to talk to. Her mother clearly wasn't the answer. Vina thought of John as the ultimate glory, a gentleman, a heroic figure, and my mother would never rob her of her illusions. She searched for ways to calm John's restless nature, but his escapades, demands, and expectations were never-ending, and escalated with his drinking. He wanted her to pattern her voice after Tallulah Bankhead's, which was arch and smoky, and develop her breasts so they equaled Lily Damita's, which could have taken the blue ribbon at the Iowa State Fair. He wanted her to have her skin treated so it was the texture and tone of Dolores Del Rio's. "There were times I thought he loved me as I was," she wrote wistfully.

He told her that if she ever found him in bed with someone else she should think nothing of it, that he was oversexed. Making love was essential to him. Drinking was essential to him. Bessie was essential to him.

Fay starred opposite leading men of her era: William Powell, Ronald Colman (above), Gary Cooper, Spencer Tracy, Wallace Beery, and George Raft. Between 1928 and 1934 she appeared in forty-six films and by 1933 was the busiest actress in Hollywood.

She often wondered what he and Bessie talked about. Later she described how she came to accept how things were. "John and me and Bessie makes three."

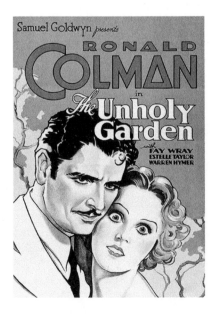

The honeymoon gave way to work. John was a top writer at Paramount. My mother was becoming the busiest actress in Hollywood. From 1928 to 1934 she starred in forty-six films. Most were happy and fulfilling experiences, some creating lifetime friendships.

She loved making *The Unholy Garden* (1931) with Ronald Colman and they became close friends. The movie, written by Ben Hecht and Charles MacArthur, was a lighthearted crime spoof set in a Sahara hotel not unlike Rick's Café in *Casablanca*. Here scoundrels, thieves, and murderers—and one honest soul, played by my mother—conducted their affairs and found sanctuary from the law. Colman is best remembered for the film my father wrote, *Lost Horizon,* and for *A Double Life,* for which he won the Best Actor Oscar. My mother also remembered him from the time she saw him in dark glasses that seemed to say, as she described it, "'I don't want to be noticed or rather please notice that I don't want to be noticed.' You couldn't help but notice."

Another who became a close friend, the urbane William Powell, taught her to play a drunk scene and how to strike an appealing pose by tilting her head up as if she were about to swallow but not doing it. In *Behind the Make-Up* (1930), she evolves from simple barmaid to the devoted and stylish wife of Powell, a vaudeville performer who in the end breaks her heart. The film was codirected by Dorothy Arzner, the only woman to direct her and someone my mother admired.

Fay costarred with Wallace Beery, George Raft, and Jackie Cooper in *The Bowery* (1933).

The same year she starred again with Gary Cooper in *The Texan*, based on an O. Henry story. It was their first sound film together and director John Cromwell, who came from the New York theater, spent a luxurious two weeks rehearsing the actors and then kept a dialogue coach on set to help my mother with her Spanish accent. Dialogue directors were a novelty, and as the sound era began there was almost always one to work with the actors. *The Texan* was well reviewed. "The lean, lanky Mr. Cooper elicits a great deal of sympathy . . . and Fay Wray has never been more captivating as Consuelo."

She loved making *Shanghai Madness* (1933)

Fay with Victor Jory in *Mills of the Gods* (1934)

with Spencer Tracy. Their emotional connection seems genuine and tender, and reflects my mother's feeling that Tracy was an outstanding leading man. "There was nothing narcissistic about him. He wore no make-up. He was so natural. So truthful."

She regretted that working picture to picture, wrapping one on Saturday and starting another on Monday, without time to study or rehearse, left her no time to work on technique. In 1933 she made eleven movies, including *King Kong,* and in 1934 made ten more. She wanted most of all that her performances be, like Tracy's, "truthful," which was far from easy in the stylized films of the 1930s.

The best of her films were very good. In the raffish *The Bowery* (1933), produced by Darryl F. Zanuck and directed by Raoul Walsh, she was pursued by both Wallace Beery and George Raft. *The New York Times* saluted the "ribald mirth, brawls, fights, noise and vulgarity" that drove the film. *The Most Dangerous Game* (1932) with Joel McCrea was a crowd-pleaser and box-office success that allowed her to demonstrate her athleticism as she ran through the jungle to escape evil Count Zaroff. In *Madame Spy*

(1934), she plays a Russian who marries a German officer only so she can spy on him; in the end, to escape the firing squad, she crawls to safety through muck and mire, a change of pace that earned her positive reviews.

On occasion she played a villainess. In *The Woman I Stole* (1933), she is a selfish, conniving, venal wife determined to rid herself of her husband so she can run off with Jack Holt. One reviewer wrote, "Fay Wray got just what she deserved when at the end she was left cooling her sinful heels on a distant pier while two men who perilously avoided her net plan to celebrate their good fortune in a quart of brandy."

Two favorites were movies she made with Victor Jory. Jory had been a rough, tough Alaska kid, quick with his fists, before becoming a polished stage actor. His energy and

high spirits ignited a special chemistry between them. In *Mills of the Gods* (1934), my mother plays the granddaughter of May Robson, who is trying to save the family mill for the workers. Jory is a charismatic mill worker who joins the cause. In *White Lies* (1935), my mother shames her father, a ruthless publisher willing to destroy a man to sell newspapers, into doing

Two actors Fay especially enjoyed working with were Spencer Tracy (below) and Victor Jory. Of Tracy she said, "He had grit. There was nothing narcissistic about him . . . So truthful." And of Jory, "His energy and high spirits were infectious."

something kind for once. Again Jory is her ally, a policeman whose integrity she admires, and love follows.

But not all her films were satisfying experiences, for her or others. Times were hard and it was important to keep working; actors, writers, directors, all had to do the best they could with what they were offered and my mother was no different. More than just keeping working, she said she felt a responsibility to bring what pleasure she could to the hard-hit country. Movies, even programmers and B pictures, were a way for people who could afford a quarter or even a dime to escape their troubles. They could live vicariously, maybe even feel they were in the presence of old friends, or Hollywood royalty.

By the early thirties Paramount was nearly out of money. To keep afloat, the studio loaned out—rented, really—the actors it had under contract to other studios, which they had every legal right to do. Some compared it to the treatment of sharecroppers or mules, but with better pay.

Paramount loaned my mother to anyone who had a script and, more important, met their price. She never complained but later wrote, "There was a roster of stars at Paramount and there was a roster of management. The roster of management made decisions for and about the roster of stars." She had no agent to protect her until 1933, when she retained Myron Selznick, and did what she was rented out to do, including several horror films where she was the woman in peril—*Doctor X, The Vampire Bat,* and *Mystery of the Wax Museum.*

John encouraged her to take every job. He developed his own economic theory that neither she nor anyone else could understand. Turning down any offer costs you double the money because, he said, "You won't get what was offered and, in addition, you would lose by that much, so if you didn't get twice as much as was offered the next time, you would be losing twice as much." No matter how hard she tried she couldn't figure it out. But he was a Rhodes Scholar and must know, so she didn't argue and went on taking whatever movies came along, sometimes having to shoot more than one at a time. The twenty-one pictures she made between 1933 and 1934, which included ten weeks of shooting on *King Kong* spread over a ten-month period, are more than many successful working actors today make in a lifetime. She suspected the exacting schedule took a toll but decided to press ahead whether it did or not. "I did not see myself as a shaper of events. I seemed to have a subconscious sense of destiny and the responsibility to meet that destiny with resilience."

Time between movies, even between scenes, was taken up by the studio's promotional machine. Publicists worked nonstop at keeping her name

Above, a 1934 photograph by George Hurrell, Hollywood's premier portrait photographer. Below, the cover of *Film Weekly*, 1932

and face in movie magazines like *Screenland* or *Motion Picture Magazine,* and scheduled endless fashion shoots and interviews about her personal life for national periodicals.

My mother was happy on the set. Makeup and costume people, her stand-in, grips, the camera and lighting crew, all cosseted her. She considered the crews the unsung heroes of moviemaking, filled with "energy, resourcefulness and ingenuity. They want to admire their leading lady and root for her success; they instantly know whether a scene works or not."

Many directors were helpful, but there were exceptions. Michael Curtiz, who directed her in *Mystery of the Wax Museum* and *Doctor X*

before going on to fame and glory with *Casablanca* and *Yankee Doodle Dandy,* was ice-cold and universally disliked. "I felt he was not flesh and bones," my mother said, rather, that "he was part of the steel of the camera." Curtiz never ate lunch on the set and forbade his cast and crew from taking a time-consuming meal break. They resented it but were powerless.

Having gone without meal breaks on his movies, my mother delighted in the story of how Curtiz was once outmaneuvered by his assistant director.

Born Kertesz Mano in Hungary, Curtiz had never lost his thick Hungarian accent. Directing Errol Flynn in a dueling scene for *Captain Blood*, he called *"Lunge! Now!"* The A.D. instantly called, "That's lunch now, everybody! Back in thirty minutes," and the cast and crew ran off the set before Curtiz knew what hit him.

Filming could be demanding work. In *The Bowery*, the script called for George Raft to slap my mother across the face. Tough guy Raft couldn't bring himself to hit her hard enough to satisfy director Raoul Walsh, who ordered take after take, twenty in all, until, with my mother's eyes watering, her face bright red and her ears ringing, Walsh finally got a slap he approved. Afterward, the shaken Raft said to her, "You're the kind of girl a man would like to have for a wife." On *King Kong*, she once was required to work twenty-two hours straight. Also on *Kong*, the director told her to "scream for your life" into a microphone for eight uninterrupted hours so he could get the exact pitch he wanted for the soundtrack. For weeks afterward she couldn't speak even in a whisper.

One other director had been difficult to work with. Paramount loaned her to Columbia for *Dirigible* (1931) when the company was still on Pov-

Working with director Frank Capra on *Dirigible* (1931) was a difficult experience.

John Monk Saunders, in 1928, with his friend F. Scott Fitzgerald, whose lifestyle inspired John to write his own Lost Generation novel, *Single Lady.* It became the basis for a film, *The Last Flight* (1931), and a Broadway play, *Nikki,* that starred Fay.

erty Row. Compared to Paramount and the other studios, my mother said in her gentle way, Columbia was "like a hungry child who needed help." She liked Harry Cohn immediately. "I saw at once there was a tiger in him; the tiger that is the driving force behind accomplishment." But she remembered Frank Capra, the director, as "a dark soul." Capra generally enjoyed easygoing relations on the set—someone described him on my father's films as happy-go-lucky but with authority. On *Dirigible* he became angry when my mother arrived on the set moments late the first day, after her hairdresser had accidentally sprayed water on her gown and taken time to dry it off. Burdened by a tight budget and short, Columbia-style schedule, and with unrelenting pressure from Harry Cohn, who was spending more on *Dirigible* than on any picture to date with the thought it might elevate his and Columbia's status in town, Capra did not let go of his resentment of my mother's tardiness and made her time on the set uncomfortable throughout the shooting.

A meatpacking company of the time had a slogan, "We get everything out of the pig but the whistle." The men who had come out of the New York garment business to run the movie studios were no different. They wrung everything they could out of those who worked for them until, by the mid-1930s, their employees were driven to action. The fight for unions to protect workers, including actors, was on.

Conditions in the movie business have improved dramatically since 1933, and today an actor slapped in the face twenty times or compelled to work twenty-two hours straight or scream for eight consecutive hours might scream instead for the Screen Actors Guild, which since its formation in the 1930s has been able to negotiate and enforce reasonable and humane working conditions. Behind-the-camera crews also have negotiated enforceable rules governing wages and working conditions. Before the unions, for grips and stand-ins, for sound technicians and set carpenters and camera assistants, it was a very hard life.

Not so much, of course, for actors who had achieved prominence. Being a star was, then as now, to be royalty, with grand homes with servants, fabulous parties, and all the perks that made the stars' lives seem so glamorous. Stars were not only looked at differently, they were treated differently. As in the army, rank has its privileges. One night while shooting *The Unholy Garden,* my mother hurried home for a champagne dinner with John. She was driving alone back to the studio with the top down, singing, when a policeman pulled her over for speeding. "I was happy and singing—and now you've spoiled all that," she pouted. Seeing who she was, the policeman apologized profusely, gave her his personal card "in case we can ever be of help," and waved her on.

John thought of himself as a member of the Lost Generation, Gertrude Stein's evocative term for those who, like F. Scott Fitzgerald and Hemingway, had come of age during World War I. He was a close friend and serious drinking buddy of Scott and Zelda and embraced their philosophy, "Live hard and die young."

Anita Loos, author of *Gentlemen Prefer Blondes,* wrote of the time the Fitzgeralds visited John during his bachelor days. After consuming serious quantities of bathtub gin they sat together on the couch, where Zelda produced scissors and said if John would only allow her to emasculate him, his earthly problems would all be over. Another time, John told my mother, Zelda and Scott came to his house and for their shared amusement the trio urinated off the balcony, aiming for distance, with Zelda somehow included.

John and my mother had been married less than a year when he informed her he was going alone to Paris to research his own Lost Generation novel. He had barely landed in Paris when he picked up a girl,

Nikki, at the Ritz Bar, and moved with her into Le Claridge Hotel on the Champs-Élysées. Soon they went off to Lisbon together. After John tired of Portugal, he returned to California with boxes of presents for my mother and told her he had stopped drinking and would dedicate himself to his new novel, *Single Lady*. The story would be about Nikki or, as it turned out, about a character who was part the real Nikki and part my mother, all mixed up together.

Abandoned in Europe, the real Nikki missed John. She sent him long pleading letters from Paris telling him that after he left she drank so much she had to be hospitalized. She said she also spent a night in a tree in her leopard-skin coat. John left the letters where my mother could read them when he went to play golf.

My mother said she was not jealous of Nikki sexually, but "wildly curious" about her as a person. John filled her in, in considerable detail. Nikki was chic. Nikki was smart. Nikki drank a lot. Nikki said she could run faster in red shoes. Nikki had a wirehaired fox terrier and turtles. John went out and bought my mother two wirehaired terriers and some turtles.

Thinking about Nikki and how to be more like her to heighten her appeal to John, one day my mother resolved to drink a great deal of bourbon, but didn't get far before she felt very unwell and decided drinking to excess was not for her.

When *Single Lady*, the novel about her and Nikki rolled into one, came out, John's dedication on the flyleaf read "For Fay."

My mother now was twenty-four years old and still having a hard time figuring out what marriage was all about.

The Depression continued to endanger the studios. Paramount and RKO saw their theater chains go bankrupt and into receivership. Fox and Warner Bros. were on the brink. There were people—many people—who couldn't afford the dime or quarter for a movie. Compounding these problems, when motion pictures went from silent to sound, foreign attendance dropped precipitously.

In 1933, Paramount started letting people go the moment their contracts expired. John was not renewed, and my mother, too, not long after. David O. Selznick, who had been executive producer on two of her pictures, gave her the news in a kindly way, telling her it was only the studio's financial troubles and no reflection on her. Other actresses, like Jean Arthur, were also being let go. It would not be long before Selznick was gone as well.

William Powell chose to interpret my mother's dismissal as good news. Now she was free. That night he came to their house on Selma Avenue and danced on the lawn with my mother and John under the stars. My mother wasn't sure the news was so good. Paramount had been like a family, but "dancing was better than crying." She was now on her own, with no guarantee of future employment.

The halcyon days of Hollywood were not just fading, they were crashing around everyone. My mother and John went to Sunday night parties at the Lasky house less often; their lavish events were scaled back as Jesse could no longer afford them. Lasky's financial advisors told him he was in grave trouble and would immediately have to cover $250,000 he owed on his margin account, plus a mountain of other debts. Harry Warner put up money to tide him over, with Jesse guaranteeing the loan with Paramount stock and the Lasky beach house. All would soon be gone, along with the New York apartment, the Rolls-Royces, the maids, and other trappings of his and Bessie's high life. The worst blow came when Paramount's board of directors fired Jesse from the company he had helped found. With consideration and renewed tenderness, Bessie turned all her attention to her husband, reassuring him that she was looking forward to a less complicated life which would not include John Monk Saunders.

John and my mother saw their own savings shrink. One day my mother heard their cook, Mattie, say on the phone, "I think my people is broke." They weren't, but they had to economize. John told his family he would be cutting back on what he was sending his mother, and my mother called Vina to say her monthly check would be reduced.

"I will sue you," Vina said.

She did not sue but Vina's words hung over my mother like a black cloud. She had been working continuously since the early 1920s, which had made it possible for her to provide for the family. Now my mother no longer depended on Vina; instead the opposite was true, with Vina depending on my mother for everything. For someone as fiercely proud as Vina, that must have been humiliating. Vina could be exacting and aloof to the point of coldness. Vina "graded her children more than she loved them," my mother said. "I knew her appreciation of good manners. Her, I never really knew."

Things never became truly financially bleak for my mother and John. She continued to work nonstop. In 1934, a year after telling her that Paramount was dropping her contract, Selznick, now at M-G-M, called to give her a part opposite Wallace Beery and Leo Carrillo in *Viva Villa*. She liked Selznick personally and admired the way he poured "his whole per-

sonality into his productions," as
he famously did with *Gone with
the Wind*.

She was cast in *Viva Villa*
thanks to what diplomats call an
international incident.

The picture was already in production in Mexico, without my
mother. After a long day's shooting, actor Lee Tracy was asleep
in his hotel after midnight when
a boisterous crowd came by. The
group included mostly soldiers on
parade, but it had been joined by some serious drinkers and other merry-
makers out for a good time, and they were making considerable noise. It
woke Tracy, who came out onto the balcony naked and urinated on them.
All Mexico was insulted. The outrage brought demands to shut down the
picture. Selznick, acting quickly, replaced Tracy and at the same time took
the opportunity to recast the female lead with my mother.

The resulting picture, reborn, triumphed and was nominated for four
Oscars, including Best Picture, winning one. My mother had a wonderful time on the shoot and was especially in awe of cinematographer James
Wong Howe, who was a genuine artist: "He made the film look like it was
made of velvet."

John kept working. He sold an original story, *The Dawn Patrol,* to First

Viva Villa (1934), from a Ben Hecht screenplay directed by Jack Conway
and starring Fay, Leo Carrillo, and Wallace Beery (below). James Wong
Howe was the cameraman.

MUSIC BLENDED WITH AVIATION

ARCHIE LEACH, FAY WRAY and DOUGLAS MONTGOMERY sketched in a fragment from "Nikki," a stage version with music of John Monk Saunders' story, running in New York City. Miss Wray, a native of Canada, besides working in legitimate, is also a member of the screen colony at Hollywood, and when at home is Mrs. John Monk Saunders.

Nikki opened on Broadway in 1931 to mixed reviews, but Fay loved the experience, largely because of her costar, Archie Leach. In Hollywood Archie adopted his new name—Cary Grant.

National Pictures, a subsidiary of Warner Bros., which also bought film rights to his new novel, *Single Lady*—retitled *The Last Flight* for the film—and hired him to write the script. Separately, he sold the theatrical rights to the novel to a wealthy businessman who hoped to turn it into a Broadway musical, *Nikki,* to furnish his daughter with her stage debut in the title role. When the daughter turned out to be inadequate, John suggested my mother for the part. The producer was delighted. The play's reviews were generally poor—my mother did get one rave for being "the saving grace of the evening"—and it closed after thirty-nine performances.

John's skill lay in writing male characters, especially men in war. He had less success writing women. My mother never criticized his writing, only once going so far as to say that, like many male writers of the time, John's female characters may have lacked dimension.

Still, for my mother the play was a memorable experience, not least because she was cast opposite a young actor named Archibald Leach. His character's name in *Nikki* was Cary, and soon after the play closed he changed his name to Cary Grant.

My mother later wrote, "There are some people who seem to have an incandescent light behind their eyes that turns on to the switch of their interest . . . Cary's eyes flashed as a moment excited him. 'Oh! . . . how interesting. I love what you have to say. I like you. Say that again. I love hearing that.'"

She savored her time with her leading man, especially in the play's final moment, with Nikki and Cary alone onstage, a spotlight on their upturned faces. As the lights go down, he looks into her eyes, then kisses her on the forehead, saying "God bless you, Nikki." Curtain.

Soon after the play closed, Cary Grant and my mother saw each other across the room at a party at the Waldorf Hotel. No words were spoken, but they looked at each other in a way that said neither of them wanted this to be good-bye. She always remembered him in white tie and tails that night, looking only at her . . . as if any woman who ever lived could forget Cary Grant in white tie and tails looking only at her across the ballroom of the Waldorf.

John had been frequenting New York's speakeasies during the run of the play, drinking even more than usual, and before returning to California he went to an upstate New York health farm to dry out. He wanted help, but withdrawal from alcohol made him so agitated that he soon left the farm.

My mother had stayed at their suite in the Pierre Hotel, alone but for the constant barking of the seals from the Central Park Zoo below her window. Cary Grant called to tell her he would be driving to California, arriving soon after she and John got back, and hoped to see her there. She was developing strong feelings for him, but had no idea where they might lead.

The week John and Fay got home, California welcomed them back in the most hospitable way possible, at the Academy Awards, where John was given the Oscar for Best Original Screenplay for *The Dawn Patrol*. Then they settled back into their regular routine, which for my mother meant making films nonstop.

Cary did come to town and was immediately put under contract at Paramount. He asked for and was given my mother's old dressing room and moved into an apartment with actor Randolph Scott. One night at a party Scott asked my mother to dance, and as he led her around the floor told her, "Cary's in love with you."

But nothing came of it, even as she allowed herself the warm feelings of their almost-connection. That he cared for her, that he had said he loved her, was enough. And she was still committed to her marriage.

6

Samuel Hopkins Adams' story "Night Bus" appeared in *Cosmopolitan* magazine. An unemployed chemist, Peter Warne, meets a young heiress, Elspeth, who, to avoid marriage to a man she doesn't love, runs away on a bus. Neither Warne, who is jaded, nor Elspeth, who is spoiled, is sympathetic when we meet them but they start to bring out the best in each other and reveal their better selves as they fall in love.

Capra told my father—"a bit dubiously," my father thought—about the story he had read in a pile the studio had given him. "Sounds cute," my father said. Capra went away to think about it and came back to say, "Okay. We'll do it." Remembering the first time he'd heard Capra pitch a

The fourth Riskin-Capra film, *It Happened One Night,* swept the top five Academy Awards of 1934—Best Picture, Actor, Actress, Writer, Director—the first picture ever to do so. The film elevated Columbia to the ranks of major film companies.

story ("abominably") to Cohn and his roomful of executives and writers, my father said, "Hey pal, let me tell this one." Capra agreed, and afterward Cohn said he would buy the rights—without enthusiasm, they both felt.

"And that," my father said, "is how we happened to make *It Happened One Night*."

It had not been their first choice. Thinking big, they had asked Cohn to buy the rights to *Mutiny on the Bounty* for their first from-the-beginning collaboration. Too expensive, he said; find something cheaper. *Bounty* went instead to M-G-M, coming out two years later; it starred Clark Gable and Charles Laughton and won the Academy Award for Best Picture. My father and Capra knew that, at this time, and at this studio on Poverty Row, the chance to make a big, important picture lay in the future, probably at another studio.

My father and Capra conferred on a general approach to adapting "Night Bus" and my father went off alone to write it. When not on a hard studio deadline, he took two to three months to think about a screenplay before writing it relatively quickly, always in longhand, often while sitting in the sun outside his studio office.

"Night Bus" provided a sound framework but a great deal of original thinking and hard work lay ahead. My father reimagined the premise; the heroine, now named Ellie, would be running away not from a forced marriage but because her father would not let her marry the man she loved. He changed Peter to a hard-boiled newsman who saw in the story of the missing heiress a scoop that would earn him a big bonus and salvage his collapsing career—if he wrote it. But spilling the beans would mean betraying Ellie, who is on the run, and in a bumbling, fumbling, opposites-attract kind of way, he is falling in love. Class and gender and moral distinctions—some cute, some funny, some serious—romantic tension, adventures, incidents, social commentary, all had to be imagined and stirred in to give the story substance and meaning while moving it forward to its happy ending.

Working out how to get from beginning to end in the most interesting dramatic or comic fashion has always meant for most writers starting the day with a long, hard think. My father said, "My own method is to begin by staring at the walls. Then I sharpen my pencils." He also played absentmindedly with the coins in his pocket and lit cigarette after cigarette, "and still stared at the walls." His new friend Billy Wilder's approach was similar. Wilder stood at the window of his studio office and was ready to start writing, he said, as soon as he had seen four cars with Indiana license plates drive by.

Screenwriting requires beginning with a blank page—the task is of course eased when there is a story to adapt—and then developing and integrating many elements in search of a unified whole. What to say and how to say it. Story, characters, dialogue, complications, dramatic tension, tone, setting, visuals, and putting them all together in a focused and economical way. The film has to come alive on paper before it can come alive on film. It's often hard to get it right the first time, and not just for screenwriters. Hemingway is said to have rewritten one page of his famous, probably perfect story "The Killers" sixty times.

Among the memorable moments in *It Happened One Night*, none of which was in the magazine story, were the hitchhiking scene where the leg proves mightier than the thumb, the rollicking communal singing of "The Daring Young Man on the Flying Trapeze" by the passengers on the bus, the learned treatise in which Peter educates Ellie on how to dunk a doughnut, Peter's striptease as he shows Ellie the various ways a man can undress, the scene where Peter is mistaken for and then has to masquerade as kidnapper and gangster. As always, my father put parts of himself into his scripts, giving Peter his own elliptical ways in romance, his views on class differences and of a woman trying to break free, a man who falls in love despite himself, his optimism about human nature. He portrays Ellie's wealthy father as a caring and principled man at a time when the very rich were stock villains.

The piggybacking scene has special meaning for me. My father loved giving Bobby and me piggyback rides and delighted in different variations. I remember holding tight at age three as he spun and backed us into C. C. Brown's to get hot fudge sundaes while barking like a parade marshal, "Lefterly! Weaverly! Backwards, march!" In the movie, Peter and Ellie—still in the early stages of romance but making progress—have left the bus and are approaching a stream. Without asking, Peter slings her over his shoulder and starts across. Ellie goes from being terrified to rather enjoying the experience.

"It's the first time I've ridden piggyback in years," she says.

"This isn't piggyback."

"Of course it is."

"You're crazy."

"I remember distinctly Father taking me for a piggyback ride—"

"And he carried you like this, I suppose . . . I never knew a rich man yet who was a piggyback rider . . . To be a piggybacker it takes complete relaxation—a warm heart—and a loving nature . . . Take Abraham Lincoln, for instance—a natural piggybacker . . ."

"And rich people have none of those qualifications, I suppose."

"Not a one."

"You're prejudiced . . . My father was a *great* piggybacker."

Peter hands her his suitcase. "Hold this a minute." His hand now free, he delivers a sharp smack to her backside, Ellie lets out a yelp and Peter takes back the suitcase. "Thank you," he says.

Now the romance takes off. Peter and Ellie have relied on repartee to keep their emotional distance until the inevitable happens. Here the tone changes. When Ellie asks Peter if he's ever thought about falling in love and settling down, the hard-boiled newspaperman reveals he is a romantic at heart. I hear my father's voice and his own romantic yearnings when Peter says:

> I saw an island in the Pacific once. Never been able to forget it. That's where I'd like to be able to take her . . . She'd have to be the sort of girl who'd jump in the surf with me on moonlight nights and love it as much as I did . . . You know, one of those nights when you and the moon and the water all become one—when something comes over you—and you feel that you're part of something big and marvelous . . . Those are the only places to live. Where the stars are so close over your head that you feel you could reach right out and stir them around . . .
>
> Certainly I've been thinking about it. Boy, if I could ever find a girl who's hungry for those things . . .

Harry Cohn gave the go-ahead the day he read the script.

For Peter, Capra wanted Robert Montgomery, who was under contract to M-G-M. Louis B. Mayer was contractually obligated to lend Columbia a "first-class actor" but wouldn't give them Montgomery and insisted they instead take Clark Gable. Cohn said Gable was not the kind of first-class actor he had been promised; he knew Mayer didn't like Gable personally and wanted to punish him for making excessive salary demands by sending him off to Poverty Row. Cohn finally, grudgingly, gave in and agreed to pay Gable's $10,000 salary.

Myrna Loy, Miriam Hopkins, and Margaret Sullavan turned down the part of Ellie. Cohn suggested Loretta Young but Capra said no. Capra proposed Carole Lombard and asked my father to give her the script but she had a schedule conflict. Cohn finally suggested Claudette Colbert, but there was a problem. Colbert and Capra had made a silent picture together in 1927, *For the Love of Mike*, which both regarded as one of the worst experiences of their lives. It was her first time before a camera—she came from the theater, where words mattered and pantomime was something only clowns were expected to do—and the speed of moviemaking left her feeling pressured and dispirited. Capra, on the tightest possible schedule, grew frustrated when she couldn't cry on cue and otherwise had trouble following his direction. Joe Walker, the cinematographer on *It Happened One Night*, said they "ended up hating each other."

Colbert was indignant when the offer came. No Capra–Poverty Row picture for her. Capra pleaded with her to no avail. My father tried and tried. "I almost had to get on my knees to that woman before she'd accept the part," he told a reporter. Finally, for $50,000, five times Gable's salary, plus overtime, she agreed.

An all-in budget of just over $300,000 and a tight thirty-six-day schedule were indicative of the studio's limited expectations. As with *Lady for a Day*, Capra went to Cohn on the eve of shooting and appealed to him to call it off but Cohn had made commitments to the actors and said they had to go ahead. Capra's nephew, Joe Finochio, who worked sound on the picture, said "We were all joking with one another, 'Hell, let's get this stinking picture over with.'" Joe Walker said, "Most of us were unhappy about doing this one."

Everything came together perfectly on *It Happened One Night*: story, script, director, cast. My father said, "It was a miracle." Public opinion was unanimous and positive—except among manufacturers of men's undershirts; when Gable took off his shirt in the classic Walls of Jericho scene and was seen without an undershirt, overnight virtually every man in America is said to have stopped wearing one.

When Academy Awards season came around, this time was different. Unlike the previous year, when *Lady for a Day* earned three nominations but no awards, *It Happened One Night* swept the boards. Columbia was off Poverty Row forever, and the people most responsible, including my father, were suddenly in the pantheon of Hollywood.

Everyone wanted to know how my father had achieved such big results from such a small picture.

THE FILM DAILY

ROBERT RISKIN TELLS HIS WRITING METHOD

There are writers who plan a scenario. They break up their story into hundreds of little scenes. I never do. I take the story assigned to me and sit down at the typewriter, working at it as if I were writing a

Iconic moments in *It Happened One Night* include the endless bus ride and Peter showing Ellie the art of dunking doughnuts.

play. The only difference is that, instead of having two or three scenes to the act, I have hundreds of scenes, if necessary. But I do aim at curtains. I direct the story toward a first-act curtain and a second-act curtain. If I succeed, I know I have suspense that will hold an audience.

He was also asked, now and frequently in the years ahead, about his working relationship with Capra. It was a subject he enjoyed talking about as their collaboration evolved and deepened through six pictures in the next seven years.

"We have the same basic story ideas," my father said. "We have some awful battles over how the story should be developed, but we never argue over what constitutes a story. He's a great editor. He'll give his opinion

of a scene, and in doing so toss off an idea from which I can take a dozen successful steps . . . then we get together and fight it out over changes."

Next my father would write a first draft that was usually "long as hell." After Capra read it, they went together "to some nearby watering-place, usually La Quinta in the desert, to tug at a trout" and discuss revisions. My father said they had one rule. With each scene they asked themselves, "Is this entertaining? If not, throw it out." They then returned to town where my father worked on the script alone again, usually for about a month. His final drafts were detailed and descriptive, including camera movements—close-ups, camera angles, dissolves—giving Capra whatever he thought would help tell the story. My father said, "When Frank gets out there with the camera—well, he's the best in the business. What he can't squeeze out of a scene isn't in it to begin with."

Writer-director Philip Dunne, who knew both Riskin and Capra well, said there was a unique ingredient in their partnership. "Frank provided the schmaltz and Bob provided the acid. It was an unbeatable combination."

Through the process they enjoyed each other's company, finding a brotherhood of humor, teasing, and friendship. They shared an excitement in collaboration and even enjoyed the creative disagreements, or at least survived them and kept going.

Their collaboration continued after the script was finished. They discussed casting down to the smallest part. Capra wanted my father to be on set during filming, both as a pair of trusted eyes and in case he or an actor wanted an adjustment. They suffered through previews together and talked through whatever changes they needed to make.

One journalist wrote, "When you interview Capra, all he will talk about is Riskin, and when you interview Riskin, all he wants to talk about is Capra." When asked after a half dozen pictures how their respect for each other came about, my father said, "Well, we've been married a long time."

True, they looked an ill-matched pair. My father wore a tie and jacket, with his shoes polished to a high sheen and his pants sporting a sharp crease, while Capra wore a plain pullover sweater, floppy corduroy slacks, and barely serviceable moccasins. It didn't concern them that in matters of dress and politics they were different. When they were making a movie, they were one.

7

When my mother was offered the part of Ann Darrow in *King Kong,* codirector Merian C. Cooper told her only that she would be cast opposite "the tallest, darkest leading man in Hollywood." She thought he meant Cary Grant, which would have been the fulfillment of a dream; or if not Cary Grant, as a very acceptable consolation prize, Clark Gable. She adapted to Kong and in time grew to appreciate and even treasure him. "Every time I'm in New York," she said late in life, "I say a little prayer when passing the Empire State Building. A good friend of mine died up there."

> "You will star opposite the tallest, darkest leading man in Hollywood."
>
> —Merian C. Cooper, codirector of *King Kong,* 1933

Merian Cooper, "Coop" to his friends, played a central role in my mother's career. She had already made *The Four Feathers* with him, and Coop and David O. Selznick were producers on *The Most Dangerous Game,* made at the same time as *King Kong.* Today the first two films are still very good viewing and the third, *King Kong,* is a classic.

Coop and my mother forged an enduring friendship. Whenever they saw each other, he pounded his chest like Kong, which led her to throw back her head in affectionate laughter. She described Coop as having the exuberance of a young boy whose dreams of adventure were always at the front of his mind.

By the time he made *Kong,* Coop had already lived a life as dramatic as any movie. Everything in his past laid the foundation for his epic film.

His family came to America in the 1600s. He was raised on ancestral stories which set in motion his life's restless and wide-ranging course. Honor, patriotism, war, freedom, adventure, and danger fused together to make the man.

Young Coop went to the U.S. Naval Academy, only to be thrown out shortly before graduating. Mortified that he had embarrassed his family, he set out to redeem himself. He joined John J. "Black Jack" Pershing's expedition to Mexico to track down Pancho Villa, and when America entered World War I in 1917, he went to France as a bomber pilot. On a combat mission he was shot down in flames by German Fokkers; in the seat behind him his observer was shot through the neck and rendered helpless. Cooper's hands were so badly burned he had to guide the plane with his knees and elbows, but he refused to bail out, which would have consigned his observer to death. He landed the bullet-riddled plane behind enemy lines in a crash so violent it tore off the wings. Headquarters pronounced him officially dead, but he survived in a prison camp until the end of the war. His observer also survived.

After the war ended, Cooper stayed in Europe, joining a volunteer relief expedition to bring food to starving people in devastated cities. Repaying a debt to his ancestor, he recruited an all-American flying squadron to fight in Poland's battle against invading Bolsheviks and led them in more than seventy missions. He was shot down again, again managing to land safely, but Cossacks took him prisoner and sent him to Russia as a prisoner of war. He escaped and made his way back to Poland, where he took up with a striking blonde ten years older than himself. He learned later that she had borne his child and he sent them money every month for the rest of his life.

After four years in Europe, Cooper wanted to come home. He signed on to a job on a freighter to New York, arriving with one dollar and an overcoat. He gave the coat to the first beggar he met and the dollar to the second, and set out to see what new adventures awaited him. After a brief stint as a reporter on *The New York Times,* he joined a seaborne expedition "to wander up and down the strange waters of the world." In the Solomon Islands the expedition came across headhunters who practiced human sacrifice, then went on to visit Murder Island, where he studied pygmies who hunted with bow and arrow. In a scene he re-created in *King Kong,* Coop's party came face to face with a large group of scaly prehistoric-looking

Young Merian Cooper, known as "Coop," one of the great explorers and documentary filmmakers of the twentieth century

lizards fourteen feet long. The lizards made menacing moves and noises, but the explorers killed one and the rest ran away.

The expedition's cameraman jumped ship at Ceylon and Cooper persuaded the team leader to send for Ernest B. Schoedsack, his good friend from the Great War who was filming the massacre of almost a quarter-million Greeks in the Greco-Turkish War of 1919–1922. Schoedsack, known as "Monty" to his friends, joined them in time to visit Abyssinia, today's Ethiopia, where the dramatic pictures he took convinced Coop that film, far more than the magazine articles he was sending back, was the way to captivate an audience. They agreed their next project together would be a documentary in Persia.

It was 1924. They contacted the nomadic Bakhtiari just as the tribe was preparing to embark on its annual spring migration. The dying winter grass could not sustain their herd of 500,000 cows and goats, which in turn sustained the tribe's 50,000 people, and they headed to the mountainous grass plateaus which fed the herds all summer. The migration promised rich photographic opportunities consistent with the mantra

Cooper teamed up with adventurer Marguerite Harrison and Ernest B.
Schoedsack in 1924 to make the documentary *Grass*, about the harrowing
midwinter journey of the Bakhtiari tribe to grasslands to feed their herds.
Coop and Schoedsack were the filmmakers. Harrison, a reporter and
former spy for the United States in Russia who had been held captive for
ten months in 1920, was their friend and patron.

Cooper and Schoedsack propounded for themselves—"Keep it distant,
difficult, and dangerous"—and they set off for Persia with 20,000 feet of
film stock, to which they tended as zealously as the herders tended their
animals. They also took a patron, Marguerite Harrison, herself a reporter
and former spy, and they all got more than they'd bargained for.

They went through long, howling blizzards. They became the first

Westerners ever to cross the raging, whirlpool-riven half-mile-wide Karun River, on rafts buoyed by inflated goatskins. The herders put women and children on the rafts, but swam across with the animals themselves. This year, like every year, people and animals were sucked to their deaths in the enormous eddies.

They made their way through hostile tribes who they were warned would kill them for their goods without hesitation. They hauled their heavy camera up a steep, snow-covered, unforgiving 15,000-foot mountain just as the tribe's herders sometimes carried their goats and cattle on their backs.

They shared every danger, every privation with the tribe. No one could be left behind once the migration started; old, young, infirm, all had to come or die. Cooper and Schoedsack lived as the tribesmen did, sleeping out in the open. "We goddam near froze to death in the snow," said Schoedsack. "Merian and I said, 'We'll probably die up here, but let's make the goddam picture,' and we did." They were gone a year and used all but eighty of their 20,000 feet of film. They brought the film back to New York to edit.

Cooper had seen only a few films and the editing process was new to him, but ninety years later the full-length documentary he and Schoedsack made, *Grass,* is still dramatic and thrilling in its unretouched depictions of life and death, of people and animals facing cruel and hard nature. It is as immediate as today. Jesse Lasky was present when the film was screened at a New York dinner party and immediately bought distribution rights for Paramount. He was also impressed enough with Cooper and Schoedsack to put up $75,000 of Paramount's money for them to make a film in the jungles of Siam, where man-eating tigers were terrorizing the villagers.

In Siam, Cooper and Schoedsack again made the filming of *Chang* difficult, distant, and dangerous, putting themselves in the middle of the unscripted action with the tigers and having a hair-raisingly close call after digging a hole for themselves and their camera and provoking a stampede of rampaging elephants to run by, and over, them.

As with *Grass, Chang* was a critical and box-office success and Cooper and Schoedsack had no trouble persuading Paramount to acquire for their next project a novel about a British officer accused of cowardice for resigning his commission before a battle in Sudan. They would write and direct *The Four Feathers* in 1929 and, as their first fully scripted drama with actors, it was an essential bridge in their careers.

Cooper and Schoedsack insisted the studio allow them to shoot the

The success of Cooper and Schoedsack's *Grass* and their second documentary, *Chang*, shot in the jungles of Thailand, brought both men to Hollywood. Their first feature, *The Four Feathers* (1929), starred Fay and Richard Arlen (below) and was produced by David O. Selznick. Cooper, a Southern gentleman, regularly sent orchids to Fay's dressing room.

exteriors in the wilds of Africa. Anxious about the cost and scope of what it was getting into, the studio reluctantly agreed and assigned David O. Selznick, a bright young associate producer, to keep a close eye on them. It turned out to be an inspired move. Not only did Selznick and the filmmakers grow to like and trust each other, he was essential in ensuring studio support throughout filming.

The studio withdrew its objections to shooting in Africa as soon as they saw the footage of a baboon stampede and the herd of hippopotami jumping off a bank into the river. The company then came back to California to film the interiors.

Cooper had assembled a first-rate cast to make what turned out to be the last epic of the silent era, although for the picture's release he did add synchronized sound effects of screaming chimpanzees and the hubbub of

thousands of tribesmen. Richard Arlen played the British officer whose fiancée, my mother, is distressed by his cowardice.

Cooper and Schoedsack were exacting directors. My mother and Arlen had to shoot one love scene more than thirty times. All in a day's work for her and no doubt better than being slapped twenty times across the face by George Raft. Cooper was also a courtly Southern gentleman who sent orchids to my mother's dressing room every few days.

The picture took two years to finish and was a major hit, proving that Cooper and Schoedsack were proficient in drama as well as documentaries. They were now ready to create their masterpiece.

Almost everything Coop had experienced in life was called upon in the making of *King Kong,* even harkening back to the story he had heard as a child of his ancestor who had gone to Africa to hunt an immense gorilla. Carl Denham, the adventurer-director who heads the film's expedition to Skull Island, is modeled on Cooper and his own voyage to the Solomons and Murder Island. Enormous scaly lizards, man-eating tigers, rampaging baboons, elephants and hippopotami—Cooper had seen them all up close and talked about them in detail to Schoedsack's wife, Ruth Rose, who was entrusted with writing the script from Coop's story. Even one of the iconic scenes of film history, where the gorilla atop the Empire State Building is strafed and sent to his death by airplanes, draws on Cooper's experiences in World War I. When the scene was filmed for *Kong,* Cooper piloted the plane and fired the guns while Schoedsack rode in the observer seat behind him.

Because of Paramount's money woes, the picture wound up instead at RKO. Selznick had left Paramount shortly after John Monk Saunders and my mother, also due to the studio's drastic belt-tightening, and Cooper's recommendation had helped Selznick land at RKO as vice president in charge of production. Selznick repaid the favor by bringing Cooper and *Kong* to RKO and making sure he had the budget to do it right. He also contributed something else of inestimable value to Cooper: an introduction to the great early genius of animation and stop-motion photography, Willis O'Brien.

Making *Kong* was a tremendous challenge for everyone involved. The production was hard on the actors, who were required to work unusually long hours, often in physically demanding, grueling scenes. At the same time my mother was doing extensive film tests for *Kong,* she was filming *The Most Dangerous Game* with Joel McCrea, directed by Schoed-

David O. Selznick, age twenty-nine in 1931, became studio chief at financially troubled RKO and implemented cost controls to stabilize the company. In an unusual move, he gave Cooper and Schoedsack complete artistic freedom in making their films. Concurrently with *King Kong*, Cooper and Schoedsack made *The Most Dangerous Game* (below), also starring Fay, with Joel McCrea. Fay went back and forth between the *Kong* and *Most Dangerous Game* sets, sometimes working in both on the same day.

On the set of *King Kong*, Cooper (left) with Fay (center) and Schoedsack (right). In the foreground is Willis O'Brien, the technical genius who created the eighteen-inch Kong doll and designed stop-motion photography for the film. Fay designed her own costumes and chose to be a blonde in the part.

sack. Between takes on *Dangerous Game*, she jammed on a blond wig and ran with Coop to the other set. It was Coop who had my mother work for twenty-two consecutive hours one day and scream for eight hours on another.

But Cooper was principled and a gentleman, and when his wife-to-be, Dorothy Jordan, herself an actress, took him to task for working my mother so hard, he promised never to do it again and didn't. For her part, my mother said she'd never minded. She trusted Cooper completely and knew he respected her. Unique among the many directors she worked with, he turned over to her alone the decision on what her wardrobe on *King Kong* should be and left to her the choice of hairstyle and color; she chose blond and fluffed-up, and when Cooper saw it he loved it.

New techniques of animation, rear projection, puppetry, stop-motion and process photography all had to be invented and refined for *King Kong*. Designing, manufacturing, and adjusting an eighteen-inch-high mechanical doll for Kong's body and then visually matching it to an eight-foot arm required all of Willis O'Brien's masterful and meticulous technical skills. Kong's movements were filmed painstakingly, one small, discrete action at a time.

The filming of my mother in Kong's hand carried considerable risk. "I would stand on the floor and they would bring this arm down and

cinch it around my waist, then pull me up in the air," she said. Once in the air, with a cement floor forty feet below and no safety harness, a wind machine was fired up to blow her clothes and hair, creating the sense of the wild outdoors. "Every time I moved, one of the fingers would loosen, so it would look like I was trying to get away. Actually, I was trying not to slip through his hand; then I would holler and they would let me down."

With so many technical and mechanical problems to solve, all for the first time, it was impossible to budget accurately. Knowing that RKO was facing the same desperate Depression-era money worries as Paramount, Selznick worked miracles to keep the money coming so Cooper and Schoedsack could fulfill their wildest vision.

It all worked. *King Kong* wound up costing the then-astronomical sum of $680,000, but its phenomenal success single-handedly saved the studio

Fay costarred with Robert Armstrong and Bruce Cabot.

from bankruptcy. In New York City, 180,000 people came on opening week, and even at 15 cents a ticket that was serious money.

Everything that went into making *King Kong* turned out to be worth it. Whether it was the desperate fight to the death between Kong and the enormous T-Rex, still as gripping as any five minutes of film ever shot, or the planes flying around Kong atop the Empire State Building with machine guns blazing, or the tenderness—love, really—that the primordial Kong comes to feel for Ann Darrow, no one had ever seen anything like it. What had been an intense, rigorous, two-year struggle to do it both well and economically had come together brilliantly. No viewer ever asked for his money back.

King Kong opens with an on-screen legend, a spurious Arab proverb written by Cooper that reads "And lo! The Beast looked upon the face of Beauty and it stayed its hand from killing. And from that day, it was as one dead." The film closes with Cooper's alter ego, Carl Denham, saying, "It wasn't the airplanes. It was Beauty killed the Beast." Today that line is still quoted, and my mother is remembered as Beauty.

King Kong spawned two remakes, one produced by Dino de Laurentiis with Jessica Lange as Ann Darrow, the other by Peter Jackson with Naomi Watts. It inspired a mega-ride at Universal Studios theme park and King Kong T-shirts and Halloween masks and costumes and mugs sold at the Empire State Building—an entire cottage industry in what in 1933 was the tallest building in the world. There was a time when *King Kong* screened somewhere in the world every day, and it remains on most lists of the 100 best pictures.

King Kong did not shape my mother's life, but it did have a powerful influence on her career and made her name indelible. "Fay Wray" is routinely the answer in crossword puzzles, Fay Wray and King Kong are used regularly in jokes and cartoons, and her name was even adopted by a rock band. A famous dog, Fay Ray, is endlessly photographed by her owner, William Wegman.

Growing up, I knew my mother had been the damsel in distress in *King Kong* and at times it made me self-conscious. In fourth grade, a schoolmate teased, "Hey, is your dad an ape or something?" Occasionally someone would say, "Wow, your mom's the lady in *King Kong*." I mumbled, "yes," not wanting to be the focus of special attention.

I was nine years old before I saw the film. My mother told me it was going to be on television.

"Would you like to see it, honey? You don't have to, of course, but I think you're old enough." At nine, I wanted to be old enough for everything.

I hardly recognized my dark-haired mother playing the very blond and waif-like Ann Darrow, wearing a clingy white dress, but I got lost in the drama of the crew landing on Skull Island, the beating of the natives' drums, the gigantic and terrifying Kong, the way he kidnaps the blonde lady, the destruction he unwittingly causes, his love for her, and finally the tender and gripping scenes of Kong on top of the Empire State Building.

My mother came into the living room a few times, checking on me. When the end came, I was in a heap, crying.

"Sweetheart, I hope the movie didn't upset you. Did it bother you to see your mother in danger that way?"

"I was upset for King Kong! He didn't want to hurt you. He just liked

Of the more than one hundred movies she made, Fay is best remembered for *King Kong*.

you and those men were so mean to him. He didn't deserve to be treated that way."

For three days, I brooded over how my mother could have been party to such cruelty.

Such is the power of movies.

I grew to appreciate *King Kong*'s place in film history. When I traveled to China in 1978, the picture served as my diplomatic calling card. The country was opening up to Westerners after the Cultural Revolution, and our small contingent from Hollywood, led by Norman Lear, were guests of the Chinese government. Our group included two of America's most recognizable faces, Mary Tyler Moore and Carl Reiner.

For two weeks, our movements were closely managed by the government. One afternoon we were ushered into a great hall to meet the minister of culture, an aging, steely-eyed, humorless man who was flanked by others who had been with him and Mao Tse-tung on the Long March of 1934–1935. Norman introduced our group: "This is Mary Tyler Moore, the most loved woman on American television . . . Carl Reiner, the most brilliant writer-comedian in our country," and so on around the room. The Chinese, without American entertainment since 1949, stared at them blankly. When Norman came to me, he said, "You might know Vicki's mother, Fay Wray . . . She was in *King Kong*." The aged minister of culture struggled to his feet and, smiling broadly, pounded his chest with his fists and roared like Kong. His entourage also stood, pounding their chests and making gorilla noises and laughing. The atmosphere in the room thawed.

My mother made more than a hundred films and television programs and there were times she wished people might remember her for some of her other movies, such as *The Wedding March*. But in the end, she was grateful for the gift of *King Kong*. In 1989, when she was eighty-two years old, she wrote this letter as the opening of her autobiography, *On the Other Hand*:

Dear Kong,

This has to be an open letter because I've never had a precise address for you.

A few years ago, a Mr. Auerbach wrote in the *New York Times* that he had interviewed you at your island home. But I do not want to chance addressing you at just Skull Island; today, without a zip code—who knows?

Then I saw a cover of a Directors Guild magazine showing you in a large easy chair, wearing house slippers and watching scenes of yourself on television at the top of the Empire State Building. There were banana peels on the floor beside you and on a table nearby there was a framed photograph of me. I found that quite touching. It let me know I had been some influence in your life.

I wonder if you know how strong a force you have been in mine?

For more than half a century, you have been the most dominant figure in my public life. To speak of me is to think of you. To speak *to* me is often a prelude to questions about you.

Sometimes, I am asked whether I get tired of hearing so much about you—of being asked so many questions. I say I don't get tired because I have good energy. I could go on to say that I also have respect for you. But that would be hard for people to understand, considering most would think you meant to do me harm.

I feel that you never did mean harm to me. My children knew that when they saw "our film" for the first time: "He didn't want to hurt you," they said, "he just liked you."

I admire you because you made only one film—and that became famous, whereas I made seventy-five or eighty and only the one I made with you became really famous. Another reason I respect you is that, although we never talked about it, I felt we had a tacit understanding that there were some beautiful moments in *King Kong;* that we both appreciated the location given us for the scene when you held me in your left hand and pulled at my skirt with your right hand, as though taking petals from a flower. That's the way I think of it because that's my disposition: to make a poetic metaphor. The background was inspired by the paintings of Gustave Doré, a wondrously quiet, mystical mountain right on the edge of outer space. You brought a petal of my skirt to your nose and sniffed at it.

At a recent film festival, this brought hoots from some young men in the audience: "Whoo, Whoo, Whew," they cried out. Later, outside the theatre, they ran after me and apologized. They didn't have to do that. Their reaction showed they liked it—in their boyish way.

The other scene I find unforgettable is you in your last moments just before falling from the top of the Empire State Building. You had put me down very carefully as though wanting me to be safe. You felt your chest where you had been shot, knowing you were doomed. That scene puts a lump in my throat. When I told this to an interviewer for a French magazine, he cried, "At last, then, Kong has won!"

Your influence has affected the way people respond to me. It made Leonard Bernstein pick me up when we were first introduced in the lobby of a theater. It made Freddy de Cordova (who produces *The Tonight Show*) lift me up and whirl me around in a restaurant. It made Tennessee Williams exclaim at our first meeting (as he held tightly onto my hand), "I am glad you got away from that big ape!"

Sometimes I fantasize that, with all that influence, you might be able to help bring about peace in the world. In my mind, I outline a script that has you buried under Fifth Avenue, where you fell after the airplanes shot you down. You have been sleeping there right into the 1980s! On an early morning, your furriness moves when discovered by subway repairmen. You push up, out, and across Manhattan (scaring people a lot) and wade into the Hudson River, bathing away your sleepiness. You sit for a while on the Jersey Palisades—then the top of the Empire State Building comes into your focus. You imagine that you see Ann Darrow there—so, of course, you wade back across the Hudson, causing huge waves as you go and, once again, you climb to the top of that building where you last saw Ann. Only she isn't there now and all you can do is cling to the spire and your memories.

You have accumulated so much affection over all the years that no one, absolutely no one, wants to kill you. What the whole world wants is to save you. All military attitudes are suspended while your case is considered.

At the United Nations, you are foremost on the agenda; how to rescue you; where to give you safe haven. After offers from Russia, China, and even South Africa, there is a representative from Skull Island who gently proposes the obvious: Why not return you to your native island?

A great helicopter is obtained with a huge and comfortable net attached. The representative from Skull Island goes up and talks quietly to you so that you go willingly into the net.

Now every rooftop in New York is alive with citizens watching, waving, calling out fond farewells as the helicopter circles the city before heading south. Their affection goes with you.

I had thought of letting you drop onto a rocket as you reached Cape Canaveral but that gets a little fantastic and it's better to think of you on the cover of the Directors Guild magazine.

These reflections will let you know that I think of you and feel it is only fair to tell you I am writing about a lot of times that have nothing to do with you—long before we met. Once we met, you had a pretty strong hold on me. I hope you don't look at television all the time and may read this.

Affectionately,

Fay

"Do you have any inflatable
Fay Wrays?"

8

Courage is what it takes to stand up and speak; courage is also what it takes to sit down and listen.

—WINSTON CHURCHILL

With the success of *Lady for a Day* and *It Happened One Night,* my father, Frank Capra, and Harry Cohn were catapulted into the top tier of Hollywood. "The film industry was dazzled by the prolific talent of Riskin and Capra," wrote one historian. At the Academy Awards ceremony on February 7, 1935, when *It Happened One Night* swept the top awards, Cohn generously said, "I want to thank Frank Capra. I want to thank Robert Riskin. I was only an innocent bystander."

In those days, Academy Award winners were notified in advance. My father chose not to attend the ceremony to accept his award, even though he already knew he had won. Instead, he had his golden statue delivered to his Columbia Pictures office where he used it as a doorstop, amusing his colleagues and irritating Harry Cohn. It would be years before I understood the complicated labor-management struggles that caused my father to stay away from the Awards on a night when the brightest stars in Hollywood came out to shine.

Four years after he arrived in Hollywood my father was enjoying the good life. He filled his apartment with English antiques, crystal stemware, Limoges china, monogrammed sterling silver picture frames, cigarette boxes, and ashtrays, all capturing an elegance completely at odds with his upbringing on New York's Lower East Side. He built a collection of 78-rpm records—classical, opera, and contemporary. He stocked his library with classics and read voraciously. Henry David Thoreau was a favorite, and the deep and committed humanism that ran through Thoreau's *Walden* enriched his own writing. Thoreau was a keen observer not just of nature but of human nature and believed most people conformed mindlessly to social norms. "The mass of men live lives of quiet desperation," he wrote. He encouraged people to think for themselves, find their own truths, and experience the spiritual joy available in solitude and nature. These themes would appear in *Mr. Deeds Goes to Town, Lost Horizon,* and *Meet John Doe.*

To manage his life as a bachelor, my father hired a valet, Richard, who kept his clothes clean, his handmade shoes waxed, his icebox (as it was then called) filled with his favorite foods, and his bar well stocked with expensive whiskey. Over time my father's relationship with Richard grew into a strong friendship.

His friend, screenwriter Sidney Buchman (*Here Comes Mr. Jordan, Mr. Smith Goes to Washington*), described my father during the 1930s as "a very cultivated, nonchalant playboy," a man-about-town. He had a group of close friends and enjoyed spending evenings over dinner in their homes—Kendall and Lewis Milestone, the director of *All Quiet on the Western Front* and *Of Mice and Men* who was later blacklisted, and Jo and Flo Swerling and Lu and Frank Capra.

Capra had married Lucille Warner Reyburn—"Lu" as everyone called her—a bright, charming, college-educated young woman with dark attentive eyes and a sparkling sense of humor. From the beginning, she centered her world on Capra and gave him everything he had been missing since childhood: a sense of home, safety, and love. She quelled his demons, buoyed his spirits, and encouraged him to believe that whatever he did was wonderful. My father appreciated the small, unpretentious evenings Lu hosted at their home and as a close friend was a frequent guest at the Capra table.

Other nights he was out on the town, squiring Carole Lombard or Loretta Young or another lady friend of the moment to the Musso and Frank Grill or Victor Hugo's restaurant or the Trocadero, a Hollywood nightclub on Sunset Strip.

The Troc was a black-tie club and the place to be seen. Photographs of celebrities "out on the town at the Troc," dancing and drinking, appeared every day in *The Hollywood Reporter,* whose publisher, William R. Wilkerson, owned the club.

Of the women my father spent time with in the 1930s, Carole Lombard came closest to capturing his heart. She was a lively, outgoing platinum blonde, adored throughout Hollywood for being delightful, irreverent,

witty, smart, warmhearted and profane. She was equally at home with the girls and as one of the boys. Barbara Stanwyck described her as "so alive, modern, frank, and natural that she stands out like a beacon on a lightship in this odd place called Hollywood."

Lombard and my father had met in 1931, when Paramount lent her to Columbia to star in his film *Virtue*, the story of a former prostitute trying to make a good life with her new husband. Reporting to the studio, Lombard was taken in to meet Harry Cohn, who greeted her without so much as a hello:

Cohn: "Your hair's too white. You look like a whore."

Lombard: "I'm sure you know what a whore looks like if anyone does."

Cohn was startled. Possibly he thought he was paying a rare compliment, telling her she looked right for the part. Not wasting more time, he started to unbutton his pants.

Lombard was born in Fort Wayne, Indiana, and had come with her family to Los Angeles as a child. As a stunningly beautiful teenager being pursued by too many boys and men, she had asked her older brothers to teach her profanity she could use in self-defense. Her return volley to Cohn, as she reported verbatim to her many friends around town, was direct and to the point.

"Look, Mr. Cohn, I've agreed to be in your shitty little picture, but fucking you is not part of the deal."

Carole Lombard and Pat O'Brien in *Virtue* (1932). Lombard told Harry Cohn she insisted on having screenwriter Robert Riskin on the set daily. Four years later, they were dating seriously.

Looking hurt, Cohn buttoned up: "That doesn't mean you can't call me Harry."

But true to his practice of respecting talented people who stood up to him, Cohn gave Lombard the largest dressing room on the lot and agreed to her request that the screenwriter of *Virtue,* Robert Riskin, be on the set to make any dialogue adjustments she wanted. From the beginning she and my father were good friends.

Three years later, after his romance with Glenda Farrell ended and after Lombard had come out from under the shadow of the accidental shooting death of her great love Russ Columbo, a leading singer of his time, my father and Lombard got together romantically. Soon they were inseparable. Journalist Dudley Early wrote, "There used to be a time when you couldn't pick up an issue of any movie magazine without seeing Bob Riskin's picture in it, always sitting, standing or walking with Carole. To the world at large, just shining in the light of reflected glory; in Hollywood, being more famous than Lady Lombard and equally important, if not more so."

My father regularly sent Lombard baubles for her charm bracelet: a tiny gold telephone that he said symbolized his luck in getting a date the first time he called . . . a gold lily after learning it was her favorite flower . . . a tiny tennis racket because she loved the game . . . a golden question mark, apparently asking if she felt as he did, which was increasingly close.

One of Lombard's many delights lay in hosting her own brand of inventive parties, an ambition my father did not share but found charming. She threw an enormous black-tie birthday party for him at her house, where arriving guests found the living room knee-deep in hay, with mules and chickens wandering through the rooms, ducks paddling in the swimming pool, and a country band playing western music. The idea of her guests tromping through her home in black tie and evening gowns while trying to avoid the mules, and where the mules had recently been standing, was vintage Lombard mischief and it became one of the most talked-about Hollywood parties of the year.

They went nightclubbing, dancing, to the racetrack. She joined him on weekends in the desert when he was working with Capra. He spent days sunning himself and reading and writing in the backyard of her Hollywood home. When his office at Columbia was suffocating in the summer heat, he escaped to her house to work in comfort.

Lombard told friends she loved my father's repartee and elliptical wit, so like the dialogue in his scripts. "I started in reading books. I don't mean just bullshit books, I mean *book* books. Aldous Huxley, Jane Austen,

Lombard and Riskin
frequented Hollywood
nightclubs, restaurants, and
the racetrack, and escaped on
weekends to Palm Springs,
causing the press in 1934 to
anticipate a Lombard-Riskin
marriage. At the Trocadero
(bottom), with Norma
Shearer and Irving Thalberg

Dickens, Faulkner. Because Bob was an intellectual and I felt I had to keep up." She asked him to teach her how screenplays were constructed. Her friend Adela Rogers St. Johns said, "She was full of ideas and had intense curiosity about everything." Lombard said she wanted to be an inspiration for my father's writing and perhaps she was.

The year they were together was pivotal for Lombard. She had appeared in several pictures which had gone nowhere and was worried her career was waning. She pleaded with Harry Cohn to give her a good and important part and he came through with the starring role opposite John Barrymore in an adaptation of Ben Hecht and Charles MacArthur's play *Twentieth Century*.

It was make-or-break for Lombard. The great director Howard Hawks told Cohn he thought Lombard was the worst actress in Hollywood—but if she stopped acting and was just herself, she could be sensational. Lombard took Hawks' words to heart and was brilliant. The film reignited her career and from then on she was a first-rate screwball comedy actress.

Gossip columnists were pressing my father and Lombard about marriage. One wrote, "They are telling chums that they'll do it when nobody's looking. She conceals the blinding ring he gave her." He also gave her a sable coat and ruby earrings, or so said the press. She gave him a gold cigarette case inscribed FOREVER, CAROLE. My mother told me that when she and my father married, he gave away everything given him by former girlfriends, but fortunately one thing slipped by him—the Lombard gold cigarette case. I still have it.

Everyone including my father was crazy about Lombard. It was impossible not to be. She lit up a room. She told everyone she adored my father and everything about him, including that he danced like a dream and played top-notch tennis. According to Everett, Carole proposed to my father but, still and again, he hesitated; the pattern established with Edith Fitzgerald and Glenda Farrell, of marriage considered but not embarked on, held firm.

What was it? Was he innately cautious? Was he looking for something different, perhaps a sense of belonging rooted less in excitement than in intimacy? Was there something in the idea of marriage that frightened him? Lombard's mercurial, madcap nature may have made him wary.

Whatever the reason, by the end of 1935 they ended their relationship. They remained friends, and two years later a photograph of her still sat on the top shelf of the bookcase in his Columbia office. Everyone in Hollywood, my father included, was delighted when Lombard found in Clark Gable the man who fulfilled her. They married as soon as his divorce became final. My father and the world mourned when she was killed in a plane crash on her way home to Gable after a tour selling war bonds in 1942.

My father loved to talk into the early hours with friends, most of all with Jo Swerling—story ideas, politics, and, doubtless, horses and gambling. They talked about others' stories, too; each was regularly asked to help writers and directors and producers and studio executives who came to them with script problems. If one of them couldn't find the solution, they talked together until they did.

My father was prolific but Swerling was superhuman; in the 1930s alone, he wrote on forty-eight produced pictures, sometimes every word, sometimes contributing scenes or a subplot or dialogue polish, sometimes creating or sharpening a character. Some of the pictures he wrote on, often without credit, including *Gone with the Wind, The Westerner, Pennies from Heaven,* and *It's a Wonderful Life,* were landmark films; others were ordinary or less, to help a friend or do a favor or just because it was a job. Swerling was never very concerned about receiving credit even when he deserved it, a cavalier attitude which drove Flo crazy. She understood credits are the lifeblood of the writing profession and affect reputations, future prospects, bank accounts, and relationships, not to mention reflecting the truth.

My father lived near Everett and they remained close. Everett and Katya's marriage lasted over thirty years but was destined never to be happy. Katya was flamboyant and unpredictable, a human cyclone who suffered from manic-depression, careening between periods of exuberant activity and spells of withdrawal and heavy drinking. The strains between the taciturn Everett and the turbulent Katya featured slammed doors and hurt feelings and were a source of continuing pain to my father. They confirmed his fear, he later told my mother, that marriage was risky business.

My father arranged for Everett to become a scout for Columbia Pictures, and he regularly went to New York to find new plays and talented writers for Cohn. On his trips Everett always visited Bessie and Jakob and his sisters, Essie and Rose, now grown and married. Murray, the youngest, had graduated from law school and also was married.

Everett shared my father's hope that the entire family would join them in California. Essie did come west and my father arranged a job for her in

Riskin at work and play

Columbia's film library. Just when it seemed Columbia was turning into the Riskin family business, Murray and his wife, Rose, came out too, but aware of Harry Cohn's reputation for being hard on employees, he opened his own practice rather than become a Columbia lawyer.

In 1935, at age sixty-nine, Bessie died after suffering a series of crippling migraine headaches and Jakob came to Los Angeles, alone. His children did everything they could for Pops. He lived briefly with Murray and Rose, but they had two young boys and he didn't want to be underfoot. My father and Everett got him his own place in the outsized Hollywood Hotel, where he could be as independent as he wanted. All the children invited him home to meals, called every day, dropped in to see him with their children.

In time he started to adjust. He had a favorite seat in the hotel lobby where, in his still-pronounced Yiddish accent, he would share his stories and progressive ideas with the staff and other residents. He became a regular in the hotel's small-stakes poker and cribbage games. Always, winter and summer, Pops wore one of the fine, heavy three-piece suits he had made for himself years earlier.

My father also loved poker but when the stakes were much higher. He was a regular in a game that included Samuel Goldwyn; Jacob "Jay" Paley, the cigar magnate and father of CBS's William Paley; Zeppo Marx; M-G-M vice president Eddie Mannix; Sol Wurtzel, one of the founding executives of Fox Films; producer Hunt Stromberg; and my mother's former agent, Myron Selznick. On one occasion Myron Selznick was a big loser. A letter in my father's files tells of Myron leaving the game owing $53,450, which he did not have. For weeks, correspondence circulated among the players about what to do. "It's unfair that Myron's reputation should be ruined due to his being short of cash," wrote Eddie Mannix, who suggested a payment schedule that was probably wishful thinking; Myron's debts were too big and it's doubtful my father ever received his $5,911 share.

My father made sizable investments in thoroughbreds, both at the betting windows and for a few years as an owner. He said his style of betting was based on the Book of Ecclesiastes—"The race is not always to the swift nor the contest to the strong," to which he appended the wisdom of sportswriter Grantland Rice: "but that's the way to bet." My father told a newspaperman he planned to name his next horse Gamut so he could say, "I ran the Gamut."

Whenever one of his own horses was entered, he took Pops to the track and before the race tucked a hundred-dollar win ticket into the breast pocket of Pops' suit. His best horse was Dogaway, a four-year-old who in 1938 set a Hollywood Park track record in winning the prestigious Will Rogers Stakes. His prize was a trophy and the owner's $2,025 share of the purse, but what made him happiest was that, at odds of 11–2, Pops cashed his ticket for $650, the equivalent today of $11,000.

The Hollywood labor wars all but consumed the movie business in the 1930s.

The Depression was still taking a terrible toll in the country. People wanted answers, change, saviors. Some thought the country's hope lay in President Roosevelt or Huey Long or some newly minted prophet. Others looked to a new economic order, socialism or communism. There was growing concern about the rise of fascism in Germany. People everywhere were caught up both in their individual plights and the larger problems of the distressed country and the world.

Hollywood was in the middle of the storm, with writers often at the forefront. The 1930s saw a large influx of writers to Hollywood, many from New York, all hoping for movie work as Broadway theaters, publishing houses, newspapers, and magazines went under. Many of the Hollywood-bound writers were already established—some feisty, some independent, all politically aware. They included John Dos Passos, Robert Benchley, Dashiell Hammett, Lillian Hellman, Marc Connolly, S. J. Perelman, Anita Loos, John Howard Lawson, Lester Cole, Dorothy Parker, and F. Scott Fitzgerald, and all were accustomed to having opinions and expressing them freely. The impact when they hit Hollywood was predictably combustible. There was hardly a studio lunch table or dinner party where, after the day's headlines had been pored over, the lot of writers working in the studio system wasn't the subject of heated conversation.

Louis B. Mayer, the autocratic head of M-G-M and no fan of liberals or labor, helped ignite the fire in Hollywood, or at least threw gasoline on it, when he announced a 50 percent pay cut for all employees, a move swiftly adopted by the other studios. One brave writer publicly asked Mayer, at the time the highest-paid executive in America, if he would be taking the same cut. Mayer said he would not, which led screenwriter Albert Hackett (*The Diary of Anne Frank, Seven Brides for Seven Brothers*) to say Mayer may have "created more communists than Karl Marx and made more Democrats than anybody else in the world."

Within days of Mayer's decree the stagehands' union, the International Alliance of Theatrical Stage Employees (IATSE), called a work stoppage and ordered members not to return until the pay cuts were rescinded. When Mayer and the studios backed down, all labor cheered.

It was evident to other studio employees that it was time to band together. Within a month the Screen Writers Guild was founded, with my father an early member. Two months later eighteen actors formed the Screen Actors Guild and my mother soon signed up. It took directors longer; it was three years before the Directors Guild was founded, perhaps because many of them, used to being in charge on the set and having others follow their orders, were not sure they were part of labor.

The studios may have had to give in to stagehands, who had the ability to stop production immediately. Writers were different. The studios all had scripts in the bank and if necessary could do without writers in the short term and perhaps in some cases for an extended period. They were adamant that they would never recognize the Writers Guild, never bargain with it. The air was filled with writers demanding minimum wages, improved working conditions, and professional respect, and the studios saying "Never!" But the gauntlet had been flung.

John Howard Lawson was elected first president of the Screen Writers Guild. His inaugural speech laid out what writers sought. Principally, he said, they wanted to own their own material and receive royalties whenever it was used. The demand outraged the studio heads. Other writers talked of asking for one percent of gross revenues and fair accountings of studio revenues, proposals which would still be considered incendiary today. At M-G-M, Irving Thalberg may not have been the first, but he was widely quoted as saying, "The inmates are trying to take over the asylum." He also said, "The writer is the most important person in Hollywood and no one must let him find out."

However, when the first demands of the writers were formally presented to the studios, they were modest. They asked not to be loaned out to other studios without their consent; not to be asked to write on speculation, that is, for free; to be given warning in writing of a layoff; to have their meals and hotel paid for when on location; to receive screen credit according to their contribution; to be told if another writer was working on the same material; and an end to studio-generated blacklisting—not the political blacklisting which lay in the future, but the practice of one studio telling another not to hire a writer they said was difficult or who just wanted more money. The studios quickly rejected every proposal.

Hoping to gain strength, Hollywood writers talked of merging with the Authors League and the Dramatists Guild in New York, two organizations where playwrights did indeed have control of their work. Studio moguls damned these organizations as nothing more than breeding grounds for communists. To thwart the Screen Writers Guild, Thalberg promoted an alternative, studio-sponsored union, the Screen Playwrights, offering a contract giving its members a few minor concessions. He convinced a number of screenwriters to join rather than fall under the domination of "those Eastern Reds."

The SWG fought back, characterizing the Screen Playwrights not as a union to benefit writers but as a non-union to benefit the studios.

The SWG seemed to be winning the internecine war, signing up many more members than the Screen Playwrights. For the first time a majority of writers, the people Jack Warner called "shmucks with Underwoods," had a sense of unity. It was not unanimous, but a start.

From the beginning, my father's heart was with the Screen Writers Guild. To his thinking, its purpose should be principally to improve conditions for young and inexperienced writers, those with the least bargaining strength and most frequently taken advantage of. While earning a handsome salary himself, he knew what it was like to live on the edge and he joined an early SWG committee to establish guidelines for better working conditions.

At the same time, he was wary of some of the outspoken firebrands in the Guild like Dalton Trumbo, who turned his powerful rhetorical guns on the powers-that-be: "Bankers, nepotists, contracts and talkies . . . On four fingers one may count the leeches which have sucked a young industry into a state of almost total paresis." Others may not have been able to match Trumbo's rhetoric but did share his passion, and not only about writing conditions. Through the 1930s, many writers identified themselves with faraway causes, such as Ethiopia, defenseless against Mussolini's assault, and the Spanish Civil War. Others, including my father, felt the Guild should focus only on working conditions for writers.

During the first three years of the Guild, my father maintained friendships in both the Screen Writers Guild and Thalberg's company union. Because of his stature in the industry, both courted him. Screenwriter Philip Dunne (*How Green Was My Valley*), a tall, red-haired patrician with a Harvard education and my father's close friend, said, "Bob's social character was that of an extremely cautious, conservative man, but politically he was a natural liberal. He was a solid New Deal liberal. He was a Rooseveltian . . . He was not radical. He was a very pure democrat with a small *d*."

The labor wars led to my father's decision not to attend the 1935 Academy Awards ceremony.

In the 1930s the Motion Picture Academy was dominated by the studios, who used the Academy to enforce binding industry-wide standards. Beyond controlling working conditions, they used the Academy to impose salary caps and anti-raiding clauses, even decreeing that no studio could approach talent whose contracts expired until the original studio had decided to keep them or let them go. Writers and actors protested, to no avail. One writer said, "I thought slavery ended with the Civil War."

When actors and writers, led by the embryonic SAG and SWG, protested to no avail, hundreds resigned from the Academy. They also boycotted the Academy Awards. My father was one of them.

Frank Capra was on the other side of the fight, and closely aligned with the studios and the Academy. He headed the Academy Negotiating Committee that in 1933 tried to promote the 50 percent pay cut to studio employees, assuring them it would be temporary. Years later Capra would

In 1933 writers struggled to form a union to represent them against their employers. Riskin, now a top screenwriter, supported the fledgling Screen Writers Guild. Above left, his good friend, the screenwriter Philip Dunne. John Howard Lawson (top right) was elected first Guild president; he was later blacklisted. Dudley Nichols (right) joined Riskin as a moderate trying to build bridges between warring Guild factions.

say that he risked his reputation by his loyalty to the Academy because it led some to think he was stooging for the companies. Many writers did criticize Capra, some calling him a scab. Not my father, who felt Capra was only expressing his honest beliefs.

Still, during the labor wars, with studios battling employees and the rise of unions, life in Hollywood went on.

For my father, as with most writers, that meant writing, and thinking about what he was writing, all the time. He constantly turned stories, words, phrases, ideas around in his head, shaping and refining characters and plot lines while in the shower, driving to work, on the golf course. He amused himself with puns, bon mots, and double entendres that found their way into his screenplays. He kept a long list of useful adverbs and adjectives whose sound he liked—*enthralled, lively, reticent*—for future use. When it was time to sit, to put the words on paper, he wrote in the morning when he was freshest, always with a Lucky Strike in his free hand. Having done his thinking largely in advance, he wrote quickly. His writing was tiny, slanting right, the words seeming to fly across the pages of his yellow legal pads, with corrections rare.

At the studio, he sometimes wrote on the porch of the Writers Building, where Sidney Buchman, Ben Hecht, Charles MacArthur, Billy Wilder, Norman Krasna, Jo Swerling, and Dorothy Parker gathered to talk out script problems. There was an easygoing collaborative spirit among them, with my father often at the hub.

Sometimes he spent mornings at home, writing in bed after his valet had brought him breakfast. Richard brought him the newspaper, too, until my father's picture *Mr. Deeds Goes to Town* came out; then my father got a dachshund, named him Deeds, and taught Deeds to bring him the paper in bed.

At Harry Cohn's request, my father mentored Columbia's budding screenwriters, which he always enjoyed. In his memoirs, James M. Cain quotes my father as telling him, "You seem to regard any story as a sort of algebraic equation, to be transformed and worked out until it yields the inevitable story that lurks in the idea somewhere in the theme . . . But it's not like that at all. A story has to be *your* story even if you're working for a picture company. There's no ultimate, inevitable perfect 'move' that's going to give you an outline, determine your situation. It's not mathematics. It's *you*." While Cain knew the strength of his novels lay in his carefully crafted style, he understood this insight to be critical as he tried his hand at the new form, screenplays.

My father tried to finish the day's writing in time for lunch and tennis at the Beverly Hills Tennis Club or golf at the Hillcrest Country Club. Hillcrest was founded by Jews from the motion picture industry who were not welcome at the restricted clubs of Los Angeles. It became the place to belong for Jewish actors, directors, producers, and writers. The Writers and Actors Table, also called the Hillcrest Round Table in honor of the Algonquin Round Table in New York, included as regulars my father, Jack Benny, Milton Berle, the Marx brothers, George Jessel, Eddie Cantor, the Ritz brothers, Danny Kaye, and George Burns, and also invited guests.

Film was a world where Jews were not only welcome but were a collective force that helped create an art and a business that was a vital part of Los Angeles, and ultimately of the country's cultural identity and economy. But even in a city where the motion picture industry was dominant, Jews encountered rigid social barriers until the 1960s and 1970s, when the doors to restricted clubs and organizations were finally opened. It was felt by some Jews that the social and business leaders of Los Angeles, needing funding for their museums, theaters, symphonies, and hospitals, turned to Jewish leaders of the entertainment industry, offering social acceptance in return.

The writers tables at studio commissaries, where the companies provided reasonable food at reasonable prices—mainly to ensure that writers would eat lunch without leaving the lot and quickly get back to work, it was said—were a font of stories that spread through the town. Some tales were first told there and others were without doubt invented there.

At the Columbia writers table, the favorite subject was always Harry Cohn.

Cohn was a legendary womanizer, always on the prowl. One night he was asleep next to his wife when he had a most evocative dream that caused him to start writhing and murmuring, "Yes . . . yes, my darling . . . oh yes!" His wife woke and looked at him murderously. She was reaching for a lamp to brain him when Cohn became dimly aware of the mortal danger he was in. He stopped writhing and, pretending still to be talking in his sleep, called, "Cut! Now bring in the horses!" This story was certified as true by a writer who must have been hiding under their bed at the time.

Even Cohn wanted in on the fun, or at least his own version of fun. He installed a chair with a hidden buzzer and electric shock in the executive dining room, where writers and directors were sometimes allowed to eat, and nailed several. One hot day, Capra came in complaining of the heat, ordering an iced tea as he sat. *Zaaap!* Capra didn't react, didn't even get up. When the buzzer wore down, he stood. "Shit! That stupid son of a bitch Cohn and his goddam chair." Then he lifted the chair and smashed it into kindling. Undeterred, Cohn had the chair replaced and kept it in service until writer-director Victor Schertzinger (*One Night of Love, The Mikado*) was jolted strongly enough that he had heart spasms that put him in the hospital.

What was no joke was that Cohn had a secret passageway built from his studio office down to his lady star's dressing room so he could collect on the privileges he claimed under *droit du seigneur*. It was said he was often, but not always, successful. Later, when Cohn tried his through-the-passageway gambit with Bette Davis, he barely escaped with his life and all body parts attached, and Davis left the studio and the film in a fury. Jean Arthur said that Cohn's assaults were so upsetting she seriously considered buying a gun and shooting him when he came through the passageway. She didn't, but his behavior caused her, too, to leave the studio.

Cohn treated writers better than directors and actors, but even writers were often subjected to humiliation. Cohn often demanded to read scenes before a screenplay was finished and would shout invective. "What kind of *drek* is this?!" Writers who answered back, "You don't know what the hell you're talking about. This is dramatic, this is exciting, this is great!," kept their jobs. Anyone who kowtowed to Cohn risked firing. Ben Hecht called him White Fang.

Writers loved it when one occasionally got the best of Cohn. Cohn was berating one goddam idiot who didn't know the first goddam thing about the goddam time and place his goddam movie was set in, Merrie Olde England of two hundred years ago. "You make the same dumb goddam mistake twenty times. Nobody, but nobody, said 'Yes, siree!' back then."

"That's 'Yes, sire,'" the writer said, adding, "And I'm not the goddam idiot making the goddam mistake." He later admitted he hadn't actually spoken those last words out loud, only wished he had.

Spelling was never Cohn's strong suit. For years he misspelled the name of his own studio *Colombia,* like the country. One writer said, "Why shouldn't he spell it that way? He runs the studio like he's dictator of a Latin American country."

Jo Swerling was not a man to be intimidated. When Flo, who was never a good driver, banged into Cohn's prize Rolls-Royce on the lot, Cohn yelled at him, "What the hell is your wife doing smashing into my car?!"

"She probably thought you were in it," Swerling said.

Columbia writers delighted in plotting against Cohn. Dorothy Parker came back from one meeting especially aggravated. "For four cents, I would buy the bastard out and put Cap Duncan [the studio gate guard] in charge of the studio!"

Jo Swerling said to my father, "Hey Bob, we need four pennies."

"Can I give you a quarter?"

"Nope. Gotta be four pennies."

My father and Swerling collected four pennies from every writer, director, actor, crew member, and janitor on the Columbia lot, telling them of their plan to invest the money and use the proceeds to buy the studio, then put Cap Duncan in charge. Charles MacArthur and Ben Hecht offered a percentage of their next play to the cause. Swerling even got Cohn to contribute, interrupting a meeting with a European distributor. "Hey, boss, want to give to a good cause?" To get rid of Swerling, Cohn gave him the money.

When they had collected $350, Swerling and my father went to the Dunes Club in Palm Springs where they decided to go for broke, betting their entire roll on one spin of the roulette wheel. The owner of the club, hearing what they were up to, said he'd match the sum if they won. They put their enormous pile of pennies on black and black came up. Cohn eventually heard about the scheme and the campaign ended.

The longest-surviving story from those days stars Herman J. Mankiewicz, who was at a meeting when Cohn said, "I have a foolproof device for knowing if a picture is good or bad. If my fanny squirms, it's bad. If my fanny doesn't squirm, it's good. Simple as that."

Mankiewicz said, "Imagine—the whole world wired to Harry Cohn's ass." He was fired on the spot.

There is a less-known sequel, possibly made up at the Writers Table. An hour later, having cleared out his desk, Mankiewicz stopped by Cohn's office, took off his pants, and pitched them to Cohn. "Put cuffs on these," he called, harkening back to the fact that many studio heads had started in the tailoring business. "I'll pick 'em up tomorrow." He walked out of the studio in his Fruit of the Loom shorts.

In the year following *It Happened One Night,* my father wrote three films at Columbia. The first, *Carnival* (1935), directed by Walter Lang, had romantic charm and a full complement of offbeat characters. The story of a simple carnival worker fighting his late wife's wealthy family for custody of the child he adores was firmly, if sentimentally, in the Riskin canon, as was the theme that all the money in the world is less important than a father's love. Lang said the "script was bright and amusing . . . Riskin's presence was a sign of the project's quality." The picture was a popular success.

My father's next film, *Broadway Bill,* was adapted from a story by journalist Mark Hellinger, "On the Nose," and directed by Capra. The setting was a racetrack, a milieu my father knew well, where trainer Dan Brooks (Warner Baxter) is being pressured by his wife Edna to go into her father's successful business. Dan wants to make her happy, but his heart is with the horses, most of all Broadway Bill, a habitual loser he's sure can be a winner. Edna's younger sister, as played by Myrna Loy, is spirited, good-hearted, and supportive, and she urges him to follow his dream.

Riskin and Capra collaborated on *Broadway Bill,* starring Warner Baxter, Myrna Loy, and racehorse Broadway Bill in 1934. Before filming finished, Riskin left for Europe, and in his absence Capra had Sidney Buchman write a new, tragic ending, perhaps reflecting Capra's personal difficulties in dealing with the success of *It Happened One Night.*

He next collaborated with Jo Swerling on one of the rare comedies directed by John Ford. *The Whole Town's Talking* (1935) starred his friend from New York days, Edward G. Robinson, whose breakthrough role as a gangster in *Little Caesar* (1930) had made him a major star. Here Robinson would play a gangster named Killer Manion who, to avoid the police, assumes the identity of a meek accountant, a Manion look-alike, also played by Robinson. The accountant is in love with coworker Jean Arthur, and writes her mash notes, much as my father had written for Joe Golden to Trixie Friganza years earlier. Miss Arthur pays no attention to the humble accountant until the police, confusing Jones with Manion, arrest him. Now Jones is exciting to her and the romance can begin. *The New York Times* said, "Jo Swerling and Robert Riskin, two of Hollywood's most agile scenarists, have written a riotous script for *The Whole Town's Talking*... Pungently written, wittily produced and topped off with a splen-

John Ford directed the Riskin-Swerling script of *The Whole Town's Talking* (1935), starring Jean Arthur and Edward G. Robinson (left). The picture, a rare Ford comedy, received excellent reviews. Above, Swerling, Robinson, and Riskin confer on the Columbia lot.

did dual performance by Edward G. Robinson, it may be handsomely recommended as the best of the new year's screen comedies." Jean Arthur played what had become a familiar Riskin woman, spunky, independent, willing to be caught by a man and worth catching. "She's gone blonde and fresh," *Variety* said. "She's more individualistic, more typically the young American, self-reliant and sassy."

Capra directed only one of these three Riskin films. For a while he stopped directing altogether. Years later, Capra said it was the success of *It Happened One Night* that had led him to an emotional crisis.

The reaction to *It Happened One Night* had been intoxicating for Capra. He hired a publicist to promote him in the press. He became a pitchman for Philip Morris cigarettes. But underneath his great success lurked a darker feeling. He could not digest his good fortune. He became deeply depressed, he said, and was for a long time unable to function. His anxiety was so acute that he felt afraid to make another movie. He asked himself a question he could not answer: "How could I top *this!*," he said of *It Happened One Night*.

There was another problem. Capra aspired to the biggest leagues. He knew that to make films of great scope and thematic importance, to become a director like, for example, the great D. W. Griffith, he would have to leave the comfort of Harry Cohn's studio and its modest budgets. He tried, working on loan to M-G-M and Irving Thalberg on a major project called *Soviet*. His opportunity died when Thalberg fell ill and Louis B. Mayer, finding the film politically dangerous, canceled it.

Capra was shaken by the experience, and it contributed to his depression. "I got scared," he said. "I got kicked out before I got started." Of the top brass at M-G-M he said, "They didn't know a goddamned thing . . . they were so stupid and so dumb. It was run by Jewish people at the top. It was right because *they said* it was right."

He returned to Columbia and was given my father's new script, *Broadway Bill*, and agreed to direct it. Once filming was under way, my father embarked on his first European vacation. In his absence, Capra became uncertain about the ending of the film and decided he wanted a conclusion that was darker and more dramatic. He called in Sidney Buchman, who devised and wrote a final scene in which Broadway Bill, rather than winning the big race, dies and is buried at the racetrack.

Capra got no better. His anxiety, or illness, turned into a pulmonary condition, possibly tuberculosis or pneumonia. The doctors found no specific cause, but Capra was sure he would die. His depression was unrelieved. He could barely drag himself out of bed to receive his Academy Award for *It Happened One Night*.

When *Broadway Bill* was released, the reviews, while respectful, and which a year earlier would have pleased him, hit him hard. "A sly and impertinent screen comedy, painlessly whimsical and completely engaging, *Broadway Bill* unfolds the fresh and inventive talent of Frank Capra in a mood of high good humor." This was scarcely a pan, but the popular response didn't rise to the level of *It Happened One Night* and Capra's mood did not improve.

Years later, he said he hadn't really been sick, but was frightened into what he identified as a psychosomatic illness.

But he was in fact sick, with his depression compounded by serious and unrelenting stomach pains. He had surgery to discover the cause and doctors traced the problem back to an old burst appendix, when an attempt to remove a ball of fat had left him vulnerable to infection or peritonitis. Lu, exhausted and despairing about her husband's ongoing illness and depression, suffered a fall; she was pregnant at the time with their second child, and her fall left them to wonder later if the fall had caused their child's developmental problems.

My father reached out to Capra and Lu often during this extended dark period. He sent a seven-page letter, hoping to lift their spirits. "Listen youse guys. I gave you permission to go down to Palm Springs for what is laughingly known as 'convalescing,' but nothing was said about you remaining there until the next Presidential election." He joked with Lu about her indecipherable handwriting in a note she sent accompanying a gift of champagne. He had to seek the help of a world-famous handwriting expert, he said. "I just discovered that it was *you* who sent me that tower of champagne. It might amuse you to know that I thanked Frank Joyce profusely for it. I made pretty speeches and sent gushing notes. Poor Joyce accepted thanks humblingly and bewildered. It's all most embarrassing." He signed the letter, "We miss you. Bob."

It's not clear how Capra finally escaped the darkness that enveloped him. Capra's story was that an unnamed friend had brought an unnamed "little man" to visit him in the hospital and this little man told him he was a coward to withdraw from the world because the world was in turmoil and needed him and his message of hope; this little man had given him the courage to go on. The story evolved dramatically over the years, becoming more detailed and more important to Capra, although there were those who felt the little man existed only in his imagination.

When Capra returned to work, for a time he foundered. Still wanting to make a major picture, he announced *Valley Forge,* based on Maxwell Anderson's play, and also considered *Anna Karenina* and *Crime and Punishment* and even a film version of *I Pagliacci*. None went ahead, but it was apparent he was hoping to begin working again.

My father returned from Europe in late 1934. He told Capra about *Lost Horizon,* a popular utopian novel he had read in London. He knew every studio had turned it down, but "I talked it over with Frank on getting back here. He read it and liked it. We mentioned it to Cohn, sure that after reading he would say we were crazy. But he surprised us by agreeing."

All three were eager to move ahead quickly and my father went right to work on the script. Capra wanted Ronald Colman for the lead, but when it turned out he wouldn't be available until 1936, a year away, they looked for another picture they could do in the meantime.

• • •

Of all his films, *Mr. Deeds Goes to Town* was my father's favorite. It's my favorite, too, blending romance, humanity, and decency into the distinctive Riskin view of the world. Film historians call it the quintessentially American movie of the Golden Age of Hollywood.

Longfellow Deeds (Gary Cooper) is a guileless fellow living in the Vermont hamlet of Mandrake Falls. He plays the tuba, writes greeting card limericks, and has few thoughts of the world beyond. Everything changes when he inherits $20 million from a distant uncle. In the depths of the Depression, $20 million was an attention-getting sum.

Deeds' uncle's lawyers arrive in town to tell him of his new fortune, and sweep him off to New York City, where they plan to take full control of the money—a perfect springboard for a Riskin film contrasting the basic goodness of the ordinary man with the rich and powerful who see him as just another sheep to be shorn.

In New York, Deeds finds the life of butlers and opera matrons his advisors press upon him unappealing and oppressive. He's happier alone, playing his tuba.

But the whole city is eager to learn about the mysterious new millionaire among them. Enter ambitious newspaperwoman Babe Bennett (Jean Arthur), who manages "a cute meet," fainting in front of his house just as Deeds flees from the bodyguards he has locked inside. Chivalrous Deeds rescues this lady in distress and, as they walk, he talks about his unhappiness with his new life and what he has seen in the big city. They make a date to talk again. And again.

Babe has the scoop of her career. The headlines of her daily stories tell about "Cinderella Man," but in mocking, not at all flattering, terms. Deeds, falling in love, doesn't see the connection between his revelations and the continuing uncomplimentary stories. Babe tells her roommate, "That guy's either the dumbest, the stupidest, the most imbecilic idiot in the world or he's the grandest thing alive." We now understand that, despite herself, she too is falling in love.

Deeds learns Babe has duped him and falls into a depression. He determines to get back to his roots by giving every nickel of his inheritance to people who need it; all it has done for him is cause him misery.

The lawyers, seeing their gravy train leaving the station, plot to have Deeds declared insane in court so they can take charge of the money. Will Deeds be sentenced to a mental institution? Will greed triumph over decency?

In my father's hands, the story departed in every significant respect from the *Saturday Evening Post* story, "Opera Hat," by Clarence Budington Kelland, he was adapting. He came up with new characters and plotlines, eliminated a murder, and added Depression-era themes and a modern newspaperwoman as the love interest. He gave an innate goodness to Deeds, and a help-thy-neighbor philosophy that persuades even the most cynical that community and integrity matter. In court he tells the judge:

> Every day I watch the cars climbing up. Some go lickety-split up that
> hill on high, some have to shift into second, and some sputter and
> shake and slip back to the bottom again. Same cars, same gasoline,
> yet some make it and some don't. And I say the fellas who can make
> the hill on high should stop once in a while and help those who can't.
> That's all I'm trying to do with this money. Help the fellas who can't
> make the hill on high.

Almost half a century later, Ronald Reagan incorporated Deeds' final speech into his 1980 presidential campaign to advance the cause of volunteerism.

With the support of Harry Cohn, my father had put aside *Lost Horizon*. Once again, as soon as Cohn read the screenplay for *Deeds,* he ordered production.

Gary Cooper could not have been better as Longfellow Deeds and Jean Arthur blossomed under Capra's direction. Taking time for some relaxed rehearsal before the cameras turned, Capra allowed the scenes to come to life unforced. Arthur said of Capra, "You never know he's on the set . . . He never raises his voice . . . He's a great director, and he does it seemingly without any effort. He's a very pleasant, good-looking, agreeable man."

He followed the screenplay to the letter. Only once did he consider cutting a scene, where Jean Arthur reads aloud some doggerel verse the love-smitten Deeds has sent her. Capra thought it might be corny, but Arthur protested she had worked hard on the scene and when she filmed it, she did it perfectly. My father said, "No one but [Capra] would have had the nerve to shoot that scene! Reading poetry on the screen is dangerous business. Unless it's perfectly done, your audience is likely to laugh. They didn't laugh at this scene, though."

Mr. Deeds opened in New York to enormous critical and popular approval. The New York Film Critics Circle selected it as the Best Film of the Year. Frank S. Nugent wrote in *The New York Times*:

Riskin wrote and Capra directed
Mr. Deeds Goes to Town (1936), the
quintessential populist film of the
Golden Age of Hollywood. Longfellow
Deeds (Gary Cooper), a guileless
fellow from Mandrake Falls, inherits
$20 million, complicating his life and
eventually making him miserable.
Newswoman Jean Arthur hinders him,
helps him, and then of course falls in
love with him. Riskin's frequent themes
of the basic goodness of ordinary people
and "We're all in this together" drive
the story.

Frank Capra and Robert Riskin, who are a complete production staff
in themselves, have turned out another shrewd and lively comedy
for Columbia Pictures in *Mr. Deeds Goes to Town,* which opened
yesterday at the Radio City Music Hall. The directing-writing
combination which functioned so successfully in *It Happened One
Night* and *Broadway Bill* have spiced Clarence Budington Kelland's
story with wit, novelty, and ingenuity. And, spurred along by the
capital performances of Gary Cooper, Jean Arthur, Lionel Stander,
Douglass Dumbrille, and the rest, the picture moves easily into the
pleasant realm reserved for the season's most entertaining films.

In the 1930s, with politics everywhere in the air and inescapable, left-leaning publications like *New Theatre* said the film reflected a significant advance in the social consciousness of Hollywood. The *Daily Express* in London wrote, "Frank Capra of Hollywood is as big potentially a political force in the States as Father Coughlin and Franklin Delano Roosevelt." The accolades may have been surprising to Capra, who continued to oppose FDR and his economic policies, but my father, a steadfast New Deal man whose belief was that we're all in this together, was able to accept the comments comfortably.

The Motion Picture Academy honored *Mr. Deeds* with nominations for Best Picture, Best Screenplay, Best Actor, and Best Sound. Capra won for Best Director.

Now they could get back to *Lost Horizon*.

And in my father's case, a few other things, too. Between 1935 and 1936 he wrote the screenplays not just for *Lost Horizon* and *Mr. Deeds Goes to Town;* he also wrote and directed a movie for Columbia, *When You're in Love* (1937), starring Grace Moore and Cary Grant. His little black notebook shows that he contributed to or conferred on dozens of outlines, stories, and screenplays in the Columbia pipeline, including *If You Could Only Cook* (1935) with Jean Arthur, *Love Me Forever* (1935) with Grace Moore, *The Lone Wolf Returns* with Melvyn Douglas, *I Promise to Pay* (1937) with Leo Carrillo, *Women of Glamour* (1937) with Virginia Bruce and Melvyn Douglas, and *Wedding Present* (1936) with Joan Bennett and Cary Grant. He read and gave his opinion on almost every novel and story Harry Cohn was thinking of buying, including *Fer de Lance, Marseillaise, Kingdom Come, Four Days of Wonder, Safari of Manhattan,* and *Purple and Fine Linen.* He proposed a film for Bing Crosby and suggested adapting a German film about Chopin, *Farewell Waltz,* an idea Capra loved but Cohn found too expensive. He writes in his notebook that "I pleaded with Harry Cohn for two hours to arrange a musical comedy with Frank Capra and Irving Berlin, and self." He helped produce the film and wrote Harry Cohn's speech for the company's annual sales convention and he also took off two whole days in the hospital for a tonsillectomy. When Cohn talked in *Screen and Radio Weekly* about elevating writers to stars, he singled out Robert Riskin as a "modest, unassuming chap" who was putting stories on screen the public wanted to see.

When Cohn announced to the press that Robert Riskin was "being made a producer because of his exceptional work," perhaps he thought my father would benefit from a few added assignments to keep busy.

9

Her youth and popularity, her marriage and beautiful home, were what the fans saw in the early 1930s. My mother was twenty-six years old when *King Kong* premiered in New York and she had become virtually overnight a focus of the nation's attention. The opening weekend's box office was the highest in film history, and it was the event of the year in Hollywood, too, opening at Grauman's Chinese Theater with sleek limousines, sparkling evening gowns, Klieg lights sweeping the sky, and adoring crowds. The next day's trade papers said, "Fay Wray is brilliant in *King Kong*."

What the world did not see was that John's drinking and infidelities continued unabated and made her life into something else entirely.

She hoped John would become the caring, brilliant, and productive man she knew he could be, but nothing worked for very long. Sixty years later, she wrote in her private musings how she wished she could have made John whole. He was her first love and she was fiercely loyal. Divorce, common in Hollywood even then, was unthinkable to her. Chances for romance, casual or more serious, were present, but she never pursued them.

John was now writing sporadically, in short bursts, mostly films about flying and war. He tried to manage his addiction to alcohol and, at low ebb, consulted with a Dr. Fishbaugh, a famous society doctor who recommended chloral hydrate to steady his nerves. Ultimately the chloral hydrate caused a new addiction, worsening his condition and making him increasingly erratic.

In 1935, he wrote *West Point of the Air* for M-G-M and went to San Antonio for the filming, but soon called my mother, desperate for her to bring him chloral hydrate from Dr. Fishbaugh. "I knew that meant he'd been drinking a lot," she wrote, but she did as he asked. She was never certain whether she would be met by John drunk or John sober. As her plane approached Randolph Field, she saw two small planes with open cockpits fly up and then alongside. In one was John, wearing a white scarf

Fay (left) with close friend
and trusted confidante, actress
Dolores Del Rio

and waving to her exuberantly. Her stay in San Antonio was a happy time,
rare and brief.

Alone, my mother found comfort in the Selma Avenue home. Weekends she visited actress Dolores Del Rio and her husband, set designer
Cedric Gibbons (*The Bridges of San Luis Rey, An American in Paris*) in
their beautiful art deco Santa Monica home. A dark-eyed Mexican beauty,
Dolores reminded my mother of her older sister, Vaida, whom she still
mourned. She admired Dolores' strength, her business acumen, and the
meticulous way she attended to her beauty, never drinking, smiling spar-
ingly to avoid wrinkles. While my mother and Dolores talked about their
lives, Greta Garbo slipped in for games of tennis with Cedric.

Some nights when John was otherwise occupied my mother went alone
to parties. Richard Barthelmess, virtually unknown today, was one of Hollywood's highest-paid actors in the silent era, and he and his wife were
famous party givers. One night he hired Paul Whiteman's entire orchestra
to play *Rhapsody in Blue* at their home. The musicians filled one side of
the tennis court; the rest of the court became a ballroom. Jascha Heifetz
and my mother played ping pong, and when Heifetz finally beat her for

LEFT: Fay with aviatrix Amelia Earhart at the 1932 Olympics in Los Angeles. Both are guests of Douglas Fairbanks (right).
BELOW: Fay was a frequent guest at the parties given by Mary Pickford and Fairbanks at their home, Pickfair.

the first time, he threw down his paddle in victory saying, "Now I will ask you to dance." He whirled her around the floor to Gershwin's music with a kind of "Slavic supremacy," she remembered, laughing. No matter what, she was always open to laughter.

Douglas Fairbanks and Mary Pickford, "America's Sweetheart," were Hollywood's most illustrious couple. My mother had been their guest at the 1932 Olympics in Los Angeles, riding with them onto the stadium field in their limo before the adoring crowd. They entertained lavishly at Pickfair, their 56-acre estate in Beverly Hills, and also at their beach house. When John was not available, Fairbanks and Pickford sent their limousine for my mother. Dinners at Pickfair rivaled those at Buckingham Palace, with European royalty in attendance and liveried footmen attending each guest, and the finest china, silver, crystal, and candelabras on view. Luncheons at their beach house had simple elegance, with handwritten menus at each guest's place and everything perfectly appointed.

Fairbanks liked to mock his own and Mary's formality. One night, when the guests were lost in conversation, he slid under the table, stealing everyone's napkin. "For some reason everyone, including me, thought this was hilarious," my mother wrote. From her I learned the source of the napkin-stealing antic my mother taught Bobby and me, at our much smaller dinner table.

One day Fairbanks seemed to make a pass at my mother. It was probably his playfulness that made her take in stride his unexpected visit to the Selma Avenue house at a time when he was supposed to be meeting John for golf. His chauffeur carried in a case of wine along with a great bottle of Chateau d'Yquem and left the house while Fairbanks stood in the hallway shifting uneasily, trying to make small talk before finally leaving. She wasn't sure what was happening until a few days later when she was following John, Fairbanks, and composer David Rose around a golf course. Rose took her aside. "You could have anything you want—ruby necklaces, anything—Douglas is crazy about you." She was startled and told John when they got home. John said, "It might be interesting for you. Although Bessie tells me he's not very good in bed. Always in so much of a hurry."

Fairbanks asked my mother and John to join him on a round-the-world yacht trip. When John suggested Fairbanks pay him $20,000 in advance in case he came up with "movie ideas" on the voyage, my mother was stunned and, of course, the trip never happened.

John's drunken binges were more frequent, as were his calls, his cold compresses, prairie oysters, and Dr. Fishbaugh's doses of chloral hydrate. When he was plagued by insomnia, my mother took him on long midnight walks across the Riviera Country Club golf course. When he "went under," as she called it, he was completely unresponsive and she was unable to address simple questions with him, such as fixing a leaky roof or planning an evening. On one occasion, he went to a health farm in upstate New York and came back strong and able to work again—for a while. In her mid-twenties, she took charge of their lives as best she could, soldiering on.

Offers for movies came often and easily to her, although sometimes she longed for more challenging roles—something real, intelligent, complex. She knew good writing. She went after a Jo Swerling script called *Man's Castle*, to star Spencer Tracy. Alas, *Man's Castle* went to Loretta Young,

Mystery of the Wax Museum (1933), directed by Michael Curtiz, costarred Lionel Atwill (left) and Glenda Farrell (right), who was dating Riskin at the time. Farrell and Fay played best friends and roommates.

who was romantically involved with Tracy at the time. Seeing the movie today, their chemistry is evident.

My mother also went after the lead in *Lost Horizon*. At the Beverly Hills Tennis Club, she approached a man she had never met, the film's screenwriter, Robert Riskin. She introduced herself, telling him how much she wanted to be in his new film. "His mind was on his tennis game . . . He stood, patient and kindly, holding the gate open with one hand . . . just as pleasant as he could be." He said he would talk to Capra. "He went through the gate and I went back to the chair under an umbrella and thought about his qualities: charmingly objective, a lighthearted dignity, and intelligent easiness."

It would be three years before they saw each other again. She never asked and never knew if he had talked to Capra on her behalf.

After her Paramount contract ended, she worked freelance, shuttling among RKO, Columbia, Twentieth Century-Fox, M-G-M, Universal, Warner Bros., and Paramount, costarring with Ralph Bellamy, Joel McCrea, Wallace Beery, Gene Raymond, Cesar Romero, Victor Jory, Jack Holt, and Edward Arnold. To avoid being repeatedly cast in horror movies like *Mystery of the Wax Museum*, *Doctor X*, and *The Vampire Bat*—which at least became horror film classics—she sought out character dramas and light comedies. She played damsels in distress, adoring girlfriends, spoiled heiresses, newspaperwomen, movie stars, and international spies. She was in demand and was almost never unemployed.

Fay was cast in two more horror films, *Doctor X* (1932) and *The Vampire Bat* (1933), causing her concern that after *King Kong* she was in danger of being typecast as a lady in distress in the horror genre.

In 1934, she made the farcical *The Affairs of Cellini* with Fredric March, Constance Bennett, and Frank Morgan. Directed by Gregory La Cava with pacing and style, the cast never slowed down. Morgan, who would later achieve film glory in *The Wizard of Oz,* was nominated for an Academy Award as the Duke of Florence, a bumbling stuttering buffoon, forerunner of the Wizard. The same year she starred with Miriam Hopkins and Joel McCrea in a charming comedy, *The Richest Girl in the World,* a classic role-swapping story about an heiress (Hopkins) who, believing no one will love her for herself, swaps roles with her secretary (Fay Wray). The screenplay, full of wit and punch, was written by talented newcomer Norman Krasna, on his way to becoming a master of screwball comedy, winning an Oscar in 1943 for *Princess O'Rourke.*

Her successful forays into comic roles and character dramas did not go unnoticed in Hollywood. *Motion Picture* magazine said, "We pay homage to the only actress besides Myrna Loy who changed her type midway in her career . . . She was the unanimous choice of producers for terror-and-torture . . . But now [Fay Wray is] a subtle comedienne (*The Affairs of Cellini*) and a forceful actress (*Mills of the Gods*)."

After fifteen years, my mother was not only in the motion picture business, she was very much *of* the business.

She was not radical nor an activist by nature. Like my father, her sympathies were with the working class. She remembered the wretched condi-

Fay played a mindless and self-centered peasant girl in *The Affairs of Cellini*, a 1934 farce directed by Gregory La Cava. Fay costarred with Frank Morgan, Constance Bennett, and Fredric March (left).

tions of the miners in Lark and knew firsthand how the studios were run. Casts and crews were forced to work as much as eighty-five-hour weeks without overtime pay. Actors, including stars, were coerced into signing multiyear contracts with continuing, never-ending studio options. They had no way to protest when ordered to play parts they didn't want to play, were loaned out to other studios against their wishes, or put in movies they knew might hurt their careers.

In 1933, my mother became Founding Member #1475 of the Screen Actors Guild. It was critical to the union that stars sign up early, as a letter from the Guild's secretary to the head of its membership department makes clear: "Dear Arthur, I have just been informed that Fay Wray is on Stage 12 at Universal, and that she wants to join the Guild. So do your stuff!" She was in the good company of Fredric March, Mae West, Ginger Rogers, Lew Ayres, Boris Karloff, Gloria Stuart, and Douglas Fairbanks Jr.

Studios could be hard for actors, including stars, to deal with. So was the press.

In the 1920s, stories coming out of Hollywood had been largely innocent, newsy pieces planted by the studios. No more. By the 1930s, the Hollywood press had become an industry within an industry, with enormous outreach and the ability to make careers and often destroy them. The press—radio, newspapers, fan magazines—was not shy about using its newfound power.

Every celebrity came to understand that power, and the need to advance positive stories while guarding against cheap or inaccurate news and gossip. All-powerful columnists like Walter Winchell, Louella O. Parsons, and Hedda Hopper competed for scoops and stories. Their red meat was scandal, especially involving romances and infidelities. They were not above trading positive mentions for inside secrets or using their columns to spread rumors or attack political enemies. They demanded obeisance and almost always got it.

Some talent went out of their way to feed the beast. Hollywood whooped in delight but at the same time had to feel sympathy for the young actor who, seeking to ingratiate himself with the no-longer-youthful Hedda Hopper, whispered to her at a party, "Miss Hopper, your stockings are wrinkled."

"I'm not wearing stockings," she said and turned her back on him, doubtless forever.

Fay, after a tennis game, and (below) at a costume party that was all the rage. Fay is seated in the second row at right, behind Mary Pickford, her arm around her nephew. Next to Fay is Joel McCrea and Mrs. Johnny Mack Brown, behind them Douglas Fairbanks Jr. in a top hat. In the background, John Monk Saunders is kissing Dorothy di Frasso. Below right, at the polo matches with gossip columnist Hedda Hopper

Dodging the columnists or paying proper homage to them was an artful game. In my mother's case, John's excesses, unknown to the wider world, were no secret to the columnists, and it was a sharp sword hanging over their heads. Helen Ferguson, once a silent-screen star herself, became a skilled and dogged publicist for actors. My mother was her first client and soon was joined by Loretta Young, Barbara Stanwyck, and Henry Fonda. Helen was a master at getting things in the columns and, more important, keeping them out. "Helen was in no way flamboyant or contriving in her concept of what public relations meant," my mother said, "and I trusted her. She was like a warmhearted nanny, calling at the end of the evening to 'tuck each client into bed.'"

With fame came other challenges. My mother was sent an extortion letter, threatening to kill Vina unless a large sum of money was left near the Selma Avenue house. Plainclothesmen from the Los Angeles Police Department watched from concealed positions while my mother drove to a nearby lot, flung a packet from the car and drove off. When a young man came to retrieve it, the police seized him, and the gun on the seat of his car. He turned out to be from a well-known Salt Lake City family and had been in love with Vaida, my mother's older sister, which made the incident especially painful for her. The Salt Lake City mayor intervened and the young man was sent back to his family, not to jail.

In New York while filming *Woman in the Dark* (1934) with Ralph Bellamy, she received another extortion note, this one demanding that money be placed in a room at the Waldorf. She called the head of Twentieth Century Pictures, who was in New York, Joseph Schenck, who came to her hotel with Howard Hughes and a bodyguard assigned to her by the New York Police Department. "Howard, all in summer white, altered his stance a lot, as if trying to secure a base that would accommodate his height," my mother remembered. No extortionist appeared and Schenck took her to the theater that night to cheer her up. Before the curtain went up, he whispered, "Do you love John . . . or are you in love with him?" What the difference might be was unclear to her, as was his reason for asking— curiosity, concern, interest on his own behalf, or for Howard Hughes? "Both," she told Schenck, and that was the end of it.

Powerhouse producers like Darryl Zanuck made propositions, sometimes not so subtly. He offered her a three-picture commitment, and she was thrilled at the prospect of a secure studio contract at the height of the Depression, but when Zanuck tried to impose a not-so-innocent kiss to seal the deal, she left his office in tears and the offer was withdrawn. While she wondered if the parts went to actresses who were more compliant, Zanuck did not allow her rejection to cause permanent damage between them and the next year cast her in *The Affairs of Cellini*. Had Zanuck felt that John's well-known infidelities might open her to his advances? Or perhaps like other executives, he simply had the power and felt it was his right to assert it? My mother learned, in this and similar instances, to deflect the advances, even to pretend they never happened.

She still felt confused about what was expected, or the norm, in a Hollywood marriage. John maintained a beach house where he could work and swim, tan, drink, and entertain his aviator friends and . . . others. One day my mother found the house littered with butts of French cigarettes and knew Nikki was visiting from Paris. She had come to town to be married to another man, and evidently have a last fling with John.

My mother said she never denied John his freedom, but wondered if she should be more assertive, or take charge. John's secretary was working late at the Selma Avenue house one night and John was coaxing her to sleep on the couch until my mother worked up her courage and firmly told the young lady it was late and she would follow her home to make sure she arrived safely.

> When I got back to the house, I had the sense that John admired what I did . . . But we didn't talk. We never did have reflective time for talking together. Life, when good, was mostly action. He bought me a shotgun and one for himself and we did a lot of skeet shooting. He chartered a boat and we went deep-sea fishing . . . I began to feel that even if we had had quiet times together and I had talked out my feelings and tried to make him see what I saw, his talents and great good fortunes to be, he wouldn't have heard.

Would anything have helped? It seems unlikely. One evening she stopped by the Selma Avenue house after work to pick up something on the way to the beach, where John was to meet her. A limousine was parked in the driveway. The driver said, "Don't go in there, Madam," but she did and saw John at the top of the stairs, naked but for a towel around his waist. "Don't come upstairs!" he ordered her. A disheveled and underdressed young woman raced down from upstairs, past her and out of the house. My mother retreated to the dining room and cried overdue tears. She slept on the floor until morning when John came in and covered her with contrite kisses. She struggled through filming that day, maintaining her professionalism, but her resolve was diminishing.

· · ·

John's behavior finally made the papers.

DATELINE HOLLYWOOD: ASSOCIATED PRESS, SEPTEMBER 25, 1934

HERBERT MARSHALL VICTIM IN FILMLAND ONE-ROUND BOUT: ENGLISH ACTOR "DIDN'T SMILE WHEN HE SAID IT" SO JOHN MONK SAUNDERS, GREAT WAR ACE AND FILM WRITER, FELT OBLIGATED TO LET HIM HAVE IT ON THE CHIN

Herbert Marshall was a British hero—he had lost a leg in the war—and, despite that limitation, a great film star. One night Ernst Lubitsch (*Ninotchka, The Shop Around the Corner*) was hosting a party where Gloria Swanson, Marshall's lady friend at the time, was being friendly with Saunders. John was "lit" and began an inspection of her décolletage. My mother, not wanting to witness it, drifted into a different room, but Marshall felt called on to defend Gloria's honor and said something insulting to John, who knocked him to the floor with one punch. The next day Winchell's column reported it in detail, emphasizing Marshall's war heroism that had cost him a leg. Other columnists picked up the story and ran with it.

December 1934, Fay leaving for England to make *Bulldog Jack* (1935), *The Clairvoyant* (1935), *Come Out of the Pantry* (1935), and *When Knights Were Bold* (1936) and grant herself a needed respite from Saunders

Incidents like these were painful and debilitating for John, John's friends, and especially for my mother, who may finally have seen she could benefit from some time away. When an offer came providentially to make two films in England, it was attractive on every level. London felt like a perfect place to go, and the films were with leading men she had long admired from a distance, Ralph Richardson in *Bulldog Jack* and Claude Rains in *The Clairvoyant*.

John encouraged her to go and Cary Grant sent a corsage for her voyage, allowing her to imagine distant possibilities.

Claude Rains and Fay in *The Clairvoyant*. She played a loyal wife whose husband betrays her.

Compared to Hollywood, production in England was leisurely. My mother had time to explore Buckingham Palace, the Houses of Parliament, and Westminster Abbey. She took French lessons, had quiet dinners alone or with friends, and set aside moments for solitary reflection. London was warm and comforting for her.

But her quiet time away from John was short-lived. He got an assignment from Howard Hughes to write a film about dirigibles and sent word that he was on his way to Europe to join her and do research.

My mother met his ship at Southampton. John was in terrible shape, drunk and as unsteady as the woman she found sharing his stateroom. She rushed him off to the Dorchester Hotel and arranged a nurse to look after him while she was filming. Soon after arriving, he cut his wrists in a way that seemed less like a suicide attempt than a cry for attention, or help; someone at the hotel leaked the story to a reporter.

Frequently in the past, John's unraveling had been followed by a burst of energy and exuberance, and it happened again. His mood shifted. He wanted to show her Oxford and his old haunts. He took her on a lovely picnic float down the Thames. They visited Knole Castle in Kent with its 365 rooms and joined a houseful of Lord and Lady Sackville's weekend guests at a dance.

A break in her film schedule allowed them to travel to Germany, where John planned to do his research. On the way they spent a few days in Paris at Le Claridge Hotel on the Champs-Élysée, ate at Maxim's and La Tour d'Argent, went to the Folies Bergère and visited Père Lachaise Cemetery where Oscar Wilde and Héloïse and Abélard were buried. John told her of the two ill-fated lovers buried side by side and the legend that if you find two heart-shaped stones near their tombs, your own love will endure. He found two heart-shaped stones and gave one to her; then he exchanged them, saying, as was the tradition, "No harm shall come to our true love." Times like these gave her renewed hope.

But in Munich, where John interviewed dirigible experts for his movie, my mother felt the deepest unease at the growing euphoria over Hitler. Their guide, whom they were sure was Jewish, went out of his way repeatedly to insist he was not. John's technical advisor said, "You must see the beer hall where the putsch took place . . . It's too bad you weren't here in this hotel yesterday. Hitler was here. You just missed him!" Would Hitler have wanted to meet my mother had he known she was in Munich? He was a movie buff and *King Kong* was one of his favorite films.

Hollywood. Nazi Germany. The studios. Jews. That they might somehow have escaped the furies of the 1930s was of course impossible, but the myriad ways in which they collided and affected each other have ever since fascinated, and often deeply troubled, historians and other observers.

During the years leading up to World War II, as the Nazis enacted increasingly harsh measures against Jews, the American movie industry faced pressure from the German government not to make films that would offend the pride and sensibilities of German audiences. With as many as sixty American films being distributed in Germany each year, the studio chiefs were fearful of losing the lucrative German marketplace and gave in to Nazi demands. A system of censorship was established under Josef Goebbels' Ministry of Propaganda whereby the studios allowed the German Consul General in Los Angeles to read, and comment on before production, every Hollywood script. Joseph Breen of the Hays Office, whose job it was to avoid offending any country that purchased American films, also had scripts reviewed and edited to German satisfaction. Some scripts were deemed problematic and never put into production.

Starting in 1933, it was common knowledge that the Nazis were adopting stringent laws and other extreme, extra-legal measures, including violence, against Jews. In Hollywood, where almost every studio head was Jewish, that made no difference. Only Harry Warner, and then his brother Jack, resisted and over time fought back and tried to rally the industry, and the public, against Hitler.

It was not the studios' feature films alone that were affected by the censorship. In their newsreels, studios omitted demonstrations of anti-Semitism in Germany and, later, disturbing images of war. Offering an explanation, one executive said of the moguls, "They were immigrants in a new business, repeating the pattern of capitalism in microcosm. They were religious men, many of them, but they were willing to violate nine out of the Ten Commandments to keep their studios running." It is also true that there is more to the story, and that away from their studios and out of the spotlight, some secretly funded both pro-Jewish and anti-Nazi activities.

Even *King Kong* came under the microscope, not in Hollywood but in Germany. A transcript survives in which the censors debated whether the movie about a gorilla who falls in love with a woman and then falls to his death from the Empire State Building could damage the health and well-being of German audiences. Some of the censors argued the film could agitate nerves and stir up the low, base instincts of the German people. Others said it would do no harm because it was too unreal to be believed.

The debate rose to the highest levels of the Nazi Party. In the end Goebbels, who loved the film, put his stamp of approval on it. "It was a terrific struggle between Kong and the dinosaurs and the highly developed white race," he said. Hitler saw the film, retitled for Germany *The Fable of King Kong: An American Trick and Sensation Film,* several times.

The German censors did not go down without a fight. They cut out the potentially upsetting close-ups of my mother screaming in Kong's hand and the derailing of the commuter train in New York City, lest the German people lose faith in this important mode of transportation.

The studios' appeasement of Germany lasted well into the late 1930s, until the Nazis demanded their distribution offices fire all Jews, including American Jews. Then they balked. No longer was Germany given a role in Hollywood moviemaking. Other studio heads started to follow Warner Bros.' earlier example, although Warners continued to lead the way. In 1939 they made the first overtly anti-Nazi film, *Confessions of a Nazi Spy,* with Edward G. Robinson. The picture was not successful, but after the Nazis invaded Norway and the Netherlands in 1940, Warners reedited the film to include scenes of the invasions and released it again.

John and Fay returned to London for her to begin *The Clairvoyant* with Claude Rains. Rains plays The Great Maximus, whose fake mind-reading act in vaudeville is transformed when he is suddenly endowed with real power to foresee the future. My mother is his loyal wife/assistant whose heart breaks when, because of his new fame, Maximus is lured away by another woman. "Fay Wray gives a fine performance of a sensitive, affectionate wife, disturbed by well-founded jealousy," said one reviewer, who was no doubt unaware of details of her life with John.

In May 1935, Fay returned briefly from London to Los Angeles between films to be sworn in as an American citizen. Here with Cary Grant

She made plans to return briefly to California as soon as *The Clair-voyant* was finished. She intended on her arrival to surrender her Canadian citizenship, which she had kept all her life, and become a naturalized American citizen. She was having tea with John at Simpsons in the Strand the evening before her departure when he said, "Why don't you go back to California and divorce me?"

My mother later wrote, "The words had all the weight of 'Why don't you pick up a *Times*?' I was sure he didn't mean it."

But his suggestion of divorce cut deep and turned her mind to thoughts of life without him. Blue and lonely on the transatlantic crossing, she danced, and spent the night, with a charming traveler from Italy. The experience, her first with someone other than John, only made her feel guilty.

She had lunch with Cary Grant as soon as she returned, her heart as always open to him, but they chatted only about their careers, avoiding anything personal. She felt the awkwardness of a schoolgirl.

Her shipboard encounter and lunch with Cary Grant brought something about her life into sharp focus for her: she wanted and needed someone to love. John couldn't accept her love. She would have a child. With John, of course, but if he didn't know her plan he couldn't derail it.

Her work in England led to more film offers and she returned to London, where John had taken a flat in Grosvenor Square. She filmed *Come Out of the Pantry* and began preparing *When Knights Were Bold*, both opposite British matinee idol Jack Buchanan. When she and John were invited to spend the Christmas holidays with Merian Cooper and his wife, Dorothy, in St. Moritz, John said she should go alone and he would join her later. Neither John nor my mother knew she was already pregnant.

Being with Dorothy and Coop made my mother feel happy and somehow free. Skiing all day, sitting in front of the fireplace at night, embraced by their abiding warmth and affection and Coop's ebullience were wonderfully restorative for her. The moon was bright enough one night that they all skied through the trees, exhilarated and carefree.

John came for Christmas but was agitated and irritable and quickly returned to London. My mother stayed on through New Year's Day when she experienced the nausea of morning sickness. She phoned John to tell him she was pregnant. He raged, "What the hell is that to me?"

"I went out onto the balcony," she later wrote, "and looked down into the valley and asked whatever forces might be there or in the sky above to give me the power to hate him."

Then she returned to London to finish the film.

She had never met John's Harley Street doctor when he called and asked her to come to his office. He told her he was considering reporting John's former physician to the authorities for the amount of medication he was

Fay on the set of *They Met in a Taxi* (1936) with costar Chester Morris. On the first day of shooting, the entire crew greeted her with newspaper clippings of her pregnancy pinned to their chests and gave her a welcoming round of applause.

Fay with baby Susan Cary Saunders,
born September 24, 1936

giving John. My mother was startled; she had never heard one doctor criticize another. When she told the doctor she was pregnant, he asked, "Why do you want to have a child with this man?" She told him, "I am having a child for myself."

She returned to California where Dolores Del Rio echoed the doctor's concerns. They talked about John's extreme mood swings and wildly erratic behavior, but could not identify a cause; this was before people understood the ravages of bipolar disorder. There was also the question of his addiction to drugs and alcohol. My mother told Dolores, "I have no idea of leaving John for another man, but I do need someone to love." She still cared for John, she told Dolores, although her love was now increasingly rooted in compassion and sadness.

News of her pregnancy hit the Hollywood press. When she arrived on the set at Columbia to film a lighthearted comedy, *They Met in a Taxi* (1936), the entire crew had the news clipping of her pregnancy pinned to their chests and gave her a long, warming round of applause. It was as if she had never been away.

Harry Cohn called her into his office. He gave her a bottle of her favorite perfume from the closetful he kept for his leading ladies. Then, with tears falling down his cheeks, he said, "I never had a child." Her pregnancy touched something deep and genuine in him. Cohn grieved over his wife's inability to give him a child and once offered a starlet a large sum of money to carry his child. She turned him down.

With pregnancy came a deep sense of calm and happiness for my mother. The baby arrived after a long delivery and John named her Susan Cary Saunders, Cary being a Saunders family name. My mother wrote, "It was not easy, at first, to know whether Susan's arrival was exciting to John." He talked about someday "wearing her on his arm at Longchamps," the elegant racetrack outside Paris.

"For me," she said, "her arrival meant I would have less and less concern for him."

John's decline accelerated. His pupils were often enlarged, his eyes vacant, his movements bizarrely slowed. Without telling her, John sold a lot they owned next door to the Selma Avenue house, and some of her jewelry went missing. He began to rail against the Jews who ran Hollywood and he told her he had ideas about joining Hitler. But when he left home for what he announced was a trial separation, she felt his absence.

She went through a period where she didn't work continuously, movie to movie, and could spend time with the baby. She found warmth and comfort being with Susan.

In 1937, at age twenty-nine, she was more beautiful than ever. In *It Happened in Hollywood,* she touched audiences as a movie star on a comeback, poignantly capturing the ephemeral nature of stardom and the shallow values of Hollywood. She reunited with Richard Arlen for *Murder in Greenwich Village* (also 1937), a screwball comedy about an heiress accused of murder.

In November 1937, she visited John at the beach house he had rented in Malibu. He played with Susan and took photos of her crawling in the sand. He seemed at ease, and entranced by his daughter. My mother napped in the afternoon. She was facedown on the daybed in her bathing suit when she felt a sharp sting in her right buttock and awoke to see John withdrawing a needle. Immediately a blurry sensation coursed through her. She felt she was made of cotton; a fuzzy, nasty, uncomfortable feeling, probably from a narcotic or the chloral hydrate he was taking to reduce his anxiety from alcohol withdrawal. Upset at his attempt to pull her into

Saunders with baby Susan. His addiction to drugs continued, and Fay soon asked for a divorce.

his drugged world, she packed up fourteen-month-old Susan at once and went back to the house on Selma Avenue.

Within days, after nine years of marriage, she told John she wanted a divorce. He said he would think about it.

While she waited for him to decide, she worried what he might do. Every evening her youngest brother, Victor, twenty-three, loyal and protective, stayed with her and they played endless games of cribbage. On occasion she went to parties, and one memorable night danced with George Gershwin. He said, "I see something in your eyes I've never seen before." She asked what he saw. "Truth," he said. The two of them danced without exchanging another word.

Still awaiting some response from John, she told Vina of her request for a divorce. Her mother, now aging and infirm, seemed not to react. My mother wrote, "We both remained standing. There was not that cozy confessional feeling of being seated closely together—where, perhaps, arms around one another, my unhappiness, as well as hers, could have been exorcised. It was as though she took for granted that any or all marriages could come to this."

Vina's story was coming to its own sad end. Within months, she lapsed into dementia and delirium. My mother sat at her bedside for hours and listened to her ramble on about a happy time before she was married, when she was a university student in Utah, young and beautiful, slim and daring. Vina remembered sitting sidesaddle, wearing a blue velvet habit and a plumed hat, the best rider in the county, and going to Washington, D.C., and the San Francisco World's Fair with her famous father, Daniel Webster Jones, whom she adored. Sometimes she drifted back to wonderful nights at the theater and opera in Salt Lake City.

Vina died in a sanitarium on April 28, 1938, age sixty-eight. My mother wrote, "I am sure she loved her children, but as a compensating force for what she felt to be her largely tragic life. Now, after a few years of some relief, tragedy was sweeping her up again. Vina Marguerite Jones had been a thrilling person . . . although most of the time, my beloved mother had torn and talonized my feelings often enough that I wanted to put her back into that earlier time. When she died, I was able to do that."

My mother's new agent, Leland Hayward, called to say she had been offered a role in a light comedy at a summer theater in Cohasset, Massachusetts. Hayward was the most powerful agent in movies, and he told her his other top movie clients, including stars like Helen Hayes and Margaret Sullavan, his wife, regularly spent summers doing stock in New England or upstate New York. He urged her with his usual exuberance to take the

Fay at her Selma Avenue home with her mother, Vina, and brother Victor waiting to hear Saunders' decision about divorce

summer away from Hollywood, doing theater, having fun. She asked for a day or two to think it over.

The next day, when John returned to the Selma Avenue house, he seemed in much better shape. He said he was agreeable to the divorce and he encouraged her to take the summer theater offer. He and the nanny could keep an eye on Susan, he said, and her sister Willow was nearby and could come over anytime.

My mother agreed. She left Susan at the house in the care of a full-time nurse and went off to Cohasset. The nurse wrote her daily letters of Susan's activities and John regularly sent pictures of Susan at play.

For the first time in years, my mother had a sense of freedom.

Sinclair Lewis, who earlier in the decade had won the Nobel Prize for Literature, was at the theater in Cohasset, trying his hand at playwriting and acting. He was remarkably prolific, able to create vivid and memorable characters while peeling away myths about American culture and society. His novels included *Main Street* (1920) and *Babbitt* (1922), followed in quick succession by *Arrowsmith, Elmer Gantry,* and *Dodsworth.*

Lewis was called "Red" because of the wisp of red hair on his balding crown. He was gangly and skeletal and cursed with a sallow, pockmarked face that made him physically unattractive. This summer he devoted his time to acting and my mother. He became besotted with her, pursuing her everywhere and all the time. She gave him no encouragement, but when she left Cohasset to work in Rhode Island, and then to another summer theater in Saratoga, New York, Lewis followed her to both places. In Saratoga he urged the director to cast him in a romantic role opposite her and she felt a sense of panic. "I could admire Lewis, admire his brilliance and

Fay did summer stock in Cohasset, Massachusetts, in 1938, where she met Nobel Prize–winning novelist Sinclair Lewis (above), who became infatuated with her. That year they wrote a play together, *Angela Is Twenty-Two*. Fay was an admirer of his writing but was not attracted to him.

the mind he himself defined as 'chained lightning,' but I wouldn't want him to touch me."

Fortunately Ethel Barrymore was a member of the company. She said to Lewis, "Good God, are you serious!" letting him know no one would believe him in a romantic relationship with my mother.

Lewis did not give up easily. He asked my mother to collaborate with him in writing a play, *Angela Is Twenty-Two*, about an older man falling in love with a younger girl. Being asked by a Nobel Prize–winning author to collaborate was heady stuff and she agreed, all the time struggling to maintain a friendship without hurting his feelings.

It wasn't easy. Plays were not Lewis' métier. "He wanted to be a great playwright," my mother said, "but didn't have a sense of dramatic structure. His plays were more ideas with conversation." And his obsession with her was hard to manage artfully; it felt suffocating and did not allow her to enjoy her summer of freedom from John.

Another man began to pursue her that summer of 1938.

Howard Hughes had just set an aviation record, flying around the world in an astonishing four days. Arriving home, he was lionized in a ticker-tape parade the length of New York's Fifth Avenue. He was dashing. He was without question courageous. He was also extremely shy. After the parade, he escaped the press that was hounding him by fleeing to the Long Island home of Herbert Swope. Swope, a journalist with the *New York World* and three-time recipient of the Pulitzer Prize, was one of the great newspapermen of his era, but when Hughes was a guest at his house, it was understood he was off-limits to the press, including himself.

On Hughes' first evening at Swope's home, he came into the solarium during cocktail hour, looking weary, his white shirt rumpled, his blue pants held up with a belt tied in a knot, the buckle missing. My mother, who was doing a play in the area and was also a guest of the Swopes, was there. Hughes asked her to talk apart from the others. He wondered if she knew the guests well. She said she didn't. "They will kill you," he said. To my mother, the women with summer tans in chalk-white dresses seemed elegant, but she said she knew how sharp-tongued New York society could be.

Several times that week, Hughes was waiting at the stage door after her play to drive her back to her hotel in the city, the Pierre. He surprised her by telling of his frequent disappointments when he had seen her at a golf course in California and waited by her car hoping to talk with her. He invited her to spend a weekend at the estate of his friend Sherman Fairchild, inventor and founder of more than seventy companies, including the Fairchild Aviation Corporation. She said, "No, I would have misgivings about that."

The next day a large box of gardenias with a hundred blossoms was delivered to her at the Pierre with a note: "No more misgivings."

After setting the around-the-world flight record in July 1938, Howard Hughes pursued Fay and they had a brief romance.

She had plans to return briefly to Cohasset when Hughes called to say he could meet her at the train in Stamford, Connecticut, and drive her to the Fairchild estate. He said, "You don't have to worry, there'll be a chaperone." When she stepped off the train, Hughes rushed up, saying, "Am I glad to see you! Reporters are following me. Get back on the train and go to the Pierre. I'll phone you there."

The next few hours made her feel she'd been cast in a spy movie. He

called and told her to take a taxi to Thirty-fourth Street at the East River where "I'll be waiting." Hughes met her with a small seaplane and flew them to the Fairchild estate, where a group of Fairchild's friends and his aunt greeted them. The aunt was appointed chaperone and at the end of the evening escorted my mother to her room.

Just as my mother was turning off her light, the door to the adjacent room opened. Hughes, then the most famous man in the world, was standing there, boyish, handsome, charming. She chose not to send him away.

She met Hughes again at the estate of Jock Whitney, philanthropist and publisher of the *New-York Tribune*, who smiled and asked her, "What are you doing to this poor fellow?"

The story of my mother's train station rendezvous with Hughes hit the newspapers. Helen Ferguson called to say John's very strange reaction had been to call a reporter to say Hughes was building a house for my mother on Catalina Island. The reporter had checked with Helen and didn't print the story.

An urgent telegram came from her sister, Willow. John had taken off with Susan, headed no one knew where—but first he had sold their Selma Avenue house and all its contents, leaving not a stick of furniture. My mother soon learned he had emptied their bank accounts as well, and also mortgaged his mother's home in Seattle and taken that money. She was reeling from the news; her shock was compounded when she learned John had encouraged her agent, Leland Hayward, to arrange the summer theater work for her, getting her out of town while he had implemented his designs.

Two agonizing weeks followed in which she heard not a word from or about John—two weeks in which she did not call the police. Then she received a call from John's sister-in-law telling her John was with Susan at the Westbury Hotel in New York and she could meet him there. My mother rushed to the hotel where Susan, not yet three years old, ran into her arms. Mercifully, John had hired a new nurse to look after her.

Hours after her reunion with Susan, Hayward called my mother to say she had been offered a role at Columbia beginning immediately and he strongly recommended she take it. It did not occur to her to ask if John had played a role in that offer, too.

Her mind was whirling. On the one hand, she needed the salary from the movie; after John emptied their bank accounts she had literally nothing. But a thousand questions went through her head. With their house gone, if she took Susan with her now, assuming John would agree to let her, where would they live when they got to California? How would she care for her while working all day at the studio? At least in New York she knew the nurse was capable and could care for Susan. If she took Susan without John's approval, could he accuse *her* of kidnapping? Women had little power under the law in those days. If she went without Susan to make the movie, she could be back in as little as two weeks or maybe a bit more.

But to leave her daughter, not yet three years old, with John? Mercurial, addicted, unstable, unreliable John? Whose promises had so often proved hollow in the past? How could she disregard the possibility, even the likelihood, that John was lying to her, manipulating her?

She made her decision. Leaving Susan with John and the nurse, she returned to California. Before she left, she insisted on and received a firm promise from John that he and Susan would stay at the Westbury until she returned. John's brother, Edward, a doctor she knew and trusted, lived with his wife in New York and assured my mother they would watch over John and Susan while she was gone.

My mother and I never discussed this so I don't know what she had been thinking. With all the cross-currents swirling around her, and under pressure to make her decision, is it possible one factor was that she felt sorry for John? She had told him she still wanted the divorce and Susan was all he had in the world; he had become very attached to her. If my mother was thinking of John's well-being, I think in this case her sympathy overruled her better judgment.

Probably predictably, no sooner had she arrived in California than John took off again, alone, with Susan—kidnapped her again—not telling anyone, not his brother, not the nurse, where he was going.

Her little girl was gone, which she now clearly understood she had allowed to happen. She called the district attorney of Los Angeles, pouring out her story, asking him to help find Susan. He called the district attorney in New York. For days, whenever she wasn't filming, she was in the D.A.'s office, hoping to hear something, and hearing nothing. Nights she spent alone in the Château Élyseé, a modest furnished apartment-hotel in Hollywood.

Sinclair Lewis inundated her with love letters and poetry. "Perhaps he thought that the prose and poetry would be some balm during a time of real distress," she wrote.

Filming *Smashing the Spy Ring* with Ralph Bellamy at Columbia, she found it almost impossible to concentrate. She must have looked strained and tired at work because Harry Cohn pulled her aside to tell her, "Your face is your fortune." He stopped her in the parking lot a second time to say, "I've never heard any gossip about you. But now you've got yourself talked about because of Sinclair Lewis." She told him there was nothing to the gossip, although if he had read the endless letters from Lewis, he would have wondered.

After six frantic and terrifying weeks, my mother heard John was in Charlottesville, Virginia. It wasn't the district attorney or the police who found him. He had gone to Charlottesville, where he had relatives, after a fling with newspaperwoman Adela Rogers St. Johns who, smitten with him, was now furious he had walked out on her and sent word to my mother.

Warned that in Virginia fathers had custodial rights over mothers, my mother now did something smart. She hired the most high-powered New York attorney she could find, William Donovan, universally known as "Wild Bill." Donovan had won the Medal of Honor in World War I as well as the Légion d'Honneur, the Order of the British Empire, and the Croce di Guerra, and he would soon become founding director of the Office of Strategic Services, the World War II precursor to the CIA. He was universally described as brilliant, bold, prescient, and potentially dangerous.

Donovan accompanied my mother to Charlottesville. At their request, Adela Rogers St. Johns joined them on the train; she was escorted by the two bodyguards provided by the Hearst newspapers in light of the major crime stories she covered for them.

They found John at the University of Virginia Hospital, where he had placed Susan in the pediatric ward under the care of a nurse and at the same time had himself admitted for psychiatric care. He met my mother in the hospital library and immediately began interrogating her about her relationship with Sinclair Lewis. He said she was the one who had betrayed him. She quickly stood up and left to find Susan. As she walked down the hospital corridor, she heard Walter Winchell on a radio reporting that Fay Wray had finally located her child, who had been kidnapped by her husband. Someone had already given, or more likely sold, him the story.

Again Susan ran into her arms.

Donovan was as effective as my mother could have hoped. First he told the Virginia courts she would return Susan to John whenever he wanted and then immediately put her and Susan on a train to California. He was confident that under California law he could get the courts to give my mother full custody.

Fay, reunited with her two-year-old daughter, Susan, after a two-month separation when Saunders kidnapped her and disappeared

John exploded. As soon as he realized Susan would not be returned to him, he railed to St. Johns that my mother had betrayed him and he would go to court to get custody of his daughter. St. Johns wrote back pleading that he not go to court, saying Fay was a wonderful mother and should be the one to care for their child. Finally, after much back and forth and with John anything but happy, he agreed.

My mother brought Susan to her new apartment at the Château Élyseé with a new nurse, Cornelia Beasley, called "Bea," whom she had hired in Charlottesville. Bea adored Susan and Susan adored Bea. She stayed with them for years, even when my mother had no money to pay her. She was fiercely loyal and loving, and gave my mother and Susan a sense of family.

That Christmas, in lieu of expensive decorations, Bea and my mother decorated Susan's tree with whipped soap, piling it high on the branches as though it were snow.

Cary Grant sent Susan a well-stuffed Santa Claus and for New Year's Eve took my mother to a party at Jack Warner's house. Dolores Del Rio lent her $5,000 to pay the rent and some accumulated debts, but other than that they got by with very little. My mother wrote, "Perhaps it was my having known impoverished conditions when I was young that made me not afraid to have lost the house on Selma and to have to start all over again. Affluence and acquisitions had not made a happy home for John and me."

When John was discharged from the hospital, he wandered aimlessly for months before finding his way to Fort Myers, Florida. He took a room in a boardinghouse with a nurse he had hired from Johns Hopkins. When he ran out of money, his nurse left but his landlady let him stay on rent free.

For a long time, John had been standing precariously at the abyss. Now he had reached the dark and lonely end of his journey. On March 1, 1940, several months after the final divorce decree, John hanged himself in his room at the boardinghouse. In his will he left everything to his beloved daughter, Susan Cary Saunders, but what he left was mostly debts.

My mother was in Los Angeles rehearsing a play when Helen Ferguson brought her the news of John's death. The curtain rose. She came on stage to sustained applause, "much too much," she wrote, "so that I was aware of the sympathy it suggested."

A portrait of John's last days by Adela Rogers St. Johns appeared in the Hearst papers under the headline HOLLYWOOD'S AUTHOR EXILE WHO STAGED HIS OWN UNHAPPY ENDING:

> It wasn't just the cruelty of Hollywood after he punched Herbert
> Marshall but his own feeling that he had failed in being the thing
> he worked so hard to be—the best type of what we call, for lack
> of a better word, a gentleman . . . When they hounded him out of
> Hollywood and into exile—or whether he hounded himself—it's
> hard to say . . . He thought there wasn't a friendly word or a friendly
> voice in the world, except Fay's . . . his beautiful lovely wife . . . He
> wanted her to be proud of him.

As my mother finished reading the story, she felt physically ill at seeing John, whom she had always tried so hard to protect during their marriage, now being autopsied so publicly in print. The doorbell rang. It was a Western Union telegram from Adela Rogers St. Johns. "I apologize. I had to do it. I needed the money."

Among the letters I have from my mother's effects is one from John's landlady in Fort Myers. She wrote that she did what she could to feed him and look after him, to provide John with at least a little liquor— "stimulant," she called it—to calm his nerves. He was alone and frightened, she said. "Mr. Harris [a local shop owner] and I were very fond of him and somehow he appealed to my mother heart, as he was so much like a helpless little boy. Gentle and kind and always showed he had had good rearing . . . He spoke to me of his happy ten years with you in Hollywood, adored his little daughter and I am confident he was still very much in love with you."

Of the many letters of condolence sent to my mother, two were especially poignant. One was from Clifford Odets, who was starting to play an important role in her life.

Monday, March 11

Dear Faysie,

I read the unhappy news in the paper today and am hoping that it won't cut you up too much. What happens to the men of Hemingway novels has nothing to do with their women no matter how fine the women are, as you are fine and as you were (I know!) during the past years. You are a unique and unusual woman, Fay, a dandy girl, altogether first rate.

All right, that's enough of that. Whatever you do in your room, alone, you will do anyway. But you have a lot of good friends all around and this is one of them.

Shall I burden you with my troubles? Shall I tell you how miserable I have been during the past two weeks? No, not a word.

I'm probably, in a day or two, going out of town for a week or two, starting a new play called, "A Place Called Avalon."

Dearest Fay, goodbye for the present, and all love to you and the baby.

Clifford

The other letter was from Sinclair Lewis.

Tuesday, March 12
Santa Barbara

Dear Fay,

I know that you are so sensitive to people that in the shock of John's death you will be in danger of somewhat blaming yourself—of looking around and finding a thousand ways in which, just perhaps, you might be to blame. You are NOT, in any way, and if you <u>are</u> thinking so, you must brutally stop it, at once.

I was with you in New York, all during the first kidnapping of the baby, and though you were wildly distraught, you never said one single unkind thing about John. You had for him nothing but patient pity. I was impressed to the point of incredulity by the fact, and perhaps I remember it much better than you can, because I could never have been so kind.

He was difficult; you gave him years of such sweetness as no one else ever could. Had it not been for you, I am sure he would have gone years ago. If you <u>are</u>, as I am guessing, finding recriminations against yourself—then you are wrong; and you must at once forget him, completely, in the thought of how many love you, including, I am sure, a great many people who have never seen you except on the screen. Your life and Susan's will be new now, and better–far more secure.

And–bless you!

I'm up here just for a few days, writing on my play. I'll be back in Beverly day after tomorrow. I feel that a note like this ought to be handwritten, but Fay, I'm so spoiled by the machine that I just can't write by hand any more.

Love—ever,

Sinclair

10

If a man's crazy 'cause he plays the tuba, then somebody better look into it, 'cause there are a lot of tuba players running around loose.

—*MR. DEEDS GOES TO TOWN*, ROBERT RISKIN

Life couldn't have been much better for my father's dachshund, Mr. Deeds. He padded along everywhere, tugging my father at the other end of the leash. To the studio, where he curled up on the couch beside my father as he wrote; to the commissary for lunch at the Writers Table; to the Swerlings' house for one of Flo's sing-alongs. Part of every Sunday was spent with family often gathering for brunch at Everett and Katya's, everyone's young children and dogs, or for dinner at a restaurant with a large table. At these weekly get-togethers, Pops sat at the head of the table and was the center of attention.

Political unrest, passionate causes, labor tensions, all were roiling Hollywood in the mid-thirties, affecting friendships, making and unmaking alliances, leaving no one unaffected. There was even one occasion when Frank Capra briefly joined my father as a defender of the powerless little man being victimized by irresistible forces. In this case, the little man was Capra himself.

Capra's conversion, temporary though it turned out to be, began with his anger at Harry Cohn, who had a political cause he cared about. When Cohn had a cause, he could go on rampages and act with even less restraint than usual, or none. In 1934, Cohn's target was Upton Sinclair, the popular socialist and muckraking novelist and author of *The Jungle*, who was running for governor of California under the banner of EPIC, or "End Poverty in California." His platform included seizure of property where owners had not paid their taxes, imposition of the first-ever income tax in

California with rates as high as 30 percent, government pensions for the old, disabled, and widowed, and other long-cherished progressive dreams. Early polls gave him an even chance to win. My father cheered him on.

Cohn and the other studio chiefs, led by Louis B. Mayer at M-G-M, prepared for battle. "We want no part or parcel of Sinclair," Cohn said. "We will close our studios in a minute if he is elected." As if to prove, in the words of M-G-M's Thalberg, that "nothing is unfair in politics," they ordered their employees to make fake anti-Sinclair newsreels, which they distributed in their theaters. They hired media consultants and took advertisements in newspapers that wrote anti-Sinclair editorials and provided the one-sided anti-EPIC news coverage they demanded. They took out attack ads and put up billboards.

Mayer provided another example of saying what he meant in a remarkably infelicitous way when he summoned a group of resistant M-G-M writers and told them, "After all, what does Sinclair know about anything? He's just a writer."

To finance their campaign, Mayer and then Cohn decreed that everyone at their studios must contribute one day's salary to the Stop Sinclair Fund. No one—writers, directors, actors, executives, crew—would be excused. Anyone who refused would be fired and blacklisted.

Capra, who didn't like Sinclair's progressive agenda any more than Cohn did, resented being strong-armed for the day's pay. So did my father, and together they agreed not to pay the tribute Cohn demanded. A few others did, too—notably John Howard Lawson, one of the organizers of the Screen Writers Guild and later its president, and later still one of the blacklisted Hollywood Ten. Cohn summarily fired him. Now my father and Capra knew Cohn wasn't kidding.

They held out as long as they felt they could before—there is no nice way to say it—capitulating. They contributed, with great reluctance to be sure, to the Stop Sinclair Fund.

Sinclair was trounced, getting 37 percent of the vote.

After the election my father wrote a piece for *The Hollywood Reporter* about his conflict with Cohn, titling it "The Canine Era." He was finally in Cohn's Dog House, he wrote whimsically, alongside many honorable colleagues.

> After four years in Hollywood—four years of helpless wrestling
> with a twisted distorted mind, I stormed the doors of psychiatrics.
> Searching, always searching for a grain of solace. But no one
> could help me. No one could put their finger on the source of my

malady . . . For years I've seen my friends go and come—to and from the Dog House . . . But all is serene now. All is well. Out of what was confusion and chaos is now divine clarity. Life is beginning to flow with new significance. Let it be screamed from high precipices. *Riskin made the Dog House!*

Cohn chose to remain silent.

The destruction of Sinclair and EPIC was a forerunner of battles to come. By 1936, with politics and passions filling the air, much of the Hollywood community was involved, especially when it came to union politics. My father found himself in the middle of a conflict that was raging between the Screen Writers Guild and the rival, studio-sponsored union, the Screen Playwrights.

The battle started when the newly founded, and progressive, Screen Writers Guild called on its membership to vote on a possible amalgamation with the New York–based Authors League of America. The goal, they said, was to prevent the studios from hiring New York playwrights in the event of a Hollywood strike. Writers' meetings were held at each studio to trumpet the amalgamation.

Conservative writers from the Screen Playwrights pushed back fiercely. "The right-wingers mercilessly shook me out of my pleasant apathy," my father said. They were successful in persuading him that the SWG was "placing our destinies into the hands of some sort of ogre in New York," but that was only the beginning.

Together with screenwriter Dudley Nichols (*Stagecoach, Bringing Up Baby*), my father tried to bridge the schism. At a meeting of the SWG, expected to be so heated that policemen patrolled the hallways, my father and Nichols argued that without important changes to the Authors League's constitution, amalgamation might result in the Guild losing its autonomy. Their tone was civilized and their arguments seemed reasoned, and the Guild leadership agreed to temper the language in the resolution and call for a vote not on amalgamation itself but on "the principle of amalgamation." So far so good. The conservatives asked the Guild to give them seats on the SWG's board of directors, including one for my father. One writer said, "He is one of Hollywood's foremost screenwriters and he is sane."

When studio moguls heard of the amalgamation resolution, they launched a counterattack. Summoning writers to mandatory emergency meetings at every studio, they issued threats. Irving Thalberg implied strongly that if amalgamation passed, people would lose their jobs. Jack

Warner called the Authors League "communists and radical bastards." The studios engaged in not-so-veiled vote buying, with one SWG loyalist whose wife was seriously ill and whose career was in decline given a three-year contract for a "no" vote. One observer wrote, "The smaller the writer, the bigger the intimidation," by the studios.

Supported by both sides, my father was elected to the board of the Screen Writers Guild, and the modified amalgamation proposal he and Nichols had sponsored prevailed. For writers across the spectrum there was, at last, unprecedented harmony under widely approved leadership.

Almost immediately everything blew up. A week after the vote, four of the most conservative members of the new board resigned, at least partly at the behest of the studios, and took 120 members of the Screen Writers Guild with them into the studio-sponsored Screen Playwrights. Leaders of the SWG, Dalton Trumbo at Warner Bros. and Lester Cole at M-G-M, were fired. It was soon learned that the four conservative defectors from the Screen Writers Guild board had recently been given lengthy studio contracts.

Philip Dunne claimed the Guild had "been sucker punched" by the "four horsemen," who had led the defection—James Kevin McGuinness, Patterson McNutt, Bert Kalmar, and John Lee Mahin. And the Screen Writers Guild was left with only forty members; they felt compelled to go underground and take the Guild with them.

My father was stunned. At the next Guild meeting, he stood and apologized for his involvement with the four writers who had led the coup. He wrote a searing piece in *The Hollywood Reporter* on May 7, 1936, entitled, "I Was Going Along Minding My Own Business," in which he questioned the integrity of the "distinguished gentlemen" with whom he had brokered the deal to bring about peace among writers. "Heigh-ho. What about their *own* convictions? What about their pledge Saturday night? What about their pledge to me? Oh hell, skip it!" Philip Dunne remembered Samson Raphaelson saying of the deserters, "I think the Guild has just had a bowel movement and is in excellent condition."

My father cast his lot with the SWG and remained on the board. He had nothing more to do with the Screen Playwrights.

Almost a year after he had stopped to do *Mr. Deeds,* my father got back to *Lost Horizon.* It was to be a monumental undertaking, more complex and demanding and more expensive by far than any film my father and Capra, and Cohn, had undertaken. Just *how* complicated would be deter-

Riskin working at home in 1937 on the screenplay for *Lost Horizon,* James Hilton's popular utopian novel. His dachshund, Mr. Deeds, offering support

mined only after the screenplay, set in a mythical Himalayan country, was written.

But this much was clear to my father: adapting James Hilton's imaginative 1932 novel would be challenging. Not only did no place like Shangri-La exist but the novel's subdued, understated, almost mystical style and tone were not the traditional underpinnings of movie drama. This screenplay would have to be different.

Robert Conway (Ronald Colman), a British diplomat who has grown disenchanted with politics and imperialism, is on a plane that crashes deep in the Himalayan Mountains. The survivors are rescued by a gentle soul named Chang, who brings them to Shangri-La, where a mystical High Lama, said to be hundreds of years old, leads the community. Conway's companions hope to leave at once, but he is intrigued both by this remarkable place and a lovely young woman, Sondra (Jane Wyatt). Sondra is sure Conway has been sent by destiny to be the successor to the High Lama, who is dying.

Hilton said he wrote *Lost Horizon* "to escape the darkness of the Depression" and to offer mankind an alternative. The book struck a responsive chord in many people, including my father. It gave meaning to their longing for peace and relief from the anxiety they felt at the rise of dictators in Europe and the drumbeats of war.

What the novel had was meaning. What it did not have was romance, any kind of focused intensity, or the conflicts needed for a dramatic movie. The story called out for personal relationships and plot and subplots, while at the same time retaining the idealism of the novel.

Hilton was a quiet and unassuming Englishman, dignified and highly intelligent. Now working in Los Angeles under contract to M-G-M, he understood instinctively what many book authors who relocated to Hollywood did not, and what my father had needed to learn. Sidney Buchman capsulized it when he wrote, "Screenwriting is an art, separate and distinct from good playwriting or fiction. It was a lot like trying to hitch up a race horse to a milk wagon."

It was clear to my father that changes would be necessary for the screenplay. Jo Swerling, who championed the project, told him the utopian tale would not make a great picture unless the characters were credible and the film not overburdened with philosophy. My father agreed in principle but said he would not abandon the utopian themes so intriguing to him. A *Variety* reporter who interviewed him at the time wrote, "After a night of doing the town and a steadying noontime breakfast, ponderings upon Thoreau slunk into his conversation and he wondered fleetingly if Thoreau's simple life was so fantastic and fairyland after all, or is it the real thing: and is the fantasy, actually, the mad life we live today?"

He thought for an unusually long three months before picking up his pencil. When he did, Thoreau infused his thoughts. Conway is searching for purpose and meaning and his journey, like Thoreau's, evolves into a protest against the direction he sees the world heading, at breakneck speed.

This was not a short magazine story to be adapted quickly. My father felt the serious responsibility of doing *Lost Horizon*. He talked with Capra and then with Hilton, soliciting Hilton's input.

Hilton could not have been more appreciative or encouraging. He approved my father's changes to Conway's character, making the modest British consul into an important diplomat disillusioned with the modern world and the overreaching British Empire. My father reimagined Mallenson as Conway's brother, George, so George's determination to return to England would add pressure on Conway to leave Shangri-La. To draw Conway tighter into the web of Shangri-La, my father created a love interest, Sondra (Jane Wyatt), and added a paleontologist (Edward Everett Horton) for levity. Hilton later told an interviewer, "It was really amazing to see how Robert Riskin has kept the feeling, the spirit of the book. He did a most remarkable piece of work really. Of course, he had to change several things: he asked me about them all."

My father listened to what Hilton thought. Of my father's final draft, Hilton wrote on March 23, 1936: "You will see that I have gone over the Lama speeches and have, at any rate, shortened them considerably. I hope you'll feel I have not destroyed their meaning or compressed too tightly, but I do think that they are technically the most difficult spot in the picture." My father agreed completely and incorporated Hilton's cuts verbatim.

He had been absorbed for months in the challenges the adaptation presented. "*Lost Horizon* was a tremendously exciting subject and completely different from everything else I have written. The story fluctuates up and down emotionally instead of continuing upwards until it reaches one big climax. If it's a success, you can cancel everything I've said on how to write a scenario."

As always, he was personally invested in what the movie was about. To open the film he wrote a legend to scroll down the screen:

> In these days of wars and rumors of wars—haven't you ever dreamed
> of a place where there was peace and security, where living was not a
> struggle but a lasting delight? Of course you have. So has every man
> since Time began.

The time and place were clearly now and here, as much as in the mythical Shangri-La. And the appeal the dying High Lama makes to Conway to stay in Shangri-La and preserve the values he cherishes is an appeal to the whole world.

> It came to me in a vision, long, long ago. I saw all the nations
> strengthening, not in wisdom, but in the vulgar passions and the will
> to destroy. I foresaw a time when man, exulting in the technique of
> murder, would rage so hotly over the world that every book, every
> treasure, would be doomed to destruction. This vision was so vivid
> and so moving that I determined to gather together all the things
> of beauty and culture that I could and preserve them here against
> the doom toward which the world is rushing . . . For when that day
> comes, the world must begin to look for a new life. And it is our hope
> that they may find it here.

After incorporating myth and reality, and the probably never-was with the likely never-to-be, in the screenplay of *Lost Horizon,* my father wrote

From *Lost Horizon,* Ronald Colman as the British diplomat and Sam Jaffe, brilliant as the High Lama. Below, Colman with John Howard (left) and Edward Everett Horton (right)

in capital letters that he had learned a valuable lesson. The most important rule for screenwriters, he now said, is that "THERE ARE NO RULES."

> A writer's or a director's dramatic instinct is so much more important than all the rules that can be advanced. To be guided by rules is often likely to lead one into the habit of telling every story in like manner. The scene is too pregnant a medium to stagnate it with a set of rules.

When he read the script, Capra was ecstatic. Finally he was to make the large-scale, significant picture he had always dreamed of.

He poured all his hopes and energy into *Lost Horizon.* He took an unusually long, intense four months to complete principal photography, never settling for a second-best way to tell the story. He shot the snow scenes in a rented refrigerated warehouse where the actors' vaporous breath could be seen. He shot the elaborate Shangri-La sets at the Colum-

ABOVE: Riskin's father, Jakob, on the opulent Shangri-La set with Everett's wife, Katya. BELOW: With his grand vision of *Lost Horizon*, Capra built elaborate sets, shot one million feet of film, and delivered a six-hour version, panicking Harry Cohn into thinking the film would bankrupt the studio. The cast and crew included Thomas Mitchell and Jane Wyatt (second from left). Cohn (second from right) looks unhappy, Riskin, next to him, quizzical, and Capra (center) looking eager. To Capra's right is Ronald Colman, looking distracted.

bia ranch and the Tibetan village sequences on the M-G-M lot. The scenes on horseback were filmed in the mountains above Palm Springs and the airplane refueling scenes in Victorville. He burned through a staggering one million feet of film—the profligate Erich von Stroheim had used only 200,000 feet for *The Wedding March;* Cooper and Schoedsack had used 20,000 feet for *Grass*—and his first cut was six hours long. With great pride he showed the masterpiece to Harry Cohn.

Cohn panicked. He ordered Capra to cut it drastically. Capra grudgingly pared the film to three and a half hours and, again proudly, gave Cohn what he called his final version.

Cohn's panic escalated. The financial strain on the studio, begun in the shooting, had by now become so great he asked all employees to defer cashing their checks.

Now Cohn took personal control of the picture. Ignoring appeals, as well as any input, from the outraged Capra, and not telling Capra what he was doing, Cohn chopped the film to less than two hours and scheduled a preview in Santa Barbara. When the reaction was lukewarm, he cut another fourteen minutes and restructured the opening.

Cohn was hell-bent on salvaging his investment—the film was initially budgeted at $1.2 million but came in at more than $2 million—and desperate to put the film in a form he thought would attract an audience. He did not care that his top director was in a volcanic rage. Not only had Capra's masterpiece been snatched away from him, Cohn had done it so peremptorily that no copy of Capra's version survives.

Cohn and Capra did everything but declare war on each other. Threats, bitter statements to the press, ripped up or ignored contracts, even numerous lawsuits would soon follow.

The stresses on *Lost Horizon* that caused the schism between Capra and Cohn did not create rifts between Capra and my father, or my father and Cohn. The differences between Capra and my father were moderate and the kind they always had in making a film, where disagreement led to intense discussion, frequently to compromise and always to resolution, with the differences soon forgotten. And as the war between Cohn and Capra raged, my father worked with both men, together when possible, separately when not, to resolve the disputes and make the film better.

The most significant disagreement between my father and Capra centered on the character of the High Lama. *The New York Times* reported, accurately, that my father wanted him to be a "kindly Franciscan sort of fellow, gently and indulgently appreciating the wayward world," whereas

"Capra wanted a "sterner sort . . . a Paul of the Himalayas." Capra won the first round, but the scenes with Sam Jaffe were judged by both Cohn and my father to be unacceptable, badly filmed—my father also said they could have been written better—with Jaffe's makeup poorly done and his voice barely audible. Together my father and Cohn convinced Capra to reshoot Jaffe after script changes and with better makeup and softer lighting. Capra would eventually shoot Jaffe's scenes three times; the last time, with my father off directing another picture at Columbia, he brought in Sidney Buchman to make dialogue changes. Ultimately they got it exactly right, with Sam Jaffe's performance as the High Lama a brilliant cross between my father's vision of the High Lama as gentle and avuncular and Capra's stern Jesuit ideal.

In another fight, my father was emphatically on Capra's side against Cohn. Cohn's hastily cut version, shown at the Santa Barbara preview, ended with Conway struggling away as a glow on the horizon—probably Shangri-La—seems to be summoning him back. This struck the audience as too vague, and even Cohn agreed. He ordered Capra to shoot a new final scene where an exhausted Conway returns to Shangri-La as Sondra beckons him forward. My father and Capra argued vehemently against what they called "such a soppy fade-out" and persuaded Cohn to let them recut the ending without Sondra, using instead a single shot of Conway looking with yearning at Shangri-La, leading us to understand he will find his way back.

The New York Times called *Lost Horizon* "a grand adventure film, magnificently staged, beautifully photographed and capitally played . . . It need have no fear of being omitted from the golden brackets of anyone's 'best-ten list.'" Other reviews, while mostly respectful, were less complimentary, with some complaining about lush Shangri-La sets and overwrought performances. The box office was initially disappointing but over time the film repaid its costs twice over. It received seven Academy nominations, including Best Picture, winning two, and today is considered a classic for its vision, scope, and imagination.

While Capra was editing *Lost Horizon,* my father was prodded by Cohn to rescue a project in his files with the offer that if he rewrote it, he could direct it, too. More important than Cohn's plea may have been that Everett would be the film's producer.

Everett was on his way to becoming one of Columbia's top producers.

Riskin's brother Everett (right) became a top producer at Columbia, producing *Theodora Goes Wild* (1936) with Irene Dunne and Melvyn Douglas (below), script by Sidney Buchman, and other film classics, *The Awful Truth* (1937), *Holiday* (1938), and *Here Comes Mr. Jordan* (1941).

He went on to make over two dozen films, including some major hits: *Theodora Goes Wild, The Awful Truth, Here Comes Mr. Jordan, Kismet,* and *Holiday.*

The film my father was to rewrite and direct was *When You're in Love,* a vehicle for Grace Moore, a popular singer who had taken the country by storm as a Metropolitan Opera star. Moore was a beautiful girl from Tennessee. Opposite Miss Grace Moore (as she was referred to) my father cast Cary Grant, who was still up-and-coming.

Wearing the two hats of writer and director was not my father's forte. In the middle of production he walked into Cohn's office and threw his

Riskin the writer found himself in conflict with Riskin the director. "When it came to my own script, I found I had overwritten."

own script on Cohn's desk, saying, "This is terrible. You'll have to get me a new writer!" Cohn just grinned and went on reading his mail.

Coming immediately on the heels of *Lost Horizon, When You're in Love* was in a distinctly minor key, with an unexceptional premise. Grant is stuck in Mexico, unable to pay his hotel bill, and opera diva Moore has visa problems. The solution for both is clear. She pays Grant $2,000 to pose as her husband so she can return to New York on his visa. When they fall in love, the film asks the obvious question: Will they stay together after solving their problems or will she remain single and resume her opera career? To highlight Moore's virtuosity, scriptwriter Riskin gave everything he could to director Riskin: operatic numbers, a Cole Porter love song written especially for the movie, an expensive Busby Berkeley–style extravaganza, and Moore's rendition of "Minnie the Moocher" by Cab Calloway. But the romantic chemistry between Grant and Moore never ignited and the movie was probably too small to bear all the extra production baggage. To my father's and Everett's shared surprise, reviewers liked the film. *The Hollywood Reporter* called it "a signal triumph for the [cast] and for Robert Riskin, here notably handling his first directorial assignment."

My father's own reflections were more self-critical. "I discovered, for instance, that you simply can't have too great an economy of dialogue. Frequently when we were working together on a script Capra has said to

me, 'We don't need that; we've said it before.' And when it came to directing my own script, I found that I had overwritten."

When Cohn again tried to entice him into a dual writing-directing
role, he declined.

The differences between Capra and Cohn during *Lost Horizon* exploded
into public warfare. Capra brought a lawsuit against Columbia over recut-
ting the film, although contractually Cohn had final cut. The suit also
accused Cohn of promoting as "a Capra film" another film Capra had
nothing to do with. In response, Cohn refused to pay Capra's salary of
$100,000 if he didn't make another film for Columbia, as his contract
required.

Charge led to countercharge. When Capra demanded that Cohn pur-
chase the rights to *You Can't Take It with You* for him to direct, Cohn
refused, citing the high asking price of $200,000. Capra wanted to make
a film about Chopin, but, concerned by the potential costs, Cohn again
refused.

The battle escalated into multiple lawsuits, charge following charge,
resentment building on resentment, but Capra's real grievance was that
Lost Horizon had been taken away from him. Years later, he said that when
he lost the fight with Cohn and Columbia—"the Jewish producers," he
now called them—"I could have cut their balls off."

In 1937, with the Cohn-Capra lawsuits pending, my father went with
Capra and Lu on the liner *Normandie* to the London opening of *Lost
Horizon*. My father took Glenda Farrell; they were no longer romantically
involved but had remained good friends. Also on the liner were Gloria
Swanson, Marlene Dietrich, and Douglas Fairbanks.

In London they were given royal treatment, with Charles Laughton
escorting them to the coronation of King George VI. My father and
Capra then went on to Moscow to be feted by the Soviet film industry.
They were guests at the May Day parade in Red Square and taken to a
public gathering to meet the great director Sergei Eisenstein, with whom
Capra felt a special kinship. Their conversation centered on film techniques and especially Eisenstein's famous montages.

My father admired the Soviet filmmakers but had serious concerns
about the vaunted utopia all around them. About the filmmakers he
was quoted in *Izvestia* as saying, "You, Soviet cinema workers, possess an
enormous wealth of themes and stories. You are the millionaires of dra-
maturgy," which may have gained something in translation and could cer-

tainly have benefitted from a Riskin polish. Capra, still enraged about his *Lost Horizon* battles, took the opportunity to draw parallels between the oppressive government of Russia and life under Harry Cohn and Columbia Studios.

While they were in Russia, Cohn sent Capra an olive branch. He told the trade press he might be willing to buy *You Can't Take It with You* for Capra to direct, and would even consider the Chopin project. But the olive branch had a thorn in it; the fourteen minutes cut from *Lost Horizon* after the Santa Barbara preview would remain out of the picture forever. When Capra heard the details, he said he was not interested and would await the outcome of the lawsuits.

When Capra and my father returned from Europe, Capra stayed away from the studio. He sequestered himself in his Malibu home where he raged against Cohn and struggled with his own deepening depression, and waited.

Cohn won the lawsuit. It was my father who called Capra to tell him. "Cohn's broadcasting the news on the telephone. He's laying eight to five you'll come crawling back to the studio in a week." Capra slammed down the phone in a fury and ran to the beach, yelling at his children to keep their distance. He went to the nearby cliffs and hurled rocks and driftwood into the Pacific, screaming, "Come on, all you bastards of the world!"

My father's loyalty was to his partner and friend. He told Cohn he would not sign a new contract until he knew whether Capra would stay at Columbia. Word got around that he might be available and he began to get offers from other studios, but he said he would not respond until the Cohn-Capra dispute was resolved. His loyalty to Capra put pressure on Cohn, who did not relish losing his top writer and top director at the same time.

But it was a pressure-filled time for Capra, too. No other studio was breaking down his door. He found himself "blacklisted," as he later described it. And his legal actions against Columbia—there was more than one—were being dismissed serially by the courts.

Eight months after the release of *Lost Horizon*, Cohn and Capra reached a rapprochement. Capra made a rich new deal at Columbia. Cohn bought the rights to *You Can't Take It with You*, in part to keep another studio from making the picture. The Chopin picture was back under consideration at Columbia and Cohn paid Capra the $100,000 he owed him. But serious damage had been done and the mutual trust they had once enjoyed was irretrievably in the past. Capra's relationship with Cohn would never be the same.

You Can't Take It with You (1938), the last Riskin-Capra film for Columbia, was adapted from the riotous Kaufman and Hart Pulitzer Prize–winning play. Starring Jean Arthur and Jimmy Stewart, the picture won Academy Awards for Best Picture and Best Director. The screenplay lost out to George Bernard Shaw's *Pygmalion*.

But at least for now, all outstanding issues were resolved. Savoring the peace, my father renewed his own contract with Columbia and immediately went to work on the screenplay of *You Can't Take It with You*, the wacky, wonderful, wildly popular Pulitzer Prize–winning play by Kaufman and Hart, in which Grandpa Vanderhof is the beloved head of an eccentric brood, son-in-law Paul makes fireworks in the basement, daughter Essie practices ballet in the living room, and the one certifiably normal daughter hopes to marry the son of a snooty munitions maker who wants to buy their house, which is not for sale. Exploding fireworks, a police raid, a drunk tank, night court, one banker who quits banking to make animated toys and another who plays 'Polly Wolly Doodle' on the harmonica all make their appearances. The play brought with it all the elements Riskin and Capra looked for in a film, including a witty, people-centered story, a solid structure, and the attractive offbeat characters my father was always drawn to. You couldn't ask for anything more to make a great comedy, but if you did, it's probably there already.

But adapting a popular Pulitzer Prize play promised to be a high-wire act, with reviewers certain to compare the film to the play, especially after Moss Hart publicly expressed his fear that Riskin and Capra might turn it into one of their "message movies." Not happy about the comment, my father met with Hart. According to one account, Hart "beat his chest [in protest] after he read what Mr. Riskin had done" to his screwball comedy by adding "social significance." My father "listened attentively, then thanked Mr. Hart for providing him with a couple of new ideas for making it even *more* socially significant."

My father's additions included, most notably, moments of armchair philosophy from family patriarch Grandpa Vanderhof, who rejects all conformity and trumpets the virtues of independent thinking—an urban Thoreau, as it were. Grandpa inveighs against "Ism-mania"—following "isms" such as "communism, fascism, voodooism"—and adds that when things got tough, "America's greatest thinkers, Washington, Jefferson, and Lincoln [here my father added Mark Twain] never used 'isms,' never said 'Think the way I do or I'll bomb the daylights out of you.'"

No matter what he might have felt, to his credit Moss Hart publicly praised the film, as did all the critics. Frank C. Nugent of *The New York Times* was one of many who noted how skillfully Riskin and Capra had adapted the play for the screen. It was a smash hit at the box office and earned seven Academy Award nominations, winning for Best Picture and Best Director. My father was nominated for Best Screenplay but lost to George Bernard Shaw for *Pygmalion*.

• • •

You Can't Take It with You was the last picture Capra and Riskin would make together for Harry Cohn.

For my father, it had been an extraordinary eight-year run. Countless writers had come and gone at Columbia, crushed by Cohn's belligerent, inflexible, often crude and explosive manner, but my father saw what my mother, who had her own history with Cohn, had seen as a softer side that Cohn worked hard to conceal. Cohn, she said, had, "a sensitivity to and recognition of talent. He was more likely to express this recognition behind the back of the appreciated one than to his face. His rough, unpolished style, his challenging, grinding attitude, was reeled out like a fishing line to make his listeners rise to the bait . . . Capra and Riskin disliked his manner [but] were sometimes stimulated by his energy, and knew they had his admiration and regard, even if it was delivered in adversarial adjectives."

My father had long been courted by Samuel Goldwyn, who hoped to entice both of Cohn's top writers—Jo Swerling was the other—and Capra, his top director, to his studio. He offered my father the fantastic and unprecedented annual salary of $1,000,000, the equivalent of $17 million today, plus a percentage of profits, to rewrite scripts and become his chief assistant and top studio executive. My father said he would think seriously about it.

At the same time, and for a long time before, Capra was rethinking his own future. It was not only his clashes with Cohn over *Lost Horizon,* which had been papered over but not forgotten. For a long time Capra had been frustrated by the conditions he, and others, worked under. For a director this could include everything from budgets to schedules to the inability to have final control over his own work, or insufficient rewards for his contributions.

Through the mid-thirties, King Vidor, founding president of the Screen Directors Guild, had been pressing Capra to become involved, telling him the union needed big names to protect their fellow directors against the studios. "What the hell are you doing breaking your ass for the Academy?," he said, when everyone knew the Academy was controlled by the moguls and was fiercely antiunion and, when necessary, antidirector. Capra finally joined the Screen Directors Guild board and, after Vidor's term, became its president and activist leader. One historian believes "His militancy on behalf of the SDG was an outlet for his own gnawing sense of creative impotence."

Capra, too, was looking outside Columbia to see what might be available.

For once the time was auspicious for the people who worked to make the films for the studios.

Unions had received a lifeline in 1937 when the Supreme Court upheld the National Labor Relations Act, affirming the right of employees to organize and vote for the union of their choice. It was here that my father's relationship with Capra took on industry-wide significance.

During the intense studio-by-studio campaign on behalf of the Screen Writers Guild, my father urged Capra, now president of the Directors Guild, to accompany him to M-G-M to help persuade writers to join the independent union and oppose the studio-sponsored Screen Playwrights. By a vote of 267–57, writers chose the Screen Writers Guild. The battle with the studios was far from over, but writers, and labor, had won a significant victory.

In 1938, after thanking Harry Cohn for a remarkable eight years, my father accepted Goldwyn's offer. Capra, after thinking long and hard, did not. He was hoping David O. Selznick would choose him to direct *Gone with the Wind* and wanted to wait until that played out. My father and Capra wished each other only the best. They may not have known when or even whether they would work together again, but their friendship would continue unaffected.

Reporting to a new job at a new studio for the first time since coming to Hollywood, my father knew that Goldwyn was, like Harry Cohn, a fiercely ambitious man who also had earned a reputation for respecting writers. True, he was famous for saying "If I look confused, it's because I'm thinking" or "Give me a smart idiot over a stupid genius any day" and "I don't think anyone should write an autobiography until after they're dead" and "I am willing to admit I might not be right, but I am never wrong," but while Goldwyn may have twisted the language out of shape, he knew enough to have under contract many of America's best writers. Jo Swerling took his offer at the same time my father did.

The press took notice of my father's departure from Columbia. The

Washington Daily News columnist wrote, "Some Hollywood schools of thought are clucking that Capra had better follow, for what can a director do without a good scenario."

Meanwhile, Capra and Lu now lived through a nightmare.

On the day of the press preview of *You Can't Take It with You,* their youngest son, John, age three, died at Children's Hospital following a routine tonsillectomy. Capra was at the screening when he got the news. He raced to the hospital, arriving too late. An autopsy revealed the boy had undiagnosed meningitis and a massive growth on the brain.

Capra was inconsolable. Friends said he was never the same after John's death. He was, one noted, "less cheerful, less confident, with a deeper streak of melancholia." Lu put away all the photographs of John, but years later, after she died, Capra unpacked them and placed them around his desert home.

Within a year, my father began to wonder if he had made a serious mistake. He was finding the Goldwyn Studio a gilded cage with golden handcuffs.

He was paid more than any boy from Canarsie could have imagined. He had a grand office and title. He was charged with overseeing a whole slate of projects, to produce, supervise or rewrite as he chose. In his first months at the studio, he rewrote *The Cowboy and the Lady* (1938), with Gary Cooper and Merle Oberon, and the following year produced two films, *The Real Glory,* with Gary Cooper, Broderick Crawford, and David Niven, and *They Shall Have Music,* an unsuccessful attempt to make Jascha Heifetz into a movie star. His executive abilities and story judgment were on call every day and he was as busy as ever, but he was coming to realize, on a daily basis, that he missed what he loved most—writing screenplays of his own. He was forty-two years old and asking whether this was the life he wanted.

He soon learned that longtime friend and partner Frank Capra was having second thoughts of his own.

After Capra lost the *Gone with the Wind* directing sweepstakes—George Cukor was hired and then fired, Victor Fleming was hired, Sam Wood took over, Victor Fleming came back—he had reenlisted at Columbia as the highest-paid director in the industry. His first picture, which also turned out to be his last at Columbia, was *Mr. Smith Goes to Washington* with Jimmy Stewart. The story about an idealistic Midwesterner who through a fluke of circumstance is appointed U.S. Senator and goes on to battle the corruption he finds in Washington is rooted firmly in the familiar Riskin-Capra tradition, and was written by my father's friend Sidney Buchman.

Buchman is largely unknown today except among serious students of film, and that's a pity. He lived a life of very high highs in the movie business and, as it turned out, even lower lows. He was a few years younger than my father and had stepped capably into his shoes at Columbia after my father left for Goldwyn. He went on to work for seventeen years under Harry Cohn, the man he cheerfully called "an opinionated despot who had a passionate love affair with Class." Cohn liked him because he was always willing to help on a script and because Buchman, with an Oxford education, had that class. He was a very good writer who would win an Academy Award for *Here Comes Mr. Jordan* (1942), produced by Everett, and he was nominated for *Talk of the Town* and *Jolson Sings Again* (1949).

Riskin left Columbia in 1939 when Sam Goldwyn offered him an unprecedented contract. Sidney Buchman (above) took Riskin's place as top writer at Columbia and wrote Capra's next film, *Mr. Smith Goes to Washington.*

Like my father, Buchman was a solid union man, charming, and a great raconteur. He was not just handsome but irresistibly, movie-star handsome, with a well-deserved reputation as a ladies' man—this despite the fact that he was happily married. He and his wife, Beatrice, herself as beautiful as any star, had agreed on an open marriage and he had free rein in the ladies' department. But there was one thing on which Beatrice was inflexible. She was a devout member of the Communist Party and told Sidney she would agree to have his baby only if he would take her to visit the Soviet Union; he did and she did, making him a father the following year. He also joined the Communist Party.

When they started on *Mr. Smith,* Capra knew Buchman's politics differed radically from his own and it complicated their writer-director relationship. Buchman later said, "Intellectually [Capra] was a very simplistic man. His view of life came down to that of a fairy tale: at the end the good people had to be rewarded and the evil ones punished . . . I really believe that he never knew what *Mr. Smith* actually was saying, [that] even when you think you are living in a democracy, that you should refuse to surrender even on the smallest things because their importance can be enormous. I ended by saying to Capra, 'There, that's my theme.' He looked at me and suddenly said, 'Go get fucked with your theme.' It was so sudden that I was dumbstruck . . . He tried to catch himself, [asking], 'Are you a communist?' I answered him, 'Are you a fascist?' And we left it at that."

Released in 1939, *Mr. Smith Goes to Washington* received favorable reviews and eleven Academy Award nominations, but only one Oscar, for Lewis Foster's original story.

Capra came to decide that his relationship with Harry Cohn was irreparably damaged. Cohn did all he could to keep his top director, even offering to make him a fifty-fifty partner on movies Capra produced and directed, but it was too late. Capra wanted to free himself from what he felt was the oppressive yoke of Cohn and Columbia. On the day he cleaned out his office, he brooded that Cohn never came to see him or wish him luck. The two men, who had known great success together but had battled for years, would go in different directions without saying good-bye.

The Capra-Riskin wheel now took a surprising turn.

As soon as it was known Capra was leaving Columbia, extremely lucrative offers came his way not just from Sam Goldwyn but David O. Selznick and Howard Hughes. As the industry wondered where he would land, Capra turned to my father with a proposal he felt sure my father would decline. Capra had been considering forming his own company. Would my father become his partner? My father accepted at once.

Why did he so quickly give up his multimillion-dollar five-year contract with Goldwyn to join Capra in what both men knew would be a highly speculative venture? It was more than creative chemistry, he said. "It was the sense of freedom, rather than the actual freedom, which led us to do it. Also there was the adventurous side to it, which one doesn't feel when working on a stated salary. We were just a pair of dice shooters at heart."

More than that, they were happy to be together again.

The two-and-a-half-page agreement incorporating the Frank Capra Production Company, dated July 8, 1939, called for each man to invest $25,000. Capra would have 65 percent ownership, my father 35 percent. My father was to write and Capra direct, with each to receive $1,000 salary per week. Capra would later say that he had final say on all matters, but the signed agreement reveals that the two men had equal voice in control, management, and selection of projects; Capra did have final say in matters involving filming. On the top left of the letterhead was Capra's name, on the top right my father's.

Battles between Capra and Cohn over *Lost Horizon* had done irreparable damage to the Capra-Cohn relationship. Capra decided to leave Columbia and asked Riskin to form a new company with him. Their first and only film was *Meet John Doe* (1941).

From *Meet John Doe*, left to right: Gary Cooper, Barbara Stanwyck, Pat Flaherty, Irving Bacon, Warren Hymer, and Hank Mann. The danger of an unsuspecting people dominated by an authoritarian would-be despot drives the film, released on the eve of World War II.

Before starting at their new company, my father took another vacation to Europe, this time alone. In Stockholm and Copenhagen, the press welcomed him as the famous Hollywood "auteur"; he took a ship through the fjords and visited Lapland. On his return, he came through Washington for a private rendezvous with Loretta Young. When the press saw them together, they reported Robert Riskin was in town with his wife.

The trip to Europe had not been entirely a pleasure trip. In 1939 the drums of war were sounding ominously. Anti-Semitism and the menace of the German army were everywhere in evidence. *Kristallnacht,* "The

Night of Broken Glass," had occurred less than a year earlier, with extensive government-sanctioned violence carried out against Jews by storm troopers and Hitler Youth, who killed and injured many and left the streets filled with the broken windows of synagogues and Jewish-owned homes and businesses.

My father was in Europe in September 1939, when Hitler invaded Poland, unleashing World War II. Although it would be more than two years before America entered the war, there now would be no escaping the war's impact on every aspect of American life.

For their first picture for their new company, my father proposed the life of Shakespeare. Capra leaned toward Cyrano de Bergerac. Then my father remembered a story by Richard Connell, "A Reputation," he had read years earlier in *Century Magazine*, and thought that not only would it make a good film, it had something important to say about what was now happening in the world. Jo Swerling had taken a stab at writing a play based on the story and offered my father his incomplete script, and Richard Connell and Robert Presnell sent him a screen treatment called *The Life and Death of John Doe*. Both my father and Capra liked it. They bought the rights, and my father began the screenplay.

Meet John Doe centers on Long John Willoughby (Gary Cooper), a former bush league baseball player who is now a homeless drifter. He applies for a job with a city newspaper to earn money to repair his damaged arm, which he thinks might salvage his career.

A columnist at the paper, Ann Mitchell (Barbara Stanwyck), has just been fired because her stories don't produce the fireworks the paper needs to boost circulation. Fighting for her job, Ann writes an impassioned letter to her column from a man she invents, decrying the state of the world and announcing he will commit suicide at midnight on Christmas Eve. The letter, which she signs "John Doe," leads to a torrent of concern from sympathetic readers and Ann is rehired with a $1,000 bonus. She sets about finding a real John Doe—a "little man" trying to deal with life's big problems—to keep the story going.

Enter Long John Willoughby. Each day, Ann's column features him and his message of hope and struggle. Soon he's a national phenomenon. Willoughby comes alive in his new John Doe role, saying he knows what people feel because he feels it too. "I've been lonely and hungry for something all my life."

The publisher, a self-seeking demagogue, sees an opportunity to harness the public's passion for John Doe to his own political ambitions, and to organize a new political party for him to dominate. He directs Ann to write a speech for Willoughby to deliver on a nationwide radio broadcast. As Willoughby speaks, tentatively at first, Ann's words move him and they become his own:

I'm gonna talk about us, the average guys, the John Does. If anybody should ask ya what the average John Doe is like, you couldn't tell him because he's a million and one things. He's Mr. Big and Mr. Small. He's simple and he's wise. He's inherently honest, but he's got a streak of larceny in his heart. He seldom walks up to a public telephone without shoving his finger into the slot to see if somebody left a nickel there.

He's the man the ads are written for. He's the fella everybody sells things to. He's Joe Doakes, the world's greatest stooge and the world's greatest strength.

Yessir, we're a great family, the John Does . . . We raise the crops, we dig the mines, work the factories, keep the books, fly the planes and drive the buses! And when a cop yells: "Stand back there, you!," he means us, the John Does!

We've existed since time began. We built the pyramids . . . sailed the boats for Columbus . . . and froze with Washington at Valley Forge! Yessir, we've been in there dodging left hooks since before history began to walk! In our struggle for freedom we've hit the canvas many a time, but we always bounced back . . . because we're the *people*—and we're tough! . . .

I know a lot of you are saying, 'What can I do? I'm just a little punk. I don't count.' Well, you're dead wrong! The little punks have always counted because in the long run the character of a country is the sum total of the character of its little punks . . .

And your teammate, my friends, is the guy next door to you. Your neighbor. He's a terribly important guy, that guy next door . . .

You're gonna need him and he's gonna need you . . . If he's sick, call on him. If he's hungry, feed him . . . You can't be a stranger to any guy that's on your own team. So tear down the fence that separates you . . . and you'll tear down a lot of hates and prejudices.

The speech goes on and the message was familiar: We're all in this together, and we have to stay together to get out of the mess. And because my father wanted to say all that he felt, he violated a cardinal rule of

Riskin (left) with Barbara Stanwyck and Frank Capra in 1940 between scenes on *Meet John Doe*

screenwriting and put everything in. What made the scene work was that he wrote it as a montage, intercutting Willoughby speaking and the publisher listening in his mansion, Stanwyck tearful and proud, the public listening, too, all affected and even galvanized by Long John's down-to-earth authenticity and optimism.

In 1939–1940, the country was sharply divided, not just the traditional rich versus poor, black versus white, Democrat versus Republican divisions, but between isolationists and interventionists. America was still at peace, but the world was not. France fell to Hitler in 1940. The Luftwaffe was pounding London nightly in the Blitz. The debate was passionate and intense, the stakes enormous. Should we enter the war or stay out? My father felt we should get in but had to be unified when we did. The speech he wrote for John Doe was what he thought the country needed to hear.

For *Meet John Doe,* my father and Capra entered into an unprecedented deal with Warner Bros. Riskin and Capra had absolute creative control. Warners would put up $500,000 and provide studio facilities and use of the lot. My father and Capra borrowed the rest of the budget, an additional $750,000, from Doc Giannini and the Bank of America, assuming personal responsibility for repaying it. Warners would take a 20 percent distribution fee and once gross receipts reached $2 million, for five years profits would be divided 25 percent to Warner Bros., 75 percent to the Capra-Riskin company. After five years, Capra and Riskin would own the film outright. The ownership and creative control were extraordinary.

They knew they were on the hook for $750,000. They also knew Gary Cooper was perfect for Long John. They had to pay Sam Goldwyn $200,000 to get him.

Principal photography began on July 8, 1940. My father had the task of keeping Capra on schedule and on budget. If they went over, they would have to go into their savings for the difference. On one occasion, Capra fulminated about the front office. "How do they expect us to make the picture if they keep slashing the budget!"

My father said, "You keep forgetting, Frank. We are the front office!"

My father proved to be an astute businessman. Gradwell Sears, head of the Warner Bros. sales organization, told the press, "Bob is one of the best businessmen I ever ran into . . . He takes nothing for granted, which is why every detail in the deals he makes is as clear as the details in his stories."

They finished shooting in September 1940, five days over schedule but only slightly over budget. When the picture was released, it all seemed worth it. Bosley Crowther of *The New York Times* seemed almost swept away by the spirit of John Doe, echoing its theme in his review:

> Call him Joe Doakes or George Spelvin or just the great American yap—he is still the backbone of this country and as sturdy a citizen as there is. You've seen him at the ballparks, on buses, at county fairs and political rallies from coast to coast. You've even caught glimpses of him—and seen him squarely, too—in films once and again. But now you will see him about as clearly as Hollywood has ever made him out in Frank Capra's and Robert Riskin's superlative *Meet John Doe,* which had its local première last evening at the Rivoli and Hollywood Theatres—you and countless other John Does . . . This is by far the hardest-hitting and most trenchant picture on the theme of democracy that the Messrs. Capra and Riskin have yet made—and a glowing tribute to the anonymous citizen, too.

And while other reviews were respectful, Capra and Riskin had built a reputation together such that merely respectful reviews were not enough. *Meet John Doe* was only moderately successful financially, with returns less than my father and Capra and Warner had anticipated. They had given a year, and Churchillian blood, sweat, toil, and tears to the film, and the only Oscar nomination was for Best Original Story. They both felt that all the risk they had assumed, and all the responsibility, made independent production a very dangerous game.

In hindsight *Meet John Doe* was, more pointedly than they had attempted before, a message movie, and explicitly so. The publisher, D. B. Norton, with his echoes of William Randolph Hearst, was the first purely unredeemed character in the Riskin-Capra oeuvre. There was little subtlety here but instead a clear warning about the dangers of blindly following a malevolent and manipulative leader such as were rising in Germany and Italy. Still, the times were extraordinary, and if they erred in emphasizing message over character, many understood and forgave them.

Their new partnership, so filled with hope, concluded as suddenly as it had begun. Even before *John Doe*'s release, they briefly considered a sequel, but decided not to go ahead, with that or even another picture as an independent company. Capra approached United Artists, where they would rejoin Selznick, but my father wasn't interested. Again there was no personal falling-out, no animosity in their shared decision. To Capra, one factor was the high corporate and personal taxes in 1941, which left them with little financial incentive to continue as an independent. He said, "Uncle Sam . . . took ninety cents out of every dollar, Riskin and Capra . . . ten cents. Bob Riskin and I got the hell out of the kitchen and dissolved our corporation."

For my father there was a different consideration. It was 1941 and his thoughts were far away from Hollywood. He was convinced that America had to support the British against Hitler. Historian Lynne Olson says there was "a brutal, no-holds-barred battle for the soul of the country" going on, and my father felt he could make his personal contribution to America and the cause by going to England as a volunteer to help build bridges between the two countries.

11

Could a greater miracle take place than for us to look through
each other's eyes for an instant?

—HENRY DAVID THOREAU

By Christmas 1940 my mother had virtually no money. Her divorce from
John and the loss of her Selma Avenue home, added to the fact that she
never recovered anything from his plundering of their bank accounts and
possessions, forced her to move with Bea and Susan, now four, from the
Château Élysée to the more modest Villa Carlotta.

Bea was a trained nurse, with frowsy hair and practical shoes. She
had a soothing Virginia style that created comfort in their lives. She was
extremely protective of Susan, who had been born nearsighted and with
her feet turned in, making her physically unsure of herself. By the time
Susan was four, her vision had been corrected with glasses and leg braces
had fixed her gait, and her sweetness and lively imagination captivated
everyone.

To pay the rent, my mother took a job starring in *Wildcat Bus* (1940),
a forgettable RKO B-movie about a father-daughter bus company threat-

Cornelia "Bea" Beasley
was a nurse from
Virginia who took care
of Fay's daughter, Susan
Saunders, and helped
Fay in 1938 after her
separation from John
Monk Saunders.

Richard Barthelmess, silent screen star, invited Riskin and Wray to a Christmas party in 1940 for single friends. As in a Riskin screenplay, complications ensued . . .

ened by wildcatters, and waited for something better.

Every year Jessica and Richard Barthelmess invited friends to celebrate Christmas Eve at their house. My mother had met Richard Barthelmess in 1931, when they costarred in *The Finger Points* by John Saunders and also costarring newcomer Clark Gable. He had also starred in two of John's other films, *The Dawn Patrol* and *The Last Flight*. A major silent star whose looks made women swoon, but whose career was impacted by the transition to talkies. His voice was not strong and that, together with botched plastic surgery, caused his career to slow and eventually fade. But he and his wife continued to lead their lives much as before, and enjoyed entertaining. My mother remained one of their many good friends.

This year everyone clustered around the grand piano to sing carols, and well into the evening, bubbling inside from music and champagne, my mother danced a happy little improvisational dance by herself, losing herself in the moment. As she danced, she realized a man across the room was watching. She remembered him as the screenwriter of *Lost Horizon* she had introduced herself to several years before at the Beverly Hills Tennis Club.

Robert Riskin crossed the room and reintroduced himself. By the end of the evening he invited her to see a new movie, *The Grapes of Wrath*.

She found herself in tears at the classic Depression-era tale. The dust storms that wrecked lives, that forced the Joad family and thousands more Oklahomans and others to leave their now-barren farms and head for the dream of California with their few possessions piled high onto beat-up old jalopies, were almost too much to bear. The cost to the families lay not just in losing their farms but in losing as well their sense of worth, of dignity. The film stirred in my mother memories of her impoverished childhood in Lark and her emotion touched my father, who had his own deep feelings for those tossed aside in the Depression. They shared their reactions after the movie, and he ended the evening by kissing her respectfully on the forehead.

He invited her for dinner and dancing at the newly opened Mocambo, then at Ciro's. She had, and then laughed at, a fleeting thought. Bob Riskin, known for squiring blondes like Carole Lombard and Glenda Farrell, was taking an interest in a lifelong brunette who had been a blonde only for *King Kong*.

But what mattered was that over the dinners they shared, he somehow unlocked his heart to her. He did not steer the conversation but let it go wherever it would. He confided in her his personal thoughts and feelings. He seemed not to want to keep anything secret. My mother was flattered that a man of such intelligence and insight would share such personal revelations. She did not know that he was not so open with others and learned only later that in telling her what he had long held private, he was beginning to fall in love with her.

She found him droll, witty. His communications were often oblique and, after she understood him better, she was embarrassed to think how often she had missed his cues. "He was debonair and quiet and had a way of expressing himself that was immensely funny," she later said. When he sent her a dozen roses with a card saying only "One dozen roses," he hoped she would recognize the lyrics of a popular song, "Give me one dozen roses, put my heart in beside them, and send them to the one I love." When he asked her, "Why do women wear lipstick?" it meant he wanted to kiss her.

But even if she had understood his meaning, the timing was inopportune. She had become seriously involved with playwright Clifford Odets and would soon be returning to New York to be with him.

My mother's relationship with Odets had begun a year and a half earlier in Skowhegan, Maine, when George Macready, one of America's great character actors, had invited her to join a summer stock company at the nearby Lakewood Theater.

Today the longest running summer theater in America, Lakewood was an idyllic summer home for my mother, Susan, and Bea. They nestled into a lakeside cottage and soon Bea was steaming fresh lobsters and foraging mushrooms which my mother, not wanting to poison her child, wouldn't let Susan eat until she tried them first. My mother fell into the happy orbit of gifted theater actors who embraced her. Hume Cronyn was

Clifford Odets (left) and Fay with Susan in Skowhegan, Maine, where she met Odets in 1939.

here, and Keenan Wynn and his father, the great comedian Ed Wynn, who lived in the cottage next door and showered Susan with toys.

It was at one of the company's meals that my mother met Odets, who was visiting from New York. She wrote, "He was intense—if velvet is intense—so smooth and softly thoughtful was the texture of his comments. His gray eyes widened behind his horn-rimmed glasses when an idea sparked his interest. He walked easily, rhythmically, quietly, like a moccasined Indian."

Odets had astonished and captivated New York theater four years earlier, in 1935, when the Group Theater produced his *Waiting for Lefty* with Odets and Elia Kazan in key roles. The story of a taxi strike, which portrayed unions as legitimate and a needed way of giving workers a chance, so moved audiences that on many nights, ten minutes into the performance, they stood and cheered and never sat down. Odets captured with perfect pitch the crackling dialogue of his working-class characters and their passions, and audiences responded.

Two more Odets plays—"revolutionary plays," critics called them—

were produced by the Group Theater the same year. *Awake and Sing* and *Till the Day I Die,* the latter a fervent anti-Nazi piece, were both enormously popular. His greatest success, *Golden Boy,* came in 1937, running 250 performances. He made the cover of *Time.* Wherever he went, excitement swirled around him. How could my mother not have found him interesting?

He invited her to a local Skowhegan tearoom where they talked into the night, sharing stories of their painful failed marriages. Odets' wife, actress Luise Rainer, who had won consecutive Academy Awards for *The Great Ziegfeld* and *The Good Earth,* was a volatile spirit who had run off to Europe without him. He told my mother his despair was such that he went to Mexico and in his state of agitation promptly crashed his car.

His biographer, Margaret Brenman Gibson, later wrote of the time he met my mother. "Odets was immediately attracted by her modest, sad dignity, and by a curiously virginal quality she conveyed despite the fact that—still in her twenties [she was in fact thirty-two]—she was estranged from her writer husband and the mother of a small child."

Odets took a cottage near hers on the lake and they spent hours together. He talked to her in ways she found thrilling of the Group Theater and their new, naturalistic approach to acting. She found his insights into literature and music extraordinary, especially for a man entirely self-taught. She soaked up everything. She was reluctant to talk about herself, but as he probed with fascination and intensity, she realized how much she longed to open up to someone.

One night they sat in the living room of his cottage talking well past midnight. When my mother got up to leave, "Clifford followed, and opened the door for me. As soon as he opened it, he slammed it shut and picked me up in his arms and carried me in to his bedroom. Maybe every woman has dreamed of such a romantic moment. I certainly had. And that it had happened for the first time was a sign, for me, of fulfillment."

Odets returned to New York and the Group Theater, which his work was now keeping afloat almost single-handedly. He took writing assignments from Hollywood, which his Group Theater colleagues thought beneath him, but his earnings from these jobs gave him the resources to support the always broke Group Theater and provide him a life of comfort.

Separated from him in Skowhegan, my mother read all his plays and wrote him that she was moved by his "lyrical tenderness." He sent packages with his favorite recordings of Bach, Beethoven, and jazz, and books and toys for Susan. His letters to her were often filled with angst and self-doubt, about both himself and his new play, *Night Music*. Her letters to him were full of admiration and reassurances, and reminded him that he towered above other American theater writers.

In his 1940 journal, later published as *The Time Is Ripe*, Odets' entries about my mother include one dated January 16:

> Fay Wray sent one of her special delivery airmail letters. She liked the play very much and her letter was written out of loneliness and a need for a base. It is easy to be swept away by a woman of such true womanliness, particularly when she tells you she adores you and needs you and admires you. Fay is very clever with a man—the man is everything to her and she keeps showing you that she sincerely means it. She must have been born with that real quality; nothing in her life shows that she got it from intimates. A woman like that touches me. All women are beginning to touch me, get into me. For the first time in my life, I really feel the difference between a man and a woman. What a confession to make as late as thirty-three.

In 1940, Odets came to Hollywood on a movie assignment and took a place across the street from my mother in the Château Élysée. Sometimes they had dinner with his friends, among them actors Luther Adler and Sylvia Sidney, but he preferred to cook for them alone in his apartment, usually simple meals reflecting his Jewish heritage; he introduced my mother to kugel, a noodle casserole. He was "broodingly serious," she wrote, and sometimes she wanted to shake him out of "his seriousness into carefree feelings, but I respected the talent that made him reflective." He had risen to soaring heights and now was searching for something to say, something transcendent and universal.

His worries about *Night Music* proved justified. It failed, as would his next play, *Clash by Night*. At the same time, another problem was making its first appearance.

Shortly after Odets left Skowhegan, a man posing as a journalist had visited my mother and questioned her about the Group Theater and Odets' supposedly communist ties. She could tell him honestly that she knew nothing about it.

The House Un-American Activities Committee, under Representative Martin Dies Jr. of Texas, had been casting a wide and increasingly ominous net in the worlds of theater and film. Some members of the Group Theater made it no secret that they were sympathetic to all things Russian and now the entire company came under scrutiny. Young actors and directors—Harold Clurman, Lee Strasberg, Cheryl Crawford—who had embraced the philosophy of the Moscow Art Theater and the acting methods of famed director Konstantin Stanislavski may have been evidence enough for HUAC investigators that the Group Theater had communist leanings, which they thought were also reflected in the radical working-class themes of their productions. Odets became a prime target.

At the end of January 1941, my father came to New York to promote *Meet John Doe*. *The New York Times* wrote:

> If Mr. Riskin falls into the category of mad artists there is daylight in his madness. Although he is able to set a group of characters moving believably across the pages of a scenario, he is also, when need be, as hardheaded a drummer as ever hit the road to peddle his wares . . . Sitting in the luxuriously appointed Radio City quarters of David O. Selznick, which he is using for the nonce, he seemed as dapper and assured as any promotion expert. Now and then, for a moment of indecision, his eyes would search the ceiling as he swiveled back and forth in his chair. But usually his mind worked at trigger speed and without pause. It will take a shrewd tradesman to outwit Mr. Riskin.

My father was eager to return to Los Angeles to see my mother again. He did not know he had an ally in his corner. My mother had attended a Hollywood affair hosted by Loretta Young, an elegant women's luncheon in a rose garden, where she was seated next to Flo Swerling. Flo spoke so effusively to her about my father that she wondered if Flo were in love with him herself.

When my father came back to California, he brought a gift—a golden table radio shaped like a piano with an inscription on the miniature music stand: FOR FAY, ON MY BIRTHDAY, MARCH 30, 1941. They spent considerable time together, with the result that now she had two brilliant writers in her life, one a brooding intellect, the other warm and caring.

However, Odets was clearly in first place, for the present. He had a long head start, and now his frequent letters and phone calls, his emotional need for her, were pulling her back to New York. She had been with him for a year and was nothing if not loyal. When her close friend Dolores Del Rio, who had left husband Cedric Gibbons for Orson Welles, pressed her to fly east so the four of them could attend the grand opening of *Citizen Kane* together, she agreed to go.

The night before her departure for New York, after dinner at the Swerlings', my mother told my father about Odets. While she had been sure he would be disappointed, she had not anticipated how hard the news would hit him. He was heartbroken. As they drove along Sunset Boulevard, there were no longer hidden meanings. She wrote, "I knew he meant it when he said he couldn't bear to see me go. My feelings were all twisted out of shape."

They would not see each other again for nine months.

All indications were that my mother would marry Odets. He talked of settling down in Dutchess County, in a New England–style farmhouse where Susan could play and he would write. He wrote in his diary, "I thought about marrying her. Tasted and sensed her all around me, thought of what a home with her would be like . . . She is mature, adult. It's easy to be swept away by a woman of such true womanliness . . . a real woman womanly in a lovely way, very loyal, beautiful . . . [She] makes me feel stronger and wiser. Luise, on the other hand, made me feel weaker and more ignorant, fine business for a young man who felt inadequate enough before!"

Odets seemed enchanted by Susan, now five years old. She was "blue-eyed, clear-eyed, and unworried about anything . . . a good child, swift of impulse, chattering and wonderstruck . . . She was bursting with energy, and I read her two stories from her book. Suddenly, as children do, she began to fade away; it was the time when she goes to sleep—this glimmering blue gem suddenly lost its sparkle, fell silent, became a piece of colorless glass. When I left a few minutes later it was necessary to pick her limp body up off the floor and put her in her nurse's arms."

Odets and my mother spent long comfortable hours at his Beekman Place apartment, listening to Bach and Beethoven, or walking across town to meet friends for dinner at Lindy's, or going to the home of friends like Lee and Paula Strasberg. She was happy. "I was conscious only of the easy way we walked together, my hair free and loose to my shoulders, sometimes catching at the sleeve of his jacket. A sensuous easy male and female walking."

They had dinner with Dolores Del Rio and Orson Welles before the premiere of *Citizen Kane*. My mother said Welles was a man of "towering talent" who loved to eat until, she noted, it was the *food* that devoured *him*. Odets called him "an ebullient boy," which she thought a bit condescending.

They sat next to Welles that night. Watching the film with him was an extraordinary experience. My mother said she and Odets sat silently when the movie ended, "absorbing the realization that we had just seen a powerful work. It was Clifford who first reached across to take Orson's hand and tell him that."

That fall, my mother went to Marblehead, Massachusetts, to star in a Chinese fantasy drama, *The Yellow Jacket*, with Harpo Marx, Alfred Drake, and Alexander Woollcott, who was also the play's producer. Her spirits were high, and Harpo lifted them higher. He thought his role as Stage Manager gave him license to do whatever he wanted in the middle of a performance and he would rearrange furniture, throw confetti in the air to signify snow, lounge on stage while smoking a cigarette in a long jade holder—something different every night. He may have tried to adjust to the seriousness of the drama, but with no success whatever. One night Alfred Lunt and Lynn Fontanne, the famous acting couple, came to a performance and Harpo stared frog-eyed at them, blowing smoke bubbles in their direction. The audience's laughter grew until it was thunderous. Producer and costar Woollcott was in a fury and Harpo promised to behave henceforth, but on closing night, with New York friends in the audience, he chased Alfred Drake around the stage with his horn, swept characters offstage with a broom, ogled my mother, rearranged props so actors never knew where to turn, pulled confetti out of every pocket and his shoes and socks, tossed it in the air and at the other actors, and slapped his sides to keep warm in the imaginary blizzard. My mother, unable to help herself, laughed with the audience. She adored this brilliant and funny man, and her friendship with Harpo and his wife Susan lasted many years.

She returned to New York in early fall 1941 to be with Odets and do a play, *Mr. Big*, directed by George S. Kaufman, with Hume Cronyn, Betty Furness, and Barry Sullivan, but the play went nowhere. She performed in a twenty-minute television broadcast, one of the first ever. She saw Flo and Jo Swerling, who had come to town. Flo reported that my father had flown to England to offer his services to the British Ministry of Information. After my mother introduced the Swerlings to Odets, Flo said dismissively that she couldn't "endure geniuses." Flo was not to be derailed from her mission of bringing my parents-to-be together.

Odets' proposal of marriage never came. My mother never really knew why. She did know that, like a wounded bear, he carried scars from his own failed marriage, his parents' endless battles, his father's cruel humiliations of him. Perhaps, too, my mother was too gentle for his turbulent spirit, or he may have felt unworthy of her devotion. At some point, knowing she wanted "something permanent," he pulled back. "I understand her feelings but reject them in defense. I don't want her pressing me." And now he was often depressed, the failure of his recent plays having sent him into a tailspin. My mother wondered if she might be responsible for his recent troubles, wondered whether her love was insufficient to inspire great things in him. "My presence had not enhanced his writing talent, as he had imagined it might," she wrote.

Without preamble, Odets ended the relationship, saying, "Fay, I am just not good enough for you." She later recalled, "What he said, what I said—I know there was nothing mean or harsh. I know I did not protest. I know my feeling was that I would go from this house and never come back." She went into his study, sat under his Utrillo painting and had a good cry. Then she left quietly. She had invested her heart and soul in a man who did not want them.

She had not been the first to experience this side of Odets. In writing about his marriage to Luise Rainer, Anaïs Nin described how the morning after they were married, Rainer ran toward him to leap into his arms and he drew away. Later Rainer said, "I realize that this is a symbol of our whole marriage. He was never there when I needed him, or when I longed for closeness." For my mother, it had been no different, really. She wanted a man to whom she could be devoted and with whom she could have a home and a family. Odets had been right when he wrote, "the man is everything to her."

After the breakup with Odets, she picked herself up and went to Washington, D.C., for the out-of-town tryout of a new play, *Golden Wings*. At a dinner party before the opening, she stood with her friend and lawyer William Donovan as he conferred with Merian C. Cooper and John Ford, hoping to enlist them for his new agency, the Office of Strategic Services. My mother heard Cooper say, "There's going to be trouble in the Pacific." Everyone in the nation's capital was talking about war, which was increasingly appearing inevitable.

My mother returned to New York for the dress rehearsal of *Golden Wings* on December 7, the day of Pearl Harbor. On December 8, when the curtain rose for the matinee, management announced that the president would be speaking to the nation and his address would be broadcast live in the theater. She joined the other actors on stage to listen: "Yesterday, December 7, 1941—a date which will live in infamy—the United States of America was suddenly and deliberately attacked by naval and air forces of the Empire of Japan . . ."

World events quickly overtook all other considerations. Hitler declared war on the United States on December 10. *Golden Wings* soon closed. Before the last performance, Odets came to see my mother and they spent one last evening together. There was "no longer a pull" between them, she said. Years later she was surprised to read in the autobiography of Irene Selznick that Odets had said "Fay Wray was the only woman he truly loved," but his capacity for love seems to have been limited.

For Christmas, my mother took the train to Charlottesville to be with Susan and Bea and Bea's family.

When my mother had gone to New York to be with Odets, my father was crushed. He channeled his passions into the war effort.

The British government had sent representatives to Hollywood to enlist support, and my father seized the chance to volunteer for the British Ministry of Information in London, where he could also ally himself with Edward R. Murrow and CBS Radio.

Winston Churchill had ordered his Ministry of Information to appeal to the sympathies of the American public through film, lectures, and radio. The ministry knew an overt propaganda campaign would seem to Americans an attempt to drag them into a European war and provoke "cold fury," as the British ambassador to the U.S. defined it. There was a strong isolationist bloc in Congress opposed to sending aid to England, as well as like-minded groups such as America First, led by Charles Lindbergh. Other Americans resented the British as upper-crust elitists with imperialist ambitions who had manipulated the United States into World War I.

But many others felt that without American aid, England was facing certain disaster. And if England fell, America and the world faced an infinitely more dangerous world.

The challenge for the Ministry of Information was to make films and arrange speeches and radio broadcasts to win over the American public, all the while keeping the hand of the British government invisible. Everything needed to look, or at least sound, "made in America."

A nine-minute documentary, *London Can Take It,* struck a chord with American audiences, including my father, such as few films ever had.

The film opens on London streets in late afternoon, with working-class people heading home. The narrator, American Quentin Reynolds, says, "These people are part of the greatest civilian army the world has ever known," preparing for the "nightly visitor," the Luftwaffe. We see ordinary Londoners going to listening posts on the coastline, manning search-

Influenced in part by the film *London Can Take It* and by the CBS radio broadcasts of Edward R. Murrow (above), Riskin went to London in 1941 to aid CBS and the British Ministry of Information, which hoped to persuade American audiences that the British were worth defending against Hitler.

lights that sweep the sky, laying out fire hoses to extinguish the flames in burning buildings—and then German planes filling the screen, bombing churches, places of business and homes, "destroying five centuries of British history." The film ends with these ordinary Londoners heading back to work the next morning, resilient and stoic, having done their jobs and ready to do them again tonight.

The message was simple: *These are ordinary people, courageous and unflinching. They are like you and me.* There were no titles crediting the British filmmakers, and audiences were left to assume an American journalist had made the film.

Harry and Jack Warner, with whom my father and Capra were making *Meet John Doe*, were the only Hollywood executives willing to distribute *London Can Take It*. As early as 1933, the Warner brothers had been the lone voices among studio chiefs to criticize Hitler out loud and now, in 1940, they presented the film in 12,000 theaters. To everyone's astonishment, it was an enormous success, reaching an audience of 60 million. The film won an Academy Award as Best Short Subject. It even made money. Soon other studios were showing British documentaries in their theaters and by early 1941 opinions were changing across the country. Most Americans now favored sending aid to England, even if it led the country into war.

Radio also played a central role, principally through the nightly CBS broadcasts of Edward R. Murrow. Murrow was a superior, credible journalist, a man of conviction blessed with a powerful and distinctive voice. Millions in America, including my father, had long admired him. His nightly broadcasts from brave London, London under attack, Londoners wanting the world to know they would never bow down before Hitler, were required listening in many houses.

On Christmas, he told his listeners:

This is not a merry Christmas in London. I heard that phrase only
twice in the last three days. It can't be a merry Christmas for these
people who spend the night in the shelters and who realize they
have bought their Christmas with their nerves, their bodies and
their abilities. Probably the best summary of this year that is dying
was written by Wordsworth in 1806, "Another year!—another
deadly blow! Another mighty Empire overthrown! And we are
left, or shall be left alone; the last that dare to struggle with
the Foe."

Attitudes toward Germany and the war were changing in America. By
1940 and 1941, the menace of Hitler as exemplified by his wanton destruction of people and countries, the anti-Jewish horrors he was perpetrating,
his attacks on civilization itself, could no longer be thought of only as
someone else's problems.

In the executive suites in Hollywood, people were starting to pay closer
attention. They saw what others saw, and were also seeing the destruction
of their overseas film business. The fall of France had eliminated the marketplace for American movies there. The Italian film industry had been
nationalized. Word came to Hollywood that Polish exhibitors who had
screened *Confessions of a Nazi Spy*, the antifascist film produced by Warner
Bros., were hanged from the rafters of their own theater. The German government, which had earlier demanded that U.S. studios fire Jews working in
German offices, dramatically reduced the number of American pictures they
allowed in their theaters. Some executives may have come to realize that
Britain was not just a bastion of civilization, a courageous and belea-
guered underdog going through trial by fire, it was now the only viable
marketplace for their films in Europe. Louis B. Mayer, who had long
been publicly silent, welcomed a representative of the British Ministry of
Information to M-G-M, saying "I will do everything possible to help the
great cause."

My father, too, and he pushed forward with his plans to go to London
as a volunteer. In the few weeks it took him to meet with government
officials both American and British, and film executives and others who
could make the proper introductions that would be helpful in London,
four million German soldiers took their Blitzkrieg into Russia, overrunning vast areas of the country, including the towns in Belarus where Bessie
and Jakob had been born.

He took a train to Montreal to board a B-24 bomber for London. He wrote to his brother, Everett, on the eve of his departure:

Dear Ev,

Here I am stuck in Montreal and a dreamier place I have yet to find—particularly for one who knows not a single soul and who is sitting in a hot seat eager to jump. The fact that time is relative is making itself painfully apparent to me—for every minute is an eternity plus—I have a desperate impulse to shove my shoulder against "time" and push it forward.

I may not be able to write freely (due to censorship) when I get over so I may give you a general idea of what I have found out thus far, which is little enough. However, what was interesting was that I had to buy a flying suit for the trip. They fly so far north and so high that it gets cold to what the officer of Ferry Command called, the "danger" point. The suit is patterned after those worn by the Eskimos, including a hood, and padded with cotton . . . I was given a list of instructions which included an admonition that the "aircraft is very noisy and earplugs should be used." Also, a long description on how and when to use the oxygen apparatus. Finally, I am asked that on boarding the aircraft for the take-off, I must sit as far forward in the bomb bay as is possible until the aircraft has left the ground. Similarly, on landing I must enter the bomb bay just before the aircraft touches down. All of which is comforting in at least one respect—there will be a place to sit. It all sounds terribly exciting and would be wonderful if it weren't for the goddamned delay.

In New York I hustled around and managed to keep all of my appointments. I saw the men at the British Press Service . . . from there I kept an appointment with Schneider of Warner Bros. and finally met with a man from the Ministry of Information who had just arrived from London. I had dinner, before train time, with Bill Paley and his wife.* She gave me a personal letter to deliver to Brendan Bracken, the new Minister of Information. He is a very close friend of theirs. This shall help.

Bill, who speaks to his representative in London, Ed Murrow,

---

* Bill Paley, founder of the Columbia Broadcasting System, and his wife, Dorothy, became my parents' good friends during the war. Paley would serve with the Office of War Information in the Mediterranean, and later as chief of radio in the OWI's Psychological Warfare Division (1944–45), and finally as deputy chief of the Psychological Warfare Division.

every night, is going to tell him to look me up and perhaps I can do some broadcasts. That would be swell.

As ever, Bob

P.S. Dammit to hell! I've just been notified we don't leave until Monday morning—Christ! Another day in this dismal hole. It's becoming anti-climactic as all get out!

I have been able to reconstruct only limited details of my father's four-month stay in London in 1941. He lived and worked at the Savoy Hotel, headquarters of American military advisors, diplomats, and journalists, which would subsequently become his base of operations for months during the war. He met with officials of the British Ministry of Information and worked with Quentin Reynolds to promote a documentary, *Target for Tonight,* that showed British bombers in action over Berlin. He traveled around the country and spoke to the "ordinary people" he always identified with and did two broadcasts about the people he had met for CBS.

He and Capra wrote each other, Capra sending good news from Hollywood about the reviews for *Meet John Doe* and my father responding that the movie was breaking all box-office records in London and wishing Frank well on his new picture, *Arsenic and Old Lace.*

My father wrote, "I get homesick once in a while but wouldn't think of being anywhere else but here. The whole atmosphere is electric . . . I may think differently when I have gone through a few raids—and then again I may not." Capra said how much he liked the broadcasts my father had done for CBS Radio, one from London and another from Cardiff. My father wrote, "I will not attempt to write any more about my experiences here, for they have been many and varied . . . I honestly wouldn't know where to start. I'll save it all up for some "good old evenings" when I get back. Give my love to Lu and the children . . . Bob."

The first half of one of the programs he did for CBS Radio, a recording made on glass, survived in a box of his personal effects. He tells of the bombing he's personally witnessed in London and the devastation he's seen in Coventry. Employing the narrative style of *London Can Take It* and his own *Meet John Do*e, he tries to convey that the British are good, decent people, average guys like you and me, with the backbone and determination to win the war. The unspoken message is—*and we should help them.* His voice is resonant and he has an easy warm delivery, as if talking to friends back home, but with a hint of urgency.

Here is what survives of his broadcast:

WHAT HAPPENED TO THE LITTLE PEOPLE IN THE WAR

Just a mountain of rubble . . . it took them 18 hours to clear the debris away before they could reach the two men. When they did, they found them locked in each other's arms, pinned under a huge wooden beam, unable to move.

The minute the rescuers sighted them, they called out asking how they were. Bill called back, "I'm all right."

"What about your father?" they asked.

There was a moment's pause before he answered, "He's dead."

That boy had lain for 18 hours touching his dead father in a tight embrace. Bill came out of it with a wounded leg, which got him mustered out of the army.

He has his job in the bank again, but he spends his evenings and nights doing warden duty. They told me he was their best worker. When a raid is on no job is too difficult and too dangerous for Bill. He works silently and, despite his limp, quickly.

I talked to Bill later that evening. I asked him about the future, what his plans were. He looked at me kind of strangely. He had no plans. "There is only one thing to think about right now; winning the war." There was no venom in Bill's voice, no bitterness, no hate, but a determination that was unmistakable. And Bill's attitude is typical. The people seem to harbor no hatred for the Germans. What hatred they feel is centered on Hitler and what he symbolizes.

So maybe it made me wonder what would happen if Hitler were suddenly to be eliminated from the picture. They would have to transfer their hate to some other person, or some symbol. And that may not be easy. Of course, that's only on the assumption that hatred for your enemy is a valuable weapon in the colic of a war.

The average Englishman apparently doesn't think so.

But I certainly expected to find more venom and bitterness in a place like Coventry, for instance, where they took such an unnecessarily cruel beating. But it is generally absent there, too. Incidentally in wandering around the streets of Coventry, I ran across a scene that's worth telling about. It was away from the main part of town. I found myself standing at a street crossing. And as I stared down the street, there is no sign of habitation. Every house has been leveled to the ground—nothing but a sea of wreckage, no life, no movement.

It's difficult to believe that such devastation could be possible where human beings once lived. Each mass of debris represented a home that someone has dreamed about, and planned, worked and saved for, where children were born, and old people died, where family bonds were cemented, where they shared their successes and failures, and their joys and their sorrows.

And now a pile of mortar and brick is all that is left of those dreams.

While I stood there, a child suddenly appeared. It was a towheaded youngster of about 5 years old. He came from around the corner, walked to the middle of the street, sat down and began to play. All by himself. It was a weird picture in the midst of all that emptiness and destruction. I had a feeling that civilization had been wiped out. And here started the beginning of a new life, of a new world.

I spoke to the child and asked where his playmates were. "They all moved away," he said, and then his little face brightened, "but Mom said they are coming back after the war!" . . .

. . . under constant threat of decimation, you never crush the spirit that inspired Joe London, the average man, during the worst days, through a display of courage that captured the admiration of the entire world. What Joe London did here should be a warning to Hitler that he is confronted by a force that is more powerful than all his cannons, and all his military victories—a force that will eventually be responsible for his undoing. And it is particularly significant and wonderful that Joe London is nobody special, no miracle man, no phenomenon. He's just an average guy, the sort you're likely to meet anywhere.

Joe London is Joe Bridgeport with a cockney accent, or Joe Chicago with a Yorkshire accent . . . or Joe Seattle with a Scotch accent . . . He's just folks. He's you or me or the fella down the street, or Uncle Harry who works at the Post Office who keeps getting in trouble with women. He's the soft-spoken minister at that little church down Main Street, or Mrs. Murphy who runs the boarding house, or that riveter in the iron works whose wife can't keep him away from Kelly's Pool Hall . . . He works in Macy's basement, a bank in Kansas City, and on the docks of San Diego.

No sir, Joe London is nothing special, because the average guy is never special.

Where he's a surprise, it's only to those who underestimate his strength, who never gave him credit for having what it takes. Of course, Joe London can take it. So can Joe Bridgeport. So can you. So can anybody when the thing he believes in is being threatened. And that's the impulse behind Joe London . . . He'll go on taking it and he might even wake up and start getting some of it out, but there's one thing you're sure about, you never quit until the job's done, until the force that seek to throttle this freedom are rubbed out of existence.

Voice of Edward R. Murrow: You have been listening to Robert Riskin speaking from London. I return you now to CBS in New York.

Voice of Announcer: You have just heard a special broadcast from Mr. Robert Riskin, scenarist of the motion picture *Mr. Deeds Goes to Town.* Mr. Riskin spoke from the capital on the subject of what happened to the little people in the war.

12

Hope is the thing with feathers
That perches in the soul
And sings the tune without the words
And never stops—at all

—EMILY DICKINSON

It was not inevitable that Robert Riskin and Fay Wray would marry. Although she had been torn about letting go of this "decent human being" when she went to New York to be with Odets nine months earlier, gone she had. They had lost contact with each other and each may also have lost any hope of reuniting.

It was also not clear that my father wanted to get married at all. He was now in his forties, and he had stayed the cultivated, nonchalant playboy Sidney Buchman described. He had lived for years with Edith Fitzgerald and been involved with Glenda Farrell, Carole Lombard, and Loretta Young, but whenever the possibility of marriage had come up, he had shied away. He couldn't have said why exactly, but later my mother grew to believe that "he was even more sensitive than people realized," and this may have caused him to guard against hurt, or stop short of a final commitment.

Or maybe he just liked life as it was. His accomplishments as a screenwriter had won him the admiration of his peers, and his strong friendships with the Swerlings, the Milestones, and the Capras, among others, fortified him personally. In his family, he was beloved "Uncle Bob" to the children of Everett and Katya, and Murray and Rose, and his sisters Essie and Rose.

But now, at age forty-four, something was undeniably different. For the first time in his life he had opened his heart, to my mother. He found himself telling her things he had always kept private, holding nothing back. Her sympathetic encouragement and understanding had made it safe to go on, and had apparently stirred in him the longing for something deeper and more enduring than he had known.

The days after Odets ended their relationship had been hard for my mother. She was alone, with a young child. She had no money. At age thirty-four she was beautiful—her possibly biased agent, Leland Hayward, said she was the most beautiful woman in Hollywood—and had been pursued by many men, but her devotion to Odets, ultimately unreciprocated, had left her dispirited, with the failure to make a lasting and meaningful connection deeply discouraging. All her life she had been drawn to writers, admiring their creativity and intellect and forgiving their weaknesses. Odets was brilliant, like John Monk Saunders was brilliant, but also like John flawed and injured. She longed to have a partner, and a family, although many relationships she had observed at close range—her parents', Dolores Del Rio's, the Laskys'—were hardly storybook affairs.

Still, with her ingrained optimism and determination, she believed she would one day find the right man. Bob Riskin was ideal—warm, witty, intelligent—but she feared she had ruined her chances.

When Hitler declared war on the United States three days after Pearl Harbor, everything changed for Robert Riskin, Fay Wray, and everyone else.

The December 15 *Hollywood Reporter* headline read BOB RISKIN ON HIS WAY BACK FROM LONDON STAY. More than anything, he was determined to serve the war effort, now for America. He planned to stay in New York only long enough to see Flo and Jo Swerling before heading back to Hollywood to fulfill as quickly as possible a final Hollywood obligation, the screenplay for *The Thin Man Goes Home,* while searching out where he could be most valuable. My mother, whose play on Broadway had just closed, had left New York City for Charlottesville to be with Susan and Bea for Christmas.

Fay Wray and Robert Riskin would have missed each other entirely had it not been for Flo Swerling, who insisted that my father stay until my mother returned to New York after Christmas. She told my father emphatically that my mother's relationship with Odets was over and she would welcome his call—so don't leave!

Fay and Bob at the Stork Club in New York, finally together and in love, 1942

When my mother came back to New York after Christmas, my father telephoned and asked if he could come see her. She wrote:

I anticipated his knock at the door. There he was, in a heavy blue overcoat. Faster than the speed of light, currents of understanding about why he was here, why he had gone to England, why—why—why. Strong, steady, genteel, kind. All these flashes of feeling, but I think what I said was simply, "I am so glad to see you." I was almost giddily pleased to see him. He stayed until midnight or maybe beyond. The embraces that had been so long delayed were welcome.

At the same time, her intense feelings made her vulnerable. A few days later she turned down his request to spend the night in his suite at the Pierre, because "I couldn't bear the idea of transience." Then she didn't hear from him. A day later, she phoned his hotel and he was gone.

Oh, my God! I had hurt him again! I felt panic that I was losing this very good, very intelligent, decent human being. I think, when I had spoken to him of transience, I was wishing he would tell me that there was permanence ahead for us.

At the Pittsburgh train stop on his way back to California, my father wrote her, confessing his own confusion.

January 5, 1942

Darling:

I'm dashing off to the coast suddenly, impulsively and completely confused—about you. Forgive me for not going through with the torture of saying goodbye. I couldn't stand the "schmertz" [Yiddish for "pain"]—seems I'm still protecting my ego. When am I going to see you, angel? Must I wait until I get back to N.Y.? I must arrange to make it soon. I'll be at the Beverly Wilshire. Please do write. Bob.

She must have written or cabled back because he sent her this telegram from Los Angeles.

GLAD YOU GOT MY NOTE MAILED FROM PITTSBURGH I WAS CONCERNED ABOUT LEAVING SO SUDDENLY HOWEVER ARRIVED INTACT EXCEPT FOR A VOID WHICH ONLY A CERTAIN CRAZY GOON CAN FILL TAKE CARE OF YOURSELF DARLING I STEW OVER YOU SO MUCH THAT IT AIN'T GOOD. LOVE—B.

Having declared himself, my father settled into a suite at the Beverly Wilshire Hotel with his dachshund Deeds and houseman Richard and, probably as a favor to his brother, began work on the latest Thin Man which Everett was producing for M-G-M. The detective series, based on Dashiell Hammett's novel, was enormously popular, in large part due to the chemistry between William Powell and Myrna Loy, but my father, who had created more chemistry than Dupont, struggled endlessly with the writing. He found it impossible to weave meaning or purpose into a comedy about detectives who lived the high life and drank too much, and immediately found he was treading water. He described his work on the "dreadfully dull Thin Man," to my mother, saying, "The whole thing is a weird experience for me. I find myself as remote from the very things I, myself, have written that I can't remember now, a week after the completion of the script, what scenes are all about. Everett tries to discuss them with me and sometimes I stare at him blankly—

Riskin was back in Hollywood at work on the screenplay for *The Thin Man Goes Home* and missing Fay. He wrote her daily letters while trying to find a position to help in the war effort.

trying to recall the scene mentioned—or its contents. That really is a phenomenon. I must have written it with some detached part of my being." His mind may have been elsewhere.

In the months that followed, his almost daily letters and telegrams to my mother were an outpouring of feelings about work, war, Hollywood politics, and—most keenly—his love for her. He bolstered her spirits after a tryout for a new play disappointed her. He wrote of his plans to attend a dinner where writer-publisher Ralph Ingersoll would speak on behalf of Russian War Relief. He captured the tensions and excitement roiling Hollywood with the world now at war.

Sometimes he just let his overflowing feelings spill out.

January 20, 1942

Darling,

It seems ages since I heard from you—(for that matter it seems ages since I've written) yet you've been constantly on my mind and in my heart. I think of writing you nearly every hour of every day—and thinking of it, I feel the deed is done. What I fail to realize is that you have no way of knowing. Or have you?

You must know. Such constant—such strong thoughts <u>must</u> find their way into your consciousness. Keep your consciousness open, honey, here comes a flood of thoughts. Keep it open always—or you'll miss millions of little thoughts that may batter against a closed consciousness and perish from lack of shelter.

I intended waiting for your letter before writing, but I've grown impatient. I know your letter is on the way—but it is so slow in coming.

In Hollywood, many rallied in support of Russia, which after Hitler's invasion in the summer of 1941 was bearing the brunt of the war. My father was sympathetic to the Russian people but still wary of the Soviet system and government. When Charlie Chaplin delivered a rousing political speech in San Francisco, my father had prescient concerns for his friend. To my mother, he wrote:

Charlie made declarations that were so foreign to his convictions that they might have come from the lips of Joseph Stalin himself. He electrified his audience when, upon being introduced, he waited for what seemed an eternity after the applause subsided—and then began with one word, "Comrades." Well, I understand the rafters are still shaking. He then plunged into a speech extolling the Russians—their ideology (by saying that if Communism produces men of such heroic stature, he'll take communism, etc.). He resented the organized efforts for the last 20 years to present the Russians as ogres both here and in England—and by God, if any man can't get along on $25,000 a year he is a cockeyed liar and a traitor to his country.

However, it was a successful speech and a popular viewpoint and I'm afraid Charlie is stuck with it. I am certain he got up next morning and said to himself, "Is that what I believe in? Well, maybe I do. Who knows." Anyway, it went over. So, from now on, the Charlie you once knew has been buried with honors—and a new one has been born. Let's hope the new one has everlasting life—for he will cling to it as long as that political philosophy remains popular . . .

And how I longed for you last night. I had my dinner served on the veranda directly outside my bedroom. It was cool and I sat there throughout the prolonged dusk. Why couldn't you have been there with me? You would have loved it so—even with poor Richard's cooking. It was so heavenly. I remained there throughout the entire evening—in the dark—and alone. Tonight is much, much cooler— and I am propped up in my bed, my veranda world tucked away until I can share it with you . . .

I finish the re-write in a few days—and then MGM are obliged, within a week, to state what brushing up they want done, and then . . .

And then, my darling, (I'm afraid to allow myself to think of it)— I am a free man. Oh Lord, let there be no complications.

Goodnight, angel . . . I do want to say I love you this minute. I adore you. Bob

At the end of January 1942, Columbia offered my mother a starring role in a romantic drama, *Not a Ladies Man,* to be shot in Hollywood. She accepted at once. She was getting back on her feet financially and grateful for work, but more important she was eager to be with my father again. She boarded the train to Los Angeles where her imminent arrival sent him into a whirlwind of preparation.

DARLING WILL MEET YOU PASADENA ARE YOU GOING TO VILLA CARLOTTA OR WHERE DID YOU MAKE A RESERVATION LET ME KNOW AM REALLY LOOKING FORWARD TO SEEING YOU VIRTUALLY BREATHLESS GET THAT TRAIN TO SHAKE A LEG OR WHEEL OR SOMETHING MUCH LOVE—BOB

My mother's train was delayed with mechanical problems several stations east of Los Angeles. He raced to Barstow, 115 miles east, only to find the train had been restored to health and was again on its way to Pasadena. As in a Riskin movie, he spun his car around and drove wildly to Pasadena, arriving barely in time to greet her with a huge bouquet of flowers. She wrote about "all the urgency and the fun of hearing about the big dash he had made . . . as we went to leave my bags at the Villa Carlotta and then to a house he had very recently rented."

In anticipation of her arrival, my father had moved into a sunny two-story colonial house in the Hollywood Hills that gave them privacy from Hollywood and the gossip columnists. Everett's wife, Katya, had arranged the furniture and filled the house with flowers and greenery. "There was a room for me that I would use more than my rooms at the Villa Carlotta," my mother wrote. "A feeling of order, of home, even if a bachelor's home, lessened a certain sense of wickedness I felt it was to be living there."

At last they were together. The movie she was filming was only a minor interruption in what mattered most. After three blissful weeks, she told my father she had to go east again, to New York, to do a radio show and then on to Charlottesville, where Susan was staying with Bea and her family. With the war, film production had slowed and radio, though poorly paid, filled her schedule and helped financially. My father said he understood but still tried to dissuade her from leaving. Failing, he cabled her several times during her trip east. "Darling the sun shone brightly all day, but I wandered aimlessly in dark clouds. It's a bewildering phenomenon. Please advise what action to take. Love, Bob."

He followed the telegram with a long letter:

> Something's gone out of the house. It's terrible, darling—I'm beginning to lose my enthusiasm for it. It's kept alive only by some vague and inner hope that you're coming back to it.
>
> I move around in it aimlessly. I never go down the stairs without peering into your room—expecting to hear you puttering about. Then, realizing you're not there, a dreadful, depressing feeling sweeps over me.
>
> Deeds misses you, too, and Richard. Something's gone out of them, too. It's intangible, but it's there.
>
> I tried to fill the void you left. I called up Katya and asked her to send my bird back to me. Remember the canary I had? I don't suppose you do. Well, Katya cared for it while I was away. With you gone there is no song in the house. I thought the canary might

furnish it. Not yet, angel! Not yet! It refuses to sing. It peeps but does not sing. You could make her sing—as you make my heart sing—as everything you touch, sings.

Write to me. Tell me all. Tell me more than all. I miss you and long for you.—Bob

He had finally found the one thing he had been missing all his life, that had kept him from making a final commitment. He had found love.

Like everyone in Hollywood in 1942, my father was searching for a wartime role in which he could make a difference.

Jack Warner, a man known for his outsized, flamboyant personality, had been recruited by Commanding General Hap Arnold of the Army Air Corps, to make training films, and Warner, now Lieutenant Colonel Warner, wanted my father to run the unit for him. "I was to do everything—the works—the whole thing was to be placed in my hands, etc.," he wrote my mother. "I find, the more I go into it, the more appalling is the notion of Jack being my superior officer. And more discouraging is the prospect of my spending the 'duration' in Hollywood—doing something I could accomplish as a civilian . . . And although I haven't done it yet, my intention is to bow out of the entire affair. I shall probably incur Jack's enmity. He will undoubtedly feel I have unwarrantedly walked out on him—but he will soon get over it. He is all agog over his commission and can't wait to get into a uniform."

There was an Army Air Corps job that interested him, about which he had "to be secretive," and he seriously considered another position. "I was asked the other day if I would be interested in a civilian job (full-time—dollar a year) with the OFF (Archibald MacLeish's Office of Facts and Figures). It's a very important job and I suggested that he offer it to me first, before I commit myself."

The Office of Facts and Figures was one of several agencies consolidated by President Roosevelt into the Office of War Information (OWI), a massive operation created to distribute news and produce propaganda for both domestic and overseas consumption. Even before the war, Wild Bill Donovan had persuaded FDR of the urgency of establishing a propaganda operation and FDR would assemble a team of literary giants to shape the direction of the agency: playwright Robert Sherwood (*The Petrified Forest, Idiot's Delight, Abe Lincoln in Illinois*), winner of four Pulitzer Prizes and Roosevelt's speechwriter and friend; poet Archibald MacLeish, another

Pulitzer-winning author and head of the Library of Congress; and Elmer Davis, a respected CBS radio journalist, whose audience of 12.5 million equaled Edward R. Murrow's.

My mother wrote her friend Donovan on my father's behalf. Donovan cabled back that he would "approach Sherwood for Bob." While he waited for an answer, he was hopeful and anxious in equal measure. Sherwood and MacLeish were just the sort of men my father wanted to be associated with in the war effort, doing the kind of work he wanted to do.

Although he normally shied away from gossip columnists, he gave Hedda Hopper a long interview, telling her about his admiration for the way women in England had gone to work in factories or joined auxiliaries of the military services as draftsmen, nurses, machinists, testers, or photographers, all in support of the war. He was appalled by the lack of understanding at home of the world situation that "cannot be exaggerated . . . We've got a job on our hands that we can pull off only if every man and woman in this country realizes we're in desperate danger, that every minute counts and that every delay in production is treasonable. The sooner our people wake up to the deadly seriousness of our situation, the sooner we can hope for eventual victory." His interview almost sounded as if he were auditioning for the OWI job.

As the war accelerated, so did my parents' romance. At the end of March, for his birthday, my mother sent from Charlottesville an enormous bouquet of flowers and a surprise cake delivered to Rosalind Russell's house where he was celebrating—"to publicly announce" to their friends her feelings for him. He wrote back:

March 28, 1942

Faysie darling,

The flowers arrived and still blooming. Picked by you and Susan! No thrill could be greater. They took on such a personal significance. They arrived yesterday (Thursday) and they haven't withered or died yet. I have them before me now. They seem to be saying, "We brought you love, you lummox, so be a little joyful about it . . ."

If in retrospect the war machine of the United States in World War II seems to have been enormous and all-powerful, in the spring of 1942 the picture was much bleaker. After Pearl Harbor and the fall of Wake Island and Bataan, and with the far-reaching Japanese assaults on the British

Empire in Asia that had claimed Singapore, with the Nazis sweeping across Russia and Rommel driving across North Africa toward the Suez Canal, the news was all bad. My father wrote:

I was terribly low today and yesterday. The news actually sickened me so I got that twisted feeling in the gut . . .

I have about snapped out of it—tried to analyze why I felt so strongly. Because I'm not so discouraged—(good heavens, we should've been prepared for Bataan's fall—it's been expected and widely predicted—and we should be prepared–at least I am—for many more reverses). I will never waver in my conviction that in time we must and will destroy the mad dogs, both German and Japanese. So why then do I get those pains! I know why. I am always fearful that others might become discouraged—that millions of men and women might be overcome by a wave of futility—that the fighting spirit of our people which is only now beginning to manifest itself—will be smothered before it blossoms forth—before it translates itself into a strength and force which nothing on earth can defeat. It would be tragic if our spirit to fight for and preserve some modicum of decorum on earth never had a chance to assert itself in its fullness.

What of your broadcasts? Tell me.

The Air Corps business may come to a head in a few weeks.

Deeds is asleep at my elbow and having wild dreams. Wish I knew what they were. What do dogs dream of? Are they visual, do you think? And are they complex—manifesting themselves in symbols? Poor Deeds. His thwarted sex life has probably turned him into a neurotic and his subconscious is raising hell with him.

I hope you've written me a loving letter and that it is on the way to me now.

They fill in the voids, your letters do. They brighten the gray days and lonesome (oh so lonesome) nights.

Deeds just woke up with a grunt and a snort which in dog language means, "love and kisses to Faysie."

I join Deeds, my darling. You have my love and as for my kisses, I am saving those up for when I see you. I will deliver a million a night—and oh, how many nights it's going to take to deliver all those I've been storing up. You will be delighted.

And in case I find myself too occupied to think of it then, I say it now, once for each kiss, "I adore you."—Bob

My mother was doing her radio shows in New York and my father was tethered to the unyielding *The Thin Man Comes Home*. He labored on the script during the days but most evenings enjoyed cozy dinners at Flo and Jo's house. He wrote my mother about his ongoing talks with the Army Air Corps, including an elaborate plan he had conceived to send combat camera crews and mobile units to all fighting fronts. "Air Force big-shots were enthusiastic," he wrote, "but fearful of its proportions." They ultimately adopted his plan, but put not him but Darryl Zanuck in charge. "I appear destined to start things and have them snatched by more ambitious individuals," he wrote, as his search for his own assignment continued.

Frank Capra moved to Washington to make his Why We Fight series for the Army Signal Corps, highly patriotic films to motivate soldiers at war. He asked my father to join him. In one of my father's letters to my mother, he writes: "Strictly confidential and to be told only in whispers (in fact not at all) but Frank has been phoning me from Washington recently with considerable regularity—urging me to join him—either as a civilian or in the service. The poor guy needs help. Wants me to take charge of all the writing and writers, etc. I somehow can't get interested."

What did interest him was my mother. What worried him was the war. His feelings about both filled endless pages in letters to her.

> The war news sounds better—the peace feelers, etc.—and all the talk of Italian collapse—and internal trouble in Germany—and Hitler appealing to his people and the many and diverse reports of weakness on the part of the Axis—but somehow I am skeptical and worried that too many Americans and British might be taken in by what I think is a well-organized propaganda campaign to get us to slow down . . . I hope I am wrong, but I cannot see where anything has happened to Germany to justify all our optimism at the moment. Hitler <u>knows</u> his peace suggestions will not be accepted . . . Despite these weighty problems that burden me, I still and always carry you in my heart. I miss you—and will rush to your arms as soon as it is the least bit practical or sensible.
>
> Do please take care of yourself—for my sake—and darling, darling, Faysie, know in your heart that I love and adore you. Your Bob

My mother kept in a brown leather pouch all my father's letters from their courting days and after they married. There are hundreds of his pages but sadly few of her letters to him remain, and none for this period. She did vow her love and loyalty to him in a phone call, because he wrote how happy he was that she wasn't "going anywhere near the apple tree either," a reference to the Andrews Sisters' hit song "Don't Sit Under the Apple Tree (With Anyone Else but Me)." He inquired about the details of her life— her radio shows, a play in the offing, her war bond drive work, her visits to Susan in Virginia—and he reported with breezy charm the mundane events of his own life, such as securing a sugar ration card.

> I had to go personally—they wouldn't give it to Richard. Good Lord, the questions I had to answer for a half-pound of sugar!! I had to be interviewed by four different women—and finally received a ration card which described my hair as "blue." It was abbreviated "bl" and one of the ladies, unflinchingly, marked it "blue." When I called it to her attention, was she mortified! (Incidentally, what hair?) Then to top it all, one of the ladies asked me if I was a movie star. She was certain of it because the name was familiar and she had it associated with the "movies." I assured her that I play only the character roles— invariably unrecognizable in makeup.

When my mother went to Cambridge, Massachusetts, to do a play she was uncertain about, he tried to give her courage. The production of *George Washington Slept Here* had been cobbled together so quickly that she met the cast only a few days before opening.

May 13, 1942

My sweetheart:

> What I wouldn't give to be there—at least for the opening. I would know the torture you were going through—the acute first night nervousness and panic—and I would suffer with you. My heart would beat rapidly—my palms would be moist—and I would have that awful pain in the gut. But despite it the transcendental excitement would compensate for it all. And the nearness to you would be so soothing and warm. How wonderful to be able to share such things with you . . .

Despite his lyrical letters, my mother felt unsure of their future together. She knew she wanted something permanent with my father. She went for advice to a kindly psychiatrist who served her Russian tea. She told him about John Monk Saunders and Clifford Odets and found herself wondering about her future with Robert Riskin.

"Meaning that maybe it's all *too* beautiful?" he asked her.

"No. The feelings are real. He is real," she said.

"Why don't you ask him to marry you?"

"Women don't ask men to marry them."

And there it rested. She was alone in New York. He was alone in California, hoping to hear about a meaningful role he could play in the war.

When it happened, it was almost an anticlimax or, as Bogart says to Bergman in *Casablanca,* "It don't amount to a hill of beans in this crazy world."

Writers finally got their industry-wide contract. After ten years of impasse it finally occurred to people on both sides that the country and the world now faced a fight that really mattered and it was time to start cooperating.

The contract had three major provisions: recognition of the Screen Writers Guild as bargaining agent for writers, the right of the Guild to adjudicate screen credits, and a minimum wage of $125 a week. It was to be signed on neutral territory, the Hollywood Roosevelt hotel. It didn't take the Guild's lawyer long to read it aloud.

Harry Warner asked, "Is that all?"

Sheridan Gibney, president of the Guild, said, "That's all, Mr. Warner."

Warner continued. "Any secret agreements? Anything else I need to know about?"

Some of the writers looked sideways at Gibney. They had the feeling they had sold out too cheaply and took this as confirmation.

Warner stood and spoke to his side of the table. "That's all these cocksuckers want? These Commie sons of bitches? They want to take my goddamn studio. My brothers and I *built* this studio! I came here from *Europe*! . . . My father was a *butcher* . . . !" He turned back to the writers. "You sure that's all you want, you Commie bastards . . . ?!"

Two of his colleagues stood. Taking hold of Warner, they led, or wrestled, him out of the now-silent room. They returned alone five minutes later, pale and out of breath. They conferred briefly with their colleagues. Then their lawyer said to the writers, "Gentlemen, we regret Mr. Warner cannot rejoin us. He wasn't feeling well. But we've discussed your proposal and we find it acceptable." They shook hands across the table.

In June 1942, after five long months in which my father and mother hadn't seen each other, he heard from the OWI. He came through New York on his way to Washington for the interview with Wild Bill Donovan and Robert Sherwood that my mother had helped arrange. He sent her a telegram from Chicago.

> BOARDING 20TH CENTURY AND STILL DON'T BELIEVE MY EYES
> ARRIVE 9 AM IF YOU SEE A MAN IN A DAZE THAT IS I. TIME
> MOVES SLOW DOESN'T IT GOON? MUCH MUCH LOVE—BOB

They went to his suite at the Pierre hotel. She wrote, "We were lying crosswise on the bed just before going to dinner. I was wearing a taffeta dress on which I had pinned a golden brooch he had given me earlier. The brooch was shaped like a bow, the knot set with rubies. Very beautiful, simple in design and strong. To me, it was almost like a garment, so wearable, so right . . . I thought it had come from his heart. It was not just a bauble."

They talked seriously about what was important to each of them. She wrote, "We were touching on the themes that motivated us and found that we were both free spirits, neither one bound to any denomination. He had been born to a Jewish family that found philosophical discussion more meaningful than going to temple. But, he said, to be Jewish was to belong to a club from which you never could, nor ever would, resign. "I felt a rush of admiration hearing that," she wrote. He may have become an urbane and cultured man but, he told her, he was still very much the son of Bessie and Jakob. He wanted my mother to know where he came from and the full story of his background. He knew that in much of the world beyond Hollywood, Jews were outsiders.

She listened. Because of the pain she had caused him, she felt the next step was hers. The seed the psychiatrist planted had taken hold.

"Bob, I'd like to marry you."

He thought before he spoke. "I do have some hurts to overcome," he said quietly.

As they talked through the long night, she felt increasingly sure of their devotion. While he never exactly said yes, he certainly didn't say no and, my mother went on to write, "There was a comfortable feeling knowing where we were in life." There was nothing they didn't talk about. He asked how things were financially and she told him she had a $2,000 debt she was paying off, but was managing fine. The next day he sent her a hand-delivered note with a check in that amount. "Darling: I can't, I won't, have you stewing about money. There must be so many things you need that you've had to deny yourself . . . And the thought of that makes my heart ache. I love you."

Fay introduced Riskin to Wild Bill Donovan (left), her friend and lawyer who ran the Office of War Information with playwright Robert Sherwood (right). CBS's Elmer Davis (below) headed the Domestic Branch and Riskin became chief of the Overseas Motion Picture Branch.

He went on to Washington to meet Sherwood and Wild Bill Donovan for the first of what became a series of high-level meetings. Roosevelt had given Donovan the role of coordinator of information, with authority to establish an agency to "collect and analyze all information and data which may bear upon national security" and to perform "supplementary activities." The supplementary activities were understood to include psychological warfare and other operations to undermine the Nazis and their sympathizers inside the U.S. and abroad.

As they mapped out propaganda projects, sharp differences had emerged between Donovan and Sherwood, so deep that for a time they stopped speaking. Donovan was a tough-minded pragmatist who saw in propaganda a vital wartime tool to disseminate lies, sow confusion among the enemy, and prepare mainland Europeans for invasion—"black" propaganda, some called it, the kind Josef Goebbels had perfected. Goebbels' technique of "The Big Lie," trumpeting Germany's triumphs and attributing to Germany's enemies every kind of malevolence, had unified the German people and contributed to the collapse of morale in the countries the Nazis were overrunning in Europe. Now that Hitler had carried the war to America, Goebbels' operation never missed an opportunity to portray America as weak, corrupt, and cruel.

The idea of distorting truth offended Sherwood. He was an idealist and, with MacLeish, felt passionately that America's message must always be based on truth, with the aim of educating people around the world about the American way of life, propounding democratic values as a counterweight to the anti-American propaganda of the Axis overseas.

By June 1942, when my father arrived in Washington, Roosevelt had resolved the conflict between his friends. He created under Donovan's leadership the Office of Strategic Services, which after the war became the Central Intelligence Agency, and put it under the umbrella of the military. Sherwood was given charge of the Foreign Information Service, with Elmer Davis, a top CBS newsman, as director of the Office of War Information. The OWI was further divided into two sections. The Domestic Branch was to provide the public with accurate information designed to bolster support for the war in America. The Overseas Branch, by contrast, was a kinder, gentler series of films to portray the real America to people now living under Fascism. "The easiest way to inject a propaganda idea into most people's minds," said Elmer Davis, who was squarely in the Sherwood camp, "is to let it go in through the medium of an entertainment picture when they do not realize that they are being propagandized."

My father had found what he had been searching for, an important place among men he admired and a chance to do his part in the war. He accepted the moment he was offered the job. As founding head of the Overseas Film Division of the OWI, over the next three years he produced twenty-six short movies designed to win the hearts and minds of people abroad. Everyone who saw them said they made an extraordinary contribution.

His office was to be in New York City.

He told my mother he had an idea and she went right to work, finding them a spacious and airy place in the Century Apartments at 25 Central Park West with park views and ample room for Susan. Helen Ferguson, her publicist, wrote a wistful letter about missing her and all their friends in Hollywood, which was fast becoming a ghost town. "Darling . . . The Riskin engagement story. True? False? . . . The town is thinning out. Freddie Brisson [Rosalind Russell's husband] is gone . . . Gilbert Roland, Ronnie Reagan, Bill Holden, and scads and scads more. We have nothing but hen parties now. And so far we've not scratched any eyes out. Everyone is so wonderful about everything . . . Be happy. I wish for you that you shall have your heart's desire. Blessings, Helen."

Hollywood was far away. She began a radio series, *Keeping Up with Rosemary*. My father traveled almost nonstop between New York and Washington. He built from scratch a film production unit in New York City and planned the slate of films, and spent all possible time with my mother in their new apartment. In July, he raced briefly back to Hollywood to pack his things and move east "for the duration." On the train, frustrated that he was unable to hear her radio broadcast, he cabled her. "Am completely lost without you my darling and don't know how I am going to stand it. Take care of yourself Faysie, it won't be long. I love you." He sent telegrams from every city where the train stopped. "Las Vegas says she loves you too but not as much as Riskin . . . Wonder how Albuquerque feels about you." His message from Albuquerque: "Aussi. Seems it's nationwide and mine grows deeper and deeper."

When his proposal of marriage came—or when he accepted her proposal; whichever—she missed it. From Los Angeles he wrote to ask about "Donovan's friend, the judge." When she didn't respond, he wrote again two days later. "Apparently you missed the point of my inquiry about Donovan's friend the judge. You is a silly goon but I adore you nonetheless." This was my father's proposal of marriage, characteristically indirect—i.e., "find a judge." She answered with a joyful "Yes!" and Everett cabled her: "Just heard the wonderful news and believe me dear it's the best news I have had in years. It's thrilling." Flo and Jo Swerling wrote they were over the moon as well.

Everything came together quickly. My father took the Santa Fe Chief back to New York, exhausted and happy, his dog Deeds at his side. Susan was on the train from Virginia to meet her new father for the first time. He wired from Colorado, "Susan arrives today. How perfectly wonderful. Give her a great big hug for me and a kiss and as for you—well for you I have a thousand hugs and a thousand kisses and heart filled with good old ingredient, love."

Susan, now six, adored my father the minute she met him. She was sure from their first meeting that he adored her, too. "Sometimes he made me

Fay proposed, Bob accepted, and they married on August 23, 1942.

laugh so hard I actually wet my pants. I'd start to say something and he'd repeat what I said almost simultaneously, teasing me. I couldn't stop giggling." My father asked Susan's permission to marry her mother and she answered, "Oh yes, yes, yes!" Having a sense of drama, Susan insisted they rehearse the wedding in Central Park, not once but several times. Deeds played the Justice of the Peace.

Bob and Fay married in Wild Bill Donovan's suite at the St. Regis Hotel in New York. Left to right are Owen McGivern (New York state assemblyman), Donovan, Judge Ferdinand Pecora, Bob and Fay, Irving and Ellin Berlin, David O. Selznick, and Dorothy Paley. William Paley, not seen, was the photographer.

The real wedding took place on August 23, 1942, in Wild Bill Donovan's suite at the St. Regis Hotel. My father gave Susan a ring at the ceremony, binding her to him forever.

In addition to Donovan's friend the judge, New York Supreme Court Justice Ferdinand Pecora, friends included Irving Berlin and his wife Ellin, William and Dorothy Paley, and producer David O. Selznick. A journalist wrote: "Riskin said that he and his bride had no plans for a honeymoon. 'We will make our home in New York or wherever my work takes me for the duration of the war.'"

13

We need not leave it to historians of the future to answer the question whether we are tough enough to meet this unprecedented challenge. We can give that answer now. The answer is "Yes."

—FRANKLIN ROOSEVELT, FIRESIDE CHAT,
SEPTEMBER 7, 1942

Gifts, flowers, and telegrams flooded in from well-wishers: Cary Grant, Rosalind Russell, Ernst Lubitsch, the Capras, the Milestones, Orson Welles, theater director Harold Clurman, author and journalist John Gunther, Pat Powers, playwright Clare Boothe Luce, and the Riskin and Wray families. A shiny sterling silver cigarette box, which I still have, inscribed MR. AND MRS. ROBERT RISKIN, AUG. 23RD, 1942, came from Jack and Charlie, owners of New York's famed "21" Club, the former speakeasy where they often dined. Flo Swerling sent a long and effusive letter, "Faysie and Bob, darlings! Bless the two of you. In a world full of heartache and distress, you have brought cheer and warmth and thrill. Of course, we knew all this had to happen—it was one of our most persistent—nay belligerent wishes . . . The good God hasn't been lending an ear of late. So a wish come true is a precious gift. Something to shout about. And we're shouting—thank you for getting married!"

My mother had waited to find the right man and now was ready to settle down and devote herself to him full-time. She set aside her film career. They never really discussed whether she should give up acting— my father simply said, "Angel, do whatever makes you happiest"—but she had worked virtually nonstop for more than twenty years, often as sole support of her family, and now wanted to focus on her husband and Susan. She occupied herself puttering around their apartment, arranging things to please my father—red roses in crystal vases, cupboards full of his favorite things. She greeted him nightly with a warm embrace and his favorite Scotch on the rocks with a splash of seltzer.

Also waiting at the front door was Susan, Deeds at her side, eager to give her new father a report of her day. My mother loved my father for many reasons, but I believe one in particular made their bond unbreakable. He told my mother he wanted to legally adopt Susan, and he did. He had put a note on Susan's mirror that read, "If I were choosin', I'd choose a girl like Susan."

He spent endless hours at the OWI Overseas Motion Picture Unit, building and leading his growing team in setting up production operations in the Pathé studios offices at West Forty-fifth Street, planning the films they wanted to make. They would eventually occupy four floors and expand into additional space on West Fifty-seventh.

The work was exhilarating. Together with screenwriter Joseph Krumgold, my father prepared a detailed memo suggesting a slate of films about American individualism and pioneer spirit, ingenuity, culture, community life, and democratic processes.

Titled "Projection of America," it began: "Purpose: To dramatize America for the people of allied, neutral and occupied countries. To give the 'why' and the 'how come' of the more important trends in American culture, and therefore, to demonstrate Democracy as it is understood and practiced in the Western Hemisphere—not perfect but attempting to be best for the people willing to change, and able to grow when called up." A critical early decision was to tell the story in whatever way served the story best; dramatization or documentary or a combination.

Their charter in place, my father spent several months assembling a group of men and women of intelligence and creativity, experienced storytellers who were paid virtually nothing but were lining up to serve their country. Some, like screenwriter Philip Dunne, producer John Houseman, and director Josef von Sternberg, came from great careers in Hollywood. Others were already legends in the documentary world: Willard Van Dyke, Irving Lerner, Alexandr Hackenschmied (later known as Alexander Hammid), and Roger Barlow. A number were first- or second-generation Americans who, like my father, had deep devotion to the country that had taken them in.

My father faced the task of forging a working alliance among men and women from two very different cultures: the Hollywood studio system, with its expertise in scripted movies, and the world of unscripted, reality-based documentaries. Even a communal adventure for a great common

Riskin recruited top Hollywood and documentary talent to produce twenty-six films that told the story of America to people who had spent the war under fascism. Documentarian Willard Van Dyke (top), with Josef von Sternberg (right), and with Irving Lerner, Riskin's second in command, and others in his OWI office at the Overseas Film Division (below)

cause did not guarantee smooth sailing. The high-minded documentary filmmakers, who in their professional lives looked down on Hollywood and all things commercial, were wary about where my father, a creature of Hollywood, would lead them. The great Willard Van Dyke, later director of the Museum of Modern Art's Film Department in New York, said that at first he thought "Riskin didn't know his ass from his elbow because he was a Hollywood guy." Van Dyke described a tough story meeting when they hammered out assignments. He said my father "was really a terrific guy, but not our kind of guy." The clash of cultures only intensified when my father made Philip Dunne, his close friend from Hollywood, chief of production and gave him oversight of all films.

The documentary people took pride in their ability to go into the field to capture real situations and real people without the planning, elaborate equipment, or specially constructed sets the Hollywood people needed. They had grave misgivings when my father assigned Josef von Sternberg,

In 1943, Ingrid Bergman narrates the film about Swedish immigrants in America. The first of the OWI films, it was nominated for an Oscar for Best Documentary Short.

The Cummington Story (1945), based on a true story of the small town Cummington, Massachusetts, where the local folks are suspicious of newly arriving refugees until they get to know them.

director of *The Blue Angel* and *Morocco*, to make *The Town,* about a small community in the Midwest. The documentary team mocked the film as "another one of those stories from East Toilet, Ohio, about folks from nowheresville . . . heavy on the schmaltz and light on the content." The documentarians, who were proud that they captured life as they found it, were outraged that von Sternberg went so far as to paint trees silver to capture the light; they would have just filmed "the reality."

In this case, my father, the Hollywood professional, was not happy at first, either. When he saw von Sternberg's early film sequences, a member of the team recalled:

> Riskin smoked Dunhill cigarettes with their paper cigarette holders, and according to Willard, "the point at which Riskin began to tear those things up and bite 'em and spit 'em out, you knew something was up." Night after night Riskin, Dunne and Van Dyke watched the rushes coming back from Indiana with Riskin breaking and chewing his Dunhill cigarette holders into thousands of pieces. Finally Riskin turned to Van Dyke and said, "Willard, go out there and save this picture!" And Van Dyke said, "Not on your life." Nobody was going to go and either save von Sternberg or step on his toes.

In the end, they left von Sternberg alone. He turned in what the entire unit, documentarians and Hollywood professionals alike, agreed was a remarkable and beautiful film about a small Indiana town.

The two camps began to work harmoniously. "Prejudices about the Hollywood guys faded," wrote one. "The documentary guys gradually realized that no one had a better critical eye than Riskin or a sharper ear for dialogue than Dunne . . . while the Hollywood brass, for their part, were soon impressed with the documentarists' fieldwork and cutting-room dexterity."

A whimsical tale told from the point of view of the Jeep, an ugly duckling who proves a friend to the soldier and able to do absolutely anything asked of it

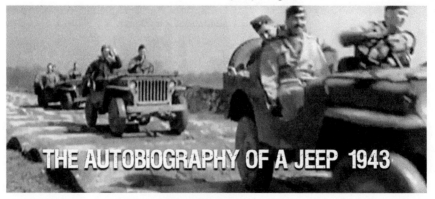

Arturo Toscanini with Philip Dunne, head of production at the OWI Overseas Motion Picture Bureau in late 1943, viewing *Hymn of the Nations* (released 1944). The film earned another Academy Award Nomination for Best Documentary Short.

Hearing that something exciting was happening on Forty-fifth Street, some of America's greatest talent in writing, directing, acting, cinematography, music, and editing signed up to tell America's story: novelist John O'Hara, dramatist Frances Goodrich and her partner Albert Hackett, actors Ralph Bellamy and Burgess Meredith, playwright Garson Kanin, director Jean Renoir, and composer Aaron Copland, some in the studio, some crisscrossing the country to find and tell the story, all working for next to nothing. Together the group was remarkable, unprecedented, never to be duplicated, and the films proved it. Over an intense three years, the Overseas Film Branch of the OWI produced twenty-six short films and dozens of newsreels. They would be dubbed into twenty-two languages and seen by millions of people around the world.

The first film was *Swedes in America*. Narrated by Ingrid Bergman, it portrayed the immigrant experience and was nominated for an Academy Award. *Cowboy* gave audiences the sense of what life on a western ranch was really like; by making an English boy who visits a ranch the story's central character, the OWI induced the British Ministry of Information to distribute the film in England, where it became a huge success. *Steel Town* highlighted a proud American laborer and captured the dramatic workings of a steel mill.

To showcase America's cities and the New York skyline, they made *The Window Cleaner,* featuring a man who with Buster Keaton–like agility scaled the Empire State Building each day to wash the windows. *The Cummington Story* recreated the tensions in a small New England town when war refugees arrive as outsiders speaking no English. Aaron Copland's evocative score captured both the experiences of the immigrants and, movingly, the emotional journey of the townspeople as they grow to accept and admire the refugees they initially rejected. In *Autobiography of a "Jeep"*, created out of stock footage, the Jeep tells in its own voice its story as an ugly duckling determined to prove its worth and its great contribution to the common cause. When the film was shown in just-liberated French cinemas immediately after D-Day, the audience, especially children, burst into applause, shouting, *"Vive la Jeep!"*

The most enduring film they made starred seventy-eight-year-old conductor Arturo Toscanini leading the NBC Symphony Orchestra in Giuseppe Verdi's patriotic "Hymn of the Nations." The film, which featured the anthems of several European nations, opened with the maestro in his living room telling how, rather than live under Mussolini and fascism, he had left his beloved Italy to come to America in his search for freedom. Then comes the performance of Verdi, recorded in NBC's Studio 8-H, with the Westminster College Choir, and great tenor Jan Peerce performing a solo passage. For a rousing finale, Toscanini added to Verdi's score the Internationale, the Russian national anthem (during the Cold War, U.S. government censors excised it from the film as pro-Soviet), and "The Star-Spangled Banner." The film was a triumph, nominated for an Oscar as Best Documentary Short, and would be shown to enormous and appreciative crowds, especially in Italy.

This was propaganda of the gentlest kind. One historian wrote, "Riskin made charity, faith and generosity of spirit his propaganda tools and the 26 short films that he personally commissioned, some of which he produced and wrote, and all of which he oversaw in their entirety, were the most visually stylish, culturally influential and politically potent of the entire war."

As Allied forces fought their way across North Africa and Europe, my father and his OWI team made sure they carried with them projectors and hundreds of OWI film cans. They would reopen theaters as they went or, if theaters were in rubble, as many were, they would project the films onto bedsheets outdoors.

My father felt that if foreign audiences loved American movies, they would love America, too, and decided also to show some Hollywood feature films in addition to the OWI films. A bureaucratic logjam between

Washington and the studios led to my father being given the additional responsibility of determining which Hollywood films would be screened. Washington trusted him to make the choices, and the studios, knowing he was one of their own, also trusted him to get their pictures back into circulation. Things went smoothly until studio heads balked about providing films without compensation. My father had to remind the moguls that the War Department had the legal authority to conscript their films and pay them nothing. He also appealed to their better natures, telling them that the war effort was more important than any commercial considerations and, after some initial grumbling, they cooperated.

The first group of films my father chose included *Flight Command, 20 Mule Team, Boom Town, Bambi, Foreign Correspondent, The Long Voyage Home,* and *Joe Smith, American.* He soon expanded the list to include *Dumbo, Mrs. Miniver,* and *The Pied Piper.* "Seeing how the other fellow lives and meets his problems is a long step toward understanding and cooperation for good," he said. By spring 1943, his list of approved films had grown to include musicals, action films, romance, and cartoons.

But along the way he vetoed a few, viewing them as potentially harmful to the war effort. One he would not approve was his own film *Meet John Doe,* which depicted a power-hungry and tyrannical newspaper publisher and a darker view of America. Another he held up, briefly, was *Casablanca,* fearing that the picture's setting in German-controlled Morocco might evoke strong political reactions in France, and worried even that Bogart's character of Rick might be a touch too cynical about the war.

The "Projection of America" effort was, both in terms of fulfilling its charter and the reception the films received, a resounding success. Neverthe-

Riskin and Fay in their New York apartment, 1942

less, in 1943, without warning, a dark cloud rose over the OWI, threatening the entire operation.

Several conservative congressmen, fearing the Office of War Information could be used as a propaganda tool in the hands of a liberal president seeking an unprecedented fourth term, and especially because it showed how good things were under Roosevelt, determined to shut down the OWI. Elmer Davis and Robert Sherwood were called before a congressional hearing where Representative John Taber (R., N.Y.) called the OWI a "haven of refuge for derelicts." Another congressman said he was outraged that OWI writers, in addition to being radicals, were earning far too much. He cited as a particularly offensive example my father, who was being paid by the government the exorbitant salary of $8,000 a year when in civilian life, one news account said, his salary had been $2,000. How could he possibly justify that?

Sherwood corrected the Congressman politely. Two thousand dollars had been Riskin's *weekly* salary in Hollywood, he said.

The proceedings were demoralizing for Sherwood, and especially for Elmer Davis and his domestic operation, where Davis had invested his personal passion. President Roosevelt, who picked his political battles with Congress carefully, chose not to intervene on the OWI's behalf, and after the hearings the budget for the Domestic Branch was slashed from $1.5 million to $50,000. Davis said that the money left for his domestic division was enough to avoid "the odium of having to put us out of business and carefully not enough to let us accomplish much."

Remarkably, the Overseas Branch was left unscathed in the budget battle. It even grew in influence, with my father now managing the relationship between Washington and Hollywood, a role that seems to have required artful diplomacy and the nerves of a gambler.

He was tested early and often. When he presented a plan by which the OWI would manage distribution of all motion pictures in formerly Nazi-controlled, now-liberated countries, the foreign sales executives of the studios rebelled in unison. Let the government control our sales business? Never! My father called an emergency meeting with the sales executives in New York and explained, again, that for the present the important effect of the films on liberated people trumped the studio's commercial wishes. The OWI would therefore handle film distribution, which would at some appropriate time be handed back to company sales representatives. When they still balked, he threatened to go over their heads to their bosses, and the discussion was over.

Fay and Bob welcome
Robert Riskin Jr. into
the world, July 1943.

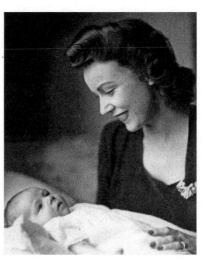

• • •

By spring 1943, my mother was five months pregnant. She wrote later, "What a delight to see my husband as happy as I was . . . Our mutual eagerness gave me a feeling of tranquility, the first I had ever known." On July 3, she delivered a boy, Robert Jr., whose arrival seemed nothing short of a miracle to my forty-six-year-old father.

Anticipating Bobby's birth, my parents had moved into a larger apartment at the Ritz Towers at Fifty-seventh Street and Park Avenue, where they lived for the rest of the war. My mother remembered how she looked out the window from the sixteenth floor as my father strode up Fifty-seventh Street to work. "Hands in the pockets of his overcoat, he went swiftly along, heels coming down first. The style and pace with which he walked had intent—and goodness. He always wore a hat. Later, we would learn that both he and Robert Sherwood scored well with investigators on that account for it was thought that communists never wore hats."

Their apartment became a stop for friends going overseas, seeking my father's guidance. Edward G. Robinson and Spencer Tracy were regular visitors. Writer John Gunther lived at 530 Park Avenue and invited them for delicatessen and conversation.

My father knew he had to go overseas to personally manage distribution of the OWI and Hollywood films and coordinate with the British Ministry of Information. He hated to be away from my mother and their new baby but was sure he would be gone no more than six weeks. Before leaving, he asked the Hollywood unions to recruit their writers, directors, editors, and actors for his films; hundreds immediately offered their services. He also asked the studios to recommend experienced people who could oversee operations and remain involved after the OWI turned distribution back to them. He took his government physical examination and vaccinations. At the last minute, his trip was delayed.

One cloud had vanished. Another appeared.

He was summoned by the Civil Service Commission to a hearing to approve him as bureau chief. The hearing, which took place in the fall of 1943, after he had been on the job for a year, was an unsettling warning of what lay ahead for the motion picture industry.

From the official transcript:

HENRY S. BECKWITH, INVESTIGATOR:

Mr. Riskin, the purpose of this interview is to allow you an opportunity to answer questions concerning information which has been received by the Civil Service Commission about alleged activities on your part. During this discussion, you are invited to make any statements of your own regarding information to be discussed which will fairly present your side of the question. A report of this interview will be recorded and upon your request a copy will be furnished you.

In the course of conducting an investigation as to your character and qualifications for the position of Chief, Motion Picture Bureau, Office of War Information, a number of matters were revealed which I should like to present to you at this time in order that a report of your answers to these questions may be made and presented to the Commission for consideration in determining your case.

After my father took the oath and gave his name, address, and birthdate, the investigator proceeded:

QUESTION: The Commission has been informed that you were a member of the Hollywood Anti-Nazi League. Inasmuch as this was a communist-dominated and controlled organization, the Commission would like an explanation.

ANSWER: I was never a member of the Hollywood Anti-Nazi League.

QUESTION: The Commission has been informed that you were active in the Screen Writers Guild. We have also been informed that this was a communist-dominated group. Do you care to explain?

ANSWER: Any statement that the Screen Writers Guild is a communist or communist-dominated organization is malicious. I am a member.

The investigator bore on, about my father's communist friends—he had none, he said—and the woman he had lived with, Edith Fitzgerald, to whom he was not married. My father answered it was "a personal matter which I don't care to go into." The investigator continued, personal and political question after question.

Should the inquisition have been so surprising? Governmental anti-communist investigations of Hollywood had begun in 1938, when the House Committee on Un-American Activities (HUAC) under Texas congressman Martin Dies Jr. had focused on alleged communist infiltration of the film business, asserting that the unions and the Hollywood Anti-Nazi League were under the control of the Communist Party. The Civil Service Commission was following their lead.

The Anti-Nazi League had been founded in 1936 in Hollywood by well-known Republicans and Democrats to raise awareness of Hitler and the rise of Nazism in Europe. Now, because to be anti–Nazi Germany was equated by some as being pro–communist Russia, its members faced obstacles in getting wartime government jobs.

My father made it through the hearings intact and at the end of November was cleared for departure, but the experience left a chill. It was a harbinger of worse to come.

Finally, he was on his way to Europe on his six-week trip. His travel papers read "Confidential War Mission" and his identity card gave him the rank of "Assimilated Colonel," giving him the privileges of a military officer. The press reported he would visit OWI offices in London, North Africa, and the Italian war zone, which especially worried my mother. She accompanied him to the airfield to say good-bye. He flew from New York to Montreal where, after a layover, he boarded a Liberator bomber for London.

She wrote him the next morning:

> My darling . . . The day [yesterday] was so beautiful. My heart had wings as I watched you off. I don't suppose you could see us on the edge of the field. The protest about our going out was just mild enough to seem perfunctory so out we went . . . One ear has been listening for the telephone all evening. You might be able to phone. But the evening's practically gone—So I wonder. I wonder where

you may be. Wherever you are, my love is wrapped around you . . .
Still no word so I suppose it means you've left. All my thoughts are
with you. Our first separation—while I am thrilled for you I feel a
gnawing hunger for you . . . I have kissed and kissed Bobby for you.
(He seems to enjoy it.) He is such a radiant baby . . . Remember to
take good care of my beloved. All my heart. I adore you. Fay

It would be a long time before they saw each other again. His six-week
trip, the first separation in their marriage, would last six months.

14

I love you simply, without problems or pride: I love you in this way because I don't know any other way of loving.

—PABLO NERUDA

Press reports said the Liberator bomber with famed Hollywood personality Robert Riskin on board had broken a transatlantic speed record. "Mr. Deeds is Here," said the *London Evening Standard. The Hollywood Reporter* wrote from London, "Funny about Bob Riskin; when he was here two years ago he got an honorable mention in the papers and not much more, but today, when newsprint is even more scarce, he is simply grabbing up space hand over fist; not that he needs or wants it." A reporter showed up at his room at Claridge's and wrote, "There is something of Mr. Deeds about him—a touch of shyness, an inquiring expression, a faintly hesitant smile." My father had never sought publicity in Hollywood, but understood its value on behalf of his OWI mission—public support of the project, the Allied partnership, Hollywood's cooperation; all were critical, and during the war he gave interviews readily.

My parents corresponded through V-mail (short for Victory mail) and telegrams. They worried their almost daily letters might not reach each other and asked friends about to cross the ocean to carry a quick written message. In one letter, my father complained about his friend Captain Irving Berlin: "I asked him to stop by my room on his way out to say goodbye . . . He said he would. I rushed upstairs and quickly wrote you a note for him to take. The rat ducked out and never stopped in." Phone calls were cherished and rare; connections were unreliable and rates were exorbitant, with 25 percent excise tax added.

My father's tiny hard-to-read script is even harder to read on the shrunken V-mail. Every letter went through an elaborate process to lessen

Riskin leaving for Europe in fall 1943 to arrange distribution of the OWI
and Hollywood feature films. His headquarters were in London, where
Hollywood and British press regularly covered his activities.

the weight of the hundreds of thousands of letters soldiers sent home
every day. After a letter was cleared by a censor, it was photographed onto
microfilm, shrunk to postage-stamp size, and blown up again to 60 percent of its original size after the letter arrived in the U.S.

At first my father wrote of spending "most of the time with the boys at
the office . . . so that except for it being colder and damper, I might as well
be in the Fisk Building [his New York office]." He worried about Bobby
and Susan. He knew Susan had a suspicion that something was different
when he left, "that my leaving was no normal departure to London. By
now she has bombarded you with inquiries—and has learned the truth."

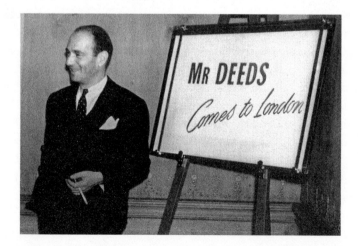

My mother wrote:

It seems strange to only imagine what you're doing and not to know at all, not to have you come home and tell me a fragment or two. When you do come home, now you will have to do your trip all over again just for me—only I'll be able to reach out and hold on to you! I love you, Bob. I love you. Goodnight.

With each letter, he found a new way to say, "I love you," to reassure her, while also telling of life in London with the war as backdrop.

Love darling,

First off, I love you. Well, for the rest of the "offs," I love you, too—so let's not go any further with that. I must stop talking about you. I'm getting to be a bore. I haven't seen that awful look on people's eyes yet—but it's bound to appear soon—(if it hasn't already—and been politely concealed). You know, that fixed expression that struggles to evoke interest but actually says, "God, there he goes again . . ."

We had an alert the other night. My first one since arrival— they didn't wait long to welcome me. It was a short one—and not particularly important (that's awful to say. I hope no one was hurt. How can a raid NOT be important?) What I mean is, in comparison to other raids this was a minor one.

First there was the siren—followed by a long, long silence—then some booming in the distance—more silence—finally very close-by, the sirens went off—but only for a few minutes . . . I considered doing something about it—downstairs—to find out where the shelter was—no perhaps I better phone—now, that's silly, no one does anything about alerts nowadays. Besides, it's very quiet—probably a false alarm. Oh-oh. What's that boom noise! Maybe I better get stirring—one can always stroll down into the lobby and appear very casual—give you a chance to just sort of look around—and see what's what—Boom! That's quite a distance away—hardly heard that last one. Silly to go dashing around the hotel. Listen. Can't hear it anymore. Silence. More silence. Long, long silence. How's about a letter to Fay? Good idea. Better take a drink first. That's it—make it a double—trickle—trickle . . .

Crack! Say, that's mighty close. Run to the window—might be some fireworks in the sky! Gosh, no! Standing by a window is stupid!

Get away from the glass! Hit the ground—that's the thing to do—
that's the way to avoid being hit by shrapnel.

By the time you make up your mind, it is silent again—and you
think, "oh, what the hell"—You sit back and review how ludicrously
you are behaving—and lo the all clear is on. That's all . . . All my love
my precious darling.

In London, to foster distribution of Hollywood and OWI films and to
fortify the OWI's relationship with the British film industry, he coordi-
nated with top brass at the Ministry of Information and especially their
key film advisor, Sidney Bernstein. Bernstein was a successful impresario,
cinema entrepreneur, and film producer, a towering figure with a vibrant
personality. He had produced the influential film *London Can Take It* for
the Ministry of Information.

They had first met in 1936, when Bernstein came to Hollywood to warn
the film community about the danger Jews were facing in Germany. The
two men had liked each other instantly.

When my father arrived in London, Bernstein sent my mother a
telegram—"Bob looks wonderful and arrived with bounty for which Zoe
[Bernstein's wife] says thank you. Family well exhibited on hotel mantel-
piece. Everybody including Bob I think wishes you were here."

Sidney invited my father to his country farm in Kent for a weekend
of fine food, good conversation, and work. They quickly agreed to work
together to create joint British-American documentary teams for the bal-
ance of the war.

My father wrote:

> My Beloved:
>
> I was out to Coppings yesterday—Sid's farm—it was heavenly—
> a penetratingly cold day—I walked for hours, but the joy of thawing
> out in front of a fireplace made all discomfort pleasurable . . .
> We talked about you a great deal—that is, I did. It brought you
> close—I could feel you all day—you hovered about and filled me
> with your warmth and love and I was peaceful. In the evening Sidney
> and I walked in the blackness—it was a moonless, starless night. We
> could see nothing and only sensed the side of the road. Yet we walked
> briskly and with confidence—and talked of many things. Now and
> again I would glance up—and receiving a shock when I realized I
> could not see him. His voice went on—I could hear the sound of his
> footsteps and feel his presence—but could see nothing. At first, the

effect was eerie and unnatural—but eventually one gets used to it—
gets used to holding a conversation with a moving body—with the
sound of footsteps on gravel . . .

You want to know something? Your letter brought a smell with
it. I shut my eyes and smell you and Bobby and the waves from the
kitchen—and Susan's hand when I kiss it in our play-acting. Funny,
that I should have to shut my eyes to recapture a "smell"—but
somehow, it seems necessary—it seems the only way it can be done.
And the smells are sharp and distinct and they differ so. Yours is
indescribable—pungent and sweet and intoxicating all at one time.

I resolved never to indulge any of the "clichés" about the censor,
but I am about to do so . . . Officers often have to censor the
mail of their enlisted men—and this friend of mine spoke of the
embarrassment it sometimes causes—knowing the writer of the letter
they censor. In any event, he spoke of reading such things as "I wish I
could feel your cold toes in bed again."

I was rather touched by this—as unpretty as this picture might
seem when it concerns someone else—the yearning of this GI—the
yearning for "those cold toes"—is the yearning of every man who
longs for his woman—his own bed, his own home—his castle. The
"cold toes" is a symbol of the closest tie between man and his wife—
of all barriers having vanished—of a oneness having manifested itself.
It is an eloquent expression of permanence and security—and so, I,
too—my darling sweetheart, long for your "cold toes" or to get closer
to the truth, I long to warm my cold toes against you . . .

My heart is yours, my lovely, darling Fay—Embrace our babies for
me. I love being your husband.—Bob

Her letters to him were loving accounts of missing him, filled with
details of everyday life—ration cards, celebrity trips to sell war bonds,
strolls in Central Park with Bobby in his pram and Susan holding Deeds's
leash, Christmas without him. She told him about the children's new British nanny, Miss Haesloop, who in Susan's mind was no replacement for
Bea, who decided to stay in Charlottesville near her family who needed
her. She retold Susan's made-up tales of suspense and action, of her
invented villain, the Black Coyote, and Bobby's repertoire of laughter,
squealing and crawling.

I go in to look at him and his big merry eyes look up at me in
the half-darkness and he gives me a warm little grin. Lately he's been
trying out a new kind of vocalizing—a high squeal or squeak. It

surprised me so. He likes it I think, likes the discovery of range in his voice and practices ever so much . . .

Well—Susan got an idea! (I took her to see the Trapp Family Singers and they sang carols carrying lanterns.) She thought I should wake her up Christmas morning by singing and carrying a candle. Then she would light a candle and sing too—then Miss Haesloop would do the same and so we would all go singing in to see the tree. Well, we did it and it worked beautifully. Her only complaint (and God knows mine) was that you should have been here to lead me singing . . .

For an hour today I went to NBC to watch the photographing of Toscanini. I was like a real "fan." It was stimulating to have him pace up and down not four feet away from me. I am eager to see the finished film. His cooperation will undoubtedly make an historical film.

My darling Bob I love you so. It was wonderful to walk with you and Sidney in the blackness . . . to know—oh how lovely—that you haven't changed your custom of tucking yourself into bed early evening. This made my heart sing. Cold toes! I will keep your toes and your heart warm. I will cherish your toes! You give me more beauty than I dreamed of—and I'm a dreamer. I love you. I adore you. Fay

He wrote her virtually every day, sometimes more than once a day, letters of ten, fifteen, twenty pages written in his hotel room at the Savoy surrounded by pictures of her and Bobby and Susan, pouring out his heart and feelings after fourteen-hour workdays. He may have been unique among Americans in London, many of whom found things to do at night that did not involve staying in and writing letters to Stateside wives. As the British complaint of the time went, "There are only three things wrong with the Americans. They are overpaid, oversexed, and over here."

As my father headed into war zones, his letters were less frequent, his whereabouts a military secret. Short notes hinted he had been in Algiers and Naples. Any period of silence worried my mother terribly. He was reported shot down in Algiers; it turned out he had only missed plane connections.

By 1943, Allied forces had gone on from North Africa to Sicily and then southern Italy, beginning the northward advance to Rome. The OWI team followed close behind, with seven mobile units operating immediately behind the front lines, moving into towns and villages the moment they were secure.

My father went with the mobile teams. For the fullest impact, speed was essential. Whole villages came out to see the films, which were morale boosters for populations still living in chaos. Admission was free. Many movie houses had been destroyed or damaged, with technical equipment missing, so the OWI brought with them projectors, screens, and spare parts, and engineers and technicians from RCA and Western Electric to repair the damage and hook up mobile generators to overcome the frequent power outages. One observer wrote, "Riskin knew time was of the essence and wanted to convey to liberated people at the very moment their freedom was being handed back to them, the sorts of ideals and the kind of lifestyle they could aspire to in a postwar world."

He returned to London in March 1944 and wrote my mother a sixteen-page letter full of pent-up emotion and observations about people and war, expressing his concern that the news of London bombings must frighten her. The "air is charged—momentous things may happen," he tells her, hinting at D-Day, although details were still unknown to him and everyone else.

March 12, 1944

My Angel, my baby, my sweetheart, my lovely, lovely wife—my reason for existence:

I haven't written you in an eternity and just wired you to that effect. Each day I would start to write and then retreat from the idea, thinking how silly—it's a matter of days . . .

I want so to be honest with you—not to give you a false impression—not to lift your hopes—yet not to unnecessarily dampen them. And to be completely honest the excitement is here—the air is charged—momentous things may happen—when? One can only guess. But, there is you—there is my beautiful family—pulling at my insides, leaning heavy on my heart—leaving me weak and lonely— unable to thrill at impending events—robbing me of the excitement my participation should give me . . .

Every time a raid starts, I think of you sitting at the radio listening to Ed Murrow describe it vividly—I see your face cloud—I see your imagination fired—I see you seeing me buried in a mass of rubble. I want to rush to a phone to tell you immediately I am whole and unhurt and not to worry and how much I love you for worrying . . . I lean back and think hard about you—until your dear, adorable face is clearly before me—and I say comforting things to you—and

I actually see your face relax and almost always you break out in a smile—an uncertain, half-comforted, nervous smile. But I do manage to break the tension. And as I lie in the darkness looking up at you and the sirens go off—with each burst you wince—and terror comes into your eyes again. Each time I look sharply at you, critically, and the nervous smile returns. And so I spend my time during a raid— Surely you must hear and feel me, my beloved.

Given the week or so of persistent raids . . . I learned something of the secret of why the British were so stoical—well, anyway <u>one</u> of the reasons. It's an injustice to the British, but a theory of mine which I will tell you about.

Actually, a great many people enjoyed the raids. Certainly the danger was there—the ever-present imminence of your own destruction—but something else was there—company. It is difficult to be lonely when you are sharing a common danger with people all about you.

I found after the first few days that I was disappointed when the alert failed to sound. I was alone in my room—removed from the world around me when nothing happened—but the moment the siren started, I was no longer alone—thousands—millions of other hearts stirred simultaneously—skipped a beat just as mine skipped— at this moment, they were in the room with me—and I was with them in a million homes in a million cellars.

At times like that—no matter how impoverished you might feel—in worldly goods or in the spirit—you are lifted to a level of equality with the most blessed of human beings. Envy of another's riches—fear through insecurity—a floundering ego—all vanish. For one moment, you are the equal of the most courageous—for one moment, the brains, the genius, the gifts—the accumulated wealth, the high positions of the mightiest disappear—and all are one—of which you are an equal part.

What a blessing this must have been to the lonely.

Think of how many sad, frustrated lives were revivified in the cellars—the subways and the shelters of Britain. People who found they weren't quite so inhibited as they thought. Words, thoughts, anecdotes poured forth. No wonder that, even when the raids stopped in 1941—humans, thousands, continued to sleep in shelters. They had inherited new families, new interests and were loath to part with them. It was so different to go back to that lonely existence . . .

His letter goes on at length about a colleague whom he likes personally but is troubled because he is:

a difficult man to know—or rather he is easy to know if he is not taken seriously. In that case—he is a simple, good, sentimental, warmhearted soul. The moment he begins to express ideas— he becomes confusing. The trouble mostly is: he is a sensitive instrument—all ideas strike a note and he has room for the whole scale . . . He is steadfast in his defense of and devotion to certain individuals out of gratitude and sentiment. In those instances, he is completely blinded to their faults . . .

I dwell on this . . . only because here is a strong vital example of what most people are. True, deep-rooted convictions are rare. They see wisdom in many ideas—conflicting ideas—their hearts and their minds leap from one concept to another. In an era of chaos—in times like these—when all the theories of social forms and changes—when every concept of economic, political and spiritual existence is dusted off and paraded before the hard-ridden masses of the world, it is no wonder that John Q Public is straddling the fence—it is no wonder he is punch-drunk and unable to assert himself. Where is that idea? Where is that big, unchallengeable, fundamentally unshakable idea, which snaps John Doe sharply out of his binge and about which he says, "now that's what I mean—that's what I've waited for—that's what I <u>stand</u> for—and the rest is bilge." Will that idea come in time to save us? I, personally, believe it will. Perhaps not in this generation, or even the next—but come it must.

I tried to say something of this sort in "Meet John Doe" and it is interesting to note (as I think, you and I have noted before) the number of books on religion which are successful in wartime. You see, people need "goodness" to lean on in times of wickedness and evil. They need to remind themselves that the human race of which they are a part, is not all evil—that its impulses are virtuous and charitable and unselfish. They need this for they cannot look upon themselves as wicked. No person except for rare pathological cases, thinks of himself as anything but a good, decent, honest human being . . .

I mustn't go on, my dearest, dearest Fay. I could, of course, but it is teatime and I didn't have lunch. I am starved. If the flesh were willing, I would sit here and scribble to you for hours and hours and would just pour out anything and everything that came to mind . . .

How I have grown since I met you. How happy you have made me.—Bob

It was another long month before my father came home. Word of his imminent return was carried in the New York *Daily News*—"Robert Riskin, who heads the OWI's overseas film set-up, will be back on Broadway from London in 10 days or so" and confirmed by a telegram he sent on Bobby's "ninth month birthday"; for a long time my parents celebrated his birth monthly.

DEAR BOBBY HAPPY NINTH BIRTHDAY TELL MOTHER I'LL BE HOME SOONER THAN EXPECTED TELL HER I LOVE HER VERY VERY DEEPLY AND JUST CAN'T WAIT TO SEE HER AND YOU AND SUSAN YOUR DADDY.

Excitement filled the apartment at Fifty-seventh and Park like air and sunlight. Susan told my mother news of her daddy's return made her feel "all twitchy." With her vivid imagination, she had conjured up all the frightening things the evil people might be doing to him overseas. She was also convinced German spies were everywhere in New York, even taxi drivers, and window washers peeking into everyone's apartment. She jumped up and down and then into his arms when he walked into the apartment, Bobby greeted him with a repertoire of his new words, including "dada."

My father resumed his long days at the OWI offices, writing and supervising scripts, giving shape and direction to the films, viewing rushes. He needed more staff and went to Hollywood on a recruiting trip, taking my mother. *The Hollywood Reporter* described him on his arrival as "bubbling with enthusiasm, and squinting in all directions for writers, cutters, editors, and other film technicians—to dispatch to his New York and London production units to make documentaries, especially for Germany, 'emphasizing the democratic way of life.'" He hoped the studios might help his Projection of America series expand by producing similar films themselves. "There are 12 such pictures we have in mind," Riskin said.

He also told the press about opening theaters in just-liberated territories. He said he had been apprehensive about the audience's response to Charlie Chaplin's *The Great Dictator*, with its vivid mockery of Hitler, still wreaking horrors without end throughout Europe, "but the reaction was almost embarrassingly enthusiastic." He also reported, "The crowds are large, for Hollywood is famous. Even in the desert 12,000 Arabs attended a showing." He pleased the moguls by committing publicly to return distribution of feature films to the studios as quickly as possible. He was able to tell them that the appetite for American films had remained as strong as ever and it was not long before the industry would again be reaping overseas profits.

In Los Angeles, my father screened four of the Projection films at the Academy of Motion Picture Arts and Sciences. Virginia Wright, drama critic of the *Los Angeles Daily News,* said she wished American audiences could see these films because "we liberated peoples could stand a little propagandizing about ourselves." Bosley Crowther of *The New York Times* described the Toscanini film as "the brilliant display of the glorious spiritual freedom, so exquisitely devoted by one man and, with him, by a musical company to the entertainment and inspiration of all . . . [It] is a tribute to American democracy and to the opportunity which Toscanini has found here." Crowther went on to praise the entire Projection series. "They narrate their story simply in a straight reportorial style. Nobody harangues or lectures; there are no fifes or kettledrums—and this, according to Mr. Riskin, is by very careful design."

Being back in Hollywood meant reconnecting with Pops, Everett, Murray, and Rose, my mother's brothers, Victor and Dick, her sister, Willow, Flo and Jo Swerling, and proudly showing them all pictures of Bobby. Irene Selznick threw a party in their honor. Loretta Young lent my mother an evening gown for an Oscar gala at Chasen's restaurant.

Before returning to New York, my father met with the leadership of the Hollywood Writers Mobilization, a group of more than 3,500 screen and radio writers, lyricists, and cartoonists who had dedicated themselves to informing the public as to what the war was about. He asked them to establish a committee of top writers to ensure "expert scripts" for his next OWI films. A month later Philip Dunne came to town to work with the committee that now included Sidney Buchman, Charles Brackett, John Howard Lawson, John Houseman, Marc Connolly, Robert Rossen, and others of similar top credentials. Dunne told the press, "Through these films we intend to tell the truth to people who have not had the truth for several years. It has been crudely expressed that we want to sell America. What we really want is to sell the ideals that make America what it is."

When they returned to New York my father, who had not had a day off in over a year, collapsed from exhaustion and my mother ordered him to bed to rest.

• • •

The first week of June 1944 marked a dramatic turning point in the war. Allied Forces landed in Normandy in the largest seaborne invasion in history, and also took Rome. My father sent fifty Hollywood and OWI films, already subtitled, with the invasion forces, where they were shown immediately to the people of liberated towns and cities. In Normandy, the French population was enjoying new American films ten days after D-Day. By September he was able to announce that 4,000 theatres had been opened in Italy, where American movies were seen for the first time in five years.

He did not have time to enjoy the comforts of home. He was needed urgently in London and Paris where he was to lay the groundwork for the new British-American newsreel teams to work cooperatively with the governments of Norway, Holland, Belgium, Denmark, and France.

Before flying to London, he spent two days alone with my mother in Montreal. After watching his plane take off, she flew back to New York. She wrote him as soon as she arrived home.

> There was a sweet and glowing comfort in knowing that we were
> both in the air and I blessed the sky and the good warm sun and
> the cottony clouds . . . and through all the details of the day loved
> you with all my heart. I feel slightly sawed in half with you gone but
> happy beyond description that I love you. Yours, Fay.

She was eager to play her own part in the war effort, which in her case meant helping Roosevelt get reelected. She left home the next day to campaign for him throughout the northeast, giving speeches in Rochester, Boston, Troy, Syracuse, Schenectady, at Vassar College in Poughkeepsie, with numerous quick stops along the way—frequently in the territory of Roosevelt's opponent, Governor Thomas E. Dewey of New York. Roosevelt was a popular president who had already served longer than any in history, but stories of his failing health were circulating and for a time it seemed his chance for a fourth term was in jeopardy. Early October polls were razor-thin: Roosevelt 48 percent, Dewey 47 percent.

She had never been especially political, other than routinely voting Democratic, but she saw in the president an infectious optimism and a caring about people that inspired her. Philip Dunne, who was now also her close friend, shaped her speeches to give them "a personal quality— just the right thing to say," she wrote my father. After one day in which she gave two long speeches, she wrote, "I don't like being away from home, but I do like the reaction to the speeches and looking out at thousands who are on the right track. At the rallies, countless people were turned away."

At times she spoke to the enormous crowds standing with Vice President Henry Wallace or Senator Robert F. Wagner. After a small gathering in a Republican stronghold, she wrote, "I think we did some good! . . . It's hectic pre–Nov. 7th—but wherever I go I take you with me and I know the things we both believe in *will* win out! I love you my dearest darling."

On election eve she joined a radio broadcast produced by Norman Corwin and hosted by Humphrey Bogart for the Democratic National Committee, featuring undoubtedly the greatest cast in radio history: Judy Garland, James Cagney, Keenan Wynn, Groucho Marx, Claudette Colbert, Irving Berlin, Joseph Cotten, Tallulah Bankhead, Rita Hayworth, Walter Huston, Gene Kelly, Danny Kaye, Paul Muni, Edward G. Robinson, Lana Turner, Dorothy Parker, Charles Boyer, the Ink Spots, Milton Berle, Frank Sinatra, and President Roosevelt himself. My father cabled her:

MY BEAUTIFUL HAPPY ELECTION DAY DON'T WORRY SWEET I
DON'T THINK THE AMERICAN PEOPLE INTEND TO GO BACKWARD
I LOVE YOU WITH ALL MY HEART. —BOB

She wrote him later that evening:

My darling—

Ten minutes to twelve election night: (Wednesday morning for you). I'm in bed, both radios on. It all sounds closer than I hoped, yet there seems to be no questioning that Roosevelt will win. Counting on a landslide for a real vote of confidence I am disturbed at the strength in the Dewey vote. Just now the radio says the N.Y. Daily News has confirmed Roosevelt's re-election! 12:00 a.m.—54.7 for Roosevelt. I wish it were 75 percent. It may yet be! Do I want too much? How I wish my darling that you were here! How I wish I were sharing this moment with you! In a real sense I am. I am, as sure as shooting right beside you. The N.Y. Times has a beam light pointing due north—a signal of Roosevelt's re-election. The Herald Tribune has just conceded. It suddenly sounds like a landslide. Now Dewey says he is <u>not</u> conceding! Roosevelt leading 55.4 of popular vote. Does this give you some picture of my election night?

Your exquisite flowers and beautiful note were so reassuring this morning. How can America miss? I love you with all my heart. Tomorrow will be a great day for you and Susan and Bobby and me. I feel very sleepy, very happy. Goodnight love, Fay

Fay, who campaigned for the reelection of FDR and spoke at war bond drives across the Northeast, is seen here with a wounded soldier.

My father wrote back about the hope Roosevelt's victory gave him for a brighter future.

> The future seems more secure. Raising children doesn't seem the hazard it used to be—some of the speculation is gone—perhaps we can hand them a world with brighter prospects—perhaps there will be obliterated the insufferable inhumanity to man. I have often wondered about Susan and Bobby—and was not very jubilant over what confronted them. I feel better now.

With American soldiers now fighting in Italy and France, the war had turned in favor of the Allies, but victory must have still felt a long way off in England, where he was working with Sidney Bernstein and the British Ministry of Information. Hitler had launched the V-2 rocket, the world's first liquid-fueled ballistic missile, which flew silently and landed without warning. Five hundred hit London, causing thousands of deaths and untold destruction.

But victory was in the air, with spirits increasingly buoyant. When not making or supervising his OWI films, my father never missed an opportunity to build bridges with our closest ally, telling the British press how much Americans admired British documentary filmmaking like *London Can Take It,* from which American filmmakers had learned much, and still had much to learn. He dined regularly with good friends like Bernstein, Bill Paley, and William Wyler, the director who had begun his career making silent movies, some with my mother. In the past two years, Wyler, working with the U.S. Army Air Forces, had made some of the war's finest documentaries, including *The Memphis Belle, Thunderbolt,* and, with Edward Steichen, *The Fighting Lady.*

In August came the long-anticipated and much-prayed-for liberation of Paris. As Allied and Free French Forces troops reached the suburbs, wildly enthusiastic civilians showered them with flowers, kisses, and wine. Charles de Gaulle, who had led the French government in exile from London during the war, led a triumphant march down the Champs-Élysées and would soon proclaim a new government in France, establishing control over the extremely fractious population.

When my father arrived in Paris two months later, he found the atmosphere far from jubilant. Sitting in the Place de l'Opéra, across the street from the famous Café de la Paix, he wrote my mother:

> Paris is not as gay as some correspondents have described for the folks back home. They must have seen it from the American Bar. There is a feeling of unrest here—of pending political and economic chaos. The future of France is unpredictable—many conflicting forces are at work. All groups suspect all other groups. Collaborationists haven't begun to be ferreted out and treated with. The government seems to have a policy of moving slowly and carefully. Only the very extreme cases have been dealt with—the cases where there was no room for doubt. The hundreds and thousands of others who collaborated with the Germans—who accumulated fortunes in profiteering—who were obvious Nazi sympathizers—they are still scot free and untouched. Naturally the FFI [French underground] and the maquis [the resistance] and the masses of people who remained loyal—resent the placid inactivity of the government. I understand that in the South of France, the culprits are disposed of quickly but here in Paris and in the north—it is shameful. Investigations will take place, of course, and hearings will be held to quiet the protests—but there is no sign of summary action contemplated . . . Hold yourself in readiness for my great love for you. It won't be long.

In Paris, he generally ate with soldiers in the army mess and only on rare occasions dined with friends like Noël Coward. He was uncomfortable in elegant restaurants while so many Parisians were suffering. He did take advantage of Bill Paley's suite at the Hotel George V and allowed himself a half-hour soak in a luxurious tub—"a delightful event," he told my mother.

This would be his last real comfort for a while. He traveled to Luxembourg, Belgium, and the Netherlands, where the war still raged. In Luxembourg, the Germans had only weeks earlier been driven from the place he now went, and were still just eight miles away. His OWI team set up a screening of *Autobiography of a "Jeep"* and *The Town*, which he said audiences found "delightful." He went to Belgium in a weapons carrier that was "rough riding but better than a limousine, the way it hugs the road." He opened theaters and searched for locals who could get projectors running. "Brussels was gayer than Paris," he said, but also politically in turmoil, with rumors that a coup d'état was imminent. Fortunately, my mother had no inkling that in a few days Hitler would make his final major assault, the Battle of the Bulge, in the Ardennes where my father was working.

He moved on to Holland and jotted down quick impressions in his small notebook:

> Nemours—Bridge blown up by Germans.
> Americans crawled up hill to citadel.
> One way down—fought Germans on street.
> Owner of café stood in doorway.
> 4 Americans killed in front of door.
> Red Cross nurse came to help.
> Prisoners of war work on road guarded by Negro troops.
> Walked 1 hour hunting Dutch Minister of Information.
> No success.
> Taken to ballet.
> Small front room.
> Landlady asked would I mind not returning until children's party was over.
> Wooden shoes are put out with carrot for St. Nick's horse and gifts. Each morning children race to see what St. Nick left—might only be a bar of chocolate.
> Place just been liberated—houses demolished—half starving—fighting within 30 miles.
> It's a sad Saint Nick eve.
> Yet they tried. Sad undernourished children coming to puppet show at Dutch Military Mission.
> Church bells playing Dutch, British, American national anthems.
> Sewanee River.
> Boy in whose house town mayor was—lived underground for 3½ years—on farm—built headquarters under farm.

Shortly after D-Day in northern France, children in bombed-out towns see *Autobiography of a "Jeep"* and fill the makeshift theater with shouts of *"Vive le Jeep!"* Riskin posted on his OWI office wall the photo of the children watching.

German Camp—30,000 Dutch, 10,000 killed.

4 theaters—two destroyed. One we arranged to open the following week. Current allowed 1–3 PM. Owner in Concentration Camp. Whole family taken.

Sign on road, "Hitler secret weapons—V1, V2 and VD."

My mother was unsure where he was—"Are you in Brussels?"—or where to write him—"I sent letters to both Paris and London"—or whether he was safe and taking care of himself. "Don't forget your overcoat." She tried not to impose her fears or worries on him. In Belgium, he had tried to

The overseas Motion Picture Branch sent truckloads of films, following close behind Eisenhower and the U.S. Army in November 1942, as they liberated North Africa, Sicily, Italy, Belgium, France, and finally entered Fortress Germany. Riskin believed that if people loved American movies, they'd grow to love America's values.

write her, but the battered typewriter he borrowed rendered phrases like "Now is the time" into "Boz is the tibs." The censors presumed it was code and the letter reached her only months later.

When he finally surfaced again in Paris in December, he sent her a dozen roses—he always sent roses—and she reported she felt giddy as a schoolgirl. "Happy days are beginning. It was so wonderful to know that you were back in Paris, and that you would soon be in London. Surely another short while will have you starting for home!" The December issue of *Le Film Français* announced a reception for Monsieur Riskin, Head of Cinema for the American Ministry of Information. (Translated, the caption under the accompanying photograph read, "M. Riskin is one of the most remarkable individuals in American film.") While there, he met with leading members of the French film industry to reestablish relationships between the American and French film communities.

His work in Paris took longer than planned and by the time he returned to London, he had to write my mother of his deep disappointment that he would miss another family Christmas.

> DARLING I KNOW IT'S AN OCEAN BETWEEN US CHRISTMAS CANNOT BE SO TERRIBLY MERRY BUT DOES IT HELP TO KNOW I LOVE YOU WITH ALL MY HEART AND LONG FOR YOU AND OUR ADORABLE BABIES. BOB

He made a final entry in his notebook the day of his departure from London:

> Left London 12/26/44
> Ate at GI mess in Prestwick. "Happy Warriors waiting order for home. Men who have completed their missions."

He was destined never to see Europe again.

As dramatically and quickly as the OWI had come together in 1942, it would just as quickly unwind.

By early 1945, with victory over Hitler in view, the overseas film operation started to be phased out. No new projects were planned. My father and Philip Dunne faced the personally difficult task of releasing their writers, directors, and editors and shuttering the operation. Dunne stayed on a while longer than my father, coming to California to complete work on *Attack at Sea*. In anticipation of the battles to come, President Roosevelt had personally requested an exposé about the origins of the conflicts, highlighting the ruthlessness of the military leaders ruling Japan.

In May, Nazi Germany surrendered unconditionally. President Roosevelt did not live to see the victory, having died of a massive cerebral hemorrhage on April 12 at his Little White House in Warm Springs, Georgia. The shock of his death was felt by millions of Americans, including my parents, who talked of the chill they both felt and the grief of losing someone they loved as a father.

In mid-April 1945, my father formally submitted his resignation to the OWI. He had always said he would stay through the end of the war, but there was nothing creative left to do. Now the job entailed only postproduction administration and shuttering the operation. He deputized documentary filmmaker Irving Lerner to finish up the work of the Projection of America unit.

Philip Dunne summed up the sadness with which they said goodbye forever "to the dingy Foxholes of 45th Street . . . [and the] group of talented, dedicated people, my friends and colleagues to whom I shall be grateful for a job well done." He captured what my father surely was feeling—both the gratitude and the sorrow. As the war ended, hundreds of thousands of men and women returned to their prewar lives, often without prospects of employment. Five thousand had been with the OWI.

In retrospect, he would have been pleased by the lasting impact his OWI films had on audiences in Germany. In the 1930s and 1940s, they had been fed a diet of virulently anti-American propaganda. In 2014, a German team working with an American director, Peter Miller, made an hour-long documentary called *Projections of America*, which John Lithgow narrated, about the group he had put together and the films they made. The film was inspired by the curiosity of a German documentary film producer, Antje Boehmert, who had wondered why German civilians, who had been bombed incessantly for three years by the U.S. Army Air Forces and had seen millions of their countrymen die and their cities obliterated, could so quickly have welcomed America, her soldiers, and her democratic way of life. Of course many Germans were relieved to be rid of the scourge of Hitler, but another part of the answer, she said, lay in the twenty-six films illuminating the heart of America that my father and his team had made and shown to spellbound audiences in Germany as soon as the war ended.

• • •

With the coming of peace, life as a civilian and his screenwriting career beckoned my father. Film ideas that he yearned to put on paper churned in his head. My mother was pregnant again, expecting in November 1945. My father had always said he hoped his efforts for the OWI might contribute to a better world for his children and now there was a newborn on the horizon. Fatherhood seems to have focused his thoughts about the next generation and one of his last OWI films, *Watchtower Over Tomorrow*, held out the United Nations as a hopeful institution for maintaining global peace in the future.

My parents packed up the New York apartment and boarded the Twentieth Century train for California with Susan, Bobby, Deeds, and Miss Haesloop. As they crossed the country, perhaps they thought about the remarkable journeys of their lives to this moment—my mother's trip across the Rockies with William Mortensen when she was fourteen years old, or my father's first train trip to Hollywood on the Twentieth Century with Edith, on his way to Columbia Pictures. How extraordinary their lives had been.

Most likely on this trip, they were absorbed in the anticipation of seeing good friends and family in Los Angeles and finding a house where the children, soon to number three, could play and grow.

They were back in Hollywood by the time Japan surrendered in September 1945, and like many other men and women who had sacrificed so much, they began to rebuild their lives. Whatever they had experienced, they felt they had fought in "a good war" and had defended their nation with courage and purpose.

My parents marked the victory of the war with the naming of the new baby. If I had been a boy, I might have been Victor, but I was a girl so I am Victoria. Later my mother told me she especially liked the name because it sounded regal.

15

All the world is made of faith, and trust, and pixie dust.

— J. M. BARRIE

Postwar Los Angeles was an easygoing town, with fresh ocean breezes from the Pacific, palm trees, and wide streets without much traffic. Electric trolleys ran along the main arteries of Sunset and Wilshire Boulevards from placid communities like Beverly Hills and Santa Monica. There were wide sandy beaches and open spaces with orange groves, cornfields, and horse ranches. The city's crowning jewel was still the movie business, which was eager to get back to work now that the war was over.

My parents settled into a small house on a hill overlooking Beverly Hills that they rented from Jascha Heifetz, while they searched for a permanent home. Katya, Everett's wife, had prepared the house for their arrival with her usual flamboyance, including extravagant bouquets of flowers, and then disappeared for days in one of her stormy separations from Everett. This one was far more serious than usual. She was found unconscious in a Malibu motel with an empty bottle of sleeping pills beside her and a note saying, "I have attempted suicide. Please notify my family." My father worried about his older brother, alone in his own house yet again, and wondered if Everett should come live with them. "You know how he likes to have family around," he told my mother. But Katya recovered and came back home, and everything was calm until the next crisis.

As soon as they returned to California, my parents hosted a party for longtime friends Jo and Flo Swerling, the Milestones, Cary Grant, Loretta Young, and Irene Selznick. While circulating among the guests my mother heard Cary say to my father, "Be good to her. I was *so* in love with her!" He added in his familiar Cary Grant cadence, "I wouldn't have been a good husband. I pay too much attention to the position of the sofa. That sort of thing."

They found their dream home on Stone Canyon Road in Bel-Air, a neighborhood of winding broad and tree-lined streets with mansions, swimming pools, horse-riding trails, and the famous Bel-Air Hotel. Ours was a large Tudor house set back from the street behind a tall hedge, with wide lawns and old trees. Los Angeles royalty lived within walking distance in every direction: Greer Garson, Cary Grant, Betty Grable, Ava Gardner, Budd Schulberg, Conrad Hilton.

Three weeks after my parents moved in, I was born. A bird flew into the library the morning of my arrival, which my mother called an omen of good things to come. When she left for Good Samaritan Hospital to give birth, Susan, now nine years old, sent with her a note for me warning that when I came home there was someone in the house, Miss Haesloop, who would know and see everything I did. "Beware!" she wrote me, several hours before I was born.

Five days later, my father and mother brought me home to what she called her "forever house" where she planned to live the rest of her life. It had high ceilings, leaded windows, a wood-paneled library, a barroom, a playroom for the children, a sunroom, breakfast room, maids' quarters, and a guesthouse where my father wrote on rainy days. My mother arranged a daybed in a small room adjacent to their master bedroom for the times he woke in the night with a story idea, as he often did. The dining room, where my parents hosted frequent dinners and family celebrations, was large and formal; the children were allowed to meet the guests, but were excluded from the fanciest dinner parties, which might include Barbara Stanwyck, Jimmy Stewart, Harpo and Susan Marx, Loretta Young, Ronald and Benita Colman, Laurence Olivier, or Ronald Reagan and his first wife, Jane Wyman. On occasion my parents emptied the living room of furniture for square dancing and Bobby and I sat enchanted on the stairs, looking on as the guests whirled around to the music. At these parties, we watched my father juggle oranges, do handstands, or form a human wheel with Frank Capra and roll around the living room as everyone laughed and applauded. The one-time partners were still good friends.

On the rare rainy days, my mother brought out the movie projector so we could watch one of the OWI films or *A Night at the Opera* with the Marx Brothers, which we all loved. One night, when Harpo and Susan came to dinner, my mother introduced us.

"Sweetheart, this is Mr. Marx, that very funny man in the movie who makes you laugh so much."

Riskin and Fay
established life
together in
Hollywood after
the war. They
moved into their
new home, where
I was born in
1945, and set
about raising their
children.

"How do you do?" he smiled, bending down and holding out his hand.

This Mr. Marx didn't have curly hair or a trench coat. He sported an elegant suit and silk tie, and had hardly any hair at all! I knew he must be an impostor. "Nice to meet you, Mr. Marx," I lied, and fled to my bedroom.

In summer, my parents organized Fourth of July fireworks and croquet matches on the front lawn. All day Bobby and I played cowboys and Indians or soldiers fighting the Germans. I was often the nurse and deployed my box of Band-Aids to care for the wounded. In our backyard, with its swing set and slide, my mother arranged pony rides and puppet shows and recruited magicians for our birthdays. On these occasions, two dozen toddlers from the neighborhood, each with a nanny, filled the yard. My uncle Victor recorded each birthday with his 16mm camera. Pops, older and less firm, came by most Sundays, arriving by yellow cab and wearing one of his same old three-piece suits, which my father swore were made of iron. He always brought one toy for Bobby and me to share, a concept we both had trouble adjusting to.

One Sunday Pops wasn't there. Then the next Sunday and the one after that. No one said anything beyond a vague "he's not coming today." We were too young to understand and after a few Sundays stopped asking. Years later I found records that show he died of natural causes.

Our childhoods were idyllic, tended to by my mother and with my father providing his own special brand of humor and imagination. Our parties seemed grand to me, though, if the truth be told, not nearly as grand as those of the family next door.

A giant hedge separated us from the magnificent English-style country home of writer-producer Charles Brackett, Billy Wilder's frequent creative partner (*Ninotchka, Sunset Blvd., The Lost Weekend*). Brackett had a butler, maids, a cook, and a chauffeur to drive him to the studio in his Jaguar. He was avuncular, generous, kind, and extravagant. At his annual Easter egg hunt, attended by Hollywood's elite, his large garden was filled with pink-cheeked toddlers, balloons, musicians, giant arrangements of chrysanthemums, a sumptuous buffet with caviar, and a steady flow of mimosas served on silver trays. Rumor had it that the Easter eggs were handmade by Fabergé himself. The hunts were designed to delight his grandson, Tigger, on whom he doted.

Even though Bobby and I routinely slipped through the hedge to play with Tigger and his giant stockpile of toys, he was a source of our nightmares. He was about Bobby's age and dominated our games, ordering us around, demanding I kiss him, hitting Bobby hard and without provocation, bullying and tormenting us. We were too young and frightened to defend ourselves. And we learned one of the most important and painful lessons of childhood, that there were times when our parents could not keep us safe.

When I was four, I was married to Tigger, Hollywood style.

It was Easter Sunday and movie royalty had gathered in Charlie's backyard. Cary Grant was there, and Loretta Young and Joan Crawford. I wore my soft yellow Easter dress and new white patent leather shoes. When my mother led us through the hedge, Charlie, dressed in a gray morning coat with tails and top hat, handed me an enormous bouquet of white roses and before I knew it had steered me down a flower-strewn aisle to where Tigger waited in a tuxedo. Violinists struck up the wedding march on cue. Tigger grabbed my hand and held me in an iron grip. Charlie performed the marriage ceremony and instructed Tigger to make it official with a kiss. I fought back tears as everyone laughed and applauded.

I was sick with anxiety and confusion. Was this real? I looked for my mother and couldn't find her in the crowd.

I was still shaken when she took me home. She said it had all been an innocent game. Then, looking more closely at my sad face, she said perhaps it had been ill-advised. I knew she failed to grasp how upset I was.

A year later, Bobby and I were playing croquet when Tigger came through the hedge and as usual demanded to be included. We tried to ignore him, which we agreed would be the best tactic. I was attempting to emulate my mother's sweeping golf swing and swung the mallet behind me full force. I accidently hit Tigger flush in the mouth, knocking out his front teeth and leaving him bleeding and writhing on the ground. He ran home in tears. Bobby, certain I had done it on purpose, was elated. "Wow! That was great! Wow! You really whacked him! Did you see that? Wow!" I protested I hadn't meant to do it, but Bobby would have none of it. He jumped around excitedly, windmilling his arms. "Wow! That was soooo great. What a whack! You really whacked him!"

To win the admiration of my big brother made me feel heroic. For a few days, my step had a little swagger in it, although underneath I was sorry about what I had done. I sensed even then Tigger was a dangerous child and that he had problems which drove him to behave in ways inexplicable and frightening to others. As a teenager he was arrested for assaulting a young woman and was addicted to alcohol. Charlie, who doted on him to the end, had him admitted to the Menninger Clinic in Kansas and over the years spent a considerable part of his fortune on psychiatrists and lawyers to keep Tigger out of prison. Bobby and I never got over our childhood fear of him, and when we heard that he had died, in 2017, we both felt a sense of relief.

My father resumed his routine of writing in the morning and playing tennis or golf in the afternoon. The Santa Anita racetrack beckoned. "Gentlemen," he wrote to the Los Angeles Turf Club, "Before the war I was the holder of one of the boxes near the finish line. Having been away in government service the last three years . . . I am interested in obtaining a box for the fall season." They said they would try their best to accommodate him.

Like everyone returning from war, he was rebuilding his life, and my mother wanted to be a perfect companion. She took up golf seriously and they played together often. I have some 16mm film my father took to help her with her golf swing. She also became a top-notch horse handicapper. They occasionally escaped to Palm Springs to be alone.

"I spent as much time with him as I could," she once told me. "Somehow I felt I might not have him for very long." All her life she had premonitions, and often they were eerily prophetic. She said she never said a critical word to him. She barked at him only once in their marriage and that was involuntary when, lost in thought, he swerved while driving back from Palm Springs. Even though it was an impulsive reaction, she instantly regretted it.

His wartime experience continued to influence his thinking. Even as he was submitting his resignation to the OWI, he pondered how movies could help repair the postwar world and make friends for America. The OWI films had clearly proven their value, and abandoning their worthwhile mission because the war was over made no sense to him. He envisioned a partnership between Hollywood and the government to make nonprofit movies like the Projection series for both domestic and foreign consumption. An editorial board of writers, directors, and producers, along with distinguished educators and scientists, could review and approve the projects. Movies would be provided free to organizations, schools, and universities, and the studios could also distribute them commercially to make the venture self-sustaining.

Germany was still on his mind, he told the press. "After the initial period of occupation, when some semblance of normal living returns to Germany, the occupying governments will be confronted with the necessity of getting people into theaters by attracting them . . . with films of entertainment in order to get them in to see the newsreels, documentaries, and educational films." It had been thirteen years since Germans had seen American movies, he said, and during that time they had been fed a steady diet of lies and distortions.

The leaders of the Hollywood Writers Mobilization embraced my father's proposal and were ready to join him, but faced opposition from Lester Cole, president of the Screen Writers Guild, who saw the program as opening the door to government interference in Hollywood. Emmet Lavery, who would write *The Court-Martial of Billy Mitchell* and *The First Legion*, and served as head of the Mobilization, responded to Cole: "You make this intelligent proposal sound like a bureaucratic plot in which the government would have control over the industry and would become a propaganda arm of the government . . . We are not trying to force our documentary thumbs down other people's throats, as the Nazis did in Norway, Holland, Belgium and France. We are trying to meet a need and insistent demand among hundreds of millions of people for a better understanding of America and our democracy."

Cole's concern about government involvement in Hollywood was, in a personal way at least, sadly prophetic. A member of the Communist Party, his screenwriting career vanished because of the blacklist three years later. One of the Hollywood Ten called before the House Committee on Un-American Activities, he refused to answer their questions and was sent to prison for a year for contempt of Congress. After his release, for a long time he could work only under a pseudonym.

My father's idea of a nonprofit partnership modeled on the OWI of World War II found no traction in Washington, where conservatives in the government believed communists ran Hollywood and had to be suppressed. Others soon agreed and the fear of communism would dominate the American scene for more than a decade.

In Hollywood the question of whether films that would influence public opinion should be made at all became a divisive topic. People like my father believed a good film had to be built on an idea and any restraint on that idea was infringement on free speech and creativity. Others saw dangerous, and usually leftwing, ideas creeping into the movie business.

During a nationwide radio debate, my father made his position clear: "All effective dramatic films must start out with an idea—not a plot idea, but a viewpoint. Without it you have no structure, no opportunity for character development, no conflict, no third act, and the chances are, no audience."

He promoted his idea of a nonprofit partnership well into 1946, bringing Frank Capra on board and reaching out to David O. Selznick, now president of the Society of Independent Motion Picture Producers. But with the advent of the Cold War, the domestic political climate became increasingly tense and confrontational and any impetus for the plan faded.

My father's contributions to the war effort did not go unappreciated. He received countless laudatory letters after he left the OWI, including a note from French producer Simon Schiffrin, who nominated him for the French Légion d'Honneur for "his service during the war." My father wrote back, "I cannot imagine on what basis the French government would wish to tender me a Légion d'Honneur, but if they feel that I have had any small part in cementing friendly relations between our two countries, I am, of course, pleased." His *chevalier* medal, which I now keep in a safety deposit box, arrived in the mail in 1946.

In November 1945, my father took a full-page ad in *The Hollywood Reporter* announcing the incorporation of Robert Riskin Productions with my mother as vice president. Seeking to set up his company at a studio, he turned first to his old friend Harry Cohn. Whatever Cohn and Columbia offered him, my father wrote to say he had a better offer, nevertheless thanking him warmly and fondly remembering their shared past. He took his company to RKO and announced a slate of three films. The first was *Magic City*, later retitled *Magic Town*.

At the same time Frank Capra started Liberty Films with directors William Wyler and George Stevens; they too made a deal at RKO. Capra later said he invited my father to join him at Liberty Films. He had long thought my father was making a mistake to go out on his own, complaining to Lu even before the war ended that "those damn writers shouldn't be making pictures," including Jo Swerling in his grievance, and going on to say that without him they should not expect to repeat their former successes.

My father's point of view was, not unexpectedly, different. Asked if he would resume his partnership with Capra after the war, he answered with a mischievous glint, "All I have to do is wait for a few weeks and then be present at the opening of the new film of Frank Capra." He might have been suggesting, in his oblique and gentle way, that "Capra films" may have had some elements of shared parenthood. He never spoke about the extent of his contributions to the pictures they had done together, only once going so far as to tell journalist Tom Pryor about *Meet John Doe,* "I did more on the film than you know."

Magic Town, with a screenplay by Robert Riskin, began production in the summer of 1946. Jimmy Stewart played ambitious pollster Lawrence "Rip" Smith, who hopes to find a perfect formula for public opinion surveys to rescue his company from bankruptcy. He comes upon Grandview, a small town whose demographics mirror the country's exactly, and convinces an important client he can deliver survey results faster and cheaper than his rival.

He travels to Grandview where Mary, a newspaper editor (Jane Wyman), is proposing a redevelopment plan to bolster the local economy. Her plans would bring more people to town and destroy Rip's perfect demographics.

The chance to poke satirical fun at consumerism and groupthink was irresistible. So was the chance to advance the cause of women. He included a mythical poll asking the question of how many people would vote for a woman president and provided the answer of 79 percent. As with many Riskin films, conflict leads to romance and resolution, and it is soon apparent that Rip and Mary will marry and live happily ever after in Grandview.

As filming proceeded my father got the sense that something wasn't working. The Stewart-Wyman chemistry didn't quite ignite and some scenes felt flat. Well into production, he spent hours tinkering with the screenplay, hoping to give it more punch and charm.

My parents traveled to San Francisco for a preview. A *New York Times* journalist who traveled with them and was present for the screening wrote: "If Robert Riskin is chewing his gum a little faster these days and more frequently dropping the coins he always is nervously manipulating in his right hand, it is because of the trials and tribulations of the 'sneak' preview." The audience was mostly teenagers, bobby-soxers who continually left the auditorium to buy popcorn. This was not as disruptive as when, with children on the screen playing hopscotch, a little girl in the audience leapt up to play hopscotch in the center aisle. "Mr. Riskin grimly closed his eyes and kept them shut," wrote the journalist.

Two more previews were lukewarm and audience testing confirmed what my father feared. Times had changed. Romantic comedies with the social commentary of Riskin's salad days were not what postwar audiences wanted. It wasn't only *Magic Town,* it was many films. Capra, too, faced a lukewarm and disappointing reception to his first postwar film, *It's a Wonderful Life.*

Hollywood took stock. Serious dramatic films with substantial themes—*The Lost Weekend, The Best Years of Our Lives, To Each His Own*—were the ones now winning audiences and awards. Americans had been

Riskin established Robert Riskin Productions in 1945 and set up operations at RKO. He wrote and produced *Magic Town* (1947) costarring James Stewart and Jane Wyman.

to war and had seen rough things, and seemed to prefer drama to escape. The old world was ending.

To add to Hollywood's challenges, a postwar recession hurt film sales, and the 1947 House Committee on Un-American Activities hearings made daily headlines and crowded out everything else in Hollywood. What came to be called the "Plague Years" were beginning just as my father was premiering *Magic Town* in San Francisco. HUAC came to town to investigate the alleged infiltration of the film industry by communists, and soon fear and suspicion were casting a long shadow over the town.

It quickly grew dramatically worse. Writers, directors, and actors were served subpoenas to appear before New Jersey congressman J. Parnell Thomas' HUAC. To defend them and the industry, Philip Dunne, William Wyler, Myrna Loy, and John Huston founded the Committee for the First Amendment, which soon included Billy Wilder, Judy Garland, Frank Sinatra, Humphrey Bogart, Edward G. Robinson, Lauren Bacall, Henry Fonda, and Bette Davis. They flew as a group to Washington to argue that "any investigation into the political beliefs of the individual is contrary to the basic principles of our democracy," but could not slow the momentum of HUAC, or what it had unleashed. In the months ahead, the Screen Actors Guild voted to require members to sign loyalty oaths to America as a condition of membership.

Our house was consumed by the drama. My parents bought a Philips television, the first in our home. The small set looked like a radio with a seven-inch screen, and had a magnifying bubble to enhance the image. My parents watched the proceedings from their red leather wing chairs. I snuggled on my mother's lap and still remember the frightening images of J. Parnell Thomas repeatedly banging his gavel and interrogating witnesses. I knew only that something dramatic was occurring.

My parents' hushed, tense voices made clear their distress. They were not personally involved but many of their good friends were. They watched friends testify on both sides. "Friendly witnesses"—friendly to HUAC, that is—such as Ronald Reagan, told the committee about "a small clique" who opposed Screen Actors Guild policy and used tactics "more or less associated with the Communist Party." Their friend Gary Cooper said, he had "never read Karl Marx but didn't like what he understood." Walt Disney asserted that the union movement in Hollywood and communism were synonymous.

My parents also watched other friends—those called "unfriendly" by HUAC—being grilled. Leaders of the Screen Writers Guild my father knew well, including John Howard Lawson, Dalton Trumbo, Lester Cole, and Ring Lardner Jr., were members of the "Hollywood Ten," all of whom went to prison for refusing to answer Thomas' questions.[*]

My parents were outraged by the governmental inquisition. They felt the witnesses had a constitutional right to refuse to answer on the First Amendment grounds of freedom of speech. Ultimately the U.S. Supreme Court did not agree.

No one felt safe. Unknown to my father, the FBI compiled a file on him starting in 1947. It included, alongside accurate reports that he had worked for the OWI and had tried to create a nonprofit organization to tell America's story to the world, such charges as having once been interviewed by the American Communist Party's newspaper, *The Daily Worker,* and having joined the American Arts Committee to support the immigra-

---

[*]   J. Parnell Thomas was found guilty of corruption in 1951 and sent to the same prison as the Hollywood Ten, where his prison job involved tending to the chickens. Kate Lardner said that her father, Ring Lardner Jr., came across him in the prison yard and said, "Hey, Parnell, I see you're still dealing with the chickenshit."

The House Un-American Activities
Committee under Congressman
J. Parnell Thomas (below, with
Robert Taylor) investigated alleged
communist influence in Hollywood
in October 1947. Some members of
the movie community, including
Ronald Reagan, top right, were
friendly witnesses—friendly to
HUAC—while ten, including Ring
Lardner Jr., bottom right, refused to
answer the committee's questions on
First Amendment grounds.

tion of displaced Jewish refugees to Palestine. He was also credited, inac-
curately, with being one of "the rebels" who led the 1936 revolt against
communist domination of the Screen Writers Guild.

With the weapons of Congressional subpoenas and hearings and wide
publicity, the inquisitions brought Hollywood to heel. Studio heads saw
early on which way the winds were blowing. Fearing public reaction and
loss of revenue, the moguls, including Harry Cohn, Louis B. Mayer, and
Sam Goldwyn, issued a proclamation memorialized in the 1947 "Waldorf Statement"—their meeting had taken place at the Waldorf Astoria
Hotel in New York—condemning the Hollywood Ten and pledging not
to "knowingly employ a communist or a member of any party or group
which advocates the overthrow of the government of the United States by
force or by illegal or unconstitutional methods."

The blacklist had begun.

It spread through the industry, the town, the country. For a decade or more, no one was immune. The principal at Los Angeles' exclusive Westlake School for Girls distributed a pamphlet identifying people in the motion picture industry she said were communists, and exhorted students not to see their movies. The list was staggering in its scope and recklessness: actors Burt Lancaster, Henry Fonda, Gregory Peck, Orson Welles, Katharine Hepburn, Danny Kaye, Rita Hayworth, Kirk Douglas, and dozens more; writers and directors John Huston and Philip Dunne, Ira Gershwin, Moss Hart, Garson Kanin, Oscar Hammerstein II, James Thurber, Billy Wilder, and dozens more. There was no evidence to support any of the charges.

"Scoundrel Time," Lillian Hellman named it. Studios, guilds, individuals, even ticket buyers—all seemed in one way or another caught up in the madness. Two writers among the many were Sidney Buchman and Clifford Odets.

Buchman was my father's close friend and had followed him as Columbia's top writer. Ordered to Washington to face the committee, Buchman told HUAC all about himself. "I joined the Party when the world was troubled by fascism, the rising tide of fascism abroad," but he refused on principle to name others in the Party. For this he was cited for contempt, given a suspended prison sentence, and fined $150; his more meaningful punishment lay in the fact that his testimony before HUAC made him immediately unemployable in Hollywood.

His story parallels those of numerous others, with only personal details changing. He moved to New York and then London before settling in France. After a decade in the wilderness, during which he and Beatrice divorced, the blacklist finally ran its course and he was again able to work, earning screen credits in the 1960s for, among other movies, *The Mark, Cleopatra,* and *The Group.* Buchman stayed in Europe, where he remarried and had a second child. In 1965 he was awarded the Writers Guild Laurel Award for Lifetime Achievement. He died at his home in France in 1975.

During their time together, my mother had never known whether Clifford Odets had been a member of the Communist Party. Twice she had asked him and both times he said he had not belonged. But a decade after their split, when the anti-communist fever reached its heights, he was called before the committee. Like his friend and colleague Elia Kazan, Odets identified friends and colleagues who had already been named by others as fellow party members. In taking this path of limited cooperation with HUAC, Odets was able to keep working and avoid the blacklist but lost the friendship and respect of many of his colleagues.

The last twenty years of Odets' life—he died of stomach cancer in 1963—were anything but easy. Two years after his split from my mother, he married actress Bette Grayson. They had a daughter, who was plagued by numerous developmental issues, and a son, Walt, now a psychologist. Odets and Bette divorced in 1951, a year prior to his testimony before HUAC. He remained productive until his death, not in theater but in film and television. But after his testimony he no longer wrote about politically sensitive subjects, and the passion that had infused his early work faded. An earlier witticism by George S. Kaufman might have served as his epitaph: "Odets, where is thy sting?"

On his deathbed he told his son Walt that he had regrets about ending his relationship with my mother. But he said, "I would have damaged Fay's goodness and integrity if we'd stayed together."

The anti-communist madness hit close to our home.

The Swerlings and Capras had houses on the same beach in Malibu. One day the Swerlings' older son, Peter, hosted a party for Cal Tech friends who, thinking to be funny, and mocking the political paranoia of the time, arrived in a car flying a banner reading "Communist Youth Outing." They parked in front of the Swerling house. Peter was not amused but didn't think more about it.

Later that week, my parents were having dinner at the Capras' house when Capra said, "Did you know that Peter Swerling is a communist?" My parents were appalled that Capra would say such a thing and before going home that night stopped by the Swerlings' and gave them a full account.

Several days later, Flo was at home when the phone rang. It was the FBI, saying they had received a call from a neighbor reporting Peter's "possible communist activities." In a fury, Flo demanded to know the neighbor's name. The FBI agent said he could not disclose it . . . but then he hesitated.

"Do you know Frank Capra?" he asked.

Capra and his wife Lu were the Swerlings' close friends, always welcome for dinner in their house, with the Swerlings hosting them as often in return. The men had worked together on numerous pictures for almost two decades.

The Capra-Swerling friendship ended that day, but the charge remained in the government's files, affecting the Swerling children for years, especially Peter. He was a brilliant boy, with great scientific aptitude. When

Capra informed the FBI of his suspicions that Peter Swerling (second from left), the college-aged son of his friends of twenty years Jo and Flo Swerling, was a communist. The Swerling family (from the left): Jo Junior, Peter, Jo Senior, and Flo.

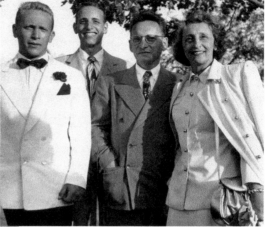

The Capra Malibu beach house where Capra taught Bobby headstands with Susan in the background, watching, 1950. Riskin and Capra were still friends.

he turned ten, Flo asked what he wanted for his birthday. To meet Albert Einstein, he told her, and she enlisted Jo's help in arranging it. Peter and Einstein sat together in Einstein's parlor in Princeton discussing physics and higher mathematics, which Flo said left her totally bewildered but proud. What made her happiest, she said, was when the hour-long meeting ended and Einstein offered Peter this advice: "Young man, pursue mathematics, but never forget the important things, like baseball."

Peter entered Cal Tech at fifteen and received degrees in mathematics and economics from Cornell and UCLA. He went on to become preeminent in the field of radar. He was constantly in demand to work with the RAND Corporation and the U.S. Department of Defense, but every time, before he could be issued a security clearance, he had to go through a long government-mandated process to clear his name anew. The same suspicions followed his younger brother, Jo Junior, who entered the California Maritime Academy to prepare for the Merchant Marine. Students were required to take a training cruise with the Coast Guard and needed a security clearance. Among all the academy's students, only Jo Junior's request for clearance was denied by the government. Flo and Jo had to hire a lawyer who demanded a hearing with the security bureaucracy, which eventually led to Jo Junior's being cleared.

The blacklist ruled Hollywood for more than a decade, ending only when movie star and producer Kirk Douglas boldly awarded Dalton Trumbo the screenwriting credit for his movie *Spartacus* in 1960. When others followed and there were no consequences, the blacklist was shown to have lost whatever power it was thought to have had.

One final vestige of the blacklist era survived until 1977. For a quarter of a century the studios had insisted on a morals clause in all writers' contracts, which was part of the studio's arsenal to rid themselves of writers who had been summoned before HUAC or had otherwise been tarred as communists or fellow travelers. My husband David was president of the Guild in 1977 and was determined to have the clause struck from writers' contracts. As negotiations with the studios commenced, he was prepared to demand reciprocity, insisting if the clause remained in writers' contracts, that producers be held to a morals clause as well. He never had to make the argument. The morals clause was deleted from all writers' contracts in the negotiations, never to reappear.

During these difficult postwar times, my father was determined to stay the course with his new independent company. As an important participant with major responsibilities in the war, the idea of again becoming a cog in a studio machine was not appealing. "The independents have been around for a long time," he told *The New York Times*. "They built up this industry and there is not a danger of them going out of business now. In fact, they're in a much better position than the majors, because they are not burdened with expensive operating costs and therefore can make adjustments more readily." He was especially optimistic that, although it was not the area in which he usually worked, fine dramas would come from those writers and directors who had been to war once they had time "to

rest and relax emotionally and sentimentally to the point they can trans-
late those experiences into perceptive drama." *The Best Years of Our Lives,*
written by his OWI colleague Robert Sherwood from MacKinlay Kantor's
novel, and directed by William Wyler, was released in 1946 and was, he
said, a preeminent example of what Hollywood could do.

But his own first independent project, *Magic Town,* was not a success.
Domestic box office receipts were modest, nothing more, and other anticipated overseas revenue was unexpectedly undermined by a new 75 percent
tax on foreign films imposed in England. He developed two more scripts
under the Robert Riskin Production banner: *You Belong to Me,* later retitled *Here Comes the Groom,* from a story by Liam O'Brien, and *The Girl
from Bogardus,* also from an O'Brien story. In a memo in June 1948, Ber-
nie Kamins of RKO wrote of my father's *Bogardus* script, "Best story of
its kind I have ever read and convinced it will be crackerjack of a picture."
He proposed June Allyson or Lana Turner to star. Production that summer seemed assured.

Bogardus never got off the ground. My father, faced with rising costs,
did what he had tried so hard not to do, suspending his independent
company in 1948 and going to work for Darryl Zanuck at Twentieth
Century–Fox.

The upside of independence was obviously creative freedom, and the
financial advantages of ownership could be meaningful. The downside
was that independent companies doing one or two films at a time had
no margin for error. With costs outpacing revenue, my father felt he had
to liquidate the company's assets, just as Capra had been forced to do a
year earlier when 50 percent cost overruns and poor box office for *It's a
Wonderful Life* forced Capra, Wyler, and George Stevens to fold Liberty
Films. Capra signed on as a contract director at Paramount. In this cir-
cuitous way the Riskin-Capra wheel took yet another spin and they were
soon reunited.

My father sold *Here Comes the Groom* to Paramount, who assigned
Capra to direct the film with Bing Crosby and Jane Wyman. Memorably, the movie introduced the great Hoagie Carmichael–Johnny Mercer
song, "In the Cool, Cool, Cool of the Evening." The movie was a moderate box-office hit in 1951. My father and O'Brien received an Oscar nomination for best original story, with *Variety* calling it a "top-notch piece of
comedy" and saying Riskin and O'Brien had provided a "merry yarn" for
Capra's direction, although other critics were less charmed.

Capra next secured rights to remake *Broadway Bill,* the film he had
directed from my father's screenplay in 1934. He asked my father to work

on the new version, and Paramount offered him a generous fee, but he was working on a script at Twentieth Century–Fox and unavailable. Melville Shavelson and Jack Rose did a rewrite on the script, now called *Riding High*. Capra asked the Screen Writers Guild to award him writing credit, based on the changes to the 1934 film's ending which he neglected to tell them had been written not by him but by Sidney Buchman, now black-listed and living in Europe. The Credits Arbitration Committee, after a thorough review of the original screenplay and the remake, determined the credit should read "Screenplay by Robert Riskin with additional dialogue by Shavelson and Rose."

After fifteen years of close collaboration and friendship, this led to the first rift between my father and Capra, whose only remaining avenue for authorship was if my father now volunteered to share his own credit. Capra asked and my father, known for his generosity, said no.

The *New York Times* review of *Riding High,* released in 1950, was unfavorable. "For this promisingly titled musical picture is pretty much of a slap-dash affair, knocked together by a gang of joke-book carpenters and a whole slew of jingling tunesmiths. What it lacks in wit and spirit it tries to make up with big production splash, and deficiencies in that department are glossed over with a Technicolor splurge."

My father's decision to accept employment at Twentieth Century–Fox may have been influenced by the family's economic circumstances following the war. For three years he had earned only his annual $8,000 government salary, and my mother did not work at all. Still, he remained upbeat and optimistic and if he felt the stress, he gave no indication. With close friends there was constant banter and play. A memo to my father and Jo Swerling from their friend, writer-producer-executive-playwright Dore Schary, captures their rapport following a 1947 bridge game:

Messrs. Swerling and Riskin,

Herewith resumé of various bets made at Mr. Swerling's house the night Mr. Riskin and I beat him so decisively at bridge. 1) $25.00 even bet. Swerling says there will be third party in 1948. Riskin says no. 2) $50.00 to $25.00. Swerling bets 2 to 1 that the Republicans will win the 1948 Presidential election. 3) $10.00. Swerling says the Senate will over-ride the veto on the Hartley-Taft bill. Schary says no. 4) $75.00 to $25.00. Riskin bets 3 to 1 that Vandenberg will not be the Republican candidate for President in 1948. 5) $75.00 to $25.00. Riskin bets 3 to 1 that Warren will not be in the Vice-Presidential campaign in 1948.

For the record, there was a third party in 1948, the Democrats won the election, the Senate did override Truman's veto of the Taft-Hartley Act, Vandenberg was not the Republican candidate for President, and Warren was the Republican candidate for Vice President. My father broke even on the political bets but made a few dollars at bridge.

Once he settled at Fox, my father completed two new scripts, writing in his studio bungalow and in our backyard, where Bobby and I ran around playing while he wrote on his long yellow pads, serenely undistracted.

His first script for Zanuck was *Mister 880*, based on a St. Clair Mc-Kelway article in *The New Yorker,* which told the real-life story of a man who counterfeited badly, small sums of money, just enough to live on modestly. Before starting the script, my father reviewed the minutes of a court hearing on the mental acuity of the man, Emerich Juttner, which he saw at once had all the elements of a great Riskin story in the mold of *Mr. Deeds.*

For years Juttner had been printing one-dollar bills, a few at a time, on cheap paper available at any stationery store. The artwork was crude, even childish, with a black splotch for Washington's left eye, with letters and numbers poorly formed and illegible, and words misspelled, i.e., "Washiston." A master criminal Juttner clearly was not; an endearing, lovable, typical Riskin "little guy" he became in the screenplay.

Zanuck loved the script. "I think it worked out magnificently," he wrote my father, and the film was slated for production with Edmund Goulding to direct. The only notes Zanuck gave concerned the original title, *Eight-eighty,* which was the case number for the Treasury Department's investigation. Would it attract an audience? They endlessly volleyed alternatives back and forth: *The Dollar Man, Face Value, Dream World, Wishful Thinking.* My father included one suggested by my mother, *He Went a Crooked Mile,* playing off the nursery rhyme. Finally agreeing that simpler was better, they called the picture *Mister 880.*

Edmund Gwenn played the elderly counterfeiter and Burt Lancaster the treasury agent assigned to track him down. The plot revolves around Lancaster tracing one of the bills to a friend of the counterfeiter, played by

Dorothy McGuire, and as Lancaster pursues her romantically, of course they fall in love. She convinces Lancaster not to send the poor old man to prison for the rest of his life and everyone lives happily ever after.

Upon its release in 1950, the reviews for *Mister 880* were rapturous. *Variety* wrote, "Here's a film of gentle humor, pathos and entertainment . . . never has there been so enchanting, so benevolent a film . . . A can't miss at the box office." Bosley Crowther of *The New York Times* said, "Mr. Riskin has turned out a funny and poignant exposition of a hoax wherein our native gullibility is cheerfully ridiculed. Most valuable in this presentation is the talented Edmund Gwenn, who plays the kindly counterfeiter with charming ingenuousness." Gwenn was nominated for an Oscar and won the Golden Globe.

Riskin went to Twentieth Century–Fox under Darryl Zanuck (right) and wrote *Mister 880* (1950) starring Dorothy McGuire, Burt Lancaster, and Edmund Gwenn. Gwenn (below), in the role of a guileless counterfeiter, was nominated for an Oscar and won the Golden Globe.

While *Mister 880* was in production, my father also worked on a script called *Half Angel* at Fox. Zanuck had misgivings about the first draft and might have let the project go, but Loretta Young loved the story of a demure nurse who sleepwalks at night, when she transforms into a sexy woman. Young, who routinely had final say on her leading man, told my father she would commit without final approval, which rekindled Zanuck's interest. Four months later, my father turned in revisions and Zanuck said, "It is wonderful . . . I cannot for the life of me see why this cannot set a record on this lot and be one of the fastest production jobs on record . . . Shooting time is the essence of cost." The popular Joseph Cotten was set as the leading man and the film went into production with Richard Sale directing. The production happened so hurriedly that the film itself looked rushed. Young's performance was overwrought, and the film, released in 1951, closed quickly.

Perhaps it was the years leading the Overseas Film Division of the OWI and then his own independent company, but by late 1950 my father's memos reflected a growing impatience with the layers of studio bureaucracy. He agreed to write a screenplay for the Mister Belvedere series starring Clifton Webb, but Samuel Engel, the Fox executive in charge, was swamped with other projects and perpetually distracted. Increasingly restless to set the direction of the picture and begin writing, my father wrote a number of amusing memos trying to arrange a story meeting and finally sent Engel what he called a "less frivolous" message: "The long weary wait has at long last played havoc with my sense of humor . . . Had I known what I know now, I could have put the last six weeks—or part of it anyway—to some profitable use. I could have taken my family off for an oft-promised and oft-postponed vacation. Or what is even more regrettable, I could have taken a very lucrative three-week job from Frank Capra [the remake of *Broadway Bill*] which I was forced to decline because I was 'tied up.'"

His impatient memo finally got Engel's attention. He got his meeting and officially went to work. By Christmas, my father had completed his screenplay and sent it to Zanuck. "Dear Darryl, Season's Greetings. All I can give you for Christmas is the script for *Belvedere*. I hope you feel, as I do, that it came out fine and that it is just what you want from Santa." He had turned in the script in time to enjoy Christmas with our family.

I have one last childhood memory from the pre-Christmas period of that year, of an animated discussion around our dinner table with Jo and Flo Swerling. They were talking about *Guys and Dolls* and I understood from the tone of their conversation it was something serious and important. Recently I asked Jo Swerling Jr. what he could tell me about it.

Guys and Dolls was about to open on Broadway. It was already the talk of the town, and would be a triumph for Swerling, who had written the book based on two Damon Runyon stories. For once, the advance word had it exactly right. The play would be a smash hit, one of the greatest musicals ever, with music and lyrics by Frank Loesser that have never gone out of style.

According to Jo Junior, the credit for writing the play's book was the subject for heated discussion, and Flo was threatening to murder Jo, if this time, again, he was cavalier about claiming his deserved credit.

The producing team had acquired theatrical rights to all Runyon's short stories—more than 700 of them—and turned to Swerling, who suggested combining "The Idyll of Miss Sarah Brown" and "Blood Pressure," integrating the romance of gambler Sky Masterson and missionary Sarah Brown, and another between Nathan Detroit and Miss Adelaide, and the Oldest Established Permanent Floating Crap Game, as the spine. The producers loved the idea and told him to go ahead. When he finished, they raised all the production money, hired George S. Kaufman to direct and, still relying on Swerling's book, put together a brilliant cast.

As they were about to go into rehearsal, the producers and Swerling talked. The producers saw the play more as a comedy, Swerling more as a love story. The producers asked if they could bring in Abe Burrows, the producers' good friend, to punch it up. Swerling was not a joke writer, but was a fan of Burrows, and he gave his permission, which the producers needed before they could proceed.

Burrows did write some wonderful jokes and brought in one additional Runyon character, Big Jule (Runyon had called him "Rusty Charlie"). All the bones—which of Runyon's 700 stories to use and how to use them— remained exclusively Swerling's.

Several weeks passed. The producers called Swerling and said they thought Burrows deserved shared credit for writing the book. Contractually, Swerling had the right to say no—in theater, writers have very strong credit protections—but, over Flo's protests, he agreed. More time passed. The producers called again, saying Burrows was still writing and asking Swerling to give half his royalty to Burrows. Ignoring the smoke coming out of Flo's ears, he gave Burrows a quarter of his share if the producers would match it, which they agreed to do. The producers called Swerling a third time, asking him to give up the first position so the credit would now read "Book by Abe Burrows and Jo Swerling."

That was where matters stood when the Swerlings came to the Riskin house. Here, according to the Swerlings' son Jo Junior, Flo said she would most certainly kill Jo if he agreed to take second position. My parents said she was absolutely right and they would stand up with her in court and say so. With everyone telling Jo he should hold his ground, he did. The final credit read "Book by Jo Swerling and Abe Burrows." For a long time afterward, the producers spoke publicly—and of course painfully for Swerling—of Burrows as the author of *Guys and Dolls*. They finally stopped when they needed Swerling's signature on a contract and Swerling threatened to withhold it unless they started to behave.

According to contemporary accounts, *Guys and Dolls*—which won the Tony Award—was selected by the Pulitzer Prize Drama Committee as winner of the Pulitzer Prize for 1950, but the Trustees of Columbia University, who administer the prize, were aware of Burrows' recent appearance before the House Un-American Affairs Committee in which he had confirmed his involvement with the Communist Party, and vetoed the selection. No prize for drama was given in 1951. Recently a spokesman for the Pulitzer committee said they have no record of this happening.

Writers have been known to face severe pressure from producers, directors, or executives, often with serious consequences for their careers. In the case of my godfather, Jo Swerling, if he had insisted on sole credit for *Guys and Dolls* from the beginning, as was his right, he might have won the Pulitzer Prize.

The day after Christmas, 1950. My father returned home from the studio in the morning with a blinding headache.

For six weeks, he had been aware of a weakness in his left hand and arm and knew he needed to see a neurologist. A golfing friend, a doctor, had given him the name of a specialist. Now my mother called and made an appointment with the specialist right away, for that morning. She wrote:

> I drove him carefully . . . carefully, believing, crazily, that a sudden
> stop or lane change might make his condition worse. The first
> indignity was having to walk barefoot in an examining gown while
> the doctor observed his gait. Yes . . . a little off. Uneven. A further
> indignity was a spinal tap. The headache that followed, they said,
> was to be expected. We went home, where he lay flat in a dark room
> to try to control the headache—a minimal consideration amid the
> enormous dark feelings about what might lie ahead.

The doctors recommended hospitalization. Flo and Jo arrived with a limousine to drive him to Cedars of Lebanon Hospital. No one spoke in the car. The hospital said they would track down the staff neurosurgeon, Tracy Putnam, but that might take time. At the end of the day, my mother went to the Swerlings' house, not far from the hospital, to wait for the doctor's call, which came late in the evening. He reported he was optimistic.

When she returned to the hospital the next morning, she found my father on the floor, his right side paralyzed. He was holding his head, saying, "Tight . . . tight." The nurses lifted him onto the bed.

Dr. Putnam thought my father had a brain tumor and performed emergency surgery on December 27. There was no tumor but instead blood clots in the carotid artery—a thrombosis, a knot of blood vessels causing lack of blood flow to the brain. The damage was in the "quiet part of the brain"—as if any part of my father's brain was quiet—and the doctor thought he would make a full recovery.

16

Morning without you is a dwindled dawn.

—EMILY DICKINSON

After my father's surgery, my mother stayed at his bedside continuously, holding his hand, talking to him, helping the nurses bathe him. The hospital arranged the room next to his so she could be with him day and night.

I still have the notebook she filled with the details of his daily progress or setbacks, certain that when he recovered he would find her observations of his recovery fascinating. Her handwriting is strong, elegant. The morning after his surgery, she wrote:

> Thursday Dec. 28th—Dr. Putnam said condition excellent. You winked at him . . . [He said] I could go in and hold your hands and let you wink at me . . . You run your hand along my upper arm. I say, "I'm here. You are wonderful." . . . You stretch your arm high and let it fall down over my shoulder. I sink down close to you and your arm holds me close, your hand feeling my face and stroking it.

Over the following days my father lapsed into a semi-coma. When he was more or less alert, he was still confused and unable to communicate. He pushed at the bedrail that penned him in. His helplessness made him weep. My mother noted:

> You begin to talk, lots of words, nothing I can understand. Then you begin to cry. I hold you and tell you it's all right. You say, "It's all right." I hold you and keep talking to you, put my face against yours, you kiss me, put your arm around me, pat me. Keep crying. I keep reassuring you.

Dr. Putnam prescribed sedatives, telling my mother his agitation was normal after brain surgery. "It shows how deep a man's emotions go. They are strong and apparent even before he is fully aware," Putnam told her.

My mother calmed and reassured my father, tried to help him focus.

> I tell you to say "mmm" if you know it's me. You say "mmm" and I say it back. You repeat it and we say lots of "mmms" back and forth, looking into each other's eyes. You stroke my face . . . I stand beside you and you put your hand on my breast. I ask you to say my name and you make your lips to form an F . . . I hold you and kiss you. You become quiet again . . . I say, "All we need is a little time and rest and we'll be fine."

Ten days after the surgery, when he opened his eyes, she again asked, "Darling . . . can you see me?" He held her gaze and said, "See clear . . . Seen you for years . . . long before anyone realizes." She knew he was telling her that for a long time he had loved her from afar.

The nurse asked, "Can you see *me*, Mr. Riskin? What do I have on my head?" No response. The nurse said to my mother, "He looks like he's thinking . . ." He said to the nurse, "I am always thinking . . . of a bon mot. Never answer a question directly if I can help it." My mother was elated. This was the clearest sign yet of recovery.

Doctors and nurses came in constantly. "How do you feel? Are you in pain?" As he improved, their repetitious questions aggravated him. One morning he refused to answer and whispered to my mother, "They won't get a straight answer out of me." She laughed uncontrollably, almost weeping. Another sign of progress. The doctors saw the progress, too.

His moments of clarity, however, were sometimes followed by the impression he was in England with the OWI. He said:

> Who's in charge of the OWI here . . . ? The Palladium is just down the street. That's where the boys play when they come here. Harpo—
> Danny . . . They love Danny Kaye over here . . . Call up Sidney
> Bernstein and we could go to his farm . . . We could watch the air raids of the next war from there.

He wanted to recruit Dr. Sanford Rothenberg, a redheaded neurosurgical resident training under Dr. Putnam, to the OWI. He called him "carrot-top" and "the boss man" and said, "He thinks straight." He liked Dr. Rothenberg and found comfort in his self-confidence. "You will get well. Do you understand me?" Dr. Rothenberg told my father, who nodded and relaxed.

In the days ahead, my father's thoughts drifted disjointedly: a play idea for Harpo, a GI he picked up on the road from Paris to Luxembourg, transportation for the children, Susan's writing, a fat little boy, Germans, the Nazis, Fleet Street, a war song he was remembering . . .

What would you think would be the greatest war song? I was walking along, minding my business, when out of an orange-colored sky, flash, bam, alakazam, beautiful you came by . . . and . . . love walked up and hit me right between the eyes. No language barriers. You can fill in whatever you want with slam-bam alakazam.

It's a kind of philosophy . . . Walking along, minding your own business, you get hit with love or with a bomb.

My mother recorded every detail. She wrote:

As the nurse is washing your lower parts you say, "This could be a game called Low Man on the Scrotum Pole . . ."

I ask if you feel my love pouring all over you and you say, "Yeah. Here I am like chicken on a spit and love is the gravy pouring all over me." I say, "What an image. Perfect. And so much gravy! Luckiest gal in the world to have a husband like you."

His recovery was slower than the doctors expected. He wanted to be "a good patient," he said, but didn't know what to do. Three weeks after surgery, the medical team again worried about a brain tumor. To everyone's relief, further tests determined there was none. Dr. Rothenberg wondered if he was in pain from the spinal tap. My father, weeping, answered, "Only the pain of creation, only the pain of composition, only the pain of creation."

After a month of hospitalization, with all tests done and his condition sufficiently stabilized, it was decided he could face the herculean challenge of physical therapy for his paralysis at home. My mother went into a flurry of preparations for his homecoming: a hospital bed, a wheelchair, physical therapy equipment, twenty-four-hour nursing care.

Nurses and physical therapists invaded our home. Outwardly, my mother maintained her optimistic spirit. She managed the nursing rotations, did the marketing, paid bills, took me to dance lessons. She took Susan to opera singing lessons with Marie Rappold who, when I tagged along, taught me how to play stud poker. She took Bobby to Cub Scout meetings where he learned to make knots. Facing unaccustomed financial pressure, she had to let go of the household staff except for Bertha, who cleaned and did the laundry, and the Nisei gardener, George, who had been released from an internment camp when the war ended. My mother made breakfasts, prepared lunch boxes for Bobby and me—peanut butter and jelly or tuna fish sandwiches—and drove us to school.

Everett, who had come to the hospital daily, visited regularly. He seemed lost without his brother. Katya volunteered to take Bobby and me on occasional outings and trips, where she drank too much alcohol; on one horseback ride she gave me a beer, a dizzying experience. Essie, Rose, and Murray were at the house constantly, and the Wray family, too. Friends Irene Selznick, Jack Benny, Harpo and Susan Marx, Edward G. Robinson, Sidney Bernstein, Ellin and Irving Berlin stopped by. To relieve my mother, Flo and Jo entertained us at their beach house and treated Bobby, Susan, and me at Wil Wright's Ice Cream Parlor.

My mother was upbeat with everyone, although later she wrote:

One night, after saying good night to the children, I went downstairs where no one could hear me if I cried. I sat in the breakfast room in Bob's chair. This was the room that we used for family meals around a large lazy Susan table. I needn't have been concerned about anyone hearing me cry. Silent tears poured steadily, steadily down my face and fell into my folded hands as they rested in my lap. Four weeks of the deepest concern had to be released. It may have taken an hour to do that. I'm not sure. I felt as though my own clock was broken. But I also felt that emptying out the tears would make space for new energies to begin the long pull toward helping Bob recover.

I have my own memories of the days after my father returned home.

The dining room had been converted into a convalescent room. I wandered through the sunroom to the closed dining room door. I heard a man's muffled voice inside. Unsure what to do, I watched the sun stream through the window, carrying particles of dust that look like tiny stars. I listened again and knocked.

The door opened and a strange man in white, a nurse, peered down at me as though I was an intruder. "Not now," he said quietly and shut the door.

My mother slipped out. "Maybe later, darlin'. They're just fixing Daddy up so you can see him. Do you have something to play with?"

I nodded but what was there to play with that mattered?

I drifted aimlessly and found myself in the kitchen where Bertha was ironing, sitting at the large machine—a mangle—feeding wrinkled bedsheets onto the roller, pressing the pedal to run them through. The white sheets came out perfectly ironed.

She looked down at me and for the first I was struck by her beauty. Later when I saw images of Nefertiti I thought she looked like Bertha.

"You all right, honey lamb? How 'bout you give me that pillowcase over there in the basket." For a moment, I felt useful.

"I'm waiting to see my daddy."

"Well now, isn't that wonderful. He's gonna be so pleased to see his little girl."

"They're fixing him up."

"That so? He's so lucky to have you and momma."

The dining room door was open when I returned. My mother saw me peeking in.

"Come in, sweetheart. Daddy wants to see you."

I tiptoed in so I wouldn't disturb him. I was trembling with excitement. The bed my father was lying in dominated the dimly lit room. The nurse elevated the bed so he could see me. He hadn't been shaved and his face was rough, but blessedly he was wearing the tortoiseshell glasses I loved so much and that made him look his familiar self. With great effort he turned his head toward me and tried to smile. "Hey rascal. How ya doin'?" The right side of his face was frozen in paralysis, giving his mouth a lop-sided grin. His effort exhausted him and he closed his eyes again.

"What can I do?" I whispered to my mother.

"Not a thing, darlin'." But my disappointment must have struck her. "Maybe you'd like to fluff his pillow. It needs fluffing."

My mother found a footstool and helped steady me on it. I patted my father's pillow several times, not quite able to achieve some imaginary degree of perfect plumpness that would make him well. I couldn't be sure but I thought I saw him make a slight nod of approval, which encouraged me.

"That's fine, my angel," my mother assured me. "Good job."

As I stepped off the footstool I saw a shiny silver bell tied to the bed railing. "What's that for?" I asked.

"For Daddy to ring if he needs anything."

A month before, I had seen him touch the bell under the dining room table with his foot, signaling the kitchen help. The same foot that flew through the air when he did cartwheels for me and Bobby and Susan, that pivoted as he swirled my mother gracefully around the dance floor, the foot that was now immobile and useless.

I left the dining room for the library with a sense of mission. I dragged my small ladder-backed chair to the now-closed dining room door. Here I would be ready when my father needed me. I could hear the bell or hear him call when my mother might be away, or the nurse momentarily absent. From here I could come to his rescue.

I sat outside his door for a long time, at least a long time in a six-year-old's mind. I watched two bluebirds cavort outside the sunroom window.

My eyes turned to the ping-pong table in the sunroom where I had seen so many fierce games. I admired my mother's forehand slice and her full-throated laugh when she won, and even when she lost. My eye went to the far end of the room, the battlefield where Bobby and I had our wrestling matches that sometimes ended with me in tears, or where Susan sometimes read to us.

Bobby had no knowledge of my Florence Nightingale assignment. He was planning to explore the forbidden woodpile by the guesthouse and wanted an accomplice. Knowing I'd be back soon, I ran outside with him and became engrossed in play for the rest of the afternoon. Then dinner and my bath, and bedtime, and the next day school, and in the following days dancing lessons and neighborhood kids having parties, playdates, day camp, and my mother's determination that our routine be normal.

I resumed my vigil by the dining room door sporadically, for ever shorter periods. Soon it faded from my daily planning. The cost to me was subtle but real, a recurring guilt that I was a soldier who had gone AWOL from an important mission, to heal my father and make things right for him again.

He didn't get better. Physical therapy did little good. A year later he had another devastating stroke and several seizures. Dr. Putnam's final report, which I still have, made clear that his prognosis was poor. It became hard and then impossible to provide all the care he needed twenty-four hours a day. My mother arranged for him to be cared for in a nursing home a few miles from our house. She had the male nurses from home go with him, but in the end, they proved unreliable. One found a bottle of my father's favorite Scotch, which Irving Berlin had brought him, and disappeared for a few days with the Scotch and my father's car.

Eventually Everett met with the board of directors of the Motion Picture Country Home and Hospital to ask if my father could be cared for in the rest home that had been established by the film industry. Built on a sprawling piece of land in Woodland Hills, the Home accepted film people based on need. Our resources had dwindled due to medical expenses—

there was no personal or studio medical insurance then, no Writers Guild insurance—and after the Country Home reviewed my mother's situation, it agreed to take my father.

The Home was a godsend. Even so, the expenses of our house were an insupportable burden and my mother began the search for a smaller home. With Ellin Berlin's help they found a modest midcentury house in the Brentwood Hills of the Santa Monica Mountains, and in 1953 my mother reluctantly packed us up and we left Bel-Air.

Each of us had our own room in the new house, with a workshop and a darkroom for Bobby, but we missed our old home. In bed at night, to comfort myself I turned my Philips radio to one of my favorite weekly dramas like *The Shadow,* whose stories of terror and mystery were strangely soothing. I relaxed as soon as I heard the radio announcer with his throaty voice ask the galactic question *"Who knows what evil lurks in the hearts of men? The Shadow knows!"* followed by the maniacal laugh. I rolled over and hugged my pillow and pulled the sheet over my head to make a cocoon, and would lose myself in tales of peril as the announcer reminded me, "The weed of crime bears bitter fruit."

Or sometimes, when another of my favorite radio serials—*Dragnet, The Whistler,* or *Sergeant Preston of the Yukon*—was unable to help me sleep, I turned down the volume and let my thoughts drift back to the beautiful Tudor house we had left and the life we had lost. I pictured each room in careful sequence, sometimes escorting an imaginary visitor, as if remembering the details would magically transport me back there. In my fantasy, I slid down the banister to show the visitor how much fun it could be. We walked into our sunroom, the bar, the cozy wood-paneled library with the Oscar on the fireplace mantel, the sun-drenched breakfast room with our parakeet in its cage, the warm kitchen and elegant dining room, and up the back stairs to the landing where I showed off the miniature set of *Magic Town* stored there, and walked past the attic. I pointed out our nursery, of course, with its dumbwaiter, and lingered in my room with its window seat that held my toys. I wandered through Bobby's and Susan's bedrooms, and my parents' wing where we had the children's hour.

With so much ground to cover, the exercise was tiring. Before I fell asleep I made a mental note to visit our old guesthouse first thing tomorrow.

My mother went to see Lew Wasserman, the top agent in town who also ran MCA. He had represented my father and been a loyal visitor when my father fell ill. She said she wanted to go back to work, needed to go back to work.

In the 1950s, Wasserman and his partner Jules Stein were transforming the entertainment industry. They not only embraced television, a business other moguls considered a passing fad, they doubled down on the new medium by purchasing Revue Productions and Universal Studios. With their impressive roster of talent, they supplied their television productions with writers, directors, and actors.

Their foresight was rewarded. By 1953, sales of television sets were booming. Advertisers could reach millions of consumers nightly. General Electric, Westinghouse, Kraft, Proctor and Gamble, and other giants were investing enormous sums in programming.

As a friend, Wasserman was eager to help my mother, and the name Fay Wray still had marquee value. After a decade in retirement my mother, now forty-six, resumed her acting career. From the first day, she said, "I felt arms around me that I could not see, supporting me."

Over the next ten years, the Golden Age of Television, she worked steadily in dramas: *Jane Wyman Presents The Fireside Theater, Alfred Hitchcock Presents, The 20th Century–Fox Hour, Playhouse 90, General Electric Theater, Kraft Theater, Studio 57, Screen Directors Playhouse.* She had matured as an actress and a person, and was frequently called on to portray mothers or regal but still-accessible women, and occasionally villains. With her high cheekbones and beautiful eyes, she was more attractive than ever. She adjusted quickly to the fast pace of television with cameras and actors always moving and less time to do everything with care.

She took virtually anything that was offered. A handful of teenage rock-and-roll movies that were the rage: *Rock, Pretty Baby* and its sequel, *Summer Love,* and *Dragstrip Riot.* Family movies like *Tammy and the Bachelor* with Debbie Reynolds, who was pregnant with Carrie Fisher at the time; my mother adored Debbie. Now that she was older, she liked to mentor young actresses.

She had roles in pictures like *Hell on Frisco Bay* with Edward G. Robinson, my father's onetime roommate and friend for years, who was now struggling to find parts because of the blacklist. She said how truly scary he was in the role as a gangster, even to her. She did *Treasure of the Golden Condor* with Anne Bancroft, *Queen Bee* with Joan Crawford and Barry Sullivan—Miss Crawford handed her a note that read "Welcome back. We need you!"—and *Small Town Girl* with Jane Powell. She was in *The Cobweb* directed by Vincente Minnelli with Richard Widmark, Lauren Bacall, Charles Boyer, and her childhood idol, Lillian Gish. She frequently

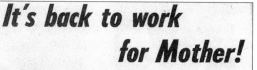

From stardom to retirement and domesticity . . . back to star status again . . . this is the story of Fay Wray . . . courageous wife . . . devoted mother . . . successful career woman. . . .

"Read me a story please," says Vicki to her mom. Fay obliges with a selection from her daughter's favorite collection.

Getting a teen-age daughter ready for her first big party is only one of the duties that Fay carries out so well.

Fay went back to work full-time in 1953, starring opposite Paul Hartman in a Universal series, *The Pride of the Family* (1953–1954) with Natalie Wood (age sixteen) and Robert Hyatt. A television magazine described Fay as "courageous wife, devoted mother, and successful career woman." Left, with me, age eight guest-starred in series like *Perry Mason, 77 Sunset Strip, The Real McCoys, Hawaiian Eye,* and *The David Niven Show,* and for a time had a series of her own, *The Pride of the Family,* playing a practical and caring mother with a bumbling husband and two children, one a sparkly-eyed teenager named Natalie Wood.

It was a replay of her earliest days in Hollywood when she worked for Carl Laemmle. Mornings, before dawn, long before I awoke, she drove her green Chevrolet over the hill to Universal Studios just as she had done decades earlier. She left my lunch box on the kitchen counter with a note: "Have a wonderful day, darlin'." I caught the school bus myself. We had a roly-poly housekeeper now, Rose Paradise, who did the marketing, car-pooling, and cooking. Her specialty was strawberry shortcake and a secret salad dressing she planned to sell one day and make her fortune.

My mother stayed away from Hollywood parties. She was home from the studio in time to have dinner with us, sometimes still in her television makeup. She never complained about the long hours. She never expected life to magically take care of her.

On occasion, I went to the studio with her. The makeup lady, the cos-tume people, the carpenters, lighting crew, cameraman, and actors, all were effusive the way movie people can be. People rushed to bring her a chair, to powder her nose or touch up her lipstick, to hold her purse between takes. "Miss Wray, are you comfortable?" . . . "We'll need you in five minutes, Miss Wray." She was like a long-lost relative who had returned to the family.

She, in turn, was a reliable professional, warmhearted with everyone, considering it her duty to help create an esprit de corps. Most important, she still knew how to charm the camera. "I was secretly pleased that, at least technically, I was still aware of camera angles," she said.

Helen Ferguson, her publicist for many years, pitched in, managing press stories and her mail. Fans wrote about their joys and heartaches as if she were a mother confessor. Little boys still fell in love with the damsel in distress from *King Kong.* She sometimes answered with handwritten notes and bits of asked-for advice. A few fans just wrote, "Please send ten auto-graphed photos. Thank you," in a form letter designed to amass movie star photos to sell for profit.

She visited my father at the Motion Picture Country Home and Hos-pital after work or, if her hours were too long, on Saturdays. I went occa-sionally to keep her company. My father was in his wheelchair on the patio, sometimes smoking through a long rubber tube. The cigarette, wedged into one end of the tube, stayed in the ashtray on a side table

Fay appeared as a guest star in film and television through the 1950s: *Queen Bee* (1955) with Joan Crawford (center left); *Tammy and the Bachelor* (1957) with Debbie Reynolds (top); *Hell on Frisco Bay* (1955) with Edward G. Robinson (left); and *77 Sunset Strip* (1960) with Roger Smith (center right).

as he inhaled at the other end. This way he wouldn't burn himself. The contraption made him look like a snake charmer from an Arabian Nights movie. Doctors didn't yet understand the connection between heart disease and smoking, but if they had, they still might not have wanted to deny him the pleasure.

Because the right side of his face was paralyzed, he would give a half smile. I remember offering him a hug but, seeing him so immobile, I stiffened slightly fearing I might cry.

Often my mother visited him alone, or sometimes with Flo, or her sister, Willow, or Everett, but soon even they came less frequently. It was a long ride from Beverly Hills to Woodland Hills before the days of freeways.

There was little my mother could do for my father but show him she was keeping up her cheerful spirits. When an idea for a story bubbled in his imagination, she wrote down every word, knowing he might repeat the same sentence and lose his way a moment later.

At his request, she sent his only unproduced script, *The Girl from Bogardus,* to Frank Capra, twice, both times with personal notes, saying he hoped Capra would be interested in directing it. Capra never responded. The notes from my father sit in the Capra archives.

For a long time at night in my bedroom, when I drifted into the twilight of sleep, I found comfort in a recurring fantasy that my father wasn't ill at all but living far away, somewhere in the South of France. I had seen photographs taken during his travels to St. Tropez before the war and I imagined he was there, waiting for me. I knew one day I would find him. In my imagination, I boarded an ocean liner to Paris and took a train through the French countryside until I reached a small coastal city where he was living. I walked the beaches searching for him until I finally saw him in his terry-cloth robe, tanned, alone in front of a cabana. I ran to him, threw my arms around him, and he hugged me hard and said we would never be parted again. Night after night I replayed the story like an old familiar song, sometimes delaying the ending to savor its conclusion before falling into a deep sleep.

On afternoons when my mother wasn't working, she sometimes made a pot of tea and cinnamon toast for the two of us. I chattered about school and she usually asked, "Vicola, shall I tell your fortune?" I listened intently as she read the tea leaves and made optimistic predictions about my future. "You will take a wonderful trip . . . You have lots of friends . . ." She wanted to paint a whole and cheerful future for me. If I caught her with a worried expression, which I often did, I saw how she tried to hide it from me. I did whatever I could to ease her burden.

A phone call came to my mother in early 1955 from the Writers Guild of America West. My father was to be given the prestigious Laurel Award for Screenwriting Achievement. The *Variety* headline read ROBERT RISKIN WINS WGA'S LAUREL AWARD. The article went on: "The Laurel Award is given to the screenwriter who through the years has made outstanding contributions to his industry and profession and advanced the literature of motion pictures." My mother attended the gala ceremony at the Moulin Rouge nightclub and received a standing ovation. She was moved to know my father was not forgotten. When she brought the award to him the next day, he said to her with a wry, lopsided grin, "Do I get to keep it?"

On September 20, 1955, a doctor telephoned from the Motion Picture Hospital. The end of my father's life was near. My mother wrote, "I was able to get there and sit with Bob for about a half hour before he went. There was no talking; I imagine I was helping him make a transition. Bob had been ill for five years." How my mother told us is vague to me now, but I am sure she used a euphemism like "Your daddy is gone."

The memorial service was held three days later before an overflow audience at the Grace Chapel at Inglewood Park Cemetery. Bobby and Susan stayed home, finding it emotionally too difficult. I accompanied my mother, not wanting her to be alone.

According to the *Los Angeles Examiner*, a "galaxy" of friends from the film industry attended. Stories around the country read, "One of Hollywood's all-time great screenwriters dies." Rabbi Edgar Magnin, "rabbi to the stars," officiated. I had never seen a rabbi before and when he recited the Mourner's Kaddish in Hebrew, the words were foreign—"*Yisadal v'yiskadash shmei rabbah* . . ."—but at ten I grasped for the first time that my family was Jewish.

Writer and comedian George Jessel said in his eulogy, "The story of Robert Riskin is in three acts," he said. "You can write the first two on a joyous note; you will have to write the last with a tear."

Frank Capra did not attend the memorial service. For those aware of the closeness of their friendship and partnership, his absence was mystifying, just as it was bewildering that during the five years of my father's illness he had never visited, either at our home or the Motion Picture Country Home. When my mother ran into Capra years later at the Universal commissary, she asked why. "I wasn't sure it would be good for

Bob," he said. He also said people told him that he shouldn't come, that he wasn't wanted, which is untrue.

Capra's failure to visit rankled Jo Swerling. One day, pacing in front of my father, he said, "It's appalling that Frank has never been to see you. He should have been here. He should be here now." From his wheelchair, my father looked up, "You're talking about my good friend, Jo."

For a long time I, too, wondered about Capra's absence during my father's illness. Perhaps the death of Frank's own son, which had been devastating to him, was the reason. Maybe my father's stroke had been too painful to accept. Writer John Gunther had planned to visit our house while staying at the nearby Bel-Air Hotel, but told my mother he was unable to find the courage to see my father. Gunther's son, who had also been operated on by Dr. Putnam, had died, and he couldn't bear revisiting the pain.

My mother said she believed Frank was torn up by my father's illness, and that it may have been too tough to face.

Was there perhaps another reason? Perhaps their friendship was less important to Capra than to my father. Could Capra have been angry with him, possibly for denying him writing credit on *Riding High*?

I believe now my father understood what it has taken me a lifetime to figure out.

Capra was a talented director with an impeccable sense of timing and a lively visual style, and he was masterful with actors. He also was filled with insecurities that led him to believe, especially later in life, that he was in a world where the limelight anyone else got somehow detracted from his own. It was a zero-sum game.

My father never felt another's glory detracted from his own. He was generous by nature and he liked others to succeed and get full credit. He also may have looked at Capra as a brother, or maybe as he looked at one of his characters—Dave the Dude, Apple Annie, Peter Warne, Longfellow Deeds, Long John Willoughby come to mind—good people with human foibles and fears whom he cared about and wanted to see find their place in the sun.

Writer Sidney Buchman told an interviewer, "Robert Riskin had a saying: 'When he works on a film, it is impossible for Capra to sleep.' In the morning, Capra would arrive with twenty or so pages in which he'd written down all his ideas. Most were terrible," Buchman said, and then—and here he said he agreed with my father—"all of a sudden there would be one which was astounding." Like Buchman, my father disregarded the bad and took Capra's good ideas and made them work, but it frustrated

Capra that he was never able to write screenplays himself, or get what he thought was his due credit.

The final word, coming years later, long after my father had died, was inexpressibly sad. With Capra's films increasingly poorly reviewed and failing at the box office, his opportunities dried up. He moved to Palm Springs and seemed to grow bitter about the film industry and especially writers. His obsession with the "one-man-one-film" theory grew. In interviews, he batted away questions about what writers had brought to the films he had directed, minimizing the contributions of Robert Riskin, Jo Swerling, and Sidney Buchman. He paid my father a backhanded compliment. "Riskin was a giant among screenwriters—at least when he worked with me." Late in his life when Capra was asked about writers he had worked with, he said, "Fuck the writers!"

As an adult, I saw Capra only once. At the invitation of a friend, I went to a talk he gave at the American Film Institute campus in Beverly Hills. When I saw him, a short white-haired man with a crowd of students around him, I wasn't sure whether to approach. Then the crowd fell away and I was standing alone next to him, just the two of us. "I'm Bob Riskin's daughter," I said. "I wanted to say hello." He seemed happy to see me, but at that moment the moderator called him to the terrace for the lecture. He said we could talk later.

I listened as Capra talked about his life and career. He never mentioned my father or any of the writers he worked with or others who contributed so much to the films he directed. During the question period, he was asked about the witty dialogue his pictures were famous for, and the novel use of words such as "pixillated" and my father's invention of the word "doodle" for *Mr. Deeds.* Capra deflected the question artfully, never mentioning a writer, saying only that he was responsible for the whole movie.

As I sat there, I reflected on something my father had told an interviewer years before. "So little is known of the contribution that the screenwriter makes to the original story. He puts so much into it, blows up a slim idea into a finished product, and then is dismissed with the ignominious credit line—'dialogue writer.'" I slipped away quietly and never saw Capra again.

In 1977, when Samson Raphaelson accepted the Writers Guild Laurel Award for Screenwriting Achievement, he captured the essence of a good and successful writer-director relationship. He and director Ernst Lubitsch had created many wonderful films together: *Angel, Trouble in Paradise, The Shop Around the Corner, Heaven Can Wait.* "Looking back over my career," Raphaelson told his fellow writers, "I can truthfully say that Lubitsch was responsible for some of my best lines." He paused a moment. "And I can equally truthfully say I was responsible for some of his best shots and visual moments."

I believe this was true of Frank Capra and Robert Riskin.

After my father's death, we muddled through as a family. Bobby devoured books and mounted science fair projects that all won prizes. The closeness we felt when we were young faded. He stayed up all hours hibernating in his workshop. His room was an unholy mess where he never picked anything up or put anything away, and the bathroom we shared looked like a war zone. We grew distant, ships passing in the night.

Sometimes I saw him in the kitchen around midnight, making himself a peanut butter and jelly or grilled cheese sandwich. He was often grumpy, no doubt fighting off his own sadness. But sometimes he was animated, eager to talk, and he went on for hours about a scientific discovery or amazing new fact he had uncovered. I was in awe of his intellect and range, and still am. In high school, he built his own early computer and taught himself to play the acoustic guitar. After a year at the University of California at Berkeley, Bobby returned to Los Angeles to run and eventually own McCabe's Guitar Shop, a legendary haunt where Linda Ronstadt, Odetta, Jackson Browne, John Lee Hooker, Arlo Guthrie, Joni Mitchell, T Bone Burnett, the Blind Boys of Alabama, and other musicians hung out and gave concerts. It was the heyday of folk music. "I always wanted to create a place where musicians would feel at home," he said, and he did. He married Esperanza, a bright and warmhearted woman of Mexican heritage, and they have two children and four grandchildren who are a regular and energetic presence in their home. When I talk with Bobby, which is now more and more often, I am reminded of his integrity. A good man.

Susan studied theater arts in high school and at UCLA and went to New York to pursue an acting career. I saw her on Broadway, filling in for both Geraldine Page and Elizabeth Ashley in *Agnes of God*, and her performances were electric. Each summer for nearly thirty years, Susan went to Tamworth, New Hampshire, to perform in summer stock at a theater run by Francis Cleveland, son of President Grover Cleveland.

She was never happier than when acting, unless it was when she was teaching acting to young people. When Bobby and I were very small, she gave us parts to play in her own made-up stories, and when she was at UCLA, she recruited us as extras in her friends' student movies. Later I

Susan (left) at the Barnstormers Theatre, a summer stock troupe in Tamworth, New Hampshire, where she directed Fay's play *The Meadowlark* (1985), about Vina's youth in Lark, Utah. Robert Riskin Jr. with his wife, Esperanza, owners of the legendary McCabe's Guitar Shop in Santa Monica (2016).

visited her at the City Center in New York and was awed by the way Susan, sometimes so tentative in life, had charismatic command over three hundred unruly inner-city kids. Now that she's nearing eighty, I've arranged for her to live nearby in Santa Barbara. I hear my father saying, "Glad you're looking after your big sister, rascal. She sure looked after you."

Growing up, my mother wanted me to be happy and mostly I was, at least on the surface. During my teens, I lost myself in girlfriends and boyfriends, pursued popularity, joined a social club, spent summers at the beach in Santa Monica or at summer camp, ran for class office, mastered geometry (sort of), danced to Johnny Mathis and did the Twist, fought pimples, learned how to drive my yellow Chevy convertible, smoked menthol cigarettes, and drank beer—all the teen stuff of the early 1960s.

After two years of college, I did a junior year abroad in Aix-en-Provence, France. I felt free and happy in Aix, in love with the whole country, France, Frenchmen—one, Paul, in particular—the old stone buildings, Jacques Brel, the melody of the language, the savory and musty smells. Was it coincidence that I gravitated to the country where I had imagined my father living when I was a child?

During those years, and even before my father died, my mother relied increasingly for guidance on my father's red-headed doctor, Sanford Rothenberg. Sandy stopped by on his way home from the hospital so often that it soon became evident his place at the dinner table was becoming permanent. His visits were not always motivated by a wish to discuss my father's condition; it was clear he was interested in my mother. Bobby, Susan, and I were unhappy that he sat in Daddy's seat at the head of the table. We found him self-assured, opinionated, lacking the easy charm and wit of our father, but my mother needed someone and felt secure having a man in her life. He helped her invest her earnings in income-producing real estate to the point that eventually she didn't need to work. They went to good restaurants in Beverly Hills together and to the Turf Terrace at Santa Anita Park on weekends. Wherever they went she was treated like royalty, not just because of her celebrity but because her vibrancy could still light up a room.

After returning from France and graduating from the University of Southern California, I went into a tailspin. The sadness of losing my father and its impact on my life was still buried deep. I went to a psychiatrist who listened passively—he was trained as an analyst—but when he provided little help, I moved on. I earned a master's degree in psychology and in the process searched for answers and sorted out my own feelings. I became a psychotherapist. In my practice, patients talked openly, revealing secrets, confusions, longings, and fears. Perhaps my own early life loss made me sensitive to their suffering. I navigated them through their depressions, anxiety, dreams, and ambitions, their stories shaping a remarkable mosaic of human experience.

Then marriage. First a short one that didn't gel, to a gifted producer, Alan Sacks, who created *Welcome Back, Kotter,* and then the one that has given me love and contentment, to my husband of thirty-nine years, David Rintels. Our social circles had overlapped in the early 1970s, but we had lost contact after my early marriage. When we're with friends, David sometimes tells how he won my heart.

In 1975, as the newly elected president of the Writers Guild, he wrote an article for the *Los Angeles Times*. "I wanted to take up the cause of writers everywhere so I wrote about the auteur theory, the idea that directors, not writers, deserve to be called the authors of movies. That use of the word auteur rankles all screenwriters. My idea was that if directors could be called auteurs, then writers, who give direction to the entire film when they write the screenplay, should be called *directeurs*. It was tongue-in-cheek, of course, but I hoped to make a point." He did, and numerous writers responded happily to the article. A group of producers, expanding on his idea, sent a letter to the *Times* offering their own "Produceur Theory" of film. Directors were not as happy.

David ended his piece with a story, possibly apocryphal, about my father. "Robert Riskin had worked for years with Frank Capra, and all this time Capra gave interviews about Capra films, the Capra touch, Capra this and Capra that, often without mentioning that another man had written his films. One day, after reading one Capra interview too many about the Capra touch, Riskin put 100 pages of blank white paper on Capra's desk and said, 'Here Frank, put the Capra touch on this.'"

Hollywood writers have told and retold this story for decades, and even today ask me if it really happened. I don't know. My father always denied it, but Everett swore it was true and spread the story more widely.

"After the piece appeared," David says, "I got letters from Vicki's mother, her uncle Everett, her brother and sister, and also Vicki, all thanking me for reminding people of Robert Riskin's place in film history. I asked Vicki to lunch. What I didn't tell her for ten years was that I hoped she'd see the article and get in touch with me."

I did more than get in touch with him. Two years later I married him.

I tell a different story about how we were destined to come together. I had gone to the first reading of *Clarence Darrow*, David's one-man play starring Henry Fonda, directed by John Houseman. There were perhaps twenty people in the small theater in West Hollywood. Almost as soon as the lights went down I was enthralled by the writing, the ideas about justice and humanity, and Fonda's performance. "Whoever wrote this play is a fine man," I thought. Later, Henry Fonda opened *Clarence Darrow* on Broadway to glowing reviews.

As a television writer, David's Harvard education in history served him well. His award-winning writing career has included *Fear on Trial, Gideon's Trumpet, Sakharov, Day One, Andersonville, Nuremberg,* and *World War II: When Lions Roared.* In 1997, when he was given the Writers Guild Laurel Award for TV Writing Achievement, my mother came with me to lead the cheers.

After we married, I earned my doctorate in psychology and continued in private practice for several years. I had as one patient Pat, a woman in her mid-50s, dignified, private, never married, living alone. When she was referred to me she had just been diagnosed with terminal cancer.

Before I agreed to see her, I thought about the powerlessness to save my father I had felt as a child. Would I be able to help her? And at what cost?

During our nine months together, I grew to care deeply about her, as a patient and a person. I encouraged her to be open, to share what she was going through with a few people around her she could trust. As she did, a circle of devoted caregivers formed around her, enriching her life in ways she had never known. During our time together, she also searched for and found a child she had given up for adoption as a young girl, and was overcome with relief and happiness when she learned her son was thriving.

When she died, this previously private woman was surrounded by friends and family who cared deeply about her, which made her passing easier for her. And I had learned from Pat finally to come to terms with death, including my father's, to understand that it is a part of life that can be faced and accepted. I tried to put what I had discovered in our time together down on paper, but when I found it difficult, David asked if we could do the story together as a movie for television.

It was the perfect resolution. David crafted my story into a lovely teleplay we titled *The Last Best Year* (1990), and we went to Canada to film it for ABC, with Mary Tyler Moore playing me and Bernadette Peters the patient. Director John Erman did a superb job, and Mary and Bernadette were outstanding. *People* magazine wrote:

> It's a singular TV movie both for the emotional complexity of
> its characters and for its poignant performances. Peters is utterly
> convincing as a sweet, timorous woman who has sealed herself off
> from her feelings. Moore, in her meatiest role since *Ordinary People,*
> is strong as a shrink whose professional facade is threatened by
> memories of her own father's death from cancer.

The world of filmmaking was suddenly intoxicating to me, just as it had been for my parents. I wanted to do more. David and I had enjoyed working as a team and we made plans to do more together. We produced *A*

Town Torn Apart (1992), a true story about a remarkable educator, starring Michael Tucker and Jill Eikenberry. I began slowly to close down my practice.

I was eager to write and next I adapted Willa Cather's classic novel *My Ántonia* for David and me to produce. The USA Network bought it and David and I headed to Nebraska, land of Cather, to produce it with an outstanding cast: Jason Robards, Eva Marie Saint, Neal Patrick Harris, and a Romanian-born actress, Elina Löwensohn, who played Ántonia. *Variety* called it "a fine job of compressing the passion, personal sacrifice, joy and love of the land depicted in what some think is the author's finest book into a classy telefilm."

My world was changing from the quiet intensity of a psychotherapist to the whirl of writer and producer. This was a time when movies for television were a staple, and David and I went on to produce *The Member of the Wedding* with Alfre Woodard and Anna Paquin, based on his adaptation of Carson McCullers' novel. We did *World War II: When Lions Roared*, a 1994 miniseries David wrote about the relationship of Roosevelt, Churchill, and Stalin; it starred John Lithgow, Bob Hoskins, and Michael Caine and won the Long-form Television award from the Producers Guild of America. During the late 1990s, I wrote television scripts for the networks and *Hallmark Hall of Fame,* but by then the movie-for-television business was winding down, and to my disappointment, projects I wrote were not filmed.

I had been proud to join the Writers Guild of America, the union my father and his friends and colleagues had fought to establish in the 1930s and 1940s. The modest two-page contract the writers and the companies first signed has in a half century grown to where it is over 600 pages long, covering every aspect of a writer's employment. I volunteered for Guild committees, went to Washington to lobby, gave testimony before the Federal Communications Commission on the dangers of having too few media companies with too much power, fought on behalf of the rights of underrepresented animation writers, and served as a trustee of the health and pension plans of the union, knowing firsthand the importance of a safety net for families.

I have often thought about the writers who put their livelihoods on the line for the benefit of their colleagues and all writers in the future. Writers went on strike in 1960 to win pension and health benefits that, had these plans existed earlier, could have helped my family. The companies contributed $600,000 to start the fund in 1960, which today has grown to more than $2.5 billion. To make the deal to get health and pension plans, the unions had to surrender all claims to television residuals on movies and television made before 1960, meaning my parents, like other writers, directors, and actors from Hollywood's Golden Age would get no continuing income from their movies. Considering the enduring popularity of some of their films, the royalties might have been considerable. That seemed not to bother my mother, who once told Monty Schoedsack, "If we had made a lot of money on the film, we might not have been such nice people," and then they laughed together.

David and I took my mother to Washington, along with Julius Epstein, screenwriter of *Casablanca*, to lobby legislators, hoping to persuade them that if the period of copyright for movies was extended an additional fifteen years, as they were considering, some modest royalties should finally go to old-time writers, directors, and actors. We did not prevail, but as a consolation prize my mother and Epstein were given a standing ovation when Congressman Henry Hyde stopped a hearing to welcome "the legendary guests from Hollywood" who had entered the committee room.

My involvement with the Guild included two years as president, when I butted heads with the leadership of the Directors Guild over the "A Film By" credit that many directors demand. I led meetings at which we asked what movies would have been like without screenwriters such as Paddy Chayefsky, Preston Sturges, William Goldman, Bo Goldman, Frank Pierson, Robert Towne, Ring Lardner Jr., Alvin Sargent, Nora Ephron, Billy Wilder, Dudley Nichols, Dalton Trumbo, Ben Hecht, Jo Swerling, and Robert Riskin and on and on. Without these men and women, a director has a hundred pages of blank paper, although I restrained myself from saying that out loud to the DGA.

During my term, the Guild launched a campaign calling "A Film By" a "Vanity Credit." The effort was inspired and led by Oscar-winning screenwriter Marc Norman (*Shakespeare in Love*) who spoke for writers hoping to persuade directors to stop putting their names—and only their names—above the title of the film. The Guild placed billboards around Los Angeles, each with a photograph of a screenwriter and a famous line of dialogue—"I'm mad as hell and I'm not going to take it anymore," from Paddy Chayefsky's Oscar-winning script for *Network* was one example—with the legend on the billboard saying "Somebody wrote that!" We pointed out to the DGA in private discussions that some of their best directors—including William Wyler and Sidney Lumet, both all-time greats—refused to take a "Film By" credit, considering it disrespectful to writers and all the others who contribute their talents to a film. Credit is about fairness, justice, and respect. No one person does it all alone, and to say a film is by one person devalues the work and the worth of others.

In truth, a screenwriter is blessed to have a partnership with a talented director, as my father had with Capra and as I did with Joseph Sargent on *My Ántonia*. Writer and director each make a unique and invaluable contribution. One has the story to tell and the other a way to tell it. Each can make the other better.

My time as Guild president coincided with the attacks on the World Trade Center and the Pentagon on September 11, 2001. A few months later Karl Rove came to Hollywood to discuss with corporate and union leaders what the entertainment industry might do to fight the "war on terror." The tragedy of 9/11 was one of those moments when all Americans wanted to serve their country, and Rove led the discussion, making clear the government was not trying to censor Hollywood, but suggesting that movies could promote stories and ideas that would be helpful to America abroad. He cautioned the room that this was not a war against Islam.

The companies were represented by their top brass, the unions by their presidents. I suggested that we have a responsibility in the stories we tell and might consider exporting fewer violent movies and developing more stories about ordinary people and real American life. At the time of the meeting, I knew little of my father's work for the Office of War Information, but in retrospect I see that I was only echoing what he had said so eloquently. Films are powerful, and American films influence the understanding of America around the world. As my father told a postwar radio audience, many people around the world know about America only from movies.

Nothing constructive came from the meeting, and certainly no serious reconsideration of the films studios send overseas, or the capacity of film to influence views of America globally.

My father was concerned about the world he would leave his children and I have clearly inherited some of his passion and worldview. For years, I have served on the board of directors of Human Rights Watch, an organization dedicated to advancing global justice. Their offices are in the Empire State Building and I am often there for meetings. I don't like heights so I've never gone to the top, where Kong put my mother down before he was machine-gunned by the airplanes circling around him, but in the lobby of Human Rights Watch there is a *King Kong* poster signed by my mother in her strong handwriting: "For my friends at Human Rights Watch, Fay Wray."

17

We wander, question. But the answer waits in each separate heart—the answer of our own identity and the way by which we can master loneliness and feel that at last we belong.

—CARSON MCCULLERS, "LONELINESS . . .

AN AMERICAN MALADY"

My mother married my father's neurosurgeon, Sanford (Sandy) Rothenberg, in 1971. He was fifteen years her junior but she outlived him by more than a decade. I appreciated the way he cared for her, and David and I enjoyed dinners with them at Chasen's or Spago or lunch at Jimmy's or at the Santa Anita racetrack. A brilliant doctor who performed thousands of brain and spinal surgeries, saving many lives, he paradoxically avoided his own medical checkups and learned too late he had metastatic colon cancer. His last days in 1991 were at home with my mother at his side holding his hand, giving him every ounce of the comfort and care she knew how to give. When I came to visit him, he told me, "Your mother is my best friend." After he died, she lived alone for her remaining thirteen years.

Her final years were spent mostly in New York City, where she lived on the fifty-third floor of Trump Tower at the corner of Fifty-sixth Street and Fifth Avenue. She preferred New York to Los Angeles. Driving around Los Angeles was less safe for her as she grew older and New York was invigorating.

Over the years, whenever we went on location, David and I asked my mother to come with us. She enjoyed being on a movie set, and the cast and crew loved her. The first time she met Bernadette Peters, she watched her do a poignant scene with Mary Tyler Moore in our TV movie *The Last Best Year*. As Bernadette walked off the set, my mother took her in her arms and said, "I love you and I love everyone you love." The crew fussed over my mother, just like the old days. "Are you comfortable, Miss Wray? Can we bring you something, Miss Wray?" And always, "Miss Wray, I fell in love with you when I was a little boy and I saw you in *King Kong*."

Despite many offers, she came out of retirement only once, as a favor to David whom she always called "My David." He asked her to play Henry Fonda's landlady, a kind woman of simple tastes—no makeup, a simple house dress, a plain straw hat—in *Gideon's Trumpet* (1980). The role was small, with not a moment of flash, but the chance to work with Fonda and her David was reason enough. After a lifetime of starring roles, she found no difficulty in leaving the stage in a small and humble part.

In the late 1980s she came with us to Montreal where we were shooting David's script *Day One,* about the making of the atomic bomb. Months later, she was having lunch in a New York restaurant when a member of the crew saw her through the window and came in. "Miss Wray," he began, "I just want to thank you for being so nice to me and everyone else in Montreal last year." He had been born in the Bronx, where he still lived, he told her, and he owed his career to seeing her in *King Kong,* which had led him into the film world. He added, "And I think the film turned out well, too. I heard it was nominated for the Emmy."

"I remember very well," my mother said. "*Day One.*"

"Oh, dey did?" said her new Bronx friend. "I didn't know dat."

For a long time after that, whenever we visited her in New York, she would open the door, throw her arms in the air and laugh, "Day One!" Or maybe it was "Dey Won." Either way was fine.

We took her to the theater frequently and learned to be selective. We

Fay retired in 1965, and came out of retirement only once, to play a small part in *Gideon's Trumpet* (1980) with Henry Fonda, as a favor for my husband and her son-in-law, writer-producer David W. Rintels.

Fay Wray, age ninety-five, speaking to an audience about her love of Hollywood at the Palm Beach International Film Festival, 2003, after receiving the Legend in Film Award

steered clear of some contemporary dramas, including those written by David Mamet and others who used salty language. She had heard all the words but never used them herself and found them jarring and unnecessary.

She never lost her youthful enthusiasm. When she was in her late eighties, I asked if there was anything in her life she'd wanted to do but hadn't gotten around to. There was one thing, she said. She had always wanted to see Santa Fe, the outpost where her grandfather, Daniel Webster Jones, had signed up to herd sheep through Ute country to the Utah nation. I booked airline tickets for the two of us that weekend. We flew to Albuquerque and rented a car. As we came to the city's outskirts, there was an enormous roadside sign, WELCOME TO SANTA FE, with the city visible in the distance. My mother clapped her hands and said, "Oooh, I can't wait to come back here."

In New York, she befriended a young journalist and documentary filmmaker, Rick McKay (*Broadway: the Golden Age, By the Legends Who Were There*), who took her to dinner, to the movies, and to film festivals in Hollywood, London, Miami, and San Francisco. He escorted her and me to the Oscars in Los Angeles, where Billy Crystal left the stage and came to where she was sitting and introduced her as one of the great screen stars of the Golden Age. She gave dozens of interviews and enjoyed life as a legend of film history.

Sitting at the windows of her apartment overlooking Manhattan, she wrote for hours on her yellow pad, inventing characters, dramas, making notes about life and people, writing poems and doggerel. She wrote her autobiography, *On the Other Hand,* and short stories and articles like "My Manhattan," that appeared in *The New York Times Magazine.* She rewrote her play based on Vina, *The Meadowlark*, about a woman trying to survive with dignity in a small mining town, and she worked with Susan, who performed the lead role in New Hampshire and Pennsylvania.

Sometimes she read Emerson, who was always on her bedside table and still inspired her reflections about the human spirit. She sailed through the *New York Times* crossword and acrostic puzzles. When she thought of lost friends, she scanned the atlas and made notes about where they might be reborn. John Monk Saunders—2 rue Cail, Paris; Robert Riskin—Fairview St., Detroit; Dolores Del Rio—Santa Rosa, California. She talked on the phone for hours with Sandy's son, Steve, whom she adored and who often visited her with his wife, Sandra, and their children. Sometimes she shared meals with special friends, including Clifford Odets' son, Walt, who visited her when he was in New York. He recently told me, "Your mother was so warm. I could have talked to her for hours." Occasionally she came back to Los Angeles to visit Bobby's family and her grandchildren, Nora

With my mother, age ninety-one, and Rick McKay. Fay was invited to be a special guest at the seventieth annual Academy Awards, 1998. Here greeting Anjelica Huston

and Jacob, whom she loved, and came to Santa Barbara to stay with David and me.

Then came the first turning point in spring 2000.

The phone was ringing when David and I got back to our hotel room where we were vacationing near Lyons, France. Susan was calling from New York to say our mother had fallen in her apartment and badly broken her femur; she had been unable to get up or summon help and lay there for unknown hours until discovered by a housekeeper. She had undergone emergency surgery and was in the hospital. We made arrangements to get to New York as quickly as possible.

Trapped in her room at the rehabilitation wing of New York Presbyterian Hospital, my mother looked pale but lit up when we walked in. "Oh, darlin'," she said and grabbed my hand hard. "There you are! And my David."

"Hi, Faysie, how you feeling?" David asked with concern. Faysie was how he always affectionately addressed her.

"My goodness, Mom, how did you get here?"

"Not by cab," she laughed. "I want to go back home, darlin', but they say I have to stay for rehabilitation. This is ridiculous."

My mother had not been in a hospital since I was born. She attributed her good health to her lifelong practice of avoiding annual physical exams and visits to doctors, and eating well.

"I need to be in San Francisco in six weeks," she said. "I promised those nice people I would come. The Castro Theatre invited me to a special screening of *The Wedding March*, you see." Her mind was fixed on going, but it now seemed impossible.

"Why don't I see what the doctor has to say?"

The doctor said my mother might not walk again unless she worked on her rehabilitation, and even then he was uncertain. She was fragile. "Maybe you can help her get on her feet a little. And oh, by the way, she needs an aortic valve replacement which we should get done while she's here in the hospital, but so far she's said no." He delivered his opinion matter-of-factly, like ticking off a grocery list, but a chill came over me.

"If she has the heart surgery, what good will it do?" I asked.

"Her aortic valve has calcified and the blood doesn't get to her heart. She'll have more energy and live longer. Simple as that."

"But she just went through major surgery on her leg and now if you open up her chest—put her under major anesthetic again—at ninety-three? Is there a risk she might not survive it?"

"At her age, there's always a chance something could happen in surgery."

"How long might she live if she doesn't have surgery?"

"A year, maybe. It's hard to say." He tucked his pencil back into the breast pocket of his white lab coat, indicating the conversation was over.

I went back to sit on my mother's bed. I fluffed her pillow and gave her some orange juice.

"What do you think, Mom? What do you feel about the surgery?"

"Ridiculous. A doctor told me a few years ago I should have heart surgery. He was a stupid man. Here I am and just fine." I knew she trusted me and if I pushed, she would have the surgery. But was it right to do at her age? I told her we should think about it.

"But if you want to go to San Francisco, there's no getting around rehabilitation. You'll have to walk," I said. "If it's okay with the doctor, why don't we give it a try? I figure if you can walk around the entire floor, you'll prove to them you can go home."

"We'll do it!" she said.

The physical therapist came to help us get her out of bed. She put weight on her leg and tried walking to the door. It must have been agonizing because she clamped her face rigidly as she put one foot in front of the other, me on one side, the therapist on the other, David following close behind with a wheelchair if needed. With all the willpower her frail body could muster, all the courage and determination that had been her lifelong way, she made it to the door. The therapist put her in the wheelchair to rest.

The next day we came back and tried again. She made it to the door again, and this time walked all the way back to the bed. Another victory lap! The next day we walked down the hallway. In a week, she was making the circle around the entire floor fairly easily. It was wonderful to behold.

"I couldn't do this without you," she said to me. I had grown to be her best friend.

Between our walking sessions, I arranged for a nurse when she came home and I recruited her housekeeper to come extra hours rather than have more strangers around.

I called a friend and asked if he could arrange for me to meet with his friend, a widely respected New York cardiologist, to discuss the heart surgery.

"It's not an easy decision," the doctor said.

"But what are the odds she'll survive surgery? That's what I want to know."

"I'd say fifty-fifty."

"If it were your mother, what would you do?" I asked him.

"I don't think at her age I'd take the chance, honestly. One thing to consider is that she's had a good life and maybe let her enjoy what's left of it."

A week later my mother was back in her New York apartment with rotating, around-the-clock home care that she accepted gracefully. Her rationale was: "If it makes you feel better, sweetheart, I don't mind having these ladies here."

Six weeks later, on July 7, 2000, David and I walked into the ornate Castro Theatre in San Francisco for the special screening of *The Wedding March* that my mother had promised to attend. There was an overflow crowd and I heard someone say they had queued up before dawn to get in. We took our seats and as the lights went down a hush fell across the audience like a gentle wave. The man in front of me whispered audibly to his neighbor, "Someone said Miss Wray might be here!"

The emcee came on stage and took the microphone. "It had always been our hope to have Miss Wray grace our stage tonight. I must tell you that recently, just a few weeks ago, she went through major surgery. Travel was not easy for her. That's why it gives me such pleasure to introduce to you our special guest this evening, Miss Fay Wray."

With that my mother walked on stage, just as she had planned, regal and smiling and waving to the crowd, which rose and applauded her. She wore a lovely white silk suit and pumps, her silvery hair perfectly coiffed, her bright red lipstick in place. She came slowly on, with her friend Rick by her side to steady her, until she found her key light center stage. When he took a gentlemanly half step back, she wobbled.

An audible gasp came from the still-standing audience. To put them at ease, she said, "Never mind getting old. I love my life. Every day gets better and better." She opened her arms wide to the audience as if to embrace all of them. The crowd went wild and gave her another sustained ovation.

As the audience cheered I stood slowly, leaning on David, managing the surge of relief she had made it onstage at all. It had been a challenge getting her to San Francisco, with Rick and a nurse and wheelchairs and airports, but her fierce determination made it possible. She made a few more charming remarks to the crowd and walked back offstage with Rick, who eased her into a waiting wheelchair. Once the movie began, he quietly wheeled her down the aisle of the darkened auditorium and helped her into the empty seat next to me. The organist was playing the original score from *The Wedding March* with melodramatic punctuations.

"Are you sure you want to watch this thing again?" she whispered to me impishly.

I took her hand. I cried quietly through the movie, as I always cry during *The Wedding March,* that heart-wrenching masterpiece. I cry especially from seeing my mother so young and beautiful as Mitzie. A scene in the quiet corner of a beer garden where von Stroheim romances her under falling apple blossoms leaves me choked up, as does the ending, when he marries Zasu Pitts. How could he have married Zasu Pitts when he loved my mother! David kept a comforting arm around me during the film as the three of us snuggled close to one another in the dark theater. My gratitude for him that night, the way we had braided our lives together, was overwhelming.

My mother never went through the aortic valve replacement surgery. The surgery was less important than making sure she had moments like these to look forward to. While there would only be three more years, they were enough for her to still savor.

At the end of her life, she was still Fay Wray.

Director Peter Jackson had been so smitten with *King Kong* as a young man that he decided to remake the movie on the heels of his triumph with *The Lord of the Rings.* As he prepared the new *King Kong,* he was insistent about offering my mother a small part as an homage to the original. I met with him and his wife, Fran Walsh, and their writing partner Philippa Boyens at their luxurious bungalow at the Beverly Hills Hotel, where he showed me some of his computer-generated scenes and told me how he would like my mother in a crowd at the end, to say the famous final line, *"It was beauty killed the beast."*

The three of them were keen to meet her. I liked them immediately, but it had been more than a year since my mother's fall and she was frailer, more confused, tiring easily, and had trouble hearing and remembering. I feared they might be disappointed.

Rick arranged for them to have dinner together in his small New York apartment. Peter, Fran, and Philippa flew back to New York the night after *The Lord of the Rings* swept the Oscars. Naomi Watts, who was to play Ann Darrow, joined them. I called my mother before their dinner to tell her about Peter's triumph at the Oscars, but I wasn't sure it registered.

A few days later I was in New York to visit her and we sat at the small round dining table in her apartment as we had countless times before. She dawdled over her breakfast, her appetite now diminished, her mind unfocused. It had become harder for me to find things that interested her to talk about. I pulled out a deck of cards to play poker with her, five-card stud, and rigged the game so she won. Each hand I dealt she looked at her cards a long time, searching for clues about what to do with them.

"So how was your dinner with Peter Jackson, Mom?" I asked.

"Fine."

"What did you think of Peter?"

"He's too fat." She smiled. (Peter has since lost seventy pounds.)

"And what about Naomi Watts? What did you think of her?"

"She's too skinny," she said playfully, still staring at her cards. In fact, when she met Naomi they ended the evening with a hug and my mother said, "Ann Darrow's in good hands."

"Wouldn't you like to be in Peter's remake of *King Kong*?" I asked.

"I don't think so."

"Are you sure, Mom?

"Noooooooo," she said with a low sonorous sound, leaning forward with a glint in her eye. And that was that.

Over a lifetime, my mother had grown to appreciate *King Kong*, and no matter how wonderful the new film, she didn't want to mix the new with the old. She wanted the original *King Kong* and Fay Wray to be eternally entwined. And in my heart, I wanted everyone to remember her as the young Fay Wray playing Ann Darrow, and not the shadow of herself with her now sometimes vacant eyes and waning spirit. Peter's affection for my mother was still that of a boy in love and he respected her decision without complaint. At the end of his epic rendering of *King Kong*, he paid tribute to her with a final title card, "To the incomparable Fay Wray."

Toward the end of her life my mother often went to Central Park in her wheelchair, guided by Phuntsog Wangmo, a woman I found to live with her. Phuntsog, a Tibetan doctor, had an earthy, steady kindness. She routinely tucked a cashmere blanket around my mother's knees and pushed her to the park to watch children play and have vanilla ice cream.

They often stopped in front of a large statue of Daniel Webster, the great American senator and patriot. It was my mother's custom when she approached the statue to thrust her hand in the air and point at his massive figure, asserting ownership of him, "That is my grandfather!" Phuntsog wasn't sure whether to believe her, as my mother's mind now sometimes floated between dream and reality.

"Is it true?" Phuntsog asked me privately when I walked with them one day. "She stops here every time we come."

"It's not *completely* true," I said, knowing where my mother's mind now resided. Like an ancient crystal vase with tiny fractures from age, her mind was less sturdy and sometimes gripped by images that came from nowhere and anywhere—images of my father, and her sisters Willow and Vaida, her brothers Vivien, Dick, and Victor, old friends like Merian C. Cooper and Monty Schoedsack, Cary Grant, Janet Gaynor, and Dolores Del Rio, or Vina or Joe or Daniel Webster Jones. She told me that occasionally these people visited her, appearing like specters in her bedroom, not frightening her but as if welcoming her to the other side.

"When will I die?" she asked me one day as we walked slowly around the block of her New York apartment, which the doctor had said was good for her to do. "I don't know, Mom," I said. "That's something that happens to all of us, but sometimes we can't know when."

She now was as thin and delicate as rice paper. Until her late eighties, she had colored her hair deep brown, but now had gracefully let it go gray-white. The silvery effect set off her blue eyes beautifully. There were many lines on her face, but she had never wanted plastic surgery so her laugh was free, open and electric. The secret to her beauty, other than good bone structure and inner charm, was Pond's cold cream—a big jar that cost her eight dollars. That's all she ever used, she told me.

On the days we walked along Fifth Avenue, I took her hand to steady her. Her left knee was missing every bit of cartilage, causing the bones to rub together painfully, but she never complained. It was her custom to stop when the pain became acute, to distract herself. "You see that bird in the tree, Vicola?" pointing to a playful sparrow, allowing herself time to let the discomfort in her knee subside. Her hand no longer had much strength and was mottled with liver spots and the blue veins of aging.

That afternoon, she held on to my arm tightly and I held tightly on to hers. Missing from her right ring finger now was the Deco-style sapphire and diamond ring I had always admired; she had given it to me a few years earlier and since that day I have never removed it. Today, when I glance at it on my right hand, I see her nature reflected in it—classic, elegant, and strong.

We braved an intersection, as pedestrians bore down on us like an advancing army. I feared someone might knock her over. New York operates with an intensity of oblivious forward motion.

Moments like her dramatic gesture toward Daniel Webster that summer afternoon in Central Park kept life playful for her and energized her, helping her defy her approaching end—as if to say, the way a child does with exuberance: *Mine! He's mine!* And there was logic to her ownership of him—her grandfather, Daniel Webster Jones, was a towering figure in her childhood pantheon of heroes, the wellspring of her resilience, a great man she had revered as a young girl in Arizona ninety years before.

• • •

The call that her end was near came when I was on my way back from a sailing trip along the southwest coast of Turkey. David and I and two other couples and their daughters had spent a week cruising the warm turquoise Mediterranean, eating fresh-caught fish every day, swapping silly tales, playing games, and talking global politics.

Phuntsog was uncharacteristically agitated when she reached me at our Istanbul hotel. She was worried and sounded unsure what to do. My mother had said she was tired and needed to lie down to rest. Her breathing had become labored and then seemed to stop. Phuntsog had called the cardiologist who wanted urgently to talk to me. She gave me the doctor's home number.

"I'm afraid her heart has given out," he said. "We can call 911 to resuscitate her. She might make it until you come home, but . . ." I heard his newborn baby fussing in the background.

My head was in a whirl. "The paramedics—tell me again, what would they do?"

"They would try to use the defibrillator to get her heart going if they can, and take her to the emergency room. It might break her ribs." The old hotel phone made his voice sound like he was underwater. I took a deep breath and saw through the window the boats gliding along the Bosphorus, the waterway that divides the great Ottoman city and Asia from Europe. I was so far away. It would take at least twenty-four hours to get to New York. I wanted to be with her, but not if it meant her suffering.

"What do you think? Should we let her go?" I asked quietly. I had anticipated this moment for some time. I hoped she was ready. She was at least at home, away from the glaring lights and chaos of a hospital emergency room. I wished I could be there and hold her hand. So many times, I have told myself, *I wish I had been there.*

"I think that seems right," the doctor said. "I'm so sorry."

"Have you spoken to my brother or sister?"

"Yes. They agree."

I listened to the distant and doleful sound of the Muslim call to prayer from Hagia Sofia, the great mosque of Istanbul. David and I hugged each other hard and quietly shared our thoughts about the sweep and wonder of my mother's life. We went to bed early. There was much to do in the days ahead, with many arrangements, and sleep did not come easily.

Two days after she died, six weeks short of her ninety-seventh birthday, the rainbow-colored lights on the spire of the Empire State Building that glow brightly above the New York skyline were illuminated in tribute to Fay Wray.

. . .

A few years earlier my mother had wondered if the Hollywood Forever Cemetery should be her final resting place. While she had no interest in planning the details of her burial—that seemed too pedestrian to her—the question entered her mind from time to time. "What do you think, darlin'?" she asked, handing me a newspaper story. "A young man is restoring the old cemetery next to Paramount Studios. It's right near where I lived with my mother in a little bungalow when we first came to California. Rudolph Valentino is buried there and my friend Janet Gaynor." Her mind was circling back to a happy earlier time.

Hollywood Forever, or Hollywood Memorial Cemetery as it was once called, had been the cemetery of the early power brokers of Los Angeles, men like Harrison Gray Otis of the *Los Angeles Times,* and Griffith J. Griffith who donated Griffith Park to the city, and Cecil B. DeMille, but it had fallen into disrepair. A twenty-seven-year-old film buff from Saint Louis, Tyler Cassity, whose family was in the mortuary business, had bought the cemetery in 1997. I had read that the television series *Six Feet Under* modeled their lead characters after Tyler and his brother.

A year after my mother had shown me the article, I toured the grounds with Tyler, cruising along walkways in a golf cart and reading the headstones that told the stories of the once rich and famous of Los Angeles. There was an ecumenical spirit to the cemetery: a small Thai temple, a burial corner for children whose families were poor, a Jewish section, an Armenian section. My mother would approve of the diverse heritages.

We stopped at the edge of a pond with a fountain in the center. Its gentle sound masked the nearby traffic. Ducks paddled in the water. My mother will like this pond with a family of ducks, I thought, and the chance to be near her old friends like Nelson Eddy, Tyrone Power, and Douglas Fairbanks Jr. As Tyler and I sat together on the grass at dusk—"magic hour" they call it in the movie business—the sky turned a soft pink. "You've picked a good spot," he said. I asked him if we might plant a willow tree next to the plot in honor of my mother's sister, Willow. He offered to make the tree a gift to our family.

"Where is your father buried?" he asked. "Perhaps you'd like them to be together. You could bring your father here, if you'd want. There is room for him to be right next to her."

The idea of reuniting my parents gripped my heart, the chance to rewrite the final chapter of their lives and give a happy ending to their story. Maybe I could repair my sadness that their love was interrupted by my father's illness and death. Maybe I could restore my father to his rightful place, next to her; but then again, maybe this was just the wish of a child. I would have to think about it.

A Blackhawk holy man said 150 years ago:

> "You have noticed that everything an Indian does is in a circle, and that is because the Power of the World always works in circles, and everything tries to be round . . . The sky is round, and I have heard that the earth is round like a ball, and so are all the stars. The wind, in its greatest power, whirls. Birds make their nest in circles, for theirs is the same religion as ours . . . Even the seasons form a great circle in their changing, and always come back again to where they were. The life of a man is a circle from childhood to childhood, and so it is in everything where power moves.

We are fragile and remarkable beings woven of so many complex threads that it's hard to untangle them to see a true picture of who we are. My life seems an accidental endeavor shaped by chance, such as being born to Fay Wray and Robert Riskin. We stand on the shoulders of those who came before us, our tribe, but learn our own lessons and fashion our own lives. Some of my parents' friends tell me I've inherited their optimism and I'd like to think it's true.

Recently I stopped by Hollywood Forever to visit my mother and see if everything was in order. I had not been there in several years. The willow tree Tyler planted was healthy, with a firm trunk and lots of gangly, leafy branches that make an umbrella of shade over the bench I had placed there for anyone who wants to rest a moment. Before leaving, I wandered onto a bridge that led to the center of the pond where I found a young couple and their twelve-year-old son, camera in hand, looking around. They asked me: "Do you know where some of the famous movie people are buried here?"

"There are quite a few," I said, pointing here and there. "Rudolph Valentino, Tyrone Power, Paul Muni, Douglas Fairbanks Jr., Fay Wray."

"Really? Fay Wray?"

"Yes. She's over there, under that willow tree," I said, and they hurried off with their cameras.

Although there is still ample space for my father to be buried next to my mother, I decided to leave things as they are. I can't change the ending of their story, can't manipulate the outcome like we do in Hollywood. Whatever they had missed together, I know my parents loved each other. My mother expressed it to me time and again and my father's letters are filled with his devotion. Her approach to difficulties was often philosophical. She would say, "Sometimes things work out the way they are supposed to, darlin'," as if we cannot know the universe's grand design.

Her sunny nature carried her through so much. I can still hear her saying, "To thine own self be true," Polonius' advice to his son Laertes in *Hamlet*. It used to trouble me because it left me wondering, *What is my true self? What does my mother mean?* I grew to understand she meant we all have an inner integrity if we but listen to it and I now know she was right.

The sound I hear most vividly in my memory is still her free and full-throated laughter. Some people say I laugh that way, too. As for my father, his spirit lives on for me through his letters to her and his movies, with the unique Riskinesque humor and sense of justice and his admiration of the little guy. The dialogue in his movies is *his* voice and is there for me to hear.

Two large black-and-white photographs of them sit on facing walls of my office at home. My father is wearing a handsome three-piece suit with a silk tie and handkerchief poking out of his pocket, dapper as always, sporting his gentle, intelligent smile. In my mother's photograph, on the wall across from him, she is striking the angelic pose of a waif in *The Bowery* (1933), the soft light illuminating her beauty.

There they are, never far away from me.

ACKNOWLEDGMENTS

On a Sunday afternoon five years ago, I arrived early for a lecture at the Santa Barbara Museum of Art and introduced myself to the woman sitting next to me. She was warm, earthy, and sharp-minded and we fell into easy conversation. She said she taught memoir writing and after the lecture she invited me to join her Thursday-morning group. Life sometimes presents interesting opportunities at the right time. Writing for television was in the past and this promised to be an intriguing challenge.

Ten women gathered in Maureen Murdock's living room each week and read aloud their heartbreaking, funny, whimsical, sometimes frightening, and always personal stories. Olivia Harris, Carolyn Butcher, Hilary Klein, Hillary Kreiger, Peggy Lamb, Genie Hoyne, Peggy Garrity, Deb Gunther, Maryanne Contraras, Wendy Lukomski—each was open about her own life and, more than that, each was a great listener and eager to help and support the others. I immediately felt at home with them and began writing about my childhood—stories that often included my parents. The women, all soon friends, gave me encouragement for which I will always be appreciative. When I had enough pages to look like a manuscript, I asked a few very close outside friends to read it: Janet Wyzanski, Anita Robboy, and Pascale Beale. They all said: "I'd love to know more about your mother and father."

About that time, and to my great good fortune, a German filmmaker named Antje Boehmert contacted me about making a documentary about my father's work at the Office of War Information. "I want to understand why after World War II so many people of my grandparents' generation fell in love with America," she told me. "Older Germans still remember the films your father brought here and the wonderful portrait they painted of America. I want to know more about the man who created those films." Of course I offered to help in any way

I could. I owe Antje on two scores: for making a wonderful documentary and for giving a crucial push in my own search for my father.

I turned for the first time in years to the boxes containing the stories of my parents' lives that my mother had left me on her death. Because she had shared so much of herself with me, I did not anticipate the treasures in store. Among them were my father's notebooks and a potpourri of notes, plans, reminders, quickly scrawled story ideas, material—often fragmentary—from every part of his life from 1897 to 1955, from the Lower East Side to Broadway to Hollywood to Washington to London. I spent hours going through it all, fascinated by what I had never known. Sometimes I was able to match a find from one box to a discovery in another and a story would be born.

Then I found—pure gold—a leather pouch containing my parents' love letters. The effect on me was, and still is, overwhelming. I spent hours reading of their devotion to each other until my father's tiny script began to strain my eyes. I recruited a young woman with young eyes, Cecily Barrie, to transcribe them. I am very grateful to her.

My mother had also given some of their papers—not the most personal—to the University of Southern California Cinematic Arts Library, which organized them largely chronologically. Here were my father's scripts, often autographed by cast and crew, 16mm prints of ten of the OWI films, scrapbooks, contracts, and much besides. Here also were pictures and stories of my mother and John Monk Saunders, scrapbooks, still photos from all of my mother's films—the evidence of a long life in movies. I am grateful to the staff at the library, and in particular Edward Comstock, for their help and for diligently caring for the Fay Wray Collection all these years.

My other reliable source was my mother's autobiography, *On the Other Hand: A Life Story*. It remains, thirty years after she wrote it, an essential resource about her life until 1988. In rereading it, I was reminded continually of her resilience and optimism, never more than in dealing with some of the complicated characters she had lived among and often had to deftly manage—Vina, John Monk Saunders, Sinclair Lewis, Clifford Odets.

To make sense and order of all this material, to make two lives into one, I turned to Kimberly Rojas, my assistant, who helped me organize my parents' memorabilia into manageable form, which made possible the task of reconstructing and understanding not only the chronology of their lives and times but their personalities and emotions and beliefs. I am deeply grateful to her.

To know my parents and their times better, and to have context, I read Utah and Mormon history, the story of the major Jewish immigration to New York at the beginning of the 1890s, the history of the movie business, biographies and diaries, labor, politics, war. Some of the most valuable sources explored experiences central to my parents' lives. Mark Vaz's *Living Dangerously: The*

Adventures of Merian C. Cooper, Creator of King Kong, was not only an invaluable guide but riveting reading. Philip Dunne's *Take Two* was both an education and a pleasure to read.

Whenever possible I spoke to people who could offer personal insights about my parents. One interview I especially appreciated was my illuminating hour-long conversation with Walt Odets about his father.

Because I had not known my father as an adult, I had to rely on others who could tell me about his life and work. No one could have given more generously of his time and counsel than film historian Joseph McBride, who had spent years writing his landmark biography, *Frank Capra: The Catastrophe of Success.* McBride's book is notable for its monumental research, its meticulous attention to detail, and above all its understanding and fine nuance. He had interviewed Capra extensively and had grown to appreciate the triumphs and also the difficulties of Capra's complicated life and times. He had also delved deeply into Capra's relationship with my father and my father's role in the creation of the Capra-Riskin films and helped me understand what was myth and what was truth.

Ian Scott's biography, *In Capra's Shadow: The Life and Career of Screenwriter Robert Riskin,* is a knowledgeable, trustworthy, and absorbing account of my father's working life that provides invaluable details and important insights into his life. Ian, too, was very supportive as I set my course.

My father's screenplays, compiled by Patrick McGilligan into one volume, *Six Screenplays by Robert Riskin,* make wonderful reading just as they made wonderful films. I hear my father's voice and sense his spirit on every page. McGilligan's opening profile of my father establishes beyond argument his place in film history.

Frank Capra's own book, *The Name Above the Title: An Autobiography* gives a view into a multidimensional and not-uncomplicated man. His own spirited voice comes through most clearly here.

Film historians have written about my father's career, but it was important for me to learn everything I could about the man. My cousins Ralph, Ira, and Verna were particularly helpful in sharing their memories of my father, and also of Jakob and Bessie and life in their Yiddish-speaking home. Verna, who loved my father, generously gave me the scrapbook of clippings that her mother, my aunt Rose, had kept of the Riskin brothers' productions on Broadway. My cousins Randy Reed and Shannon Wray gave me invaluable photographs as well as insights into the Wray family.

Jo Swerling Jr. and I talked at length about our parents and their close friendship of many years; he tells me I have made his parents come alive for him again, for which I am grateful.

As I did my research, there were still missing pieces, especially regarding my father's romances in the 1920s and '30s before he met my mother. Shortly before Everett's death in 1982, I had asked him about Edith Fitzgerald and Carole Lombard. He remembered a great deal and was eager to share it; I was happy when, thirty years later, I found I still had my notes on our talks. Details about Edith's life proved challenging. Newspaper accounts from Burnside, Kentucky, where she grew up, told a little about her family, and other newspapers mentioned almost in passing Edith and my father in their New York days. Census reports told where they lived. I had the good fortune to track down a woman in Kentucky who had married into the Fitzgerald family and who offered some illuminating family stories; thank you, Debra Fitzgerald, for your time and effort. Portraits of my father's life with Glenda Farrell and Carole Lombard were easier to piece together, with plenty of stories in the Hollywood press, some more reliable than others, and in film histories.

I want to thank my brother, Bob, for his encouragement and support. I hope this book will provide his wonderful children, Nora and Jolie, and their children, Wiley, Simone, Tesla, and Tiberius, answers to some of the questions about their family heritage I had at their age. My older sister Susan's memories have faded with time but over the years she shared important recollections with me, which have found their way into this book. I am grateful to her for being my big sister.

My thanks go to film experts Anthony Slide, Frederick Ott, and Charles Wolfe for carefully reading and commenting on the manuscript. Thank you to the archivists at the Margaret Herrick Library of the Academy of Motion Picture Arts and Sciences, to the Wesleyan College Frank Capra Archives, to the Museum of Modern Art for finding and screening for me one of my father's early silent movies, *Rough and Ready*. Thanks also to Karen Boysen and Rita Belda at Sony Pictures for private screenings of both Fay Wray and Robert Riskin films and for providing still photographs from their archives for this book.

Others whose support and advice was invaluable include Aviva Layton, Joan Tapper, Kirk Douglas, Kenneth Turan, Anthony Slide, Don Bellisario, Fred Klein, Nancy Leffert, Marcia Meier, Jerry Roberts, Joe Medjuck, Jeff Barbakow, Nancy Randle, Walt and Nora McGraw, Jane Olson, Mike Farrell, Shelley Fabares, Barbara Greenleaf, John Pielmeier, Irene O'Garden, Jonathan Rintels, Marc Jaffee, Matthew Hall, Robert Elisberg, Deborah Ramo, Charles Wolfe, Jane De Hart, Allie Lebos, Larry Fineberg, Kathy Zuckerman, Emily Murphy, Iris Weinstein, Jenny Carrow, Kevin Bourke, Jill Finsten, John Steed, Molly Sturges, John Liedle, D. C. McGuire, Laurence Tribe, Elizabeth Westling, Joan Beerman, James Moore, Steve and Sandra Rothenberg, Sarah Ream, Noah Mayrand, Diann Kim, Monique Fay, Bobbie and Eddie Rosenblatt, Hassan Elmasry, Kathleen Peratis, Sherrod Brown, Connie Schultz, Jenny Allen, Davis Weinstock, and Sarah Catchpole.

Thank you to Peter Bernstein, my agent, for his friendship and wise counsel.

This book owes its very existence to my diligent and always caring editor, Victoria Wilson, who loves without reserve writers, writing, and the movies.

Finally, no one could have been more devoted during the almost five years I worked on this book than my husband David W. Rintels, who loved my mother dearly, admired my father, and offered support and thoughtful and valuable insights throughout.

BIBLIOGRAPHY

Brenman-Gibson, Margaret. *Clifford Odets: American Playwright: The Years from 1906 to 1940*. New York: Atheneum, 1981.

Capra, Frank. *The Name above the Title: An Autobiography*. New York: Vintage Books, 1985.

Dunne, Philip. *Take Two: A Life in Movies and Politics*. New York: McGraw-Hill, 1980.

Gabler, Neal. *An Empire of Their Own: How the Jews Invented Hollywood*. New York: Crown Publishers, 1988.

Marx, Harpo. *Harpo Speaks!* New York: Bernard Geis Associates, 1961.

McBride, Joseph. *Frank Capra: The Catastrophe of Success*. New York: Simon & Schuster, 1992.

Navasky, Victor S. *Naming Names*. New York: Viking Press, 1980.

Odets, Clifford. *The Time Is Ripe: The 1940 Journal of Clifford Odets*. New York: Grove Press, 1988.

Riskin, Robert. *Six Screenplays by Robert Riskin*. Berkeley: University of California Press, 1997.

Ross, Steven J. *Hitler in Los Angeles: How Jews Foiled Nazi Plots Against Hollywood and America*. New York: Bloomsbury, 2017.

Schwartz, Nancy Lynn (completed by Sheila Schwartz). *The Hollywood Writers' Wars*. New York: Knopf, 1982.

Scott, Ian. *In Capra's Shadow: The Life and Career of Screenwriter Robert Riskin*. Lexington: University Press of Kentucky, 2006.

Stegner, Wallace. *The Gathering of Zion: The Story of the Mormon Trail*. New York: McGraw-Hill, 1964.

Swindell, Larry. *Screwball: The Life of Carole Lombard*. New York: Morrow, 1975.

Thomas, Bob and Peter Bart. *King Cohn: The Life and Times of Harry Cohn*. New Millennium, 2000.

Urwand, Ben. *The Collaboration: Hollywood's Pact with Hitler.* Cambridge, MA: Belknap Press of Harvard University Press, 2013.

Vaz, Mark. *Living Dangerously: The Adventures of Merian C. Cooper, Creator of King Kong.* New York: Villard Books, 2005.

Wray, Fay. *On the Other Hand: A Life Story.* New York: St. Martin's Press. 1989.

Feature Films and Shorts

Fay Wray was under contract to Hal Roach Studios for six months (1924–1925), playing small parts in Hal Roach comedies. Titles include: *Sweet Daddy, Just a Good Guy, Sure-Mike!, What Price Goofy?, Isn't Life Terrible?, Thundering Landlords, Chasing the Chaser, Madame Sans Jane, No Father to Guide Him, Unfriendly Enemies, Your Own Back Yard, Moonlight and Noses.*

The Coast Patrol (1925) Bud Barsky Corp.
    Director: Bud Barsky. Screenplay: William E. Wing. Cast: Kenneth MacDonald, Clair de Lorez, Spottiswoode Aitken, Gino Corrado. 5 reels.

Lazy Lightning (1926) Universal.
    Director: William Wyler. Screenplay: Harrison Jacobs. Cast: Art Acord, Robert Gordon, Vin Moore, Arthur Morrison, George B. French, Rex De Roselli. 5 reels.

The Man in the Saddle (1926) Universal.
    Directors: Lynn Reynolds, Clifford Smith. Screenplay: Charles Logue. Cast: Hoot Gibson, Charles Mailes, Clark Comstock, Sally Long, Emmett King. 6 reels.

The Saddle Tramp (1926) Universal.
    Director: Victor Noerdlinger. Story by Cecil Burtis Hill. Cast: Edmund Cobb, Buck Connors, Palmer Morrison, Albert J. Smith. 2 reels.

The Wild Horse Stampede (1926) Universal.
>   Director: Albert Rogell. Story by W. C. Tuttle. Screenplay: Charles Logue. Cast: Jack Hoxie, William Steele, Marin Sais, Clark Comstock, Jack Pratt. 5 reels.

Loco Luck (1927) Universal.
>   Director: Clifford Smith. Screenplay: Isadore Bernstein, Alan James, Doris Malloy. Cast: Art Acord, Aggie Herring, William A. Steele, Al Jennings, George F. Marion, M. E. Stinson. 5 reels.

A One Man Game (1927) Universal.
>   Director: Ernst Laemmle. Story and screenplay: William Berke. Cast: Fred Humes, Harry Todd, Clarence Geldart, Norbert Myles, Lotus Thompson, William Malan. 5 reels.

Spurs and Saddles (1927) Universal.
>   Director: Clifford Smith. Story by Paul M. Bryan. Screenplay: Harrison Jacobs. Cast: Art Acord, Bill Dyer, J. Gordon Russell, C. E. Anderson, Monte Montague, Raven the Horse. 5 reels.

The First Kiss (1928) Paramount.
>   Director: Rowland V. Lee. Story by Tristram Tupper. Screenplay: John Farrow. Cast: Gary Cooper, Lane Chandler, Leslie Fenton, Paul Fix, Malcolm Williams, Monroe Owsley. 6 reels.

The Legion of the Condemned (1928) Paramount.
>   Director: William A. Wellman. Screenplay: John Monk Saunders, Jean de Limur, George Marion Jr. Cast: Gary Cooper, Barry Norton, Lane Chandler, Francis McDonald, Voya George. 8 reels.

The Street of Sin (1928) Paramount.
>   Director: Mauritz Stiller. Story by Benjamin Glazer, Josef von Sternberg. Screenplay: Julian Johnson, Chandler Sprague. Cast: Emil Jannings, Olga Baclanova, Ernest W. Johnson, John Gough, Johnnie Morris, John Burdette. 7 reels.

The Wedding March (1928) Paramount.
>   Director: Erich von Stroheim. Screenplay: Harry Carr, Erich von Stroheim. Cast: George Fawcett, Maude George, George Nichols, Zasu Pitts, Hughie Mack, Dale Fuller. 113 minutes.

The Four Feathers (1929) Paramount.
>   Directors: Ernest B. Schoedsack, Merian C. Cooper, Lothar Mendes. Based on a novel by A. E. W. Mason. Screenplay: Hope Loring, Howard Estabrook, Julian Johnson. Cast: Richard Arlen, William Powell, Clive Brook, Noah Beery, Theodore von Eltz, Harold Hightower. 81 minutes.

Pointed Heels (1929) Paramount.
>   Director: A. Edward Sutherland. Based on a short story by Charles Brackett. Screenplay: Florence Ryerson and John V. A. Weaver. Cast: William Powell,

Helen Kane, Skeets Gallagher, Phillips Holmes, Adrienne Dore, Eugene Pallette. 61 minutes.

Thunderbolt (1929) Paramount.
Director: Josef von Sternberg. Story by Charles and Jules Furthman. Screenplay: Herman Mankiewicz. Cast: George Bancroft, Richard Arlen, Tully Marshall, Eugenie Besserer, James Spottiswood. 85 minutes.

Behind the Make-Up (1930) Paramount.
Directors: Dorothy Arzner, Robert Milton. Story by Mildred Cram. Screenplay: Howard Estabrook, George Hanker Walters. Cast: William Powell, Hal Skelly, Kay Francis, E. H. Calvert, Paul Lukas, Jacques Vanaire. ca. 65–70 minutes.

The Border Legion (1930) Paramount.
Directors: Otto Brewer, Edwin H. Knopf. Based on a story by Zane Grey. Screenplay: Percy Heath, Edward E. Paramore Jr. Cast: Richard Arlen, Jack Holt, Eugene Pallette, Stanley Fields, Ethan Allen, Sid Saylor. 68 minutes.

Captain Thunder (1930) Warner Bros.
Director: Alan Crosland. Based on a story by Pierre Couderc. Screenplay: Gordon Rigby. Cast: Victor Varconi, Charles Judels, Robert Elliott, Don Alvarado, Natalie Moorhead, Bert Roach. 65 minutes.

Paramount on Parade (1930) Paramount.
Directors: Dorothy Arzner, Edmund Goulding, Victor Heerman, Edwin H. Knopf, Rowland V. Lee, Ernst Lubitsch, Lothar Mendes, Victor Schertzinger, A. Edward Sutherland, Frank Tuttle. Writer: Joseph L. Mankiewicz. Cast: Jean Arthur, Clara Bow, Gary Cooper, Maurice Chevalier, William Powell, Fredric March, Jack Oakie, many others. 102 minutes.

The Sea God (1930) Paramount.
Director: George Abbott. Screenplay: George Abbott. Cast: Richard Arlen, Eugene Pallette, Robert Gleckler, Ivan F. Simpson, Maurice Black, Robert Perry. 75 minutes.

The Texan (1930) Paramount.
Director: John Cromwell. Based on a story by O. Henry. Screenplay: Daniel Nathan Rubin. Cast: Gary Cooper, Emma Dunn, Oscar Apfel, James A. Marcus, Donald Reed, Veda Buckland, Edwin J. Brady. 79 minutes.

The Conquering Horde (1931) Paramount.
Director: Edward Sloman. Based on a novel by Emerson Hough. Cast: Richard Arlen, Claude Gillingwater, Ian Maclaren, Frank Rice, Arthur Stone. 75 minutes.

Dirigible (1931) Columbia.
Director: Frank R. Capra. Based on a story by Frank Nead. Screenplay: Jo Swerling. Cast: Jack Holt, Ralph Graves, Hobart Bosworth, Roscoe Karns, Harold Goodwin, Clarence Muse, Selmer Jackson. 100 minutes.

The Finger Points (1931) Warner Bros.
Director: John Francis Dillon. Story by John Monk Saunders and W. R. Burnett. Screenplay: Robert Lord and John Monk Saunders. Cast: Richard Barthelmess, Regis Toomey, Robert Elliott, Clark Gable, Oscar Apfel, Robert Gleckler. 90 minutes.

The Lawyer's Secret (1931) Paramount.
Directors: Louis J. Gasnier, Max Marcin. Screenplay: Lloyd Corrigan, James Hilary Finn, Max Marcin. Cast: Clive Brook, Charles ("Buddy") Rogers, Richard Arlen, Jean Arthur, Francis McDonald. 70 minutes.

Not Exactly Gentlemen (1931) Fox.
Director: Benjamin Stoloff. Based on a novel by Herman Whitaker. Screenplay: Dudley Nichols, William M. Counselman. Cast: Victor McLaglen, Lew Cody, Robert Warwick, Franklyn Farnum, David Worth, Joyce Compton. 70 minutes.

The Unholy Garden (1931) United Artists.
Director: George Fitzmaurice. Screenplay: Ben Hecht and Charles MacArthur. Cast: Ronald Colman, Estelle Taylor, Tully Marshall, Warren Hymer, Mischa Auer. 74 minutes.

Doctor X (1932) Warner Bros.
Director: Michael Curtiz. Screenplay: Robert Tasker, Earl Baldwin. Cast: Lionel Atwill, Preston Foster, Lee Tracy, George Rosener, Leila Bennett, Arthur Edmund Carewe. 76 minutes.

The Most Dangerous Game (1932) RKO.
Directors: Ernest B. Schoedsack, Irving Pichel. Based on a story by Richard Connell. Screenplay: James Ashmore Creelman. Cast: Joel McCrea, Leslie Banks, Robert Armstrong, Noble Johnson, Steve Clemente.

Stowaway (1932) Universal.
Director: Phil Whitman. Screenplay: Norman Springer. Cast: Betty Francisco, Leon Waycoff [Ames], Roscoe Karns, Lee Moran, James Gordon, Maurice Black, Montagu Love. 54 minutes.

Ann Carver's Profession (1933) Columbia.
Director: Edward Buzzell. Screenplay: Robert Riskin. Cast: Gene Raymond, Claire Dodd, Arthur Pierson, Claude Gillingwater, Frank Albertson. 71 minutes.

Below the Sea (1933) Columbia.
Director: Albert S. Rogell. Screenplay: Sy Bartlett, Warren Duff. Cast: Ralph Bellamy, Fredrik Vogeding, Esther Howard, Trevor Bland, William J. Kelly, Paul Page. 78 minutes.

The Big Brain (1933) RKO.
Director: George Archainbaud. Screenplay: Jo Swerling. Cast: George E. Stone, Phillips Holmes, Minna Gombell, Lilian Bond, Reginald Owen, Berton Churchill. 72 minutes.

The Bowery (1933) Twentieth Century–United Artists.
Director: Raoul Walsh. Based on a novel by Michael L. Simmons, Bessie Roth Solomon. Screenplay: Howard Estabrook, James Gleason. Cast: Wallace Beery, George Raft, Jackie Cooper, Harold Huber, Fletcher Norton, John Kelly, Pert Kelton. 92 minutes.

King Kong (1933) RKO.
Directors: Ernest B. Schoedsack, Merian C. Cooper. Story by Merian C. Cooper, Edgar Wallace. Screenplay by Ruth Rose, James Ashmore Creelman. Cast: Robert Armstrong, Bruce Cabot, Frank Reicher, Sam Hardy, Noble Johnson, Steve Clemente, Victor Wong. 100 minutes.

Master of Men (1933) Columbia.
Director: Lambert Hillyer. Screenplay: Seton I. Hiller, Carl Erickson. Cast: Jack Holt, Theodore von Eltz, Walter Connolly, Berton Churchill. 65 minutes.

Mystery of the Wax Museum (1933) Warner Bros.
Director: Michael Curtiz. Screenplay: Don Mullaly, Carl Erickson. Cast: Lionel Atwill, Glenda Farrell, Frank McHugh, Allen Vincent, Gavin Gordon. 77 minutes.

One Sunday Afternoon (1933) Paramount.
Director: Stephen Roberts. From a story by James Hagen. Screenplay: Grover Jones, William Stevens McNutt. Cast: Gary Cooper, Neil Hamilton, Frances Fuller, Roscoe Karns, Jane Darwell. 85 minutes.

Shanghai Madness (1933) Fox.
Director: John Blystone. Screenplay: Austin Packer, Gordon Wellesley. Cast: Spencer Tracy, Ralph Morgan, Eugene Pallette, Herbert Mundin, Reginald Mason, Arthur Hoyt. 68 minutes.

The Woman I Stole (1933) Columbia.
Director: Irving Cummings. From a novel by Joseph Hergesheimer. Screenplay: Jo Swerling. Cast: Jack Holt, Noah Beery, Raquel Torres, Donald Cook, Edwin Maxwell, Charles Browne. 70 minutes.

The Vampire Bat (1933) Majestic.
Director: Frank Strayer. Screenplay: Edward T. Lowe Jr. Cast: Lionel Atwill, Melvyn Douglas, Maude Eburne, George E. Stone, Dwight Frye, Rita Carlisle.

The Affairs of Cellini (1934) Twentieth Century–United Artists.
Director: Gregory La Cava. From a play by Edwin Justin Thayer. Screenplay: Bess Meredyth. Cast: Constance Bennett, Fredric March, Frank Morgan, Vince Barnett, Louis Calhern. 86 minutes.

Black Moon (1934) Columbia.
Director: Roy William Neill. From a story by Clements Ripley. Screenplay: Wells Root. Cast: Jack Holt, Dorothy Burgess, Cora Sue Collins, Arnold Korff, Clarence Muse, Lumsden Hare. 68 minutes.

Cheating Cheaters (1934) Universal.
Director: Richard Thorpe. Screenplay: Gladys Unger, Allen Rivkin. Cast: Cesar Romero, Minna Gombell, Francis L. Sullivan, Hugh O'Connell, Henry Armetta. 70 minutes.

The Countess of Monte Cristo (1934) Universal.
Director: Karl Freund. Screenplay: Karen DeWolf. Cast: Paul Lukas, Reginald Owen, Patsy Kelly, Paul Page, Carmel Myers, Robert McWade. 78 minutes.

Madame Spy (1934) Universal.
Director: Karl Freund. Screenplay: William Hurlbut. Cast: Nils Asther, Edward Arnold, John Miljan, David Torrence, Douglas Walton, Oscar Apfel, Vince Barnett. 70 minutes.

Mills of the Gods (1934) Columbia.
Director: Roy William Neill. Screenplay: Garrett Fort. Cast: May Robson, Victor Jory, Raymond Walburn, James Blakeley, Josephine Whittell, Mayo Methot. 66 minutes.

Once to Every Woman (1934) Columbia.
Director: Lambert Hillyer. From a story by A. J. Cronin. Screenplay: Jo Swerling. Cast: Ralph Bellamy, Walter Connolly, Walter Bryon, J. Farrell MacDonald, Billie Seward. 70 minutes.

The Richest Girl in the World (1934) RKO.
Director: William A. Seiter. Screenplay: Norman Krasna. Cast: Miriam Hopkins, Joel McCrea, Henry Stephenson, Reginald Denny, Beryl Mercer. 76 minutes.

Viva Villa! (1934) M-G-M.
Director: Jack Conway. Screenplay: Ben Hecht. Cast: Wallace Beery, Leo Carrillo, Donald Cook, Stuart Erwin, George E. Stone, Joseph Schildkraut. 115 minutes.

White Lies (1934) Columbia.
   Director: Leo Bulgakov. Screenplay: Harold Shumate. Cast: Walter Connolly, Victor Jory, Leslie Fenton, Robert Allen, William Demarest, Oscar Apfel, Mary Foy. 63 minutes.

Woman in the Dark (1934) RKO.
   Director: Phil Rosen. Based on a story by Dashiell Hammett. Screenplay: Sada Cowan. Cast: Ralph Bellamy, Melvyn Douglas, Roscoe Ates, Ruth Gillette, Joe King, Nell O'Day. 68 minutes.

Bulldog Jack (1935) Gaumont-British. U.S. title: *Alias Bulldog Drummond*
   Director: Walter Forde. Screenplay: J. O. C. Orton, Sidney Gilliat, Gerald Fairlie. Cast: Jack Hulbert, Ralph Richardson, Paul Graetz, Gibb McLaughlin, Atholl Fleming. 72 minutes.

The Clairvoyant (1935) Gaumont-British.
   Director: Maurice Elvey. Based on a novel by Ernst Lothar. Screenplay: Charles Bennett Bryan, Edgar Wallace. Cast: Claude Rains, Jane Baxter, Mary Clare, Ben Field, Athole Stewart, Felix Aylmer. 81 minutes.

Come Out of the Pantry (1935) United Artists.
   Director: Jack Raymond. Based on a story by Alice Duer Miller. Screenplay: Douglas Ferber, Austin Parker. Cast: Jack Buchanan, James Carew, Ronald Squire, Olive Blakeney, Fred Emney, Kate Cutler. 71 minutes.

Roaming Lady (1936) Columbia.
   Director: Albert S. Rogell. Story by Diana Bourbon, Bruce Manning. Screenplay: Fred Niblo Jr., Earle Snell. Cast: Ralph Bellamy, Thurston Hall, Edward Gargan, Roger Imhof, Paul Guilfoyle, Arthur Rankin. 66 minutes.

They Met in a Taxi (1936) Columbia.
   Director: Alfred E. Green. Story by Octavius Cohen. Screenplay: Howard J. Green. Cast: Chester Morris, Lionel Stander, Raymond Walburn, Henry Mollison, Kenneth Harlan. 70 minutes.

When Knights Were Bold (1936) General Film Distributors.
   Director: Jack Raymond. Based on a play by Harriett Jay. Screenplay: Douglas Ferber, Austin Parker. Cast: Jack Buchanan, Garry Marsh, Kate Cutler, Martita Hunt. 76 minutes.

It Happened in Hollywood (1937) Columbia.
   Director: Harry Lachman. Based on a novel by Myles Connolly. Screenplay: Ethel Hill, Henry Fergusson, Samuel Fuller. Cast: Richard Dix, Victor Kilian, Franklin Pangborn. 67 minutes.

Murder in Greenwich Village (1937) Columbia.
Director: Albert Rogell. Story by Robert T. Shannon. Screenplay: Michael L. Simmons. Cast: Richard Arlen, Raymond Walburn, Wyn Cahoon, Scott Kolton, Thurston Hall. 68 minutes.

The Jury's Secret (1938) Universal.
Director: Ted Sloman. Story by Lester Cole. Screenplay: Lester Cole, Newman Levy. Cast: Kent Taylor, Larry Blake, Nan Grey, Samuel S. Hinds, Halliwell Hobbes, Granville Bates. 65 minutes.

Smashing the Spy Ring (1938) Columbia.
Director: Christy Cabanne. Story and screenplay: Arthur T. Herman, Dorrell McGowan, Stuart G. McGowan. Cast: Ralph Bellamy, Regis Toomey, Walter Kingsford, Ann Doran, Warren Hull, Lorna Gray. 62 minutes.

Navy Secrets (1939) Monogram.
Director: Howard Bretherton. Based on a story by Steve Fisher. Screenplay: Harvey Gates. Cast: Grant Withers, Dewey Robinson, Craig Reynolds, George Sorrel, Robert Frazer.

Wildcat Bus (1940) RKO.
Director: Frank Woodruff. Story and screenplay: Lou Lusty. Cast: Charles Lang, Paul Guilfoyle, Don Costello, Paul McGrath, Joseph Sawyer, Roland Drew, Oscar O'Shea. 64 minutes.

Adam Had Four Sons (1941) Columbia.
Director: Gregory Ratoff. Based on a novel by Charles Bonner. Screenplay: William Hurlbut, Michael Blankfort. Cast: Ingrid Bergman, Warner Baxter, Susan Hayward, Richard Denning, Johnny Downs, June Lockhart. 81 minutes.

Melody for Three (1941) RKO.
Director: Erle C. Kenton. Screenplay: Walter Ferris, Lee Loeb. Cast: Jean Hersholt, Walter Woolf King, Patsy Parsons, Maude Eburne, Irene Ryan, Leon Tyler. 67 minutes.

Not a Ladies' Man (1942) Columbia.
Director: Lew Landers. Story by Robert Hyde. Screenplay: Rian James. Cast: Paul Kelly, Douglas Croft, Ruth Lee, Lawrence Dixon, Don Beddoe, Louise Allbritton. 60 minutes.

Small Town Girl (1953) M-G-M.
Director: László Kardos. Screenplay: Dorothy Cooper, Dorothy Kingsley. Cast: Jane Powell, Farley Granger, Ann Miller, Bobby Van, Robert Keith, Chill Wills, S. Z. Sakall. 92 minutes.

Treasure of the Golden Condor (1953) Twentieth Century–Fox.
Director: Delmer Daves. Based on a novel by Edison Marshall. Screenplay: Delmar Daves. Cast: Cornel Wilde, Finlay Currie, Constance Smith, Anne Bancroft, George Macready, Leo G. Carroll. 93 minutes.

The Cobweb (1955) M-G-M.
Director: Vincente Minnelli. Based on a novel by William Gibson. Screenplay: John Paxton. Cast: Lauren Bacall, Charles Boyer, Lillian Gish, Richard Widmark, Gloria Grahame, John Kerr. 124 minutes.

Queen Bee (1955) Columbia.
Director: Ranald MacDougall. Based on a novel by Edna Lee. Screenplay: Ronald MacDougall. Cast: Joan Crawford, Barry Sullivan, Betsy Palmer, John Ireland, Lucy Marlow, William Leslie. 95 minutes.

Hell on Frisco Bay (1956) Warner Bros.
Director: Frank Tuttle. Based on a novel by William P. McGivern. Screenplay: Sidney Boehm, Martin Rackin. Cast: Alan Ladd, Edward G. Robinson, Joanne Dru, Perry Lopez, William Demarest, Paul Stewart. 99 minutes.

Rock, Pretty Baby (1956) Universal-International.
Director: Richard Barlett. Story and screenplay: Jo Eisinger. Cast: Sal Mineo, John Saxon, Luana Patton, Edward C. Platt, Rod McKuen, Shelley Fabares. 89 minutes.

Crime of Passion (1957) United Artists.
Director: Gerd Oswald. Screenplay: Herbert Margolis, William Raynor. Cast: Barbara Stanwyck, Sterling Hayden, Raymond Burr, Royal Dano, Virginia Grey, Dennis Cross. 86 minutes.

Tammy and the Bachelor (1957) Universal-International.
Director: Joseph Pevney. Based on a novel by Cid Ricketts Sumner. Screenplay: Oscar Brodney. Cast: Debbie Reynolds, Leslie Nielsen, Walter Brennan, Mala Powers, Sidney Blackmer. 89 minutes.

Dragstrip Riot (1958) American-International.
Director: David Bradley. Story by O'Dale Ireland, George Hodgins. Screenplay: George Hodgins. Cast: Yvonne Lime, Gary Clarke, Bob Turnbull, Connie Stevens, Gabe DeLutri, Steve Ihnat. 68 minutes.

Summer Love (1958) Universal-International.
Director: Charles F. Haas. Screenplay: Herbert H. Margolis, William Raynor. Cast: John Saxon, Molly Bee, Rod McKuen, Judy Meredith, Jill St. John, John Wilder, Edward Platt. 85 minutes.

Television

The Pride of the Family 40 episodes (1953–1954).
Director: Bob Finkel. Cast: Natalie Wood, Paul Hartman, Robert Hyatt.

Screen Directors Playhouse: It's Always Sunday (1956).
Director: Allan Dwan. Story by Jesse Goldstein, Frank Fox. Screenplay: D. D. Beauchamp. Cast: Dennis O'Keefe, Sheldon Leonard, Grant Withers, Chick Chandler, Eilene Janssen, Robert Easton.

The 20th Century–Fox Hour: In Times Like These (1956).
Director: William A. Seiter. Based on a novel by MacKinlay Kantor. Screenplay: Julian Josephson, Kathryn Scola. Cast: Macdonald Carey, Mark Damon, Pamela Baird, Todd Ferrell, George Eldredge, Johnny Washbrook, Susan Luckey, Lily Gentle.

Alfred Hitchcock Presents
A Dip in the Pool (1958). Director: Alfred Hitchcock. Based on a story by Roald Dahl. Teleplay: Robert C. Dennis. Cast: Keenan Wynn, Philip Bourneuf, Louise Platt, Doreen Lang, Ralph Clanton, Doris Lloyd.
The Morning After (1959). Director: Herschel Daugherty. Cast: Robert Alda, Jeanette Nolan, Dorothy Provine, Dorothea Lord.

The Real McCoys: Theatre in the Barn (1961).
Director: Lawrence Dobkin. Story by Arthur Marx, Mannie Manheim. Teleplay: Bob Ross. Cast: Walter Brennan, Richard Crenna, Kathleen Nolan, Tony Martinez, Eva Norde, Robert Karnes, Marjorie Bennett, Andy Clyde.

Perry Mason
Cast: Raymond Burr, Barbara Hale, William Hopper, William Talman, Ray Collins.
The Case of the Prodigal Parent (1958). Teleplay: Seeleg Lester, Gene Wang. Director: Arthur Marks.
The Case of the Watery Witness (1959). Teleplay: Jackson Gillis. Director: Richard Kinon.
The Case of the Fatal Fetish (1965). Teleplay: William Bast. Director: Charles R. Rondeau.

Gideon's Trumpet (1980) Gideon Productions/CBS.
Director: Robert Collins. Based on the book by Anthony Lewis. Teleplay: David W. Rintels. Cast: Henry Fonda, José Ferrer, John Houseman, Ford Rainey, Edmund H. North, Dean Jagger, Sam Jaffe.

Documentaries

Off the Menu: The Last Days of Chasen's (1997) Northern Arts Entertainment.
   Directors: Shari Springer Berman, Robert Pulcini. Cameos with Donna Summer, Jack Lemmon, Martin Landau, Sharon Stone, Ed McMahon, Ronnie Clint, Pepe Ruiz, Jackie Collins, Angela Bassett.

Broadway: The Golden Age (2003) PBS, RCA, BMG.
   Director: Rick McKay. Cameos with Stephen Sondheim, Angela Lansbury, Edie Adams, Bea Arthur, Elizabeth Ashley, Alec Baldwin, John Barrowman, Kim Hunter, Gwen Verdon, Kaye Ballard, Mimi Hines, Hume Cronyn, Carol Burnett, Carol Channing, Charles Durning, Rosemary Harris, Derek Jacobi, Lainie Kazan.

STAGE

Nikki (1931) Musical. Book by John Monk Saunders.
   Cast: Fay Wray, Archie Leach (Cary Grant)

Angela Is Twenty-Two (1938) Written by Fay Wray and Sinclair Lewis.
   Cast: Fay Wray, Sinclair Lewis

Golden Wings (1941) by William Jay and Guy Bolton.

Mr. Big (1941) Directed by George S. Kaufman and written by Arthur Sheekman and Margaret Shane.
   Cast: Fay Wray, Hume Cronyn

ROBERT RISKIN

STAGE

The Mud Turtle (1925) Bijou Theatre. Written by Elliott Lester
    Producers: A. E. Riskin and R. R. Riskin

The Bells (1926) Revival. Nora Bayes Theatre. Written by Leopold Lewis
    Producers: A. E. Riskin and R. R. Riskin

She Couldn't Say No (1926) Booth Theatre. Written by B. M. Kaye
    Producers: A. E. Riskin and R. R. Riskin

Bless You, Sister (1927) Forrest Theatre. Written by John Meehan and Robert Riskin
    Producers: A. E. Riskin and R. R. Riskin. Directors: John Meehan and George Abbott

Many a Slip (1930) The Little Theatre. Written by Edith Fitzgerald and Robert Riskin. Director: Robert Riskin

FILMOGRAPHY

Robert Riskin was chief of production for Klever Komedies Inc. filming dozens of one- and two-reel comedies (1916–1919), mostly starring Victor Moore. They include: *Rough and Ready, Adam and Some Eves, Cinderella Husband, Flivvering, The Wrong Mr. Fox, Home Defense.*

Illicit (1931) Warner Bros.
    Screenplay: Harvey Thew. Based on the play *Illicit* by Edith Fitzgerald and Robert Riskin. Director: Archie Mayo. Cast: Barbara Stanwyck, James Rennie, Ricardo Cortez. 79 minutes.

Many a Slip (1931) Universal.

Screenplay: Gladys Unger. Based on the play *Many a Slip* by Edith Fitzgerald and Robert Riskin. Director: Vin Moore. Cast: Joan Bennett, Lew Ayres, Ben Alexander. 64 minutes.

Men Are Like That (1931) Columbia.

(Originally titled *Arizona*) Adaptation and Dialogue: Robert Riskin. Continuity: Dorothy Howell. Based on the play *Arizona* by Augustus E. Thomas. Director: George B. Seitz. Cast: Laura La Plante, John Wayne. 70 minutes.

The Miracle Woman (1931) Columbia.

Screenplay: Jo Swerling. Continuity: Dorothy Howell. Based on the play *Bless You, Sister* by John Meehan and Robert Riskin. Director: Frank Capra. Cast: Barbara Stanwyck, David Manners, Sam Hardy. 90 minutes.

Men in Her Life (1931) Columbia.

Adaptation and Dialogue: Robert Riskin. Continuity: Dorothy Howell. Based on a story by Warner Fabian. Director: William Beaudine. Cast: Lois Moran, Charles Bickford. 70 minutes.

Platinum Blonde (1931) Columbia.

Adaptation: Jo Swerling. Dialogue: Robert Riskin. Continuity: Dorothy Howell. Based on a story by Harry E. Chandlee and Douglas W. Churchill. Director: Frank Capra. Cast: Jean Harlow, Loretta Young, Robert Williams. 89 minutes.

American Madness (1932) Columbia.

Story and Screenplay: Robert Riskin. Director: Frank Capra. Cast: Walter Huston, Pat O'Brien, Constance Cummings. 75 minutes.

The Big Timer (1932) Columbia.

Story and Dialogue: Robert Riskin. Continuity: Dorothy Howell. From a story by Robert Riskin. Director: Edward Buzzell. Cast: Ben Lyon, Constance Cummings, Thelma Todd. 72 minutes.

The Night Club Lady (1932) Columbia.

Screenplay: Robert Riskin. From a story by Anthony Abbot. Director: Irving Cummings. Cast: Adolphe Menjou, Mayo Methot. 66 minutes.

Shopworn (1932) Columbia.

Story: Sarah Y. Mason. Screenplay and dialogue: Robert Riskin, Jo Swerling. Director: Nicholas Grinde. Cast: Barbara Stanwyck, Regis Toomey. 72 minutes.

Three Wise Girls (1932) Columbia.

Adaptation: Agnes Christine Johnson. Dialogue: Robert Riskin. Based on the story "Blonde Baby" by Wilson Collison. Director: William Beaudine. Cast: Jean Harlow, Mae Clarke, Walter Byron. 68 minutes.

Virtue (1932) Columbia.
Screenplay: Robert Riskin. From a story by Ethel Hill. Director: Edward Buzzell. Cast: Carole Lombard, Pat O'Brien, Ward Bond. 68 minutes.

Ex-Lady (1933) Warner Bros.
Adaptation: David Boehm. From a story by Edith Fitzgerald and Robert Riskin. Director: Robert Florey. Cast: Bette Davis, Gene Raymond.

Ann Carver's Profession (1933) Columbia.
Screenplay: Robert Riskin. From his story "Rules for Wives." Director: Edward Buzzell. Cast: Fay Wray, Gene Raymond. 71 minutes.

Lady for a Day (1933) Columbia.
(Originally titled *Beggar's Holiday*) Screenplay: Robert Riskin. From the story "Madame La Gimp" by Damon Runyon. Director: Frank Capra. Cast: May Robson, William Warren, Glenda Farrell. Academy Award Nominee: Best Film; Best Actress in a Leading Role; Best Director; Best Writing, Adaptation. 96 minutes.

It Happened One Night (1934) Columbia.
Screenplay: Robert Riskin. Based on the story "Night Bus" by Samuel Hopkins Adams. Director: Frank Capra. Cast: Claudette Colbert, Clark Gable. Academy Award Winner: Best Picture; Best Actor in a Leading Role; Best Actress in a Leading Role; Best Director; Best Writing, Adaptation. 105 minutes.

Broadway Bill (1934) Columbia.
Screenplay: Robert Riskin. Based on the story "On the Nose" by Mark Hellinger. Director: Frank Capra. Cast: Warner Baxter, Myrna Loy, Walter Connolly. 104 minutes.

Carnival (1934) Columbia.
Story and Screenplay: Robert Riskin. Director: Walter Lang. Cast: Lee Tracy, Sally Eilers, Jimmy Durante. 77 minutes.

The Whole Town's Talking (1935) Columbia.
Screenplay: Jo Swerling, Robert Riskin. Based on the story "Jailbreaker" by W. R. Burnett. Director: John Ford. Cast: Edward G. Robinson, Jean Arthur. 93 minutes.

Mr. Deeds Goes to Town (1936) Columbia.
Screenplay: Robert Riskin. Based on the story "Opera Hat" by Clarence Budington Kelland. Director: Frank Capra. Cast: Gary Cooper, Jean Arthur. Academy Award Winner: Best Director. Academy Award Nominee: Best Picture; Best Actor in a Leading Role; Best Writing, Adaptation. 115 minutes.

When You're in Love (1936) Columbia.
  Screenplay: Robert Riskin. Based on a story by Ethel Hill and Cedric Worth.
  Director: Robert Riskin. Cast: Grace Moore, Cary Grant. 100 minutes.

Lost Horizon (1937) Columbia.
  Screenplay: Robert Riskin. Based on the novel *Lost Horizon* by James Hilton.
  Director: Frank Capra. Cast: Ronald Colman, Jane Wyatt, Sam Jaffe. Academy
  Award Nominee: Best Picture. 132 minutes.

You Can't Take It with You (1938) Columbia.
  Screenplay: Robert Riskin. Based on the play *You Can't Take It with You* by
  George S. Kaufman and Moss Hart. Director: Frank Capra. Cast: James Stew-
  art, Jean Arthur, Lionel Barrymore, Spring Byington. Academy Award Winner:
  Best Picture; Best Director. Academy Award Nominee: Best Actress in a Sup-
  porting Role; Best Writing, Screenplay. 126 minutes.

The Real Glory (1939) United Artists.
  Screenplay: Jo Swerling, Robert R. Presnell. Producer: Samuel Goldwyn. Asso-
  ciate Producer: Robert Riskin. Director: Henry Hathaway. Cast: Gary Cooper,
  David Niven. 96 minutes.

They Shall Have Music (1939) United Artists.
  Screenplay: Irma von Cube, John Howard Lawson. Associate Producer: Robert
  Riskin. Director: Archie Mayo. Cast: Jascha Heifetz, Joel McCrea. 102 minutes.

Meet John Doe (1941) Warner Bros.
  Screenplay: Robert Riskin. Based on an unpublished story by Richard Connell
  and Robert Presnell. Director: Frank Capra. Cast: Gary Cooper, Barbara Stanwyck. Academy Award Nominee: Best Writing, Original Story. 122 minutes.

The Thin Man Goes Home (1944) M-G-M.
  Screenplay: Robert Riskin and Dwight Taylor. Based on an original story by
  Robert Riskin and Harry Kurnitz. From characters created by Dashiell Ham-
  mett. Director: Richard Thorpe. Cast: Myrna Loy, William Powell. 100 minutes.

Magic Town (1947) RKO.
  Screenplay: Robert Riskin. From a story by Robert Riskin and Joseph Krum-
  gold. Producer: Robert Riskin. Director: William A. Wellman. Cast: James
  Stewart, Jane Wyman. 103 minutes.

Riding High (1950) Paramount.
  Screenplay: Robert Riskin. Based on the story "On the Nose" by Mark Hellinger,
  and the 1934 movie *Broadway Bill*. Director: Frank Capra. Cast: Bing Crosby,
  Coleen Gray. 112 minutes.

Mister 880 (1950) Twentieth Century–Fox.
  Screenplay: Robert Riskin. Based on the *New Yorker* article "Old Eight-Eighty"

by St. Clair McKelway. Director: Edmund Goulding. Cast: Burt Lancaster, Edmund Gwenn. Golden Globe Winner: Best Supporting Actor. Academy Award Nominee: Best Actor in a Supporting Role. 90 minutes.

Half Angel (1951) Twentieth Century–Fox.
Screenplay: Robert Riskin. Based on a story by George Carleton Brown. Director: Richard Sale. Cast: Loretta Young, Joseph Cotten. 77 minutes.

Here Comes the Groom (1951) Paramount.
Screenplay: Virginia Van Upp, Liam O'Brien, Miles Connolly. Based on the story "You Belong to Me" by Robert Riskin and Liam O'Brien. Cast: Bing Crosby, Jane Wyman, Alexis Smith. Academy Award Winner: Best Music, Original Song. Academy Award Nominee: Best Writing, Motion Picture Story. Golden Globe Nominee: Best Actor—Comedy or Musical. 113 minutes.

Documentaries

Between 1942 and 1945 the Overseas Film Bureau under Bureau Chief Robert Riskin produced 26 documentaries. A partial list of titles includes:

Swedes in America (1943) Director: Irving Lerner. Writer: Joseph Krumgold.
Narrator: Ingrid Bergman.

The Autobiography of a "Jeep" (1943)
Director: Irving Lerner. Writer: Joseph Krumgold.

Arturo Toscanini: Hymn of the Nations (1944)
Director: Alexander Hammid. Writer: May Sarton. Cast: Arturo Toscanini, Jan Peerce. Narration: Knox Manning and Burgess Meredith.

The Valley of the Tennessee (1944)
Director: Alexander Hammid. Narration: Fredric March.

The Cummington Story (1945)
Writer-Directors: Helen Grayson and Larry Madison. Music: Aaron Copland.

The Town (1945)
Director: Josef von Sternberg. Writer: Joseph Krumgold.

Watchtower Over Tomorrow (1945)
Directors: John Cromwell and Harold Kress. Writers: Ben Hecht, Karl Lamb.

Library of Congress (1945)
Director: Alexander Hammid. Music: Alex North. Narration: Ralph Bellamy.

Documentary Profile of Robert Riskin

Projections of America (2014) PBS International. ARTE
   Director: Peter Miller. Executive Producers: Antje Boehmert, Christian Popp,
   Peter Miller. Narrator: John Lithgow.

OTHER WORKS

"Lucienne" (1959) *The New Yorker.* Published posthumously.

Page numbers in *italics* refer to illustrations.

A NOTE ON THE TYPE

This book was set in Adobe Garamond. Designed for the Adobe Corporation by Robert Slimbach, the fonts are based on types first cut by Claude Garamond (c. 1480–1561). Garamond was a pupil of Geoffroy Tory and is believed to have followed the Venetian models, although he introduced a number of important differences, and it is to him that we owe the letter we now know as "old style." He gave to his letters a certain elegance and feeling of movement that won their creator an immediate reputation and the patronage of Francis I of France.

COMPOSED BY NORTH MARKET STREET GRAPHICS,
LANCASTER, PENNSYLVANIA

PRINTED AND BOUND BY BERRYVILLE GRAPHICS,
BERRYVILLE, VIRGINIA

DESIGNED BY IRIS WEINSTEIN